# Vicegerency in Islamic Thought and Scripture

This book explores the reasons for the creation of humanity on Earth from the perspective of ancient and contemporary Muslim thinkers, aiming to lay the outlines of a Qur'anic theory of human existential function.

The author proceeds from the assumption that, until now, contemporary Islamic scholarship has suffered from the absence of theorisation about a Qur'anic conception of human existential function (vicegerency), lacking a unified philosophical and epistemological frame of reference. Challenging common perceptions among contemporary Muslim reformists regarding the human existential function, the author examines both classical and contemporary thought as well as conducting a thorough and comprehensive analysis of Qur'anic passages that ground the theory of vicegerency within a cosmic scheme. Ultimately, a new approach for understanding the human existential function from within the Qur'anic worldview is proposed. For the first time then, this book offers an integral induction and categorisation of Qur'anic teleological concepts, combining them within a coherent framework that reveals the outlines of a vicegerency theory and a Qur'anic worldview.

Suitable for both scholars and laypersons, the book serves as a landmark textbook in the fields of Islamic Philosophy, Theological Anthropology and Qur'anic Studies.

**Chauki Lazhar** is Assistant Professor of Islamic Studies at the College of Sharia and Islamic Studies, Qatar University. His research interests in the field of Islamic Studies include theological anthropology, Islamic meta-ethics and metaphysics, the epistemology of Islamic sciences, Islamic worldview studies and the methodology of contemporary ethico-religious reasoning (ijtihād). He is the author of, inter alia, *Al-Umūma wa al-Unūtha fī al-Islām wa al-Tamyīz Bayn al-Mar'a wa al-Rajul fī al-Aḥkām al-Shar'iyya* [Motherhood, Femininity and Gender Differentiation in Islamic Provisions] (Doha: Hamad Bin Khalifa University Press, 2019).

## Routledge Studies in Islamic Philosophy

Series Editor

*Oliver Leaman, University of Kentucky*

The Routledge Studies in Islamic Philosophy Series is devoted to the publication of scholarly books in all areas of Islamic philosophy. We regard the discipline as part of the general philosophical environment and seek to include books on a wide variety of different approaches to Islamic philosophy.

**The Philosophy of Religion in Post-Revolutionary Iran**
On an Epistemological Turn in Modern Islamic Reform Discourse
*Heydar Shadi*

**Analytic Philosophy and Avicenna**
Knowing the Unknown
*Mohammad Azadpur*

**The Political Philosophy of Mullā Ṣadrā**
*Seyyed Khalil Toussi*

**Knowledge and Beauty in Classical Islam**
An aesthetic reading of the *Muqaddima* by Ibn Khaldūn
*Giovanna Lelli*

**Philosophical Sufism**
An Introduction to the School of Ibn al-ʿArabī
*Mukhtar H. Ali*

**The Crisis of Muslim Religious Discourse**
The Necessary Shift from Plato to Kant
*Lahouari Addi*

**Miskawayh's *Tahḏīb al-aḫlāq***
Happiness, Justice and Friendship
*Ufuk Topkara*

**The Covenants of the Prophet Muḥammad**
From Shared Historical Memory to Peaceful Co-existence
*Ibrahim Mohamed Zain and Ahmed El-Wakil*

**Vicegerency in Islamic Thought and Scripture**
Towards a Qur'anic Theory of Human Existential Function
*Chauki Lazhar*

For more information about this series, please visit: https://www.routledge.com/middleeaststudies/series/RSINIP

# Vicegerency in Islamic Thought and Scripture

## Towards a Qur'anic Theory of Human Existential Function

**Chauki Lazhar**

Routledge
Taylor & Francis Group
LONDON AND NEW YORK

First published 2023
by Routledge
4 Park Square, Milton Park, Abingdon, Oxon OX14 4RN

and by Routledge
605 Third Avenue, New York, NY 10158

*Routledge is an imprint of the Taylor & Francis Group, an informa business*



*British Library Cataloguing-in-Publication Data*
A catalogue record for this book is available from the British Library

*Library of Congress Cataloging-in-Publication Data*
Names: Lazhar, Chauki, author.
Title: Vicegerency in Islamic thought and scripture: towards a Qur'anic theory of human existential function/Chauki Lazhar.
Description: First Edition. | New York, NY: Routledge, 2023. |
Series: Routledge studies in Islamic philosophy | Includes bibliographical references and index. |
Identifiers: LCCN 2022051052 (print) | LCCN 2022051053 (ebook) |
ISBN 9781032372211 (hardback) | ISBN 9781032372259 (paperback) |
ISBN 9781003335948 (ebook)
Subjects: LCSH: Theological anthropology. | Islam–Doctrines. |
Islamic renewal. | Qur'an.
Classification: LCC BP166.7 .L394 2023 (print) | LCC BP166.7 (ebook) |
DDC 297.2–dc23/eng/20230119
LC record available at https://lccn.loc.gov/2022051052
LC ebook record available at https://lccn.loc.gov/2022051053

ISBN: 978-1-032-37221-1 (hbk)
ISBN: 978-1-032-37225-9 (pbk)
ISBN: 978-1-003-33594-8 (ebk)

DOI: 10.4324/9781003335948

Typeset in Times New Roman
by Deanta Global Publishing Services, Chennai, India

# Contents

*Acknowledgements* vii

1 **Introduction** 1
*1.1 Research Questions, Methodological Approach and Focus 1*
*1.2 Islamic Vicegerency 4*
*1.3 Knowledge Integration in Islamic Thought and Disciplines 6*
*1.4 Islamic Worldview as Epistemological and Methodological Frame 8*
*1.4.1 Ismāʿīl al-Fārūqī 9*
*1.4.2 Ṭāhā Jābir al-ʿUlwānī 11*
*1.4.3 ʿAbd al-Ḥamīd Abū Sulaymān 12*
*1.4.4 Ṭāhā ʿAbd al-Raḥmān 12*
*Notes 15*
*Bibliography 19*

2 **Islamic Worldview in the Context of Modern Reformism** 23
*2.1 The Crisis of Islamic Thought in the Context of Modernity 23*
*2.2 Islamic Worldview as Promising Horizon 30*
*Notes 38*
*Bibliography 43*

3 **The Concept of *Istikhlāf* in Islamic Heritage** 46
*3.1 Who is Man the Deputy of? 46*
*3.2 Who is the* Khalīfa*? 56*
*3.3 What is Man Deputised For? 59*
*3.4 Vicegerency and Human Existential Function 63*
*Notes 73*
*Bibliography 84*

4 **Vicegerency as Existential Function in Contemporary Reformism** 88
*4.1 Building and Populating the Earth (*ʿimārat al-arḍ*)*
*and Utilising its Resources 90*

*4.1.1 The Problem of Vicegerency and Worship 91*
*4.1.2 The Lordship-Wordship Dichotomy 96*
*4.2 Adherence to God's Will and Commands and their Implementation on Earth 102*
*4.3 The Responsibility of Choice and Disposition 108*
*4.4 The Manifestation of Divine Attributes and Ethics on Earth 113*
*4.5 Nature and Beyond 121*
*4.6 Concluding Remarks 124*
*Notes 130*
*Bibliography 141*

**5 The Object of Vicegerency: Identifying Human Existential Function** 147
*5.1 Deducing the Object of Vicegerency 148*
*5.2 Vicegerency is Deputisation on Behalf of God 155*
*5.3 Some Hermeneutical Considerations 160*
*5.4 Identifying the Object of Vicegerency 165*
*5.4.1 Cosmic Worship 166*
*5.4.2 Human Worship 173*
*Notes 180*
*Bibliography 190*

**6 Vicegerency in the Qur᾽anic Worldview** 194
*6.1 The Major Concepts of Islam from the Perspective of Vicegerency 197*
*6.2 The Aspects of the Cosmic Balance Entrusted to the Human Being 205*
*6.2.1 Maintaining the Spiritual Balance 205*
*6.2.2 Maintaining the Collective Balance 226*
*6.2.3 Maintaining the Environmental Balance 237*
*Notes 248*
*Bibliography 260*

*Conclusion* 263
*Index* 269

# Acknowledgements

In the Name of Allah, the Most Beneficent, the Most Merciful

My first and foremost gratitude goes obviously to God, any merit in this work goes to Him only, and any mistake, inconsistency or flaw is but a consequence of the author's weakness, sin or ignorance. Throughout this work, I felt His kindness and mercy accompany me, despite my many flaws; without that, nothing would have been possible. Though I know I do not have any real merit in the potential contributions of this work, the honour that He allowed me to achieve it is priceless. May Allah's peace be upon the Prophet Muhammad, his family and his companions.

Then, I express my very strong thanks to my wife Khadija who has supported me in all my enterprises throughout the last 18 years, and here again, I could count on her support. I would also like to extend my deepest gratitude to my parents Noura and Abdallah for their love, emotional support and their prayers that may be the reason why God allowed me to accomplish this work. I am also grateful to my brother Hilmi with whom the hours of discussion on vicegerency gave me new insights and inspirations, without forgetting my deep discussions with my brother Alaidine, thank you! Thanks should also go to my sisters Rifka and Nour for their love and kindness. Not forgetting to mention here my lovely children Sirine, Tesnime and Junayd. My deep and sincere thanks also go to the rest of my close and extended family members: My parents-in-law, my brothers- and sisters-in-law and my nephews and nieces.

I am extremely grateful to Dr Mawahib, you were always there to support me. My sincere gratitude goes to all those who provided me with useful comments on the current work: Dr Dawoud Al Alami, Dr Martin Mills, Dr Istvan Kristó-Nagy, Dr Usaama Al Azami and the two anonymous reviewers.

I must also thank my longtime friends from Belgium: Tom De Bleeckere, who made an active contribution to this study, as well as Sam Bossaert and Robby De Baere for always being faithful. I am also grateful to my valuable and promising assistants Nagat, Zinnira and Tehmeena for their dedication and their skills. Many thanks to all my friends and students in Doha, Belgium and France.

Finally, I am deeply indebted to my teachers Dr Abdul Majid al-Najjar, Dr Larbi Bechri, Dr Abdullah al-Judai, Dr Ahmed Jaballah, Dr Ahmed Raissouni and all the others.

# 1 Introduction

## 1.1 Research Questions, Methodological Approach and Focus

The massive shifts in ideas and perceptions induced by modernity have challenged the Islamic tradition and compelled Muslims to critically revisit their intellectual heritage and ways of dealing with sources of knowledge, which in turn led to the emergence of reform endeavours in religio-ethical reasoning (*ijtihād*)[1] and its epistemic base, i.e., Islamic sciences,[2] for nearly two centuries. Despite these lengthy endeavours, reformists among Islamic science specialists believe that this field is still in need of further efforts to meet contemporary challenges and to regain its efficacy in addressing human reality through the ideals of the Islamic value system.

The endeavours to anchor Islam in the era of modernity required an approach to Islamic thought that makes use of classical modes of thinking and concepts by attributing to them a status that they did not enjoy in pre-modern times. The scope of application of these concepts was broadened to include that which was not usually included in classical literature. This shift was one of the requirements for overcoming the fragmentation of thought and the reductionist approaches that typified the legacy of pre-modern Islamic scholarship. These concepts and modes of thinking include *tawḥīd* (monotheism), *maqāṣid* (*Sharīʿa* objectives), *ʿimārat al-arḍ* (constructing and populating the earth), *fiṭra* (unspoiled nature), *amāna* (trust), *tazkiya* (purification), as well as *istikhlāf* (vicegerency), among many other concepts that were considered to constitute the "Islamic worldview."

The central hypothesis held by many contemporary reformists, and supported by this study, is that the main deficiency in contemporary Islamic thought is the absence of a comprehensively theorised philosophical and epistemological framework (worldview). This study argues that vicegerency (*istikhlāf*) as the human existential function[3] in Islam is a vital concept to develop this framework.

The concept of *istikhlāf* is ubiquitous in the literature of contemporary reformists and revivalists, especially in their discussion of the Islamic worldview, since most of them classify it among the major principles that make up this worldview. Nevertheless, this study argues that contemporary Islamic thought, thus far, did not elaborate an Islamic worldview and did not establish what can be considered components of that worldview in a coherent and comprehensive system.

DOI: 10.4324/9781003335948-1

This applies, to a greater degree, to the concept of *istikhlāf*. These studies did not clearly explain the meaning of *istikhlāf*, its ontological foundations,[4] its relationship to other concepts and its epistemological and methodological underpinnings. The concept of *istikhlāf* has, therefore, remained underdeveloped, despite the frequent emphasis on its importance and its ubiquity in contemporary writings. It has remained shrouded in ambiguity to the extent that many contemporary writers continue to use it as a loose, undefined concept. Despite the recurrent references to it, the concept of *istikhlāf* only played a formal role in shaping the Islamic worldview among those who tried to elaborate on it. Moreover, it did not play a role in the evaluation of Islamic thought epistemologically, despite being one of the most important factors in determining the Islamic worldview of humans and their relationship with existence, as claimed by the adherents of the theory of the Islamic worldview themselves.

This study will discuss some of these shortcomings in relation to the subject of the Islamic worldview. The purpose of this study lies in the attempt to open up new horizons for the concept of *istikhlāf* by establishing its meaning, dimensions, ontological foundations and its relationship with the major principles of Islam. With this in mind, I aim to clarify the features of this concept as a central component of the Islamic worldview. This will facilitate further discussions on the epistemological and methodological expressions of this concept in a way that reveals its ability to address some aspects of fragmentation in *ijtihād* (religio-ethical reasoning) and Islamic thought and disciplines in general.

Before embarking on this discussion, this study will seek to address the concept of *istikhlāf* from within the Islamic heritage in which it has been developed. In the process, this study attempts to analyse the perception of this concept among classical scholars in order to explore it from the perspective of the pioneers of contemporary Islamic reformism and revival. By limiting the scope of my work to the concept of vicegerency, I will explore its importance in developing an Islamic worldview and its place in Islamic Scripture, tradition and contemporary reformism.

The main hypothesis of this study is that the absence of the theorisation of the existential function of the human being in Islam, i.e., vicegerency, as one of the most prominent dimensions of the Islamic worldview, is a major lacuna in the literature on what has come to be known as the Islamic worldview and in the area of Islamic methodology and epistemology in general. This study will address this lacuna by linking major Islamic concepts and principles to the notion of vicegerency, demonstrating their cohesion under its frame as a harmonious entity, and the ability of this frame to function as a comprehensive system that regulates the particular and overall teachings of Islam.

Against this background and bearing in mind that none of the sources relied upon in this study formulated a comprehensive and consistent theory of vicegerency in Islam, I will attempt to formulate the outlines of this theory. To begin with, I will identify and attempt to overcome the shortcomings that have prevented the development of this theory to this day. To this end, a systematic approach will be adopted so as to ensure the coherence and comprehensiveness of our proposed theory to the greatest extent possible. Given that the existing literature on vicegerency and human existential function in Islam, in general, did not study vicegerency from the Qur'anic conception of existence and cosmos, this study will fill that gap. The relative Qur'anic texts will be treated inductively and analytically in an attempt to construct the said theory. Therefore, the overall methodological approach in this study can be described as critical, systematic and constructive. Considering the contemporary context that has prompted the emphasis on the issue of the Islamic worldview as the main solution for the epistemological and methodological reform of Islamic thought, the notion of vicegerency as human existential function will be the main focus of this study. Based on the above, the main question addressed by this study is: **What are the outlines of an Islamic theory of vicegerency as the human existential function within the Qur'anic worldview?**

Other key questions this study seeks to explore are: **How did ancient Muslim scholars perceive the concept of *istikhlāf*? How was the concept elaborated in the context of modern Islamic reformism? How relevant is the classical perception of the concept of *istikhlāf* to contemporary scholars? What are the limitations of contemporary views on *istikhlāf* that have prevented the concept from developing into a theory?**

These multifaceted questions are addressed in five chapters. **The second chapter**, which follows the introduction, clears the ground for the study by describing the background to the rise of the emphasis on the concept of vicegerency in the context of modern Islamic reformism. This chapter handles some of the problems posed by European modernity to Islamic thought that prompted Muslim reformists to question the classical mechanisms of Islamic epistemology and methodology. The aim is to understand how the upheavals caused by modernity raised awareness among Muslims of the necessity to develop a worldview capable of containing their fragmented thought and competing with Western worldviews. Since vicegerency is considered an integral part of that worldview according to most modern reformists, this chapter will be indispensable to understand the context of its use in modern Muslim literature. **The third chapter** explores the way in which vicegerency as an existential function was conceived in classical Islamic scholarship and the reasons behind the divergences surrounding it. This will be elaborated through the examination of the main divergences, which impacted that conception, around Qur'an 2:30. These pivotal divergences concern the identity of the person(s) or entity(ies) deputised by the vicegerent, the vicegerent himself and the object of his vicegerency. This chapter will also examine the way human existential function and vicegerency were perceived within classical epistemological paradigms, and pave the way to understanding contemporary debates about and perceptions of the concept. **The fourth chapter** is a comparative study of contemporary views about vicegerency as an existential function. This chapter will also provide a comparison between the views of contemporary and classical scholars. Furthermore, another key objective will be to underline some of the main shortcomings or distortions that have prevented the development of a coherent vicegerency theory. The questions raised in this chapter consist mainly of the following: How have contemporary scholars defined the concept of *istikhlāf* as existential function? What is the object of vicegerency (*al-mustakhlaf fīhi*) in the perception of contemporary scholars? What is the contribution of contemporary scholars to this field? In what way has the concept of *istikhlāf* been rooted in the Islamic worldview, and how have contemporary scholars related it to the major principles of Islam? How far did contemporary attempts root the concept in the Qur'an and in Islamic theology? What are the shortcomings or flaws in contemporary perspectives on the concept of vicegerency? **The fifth chapter** will lay the overall framework from which the development of the outlines of a vicegerency theory can proceed. First, one must examine the way in which contemporary thinkers attempt to relate the object of vicegerency, i.e., the nature of the human existential function, to the Qur'an and to what extent this can be relied upon. Another essential step in laying the bases of a Qur'anic vicegerency theory is to engage in the debate on the identity of the persons and/or entities of which man is vicegerent, as this will determine the meaning of vicegerency and its object. A thorough examination of this issue will thus be provided in this chapter. Besides the treatment of these fundamental questions, the chapter will develop a set of methodological and epistemological mechanisms that will be followed in an attempt to identify the object of vicegerency. **The sixth chapter** is an attempt to answer the main question raised in this study, as described above. The main purpose in this chapter is thus to develop a precise and consistent view of the human existential function and its features within a coherent Qur'anic worldview. This will be done on the basis of a holistic induction of the Qur'an and against the backdrop of the previously developed methodological and epistemological framework and identified flaws.

## 1.2 Islamic Vicegerency

*Istikhlāf* (vicegerency) is the infinitive of *istakhlafa*, which is derived from the root *khalafa*, and means etymologically to assign a *khalīfa* (successor/substitute/deputy/steward/vicegerent).[5] The root *khalafa* with its different derivatives (*khalīfa/istakhlafa/khulafā'/khalā'if/musthaklafīna*, *khalafa*, etc.) is used in different contexts in the Islamic founding texts, with the overall significance of replacing/succeeding/deputising, as per the linguistic meaning.[6]

With regard to *khilāfa* or *istikhlāf* as the existential function of the human being on Earth, the most obvious and most quoted verse in this regard is the one in *sūrat* (chapter) *al-Baqara*: "When your Lord said to the angels, 'Indeed, I am going to set a *khalīfa* on earth.'" (Q 2:30, b.o. Ali Qarai).[7] However, the Qur'an commentators did not agree about the meaning of *khalīfa*, nor with regard to whom the *khalīfa* is (Adam, his righteous progeny, the Muslim leaders, all human beings…), nor on who is being replaced/succeeded/deputised by the *khalīfa*. Some scholars even considered the idea of man being the vicegerent of God to be a violation of Islamic creed. Furthermore, the notion of *khilāfa* or *istikhlāf* as existential function received little attention in classical works and was not studied in independent works or chapters, or even as a separate topic. The only classical works including the word *khilāfa* in their title are those dealing with *khilāfa* as political function or institution, which was generally the main theme that was addressed by classical scholars when dealing with the concepts *khilāfa* or *istikhlāf*. Several academic studies have dealt with the term *khilāfa* from this angle,[8] yet most scholars conclude that there is hardly a link between the Qur'anic notion of *khilāfa* and the political function/institution of *khilāfa* as developed in the classical period.[9]

It is with the modern reformist movement[10] that the notion of *istikhlāf* or *khilāfa* as the existential function of (every) human being consisting in his vicegerency of God gained popularity, in line with the rising trend of exploring the major principles governing Islamic thought and civilisation. Most modern reformists[11] have referred to this concept in their works with a comprehensive meaning, but have limited themselves to general remarks without discussing *istikhlāf* as an independent topic or developing it in a detailed way. Only a few works discussed the issue of *istikhlāf* independently. Nevertheless, we could not find any study that developed a vicegerency theory.[12] The majority of these studies did not address it as a comprehensive philosophical system governing the teachings of Islam and regulating human thought and activity. Instead, they deal with it from a partial and, at times, reductionist perspective, sometimes in a variety of unrelated contexts, approaches and perspectives. As a consequence of this disarray, despite the abundant discussions on vicegerency, there is no agreement as to what it precisely is. The fourth chapter of this study will focus on the in-depth study of each of these works devoted to the issue of vicegerency.

It appears that the theoretical interest in vicegerency of man on Earth, as a key feature of the Islamic worldview, its scope and theological roots, is not tantamount to the momentousness of the subject matter. I have not come across any study concerned with the issue of vicegerency (*istikhlāf*) as a comprehensive philosophical system in Islamic thought that seeks to link it to all Islamic teachings in a coherent theory, taking it as a methodological basis for Islamic thought and demonstrating its importance in rationalising contemporary Islamic intellectual production.[13]

The closest study we found to the subject matter in focus is the study of ʿAbd al-Majīd al-Najjār, "The Vicegerency of Man, Between Revelation and Reason: A Critique of the Dialectic of the Text, Reason, and Reality."[14] This book focuses on the idea of vicegerency (*istikhlāf*) as the human function on Earth, with Revelation serving the purpose of enabling and empowering humankind to achieve it. In this context, human intellect is just a means to accomplish this mission. Al-Najjār discusses the doctrinal theological grounds of vicegerency as crucial to illustrate the concept, reality, nature and means of vicegerency. He then demonstrates the role of reason in achieving it – understanding Revelation as the first requirement to apply Revelation to the realities of life. For al-Najjār, the comprehensive conception of existence defines the source of the system and human function therein, as well as the aim it intends to achieve in life. Unless the ultimate aim of humanity is specified, confusion befalls human life and puts it into disarray.

Once the right existential function has been identified, one must identify the methods necessary to realise it and, finally, the way to implement these methods in human reality. As such, the author earnestly tries to identify the foundations of the methodology that can help reason understand Revelation and put it into operation in human reality. He also attempts to standardise the dialectic of text, reason and reality, and the role of each of them in specifying the values for the accomplishment of the human existential function. The focus of this book is mainly on the theological doctrinal frame of human vicegerency and the role of Revelation, reason, reality and the methods of *ijtihād* required to achieve it. The discussion only briefly touches on the quiddity and theoretical foundations of vicegerency and its association with other Islamic concepts, as well as its position in the comprehensive Islamic worldview. In short, the book does not develop the concept as an integrated theory, as we will further demonstrate in the fourth chapter.

## 1.3 Knowledge Integration in Islamic Thought and Disciplines

The challenge of going beyond the fragmented approaches in understanding the Islamic founding texts and, accordingly, addressing the problems that face Muslims from a holistic perspective, has been the main concern of the modern Muslim reformist movement.[15] The way in which this issue was addressed originated from the assessment of the historical course of Islamic sciences in general and *ijtihād* in particular. The fragmented approach has dominated this movement in the process of deduction (*istimbāt*) from and understanding of Revelation. The issue also originated from the observation of the decline of Muslim thought and civilisation in relation to the contemporary West. As such, the modern reformist movement paid due attention to the constant holistic system governing Islamic thought and the thematic unity of Islamic founding texts.

This was considered to be the starting point for reconnecting heritage and Muslim intellectual production with contemporary reality. Early reconciliation efforts emerged in the discussions and dialogues of Jamāl al-Dīn al-Afghānī and then Muḥammad ʿAbduh and his disciple Rashīd Riḍā,[16] who emphasised and developed this approach, which is essentially an attempt to discover the principles of understanding Qurʾanic norms (*sunan*)[17] in human societies and civilisations. Later, Mālik Bin-Nabī followed a similar course in his writings on civilisation. In addition, Muḥammad Iqbāl's attempt towards "the reconstruction of religious thought in Islam,"[18] and Muḥammad ʿAbd Allāh Drāz's endeavour to draw a Qurʾanic philosophy[19] were steps forward in the same direction as the early modern reformist scholars. Moreover, many contemporary scholars[20] have shown a keen interest in studying the Qurʾan in an attempt to "reconstruct Muslim religious philosophy"[21] according to Iqbāl's claim, or in attempts to discover the *maqāṣid* (higher objectives) of *Sharīʿa* from a social perspective, which in turn led them to expose the most important social challenges and problems facing modern communities.[22] Indeed, modern reformist thinkers focused on the comprehensive system governing existence and especially human action on the social level, considering that the decline and deviation that befell the Muslim community drove it away from the principles of that system, as well as the prerequisites of modern reality. In essence, the partial and fragmented understanding of the revealed texts and their rulings affected individual religiosity only slightly, but profoundly impacted communal religiosity and social renaissance.[23]

In this regard, several attempts have been made to overcome this fragmented approach through crystallising new *ijtihād*-oriented approaches for the treatment of texts and context. As such, attention was paid to the thematic interpretation of the Qurʾan, *maqāṣid al-Sharīʿa*, and the role of reality in *ijtihād*. In this context, many new approaches and disciplines appeared, such as *al-sunan al-kawniyya* (cosmic norms),[24] *al-naẓariyyāt al-fiqhiyya* (legal theories of jurisprudence),[25] *fiqh al-nawāzil wa-muwākabat al-mustajaddāt* (methodology for resolving new legal incidences and reality-treatment),[26] *fiqh al-wāqiʿ* (methodology of considering reality in *ijtihād*)[27] and *fiqh al-tanzīl* (methods of applied *fiqh*),[28] as well as methods of *muwāzanāt* (the legal balance between benefits and harms),[29] *awlawiyyāt* (priorities)[30] and *maʾālāt* (ultimate consequences of actions).[31] However, these attempts have not given rise to a real shift in contemporary *ijtihād*, although they helped it to overcome some aspects of the fragmented approaches.

Consequently, several studies emerged, especially in the *Islamisation of Knowledge* project (later renamed knowledge integration),[32] which calls to adopt modern knowledge in a way consistent with the Islamic worldview and ethical norms, contributing to the critique of both traditional and contemporary approaches of *ijtihād*. These studies argued that the contemporary approaches have not been liberated from the classical paradigm of *ijtihād* in terms of conceptual reductionism and fragmentation of knowledge. They went on to emphasise the necessity of complementing or, rather, replacing them with new approaches to liberate the Islamic intellectual production from the narrowness of partiality and legal formalities. To overcome the diagnosed methodological defects, these studies were guided by a general plan proposing the critical evaluation of both Islamic heritage and Western knowledge in order to determine the proportionality between Islam and the modern sciences. The ultimate goal was to enable the exploitation of modern knowledge in the construction of Islamic knowledge. The most important starting point for this methodological reformation was to build the Islamic epistemology and methodology on the general governing philosophy of Islamic teachings. As stated above, the philosophy that guides Islamic thought and methodology was of interest to many scholars in the modern era. However, Sayyid Quṭb (d. 1966) who explored it in his *Khaṣāʾiṣ al-Taṣawwur al-Islāmī wa-Muqawwimātuhu* (Islamic Perception: Its Characteristics and Key Elements),[33] was considered by some researchers as one of the main initiators of worldview studies in the Muslim world.[34] This interest is reflected at the institutional level and is exemplified by the work conducted by the International Institute of Islamic Thought (IIIT) in the context of the discussion of many seemingly synonymous terms like "Islamic worldview," "universal Islamic vision," "world perception," "general philosophy," "comprehensive interpretation" (*al-tafsīr al-shāmil*), "explanatory model" (*al-namūdhaj al-tafsīrī*) and "ideology";[35] however, the most recurrent of these terms remains "Islamic worldview."

## 1.4 Islamic Worldview as Epistemological and Methodological Frame

The term "worldview" (*weltanschauung*) goes back to the German philosopher Immanuel Kant (1727–1804).[36] The two concepts "philosophy" and "worldview" are closely related. Talking about "a philosophy" in its broadest sense refers, in fact, to a worldview.[37] A worldview is a "particular philosophy of life or conception of the world."[38] More precisely it is "a coherent collection of concepts and theorems that must allow us to construct a global image of the world, and in this way to understand as many elements of our experience as possible."[39] This ultimately will influence all of one's perceiving, thinking, knowing and doing.[40] Humans have always, consciously or subconsciously, explored deep questions related to existence. The formulated answers to those questions constitute their worldview.[41]

The notion of worldview attained the status of academic celebrity in the second half of the nineteenth century. In the German context, "when *weltanschauung* had reached its zenith in popularity in both common and academic discourse around the turn of the twentieth century, it finally began to receive noteworthy attention. That attention has continued right up to the present time."[42] In his historical overview of the concept of worldview, David K. Naugle surveyed its usage in the European and Anglo-American contexts concluding that:

> Since its inception in Immanuel Kant's Critique of Judgment in 1790, the notion of *Weltanschauung* (worldview) has become one of the central intellectual conceptions in contemporary thought and culture. Though the history of the term has for the most part been neglected in the English-speaking world, scholars in the prodigious German enterprises of word history and the history of ideas have thoroughly investigated its background [...] though this fascinating notion has its roots sunk in German soil, its rapid transcontinental transplantation manifests the amazing fertility of the concept. A penetrating idea that felicitously expressed core human concerns had been born. No wonder, then, that within seven decades of its birth it entered the Anglo-American discourse and became as fruitful across the channel and overseas as it had been on the European continent.[43]

The Center Leo Apostel (CLEA), a Belgium-based research institution dedicated to the development of worldviews on an interdisciplinary basis, notes that a worldview is constituted from seven basic components, which are the answers to seven questions, forming a coherent whole.[44] These questions were summarised with their corresponding traditional philosophical discipline by Clément Vidal,[45] as follows:

1. What is? *Ontology* (model of reality as a whole)
2. Where does it all come from? *Explanation* (model of the past)
3. Where are we going? *Prediction* (model of the future)
4. What is good and what is evil? *Axiology* (theory of values)
5. How should we act? *Praxeology* (theory of actions)
6. What is true and what is false? *Epistemology* (theory of knowledge)
7. Where do we start in order to answer those questions?

From an Islamic perspective, the contribution to worldview studies is scarce and does not encompass all the aspects of the discipline. In the context of modern Islamic reformism, over the past two centuries, Muslim scholars have intensively discussed several features related to the Islamic worldview, such as *tawḥīd* (monotheism), God, human nature, the "witnessed" (*shahāda*) and the "unwitnessed" (*ghayb*) worlds, vicegerency (*istikhlāf*), etc., but not necessarily under the heading of "worldview studies."[46] Although these contributions provide many answers to the above-mentioned worldview questions from an Islamic perspective, there is, within Islamic scholarship, "still no separate branch of knowledge or discipline that specializes on issues pertaining to the Islamic worldview, such as its subject matter, objectives, methods or tools of analysis, and its applications to different disciplines."[47]

Most of the works in this regard do not address the seven above-mentioned questions as a whole, in a coherent and systematic way, but only deal with partial aspects of the Islamic worldview in a more or less scattered way. A case in point is the absence of an in-depth study of the impact and requirements of the Islamic worldview on contemporary *ijtihād* (religio-ethical reasoning) and its consequent sciences (Islamic sciences). Furthermore, an essential principle of the Islamic worldview, i.e., vicegerency (human existential function), was never theorised as an integral part of that worldview, as argued in this study.

### *1.4.1 Ismāʿīl al-Fārūqī*

One of the pioneering studies on reforming Islamic methodology based on an Islamic worldview was the founding treatise of one of the leading figures in the *Islamisation of Knowledge* project, namely Ismāʿīl Rājī al-Fārūqī (d. 1986), entitled *Islamisation of Knowledge: General Principles and Work Plan.*[48] Al-Fārūqī raised critical remarks about the later jurists' narrow conception of *ijtihād*, pointing out that they had reduced the process of *ijtihād* to jurisprudential analogy (*qiyās fiqhī*) and thus reduced the various problems faced by contemporary Muslims to jurisprudential issues. Furthermore, he noted that they had entrusted the process of *ijtihād* in various aspects of thought and life to the jurists, thereby reducing scientific and epistemic research to the realm of jurisprudential sciences.

Hence, he stressed the urgent need for Muslims to adopt a broader conception of *ijtihād*, inclusive of all domains of human activity. The same holds true for the fundamentals of jurisprudence (*uṣūl al-fiqh*).

In al-Fārūqī's opinion, the early jurists understood *uṣūl al-fiqh* to signify the primary principles necessary for Islamic understanding of life and reality. Al-Fārūqī maintained that Islamic thought adopted a narrow approach regarding the concept of *ijtihād*, reducing it to *fatwā* (non-binding legal verdict) and specific rulings (*aḥkām juzʾiyya*), which thwarted the success of contemporary reformist scholars' invitation to reopen the "gate of *ijtihād*" and reinvigorate its practices for the sake of Muslim renaissance. To put it simply, the problem with the aforementioned approach to *ijtihād* was the absence of a holistic vision. As such, al-Fārūqī called for a new methodology and understanding of the principles (*uṣūl*) and sources of Islamic knowledge. The Islamisation of knowledge is the only possible way, in al-Fārūqī's opinion, to fix the shortcomings affecting the traditional methodology, which in turn, following al-Fārūqī's call, should draw harmony between the Islamic tenets and views of modern sciences and, at the same time, criticise and examine Western thought with a view to generating new Islamic knowledge. Consequently, he developed a set of principles as the framework for Islamic knowledge, revolving around the principles of monotheism (*tawḥīd*) in the Islamic conception. This is a monotheistic methodology based on the Islamic conception of the Oneness of the Creator and the unity of creatures, unity of knowledge, unity of life and unity of humanity.

The IIIT published a number of studies in the context of the above-mentioned project in serious attempts to systemise both general and specific teachings of Islam and build the methodology of Islamic thought in conformity with a coherent system generating the Islamic epistemology. One of these studies was al-Fārūqī's work *Tawḥīd: Its Implication for Thought and Life*.[49] In this study, al-Fārūqī attempted to draw the milestones of *tawḥīd* as a methodological principle furnishing man with the ability to investigate texts, universe and reality through a holistic vision. Al-Fārūqī maintained that *tawḥīd* is the only good nucleus for human vicegerency and the bearing of responsibility (*amāna*) on Earth.

Through a comparative epistemological analysis, the study demonstrates the uniqueness of *tawḥīd* using 13 perspectives on two levels: first, *takhliya* (the purgative habilitation) that liberates human endeavours in this world from the causes of corruption and imbalance; second, *taḥliya* (securing the best development) for all elements of empowerments, righteousness and reformation. The book has 13 chapters including 13 articles that are as follows:

- The essence of religious experience
- The quintessence of Islam
- The principle of history
- the principle of knowledge
- The principle of metaphysics
- The principle of ethics
- The principle of social order

- The principle of the *umma*
- The principle of the family
- The principle of political order
- The principle of economic order
- The principle of world order
- The principle of esthetics

In spite of the fact that this book is a significant contribution to the literature on the Islamic worldview, it has only superficially explored one of its most important elements, namely, the function of vicegerency.

### *1.4.2 Ṭāhā Jābir al-ʿUlwānī*

In the same trajectory, Ṭāhā Jābir al-ʿUlwānī's[50] work: *Al-Tawḥīd wa-l-Tazkiya wa-l-ʿUmrān: Muḥāwala fī l-Kashf ʿan al-Qiyam wa-l-Maqāṣid al-Qurʾāniyya al-Ḥākima* (Monotheism, Purification, and Civilisation: Attempts to Reveal the Ruling Qurʾanic Values and Objectives)[51] formulates what al-ʿUlwānī (d. 2016) called the "Governing Value System." He organised the elements of that system in three concepts to form a *maqāṣid* (objectives)-set referential ground with a view to explaining the ultimate end of the creation and developing a standard value system from which all general and specific Islamic values emanate. The most prominent aim of this endeavour was the rehabilitation of the general Qurʾanic principles and overall *Sharīʿa* principles, after long-standing concern for the particular evidence and its meticulous details, which was about to erase the great significance of these general principles and thwart their functioning.

Sheikh al-ʿUlwānī is of the opinion that the tripartite system of *tawḥīd, tazkiya,* and *ʿumrān* (i.e., Monotheism, Purification, and Civilisation) forms a governing system that should prevail over all details of Islamic jurisprudence (*fiqh*) and thought. He wanted this paradigm to constitute the methodological entry point to the endeavours of editing and verifying the Islamic intellectual legacy in order to clear it from what he considers "scriptural traces" that leaked into it from the "people of the book" at an early time and then from the "legacies of other nations." He also wanted it to be a *maqāṣid*-oriented entry point for a revisionist movement of the religious sciences before being an Islamic moral entry for a normative assessment of modern sciences. Al-ʿUlwānī also maintains that these governing higher objectives could help in the development of a general epistemological theory in all religious sciences as well as in social sciences.

However important this study may be in terms of the new horizons it opens up for reforming Islamic thought, it remains too vague and lacks some basic elements necessary for theoretically formulating the Islamic worldview. A case in point is that it neither presents a specific frame for the standards used to choose these three exclusive principles over others, nor does it provide sufficient details of these principles. It builds no system or theory on this triad alongside an illustration of how all other Islamic principles, objectives, values and rulings are included thereunder and standardised therewith. Furthermore, it draws no precise association between these three principles and others, which leaves many questions unanswered, e.g., the question of the comprehensiveness of *tawḥīd* and its inclusion of all dimensions of the Islamic conception. How could it form a division beside other principles included thereunder? The study also makes slight indications only in passing to the relation of vicegerency to these governing principles.

### *1.4.3 ʿAbd al-Ḥamīd Abū Sulaymān*

Other significant studies in the area of the Islamic worldview include ʿAbd al-Ḥamīd Abū Sulaymān's *The Qurʾanic Worldview: A Springboard for Cultural Reform*.[52] This work presents a broad revision of the issue of the Islamic worldview. Abū Sulaymān (d. 2021) traced the trajectory of the Islamic worldview through history, explaining that it was a main cause of the early progress of the first Muslim generation. He tried to uncover the kinds of distortions that befell it and the perils facing Islamic thought today because of those distortions.

This book contributes to expounding the Qurʾanic worldview and the way to realise and retrieve it in the present world, with a view to helping overcome the fragmented approaches in Islamic thought and achieving epistemological integration between the Revelation-based sciences and the natural sciences. In so doing, Muslim individuals and their community will be empowered to recover their past positive motivations, dynamics and abilities for building human civilisation. Abū Sulaymān considered the random and partial reform efforts, with their failure to understand the nature of the Islamic civilisational system and its associated laws governing its interaction with its environment, to be futile. The ignorance and intellectual neglect of this element was the main reason behind the failure of the reformers' efforts to revive and energise the Muslim *umma* (community), despite several endeavours devoted to this purpose over the centuries. The book investigates a number of concepts, viewing them as the principles of the Qurʾanic worldview, such as *tawḥīd*, *istikhlāf*, justice, freedom, responsibility, teleology and morality, among several others. However, he did not explore the details of these principles or explain how they coherently associate with one another to form a logically consistent system or theory. A thorough critique of the idea of vicegerency as presented in the above-mentioned works will follow in the fourth chapter of this study.

### *1.4.4 Ṭāhā ʿAbd al-Raḥmān*

In a register closely related to that of knowledge integration,[53] a contemporary Muslim philosopher who formulated one of the most developed Islamic ethical philosophies is Ṭāhā ʿAbd al-Raḥmān. ʿAbd al-Raḥmān captures his Islamic worldview in one central concept that he calls the "Trusteeship paradigm."[54] The Moroccan ethicist defines the trusteeship paradigm, which he developed throughout his prolific writings, as follows: "Trusteeship is a deposit of care, which makes everything that God has created for the human being a deposit entrusted to him."[55]

It is also "a spiritual connection in which external 'ethicisation' (*takhalluq*) is constructed on internal 'ethicisation.'"[56] Trusteeship is thus a deposit of care and a spiritual connection.

This paradigm is based on five principles, i.e., 1. *Al-shāhidiyya* (witnessing), 2. *Al-āyatiyya* (signing), 3. *Al-idāʿiyya* (depositing), 4. *Al-fiṭriyya* (innateness), 5. *Al-jamʿiyya* (wholeness).[57] The principle of witnessing implies that the 'ethicisation' (*takhalluq*) of the human being can only be based on the fostering of the consciousness that God is witnessing everything. This consciousness will elevate ethics from a mere Divine commandment that the human must abide by, to a pleasure that he will gravitate towards spontaneously. Thereby, he will be a witness of the unity of God, which is what Islam is about. The principle of signing means that there is no separation between the world and religion considering that both of them are God's signs. In that sense, the universe is not made of merely abstract phenomena, but those are linked to a metaphysical reality. The principle of depositing reflects the idea that things are deposits given to the human. The elements of the universe are not the property of the human but that of God. Depositing is to possess things through God as a trust that He entrusts you with so that you would care for it, which implies a considerable ethical responsibility. The principle of innateness reflects the idea that ethics are taken from the *fiṭra* (natural human disposition). The human being is innately ethical since his spirit (*rūḥ*) is linked with God. The circumstances of life can affect this innate status and replace it with a temporary status devoid of ethics. As for the principle of wholeness, it means that religion is constituted out of ethics in its entirety. Religion was only revealed to guide all human actions towards the ethical; the morality of the human being thus depends on his faithfulness to religion. Without religion, he can only moralise a part of himself, whereas religion considers all dimensions of the human being, inner and outer, allowing him to regain his fully fledged humanness and spirituality.

It becomes apparent on studying ʿAbd al-Raḥmān's trusteeship paradigm that the main issue to him is not to initially theorise a comprehensive Islamic ethical theory or worldview, but rather to immediately begin the critique of the hegemony of Western philosophy and euro-modernity from that reading grid, without focusing on developing that very paradigm in a comprehensive model. This forces the reader of his works to extricate it from the sum of his thoughts. In other words, his focus was not on building that paradigm theoretically unless it was required to deconstruct atheist secularism, modern ethical theories and political Islam.

Besides his critique of modernity, ʿAbd al-Raḥmān also aims critique at Islamic jurisprudence (*fiqh*), which he calls "injunctive jurisprudence" (*fiqh iʾtimārī*), from the perspective of trusteeship. He does not really challenge classical jurisprudence (and Islamic sciences in general), its scope, its underlying logic, etc., but rather insists on the necessity of what he calls "trusteeship jurisprudence" (*fiqh iʾtimānī*) alongside it or above it, in order for classical jurisprudence to achieve its ethical objectives. Indeed, he considers that classical jurisprudence is only concerned with the apparent human behaviour, while the purpose of the apparent injunctions should be to achieve the depth of those injunctions, which can only be realised through "trusteeship jurisprudence." ʿAbd al-Raḥmān does not question the efficiency of classical jurisprudence in fulfilling its practical function today, but only highlights the need to reconstruct it on its spiritual foundations. He believes that the coercive method adopted by the "injunctive jurisprudence" will not vivify the heart of the human when following the Divine command, contrary to the "trusteeship jurisprudence."[58]

What is important to highlight in the context of our present study, is that ʿAbd al-Raḥmān entitled his project "trusteeship paradigm" in his latest writings, long after he started developing his ethical philosophy. In that sense it appears, through his writings, that trusteeship is the title of his ethical theory rather than a concept governing it and framing all the principles that constitute it. Hence, he did not dedicate much effort in defining its meaning and its link with Islamic teachings and principles. Also, he did not try to systematically link the concepts and the principles, like the five principles mentioned above, which he developed as the main components of the trusteeship paradigm, with the concept of trusteeship itself, nor did he demonstrate the way in which they relate to it. Occasionally, it is difficult for the reader to see any clear relationship at all. Furthermore, even though he makes use of concepts that we deem central in the theory of vicegerency, such as *istikhlāf* (vicegerency) itself, *fiṭra*, *amāna* (trust/responsibility), etc., he does this without explicitly theorising the frame in which they operate and which permits categorising them and relating them to the overall Islamic value system. Moreover, I consider *istikhlāf* more suitable to govern Islamic epistemology, as it refers to the ultimate function of the human on Earth, while trusteeship does not explicitly express what the purpose of trusteeship is, i.e., what exact responsibility humans are entrusted with. In that sense, trusteeship is not the highest purpose governing Revelation and directing human action. Finally, the main purpose of ʿAbd al-Raḥmān's trusteeship paradigm is to deconstruct euro-modernity through an alternative model, defending the idea that the status quo is not the only possible expression of modernity, and claiming the right for every tradition and culture to develop its own modernity, of which trusteeship would be the Islamic alternative.[59] Instead, my purpose here is, more modestly, to consider the idea of restructuring Islamic thought and sciences through the prism of the vicegerency theory. However, my focus will be on the construction of that very theory as the first priority.

Generally speaking, critical interaction with studies on the Islamic worldview in general, and vicegerency in particular, provides a rich ground for launching the theorisation of the outlines of the Islamic worldview in general, and of the existential function of man in particular. However, most of these studies focus on developing a frame for reviewing social sciences, instead of rebuilding the religious sciences on the basis of the Islamic worldview. Hence, few studies elaborate on reform in *ijtihād* and its consequent sciences on that basis, as stated previously.

Although the term *istikhlāf* is repeatedly used in all these studies, it is not defined in a precise way nor is it theorised as an essential element of the Islamic worldview. Users of this term seem to have different views about its meanings and dimensions. Man's existential function in Islam may be clear and agreed upon in overall terms, yet ambiguity continues to befall its theoretical foundations, details, its interaction with other Islamic principles and its impact on Islamic methodology and epistemology.

## Notes

1 *Ijtihād* is used here in its general and comprehensive sense, which encompasses all kinds of intellectual endeavours that seek to orient the human perception and behaviour towards Islamic ethics.
2 Islamic sciences refers to the disciplines concerned with the study of the Islamic foundational texts, i.e., Qur'an and *Sunna*, with a view to minimising the instances of slippage and error in understanding and implementing them in accordance with the requirements of the human reality under study. These sciences represent a link between the absolute Divine Revelation and the relative human reality. The meaning of the concept of Islamic sciences, as understood in this study, relates to any of the sciences pertaining directly to the study of religious texts and their implementation in reality, including, among others, Qur'an exegesis, *Ḥadīth* studies, theology, Islamic law (*fiqh*) and its fundamentals, and Sufism.
3 What is meant by human existential function in the present study is the particular mission or task for the realisation of which God created the human being and sent him to earth. It is for the fulfilment of that mission that the universe was subjugated for him, that he was created according to an adequate natural constitution and that he was addressed by scriptural revelation through consecutive messengers and prophets sent by God.
4 The term "ontology" will be used in this study with reference to the original nature of things – what they are in their fundamental essence and how they relate to other entities – and not with reference to the homonymous branch of metaphysics in philosophy. Here, for instance, when talking about the "ontological foundations" of *istikhlāf*, we refer to the original principles that define its very existence as a concept, the underlying structures that shape its nature and how they relate to one another in that sense.
5 Muḥammad ibn Manẓūr, *Lisān al-ʿArab* [The Tongue of the Arabs] (Beirut: Dār Ṣādir, 3rd ed. 1993), vol. 9, 85.
6 See: ʿAbd al-Riḍā Ḥasan Jayyād, "Mafhūm al-Khilāfa al-Ilāhiyya li-l-Insān fī l-Qurʾān al-Karīm wa-Kitābāt al-ʿUlamāʾ al-Muslimīn" [The Concept of Man's Vicegerency of God in the Noble Qur'an and in Islamic Scholarship], *Adab al-Kūfa Journal*, no. 2 (2008), 134–35.
7 The Qur'anic verses in this study will not always be retrieved from existing translations but will often be reformulated on the basis thereof as per the understanding of the researcher according to the study of different Qur'an lexicons and to the approaches adopted in this study. Consequently, we will use the term "based on" (b.o.) to refer to the translations on which basis we developed our translation whether through major or minor amendments. The absence of the abbreviation b.o. means that the respective translation is quoted without alteration.
8 See for instance:
   - William Montgomery Watt, "God's Caliph: Qurʾānic Interpretation and Umayyad Claims," *Iran and Islam, in Memory of the Late Vladimir Minorsky*, ed. Clifford Edmund Bosworth (Edinburgh: Edinburgh University Press, 1971), 565–74
   - Wael B. Hallaq, "Caliphs, Jurists and the Saljūks in the Political Thought of al-Juwaynī," *The Muslim World* 74.1 (1984), 26–41
   - Patricia Crone and Martin Hinds, *God's Caliph, Religious Authority in the First Centuries of Islam* (Cambridge: Cambridge University Press, 1986)

- Wadād al-Qāḍī, "The Term 'Khalīfa' in Early Exegetical Literature," *Die Welt des Islams*, 28/1 (1988), 392–411
- Fadzli Bin Adam, "The Concept of Khilāfah according to Selected Sunni and Shīʿī Qurʾanic Commentaries" (PhD diss., University of Leeds, 2001)
- David L. Johnston, "The Human Khilāfa: A Growing Overlap of Reformism and Islamism on Human Rights Discourse?" *Islamochristiana* 28 (2002), 35–53
- Uri Rubin, "Prophets and Caliphs: The Biblical Foundations of the Umayyad Authority" in Herbert Berg (ed.), *Method and Theology in the Study of Islamic Origins* (Leiden: Brill, 2003), 73–99
- Eric J. Hanne, *Putting the Caliph in His Place: Power, Authority, and the Late Abbāsid Caliphate* (Madison, NJ: Fairleigh Dickinson University Press, 2007)
- Vernie Liebl, "The Caliphate," *Middle Eastern Studies* 45.3 (2009), 373–91
- Kim Searcy, "The Khalīfa and the Routinization of Charismatic Authority," *International Journal of African Historical Studies* 43.3 (2010), 429–42
- Mattias Gardell, "'Every Man and Woman Is God's Caliph': The Rise of the Islamic Democratic Mainstream," in *Fundamentalism in the Modern World*, vol. 1, ed. Ulrika Mårtensson, Jennifer Bailey, Priscilla Ringrose and Asbjorn Dyrendal (New York: I.B. Tauris, 2011), 240–65
- Abdulhadi Alajmi, "ʿUlama and Caliphs New Understanding of the 'God's Caliph' Term," *Journal of Islamic Law and Culture* 13., no. 1 (2011), 102–12
- Linda T. Darling, "'The Vicegerent of God, from Him We Expect Rain': The Pre-Islamic State in Early Islamic Political Culture," *Journal of the American Oriental Society* 134.3 (2014), 407–29
- Han Hsien Liew, "The Caliphate of Adam: Theological Politics of the Qurʾānic Term Ḫalīfa," *Arabica* 63 (2016), 1–29
- Andrew F. March, *The Caliphate of Man: Popular Sovereignty in Modern Islamic Thought* (Cambridge, MA; London, England: Harvard University Press, 2019)

9 See for instance: Rudi Paret, "Signification coranique de ḫalīfa et d'autres dérivés de la racine ḫalafa," *Studia Islamica* 31 (1970), 211–17; Watt, "God's Caliph: Qurʾānic Interpretation and Umayyad Claims"; and Liew, "The Caliphate of Adam: Theological Politics of the Qurʾānic Term Ḫalīfa."

10 For Mālik Bin-Nabī, modern reformism is the one that aims at keeping pace with modern reality and civilisation in reliance on and loyalty to the Islamic values. It is not the traditionalist reformation of belief, behaviour or religiosity in isolation from modernisation. Jamāl al-Dīn al-Afghānī (d. 1897), in Bin-Nabī's view, was the one who initiated this movement. See: Malik Bennabi, *Vocation de l'Islam* (Beirut: Albouraq, 2006), 87.

11 We will mention some of them in the section below.

12 This applies to both reformists that studied *istikhlāf* as a general human existential function and those who used it to develop a modern Islamic theory of governance, popular sovereignty and democracy.

13 I have surveyed a number of Arabic and English databases, including: Dar Almandumah, Al Manhal, JSTOR, Index Islamicus, Literature Resource Center, Scopus, AGRIS and SienceDirect.

14 ʿAbd al-Majīd al-Najjār, *Khilāfat al-Insān bayna al-Waḥy wa-l-ʿAql* [The Vicegerency of Man, Between Revelation and Reason: A Critique of the Dialectic of the Text, Reason, and Reality] (Herndon, VA: International Institute of Islamic Thought, 3rd ed., 2005).

15 In his introduction to Sheikh al-Ṭāhir ibn ʿĀshūr's work *Maqāṣid al-Sharīʿa al-Islāmiyya*, Muḥammad al-Ṭāhir al-Misāwī presents the views of a group of modern reformers, Sunni and Shiite, denouncing the fragmented approach in dealing with texts and legal rulings in complete absence of the comprehensive vision that places issues in their general framework on both theoretical and practical levels. See Muḥammad al-Ṭāhir ibn ʿĀshūr, *Maqāṣid al-Sharīʿa al-Islāmiyya* [The Objectives of *Sharīʿa*], ed. Muḥammad al-Ṭāhir al-Misāwī (Jordan: Dār al-Nafāʾis, 2nd ed., 2001), 97–109.

16 This is particularly visible in the Qur'an exegesis of Riḍā, *Tafsīr al-Manār*, which is based on a collection of thoughts of a disciple of al Afghānī, Muḥammad 'Abduh, of whom Rashīd Riḍā was a disciple.
17 These are considered to be a set of universal and constant laws governing history and human society.
18 Muḥammad Iqbāl, *The Reconstruction of Religious Thought in Islam* (Dodo Press, 2009).
19 Especially in his book *The Moral World of the Qur'an*. Muḥammad 'Abd Allāh Drāz, *The Moral World of the Qur'an* (London: I.B. Tauris, 2008).
20 Besides those we have mentioned and the coming scholars, we can add the following ones just to name a few:

- Badī' al-Zamān Sa'īd al-Nūrsī, *The Words, On the Nature and Purposes of Man, Life, and All Things*, translated by Şükran Vahide (Istanbul: Sözler, 2008)
- Muḥammad Bāqir al-Ṣadr, *Our Philosophy* (Ahlulbayt, 2014)
- Murtaḍā Muṭahharī, *Fundamentals of Islamic Thought: God, Man and the Universe* (Berkeley: Mizan Press, 1985)
- Abdul Hameed Siddiqi and Muḥammad Saeed Siddiqi, *The Islamic Concept of Religion and Its Revival* (Lahore: Kazi Publications, 1980)
- Muḥammad al-Ghazālī, *al-Mahāwir al-Khamsa li-l-Qur'ān* [The Five Axes of the Qur'an] (Cairo: Dār al Shurūq, 2000)
- Yūsuf al-Qaraḍāwī, *al-Khaṣā'iṣ al-'Āmma li-l-Islām* [The General Characteristics of Islam] (Beirut: Mu'assasat al-Risāla, 2nd ed., 1983)
- Muḥsin 'Abd al-Ḥamīd, *al-Madhdhabiyya al-Islāmiyya wa-l-Taghayyur al-Ḥaḍārī* [Islamic Doctrines and Civilisational Change] (Doha: Qatar's Ministry of Endowments and Islamic Affairs, 1985)
- Seyyed Hossein Nasr, *Ideals and Realities of Islam* (ABC International, 2000)
- Maulana Wahiduddin Khan, *Islam Rediscovered: Discovering Islam from Its Original Sources* (New Delhi: Goodword, 2001)
- Muhammed Hamidullah, *Introduction to Islam* (International Islamic Federation of Student Organisations, 1970)
- Fazlur Rahman, *Major Themes of the Qur'an* (Chicago: University of Chicago Press, 2nd ed., 2009)
- Syed Muḥammad Naquib al-Attas, *Prolegomena to the Metaphysics of Islam: An Exposition of the Fundamental Elements of the Worldview of Islam* (Kuala Lumpur: International Institute of Islamic Thought and Civilization (ISTAC), 1995)
- Abdul Wahid Hamid, *Islam: The Natural Way* (London: Muslim Education and Library Services, 2004)
- 'Abd al-Majīd al-Najjār, *Fiqh al-Taḥaḍḍur al-Islāmī* [The Jurisprudence of Islamic Civilisation] (Beirut: Dār al-Gharb al-Islāmī, 1999)
- William C. Chittick, *Science of the Cosmos, Science of the Soul, the Pertinence of Islamic Cosmology in the Modern World* (Oxford: Oneworld Publications, 2007)

21 Iqbāl, *The Reconstruction of Religious Thought in Islam*, Preface.
22 Zaynab al-'Ulwānī, *Murāja'āt fī Taṭawwur al-Minhāj al-Maqāṣidī 'inda al-Mu'āṣirīn* [Review of the Evolution of the Contemporary *Maqāṣidī* Approach] (Herndon, VA: International Institute of Islamic Thought, 2012), 4.
23 The second chapter of this study will elaborate on the context of the shock of Western civilisation which stimulated the reformist endeavours for social reformation.
24 See for instance: 'Ādil 'Īsāwī, *Fiqh al-Sunan al-Ilāhiyya wa-Dawruhā fī al-Binā al-Ḥaḍārī* [Divine Norms and Their Role in Civilisational Construction] (Doha: Qatar's Ministry of Endowments and Islamic Affairs, 2012).
25 See for instance: Muḥammad al-Zuḥaylī, *Al-Naẓariyyāt al-Fiqhiyya* [Legal Theories of Jurisprudence] (Damascus: Dār al-Qalam, 1993).
26 See for instance: Muḥammad al-Jīzānī, *Fiqh al-Nawāzil* [Methodology for Resolving New Legal Incidences] (Cairo: Dār ibn Ḥazm, 2nd ed., 2006).

27 See for instance: Saʿīd Bayhī, *Al-Taʾṣīl al-Sharʿī li-Mafhūm Fiqh al-Wāqiʿ* [The Legal Foundation of the Notion of *Fiqh al-Wāqiʿ*] (Alexandria: al-Dār al-ʿĀlamiyya, 2nded., 2005).
28 See for instance: Aḥmad al-Miʿmārī, *Fiqh al-Tanzīl* [Methods of Applied *Fiqh*] (Beirut: Markaz Namāʾ, 2015).
29 See for instance: ʿAbd al-Majīd al-Sawsawa, *Fiqh al-Muwāzanāt fī l-Sharīʿa al-Islamiyya* [The Balance between Benefits and Harms in Islamic Legislation] (Dubai: Dār al-Qalam, 2004).
30 See for instance: Yūsuf al-Qaraḍāwī, *Fī Fiqh al-Awlawiyyāt* [Understanding Priorities] (Cairo: Maktabat Wahba, 1996).
31 See for instance: Walīd al-Ḥusayn, *Iʿtibār Maʾālāt al-Afʿāl wa-Atharuhu al-Fiqhī* [The Consideration of the Consequences of Actions and Their Jurisprudential Impact] (Riyadh: Dār al-Tadmūriyya, 2008).
32 Fatḥī Malkāwī, *Minhājiyyat al-Takāmul al-Maʿrifī* [Methodology of Knowledge Integration] (Beirut: International Institute of Islamic Thought, 2011).
33 Sayyid Quṭb, *Khaṣāʾiṣ al-Taṣawwur al-Islāmī wa-Muqawwamātuh* [Islamic Perception: Its Characteristics and Key Elements] (Beirut: Dār al-Shurūq, 1997).
34 Abdelaziz Berghout, "Toward an Islamic Framework for Worldview Studies: Preliminary Theorization," *The American Journal of Islamic Social Sciences* 24, no. 2 (2007), 27.
35 See Malkāwī, *Minhājiyyat al-Takāmul al-Maʿrifī*, 98.
36 Immanuel Kant, *Critique of the Power of Judgment*, ed. Paul Guyer (New York: Cambridge University Press, 2000).
37 Clément Vidal, "Wat is een Wereldbeeld?" (What Is a Worldview?), in *Nieuwheid denken. De wetenschappen en het creatieve aspect van de werkelijkheid*, ed. H. Van Belle & J. Van der Veken (Leuven: Acco Press, 2008).
38 Oxford English Dictionary, Worldview, accessed 17 March 2018, http://www.oxforddictionaries.com/definition/english/world-view?q=worldview
39 Diederik Aerts, et al., *Worldviews, From Fragmentation to Integration* (Brussels: VUB Press, 1994), 17.
40 Ken Funk, "What is a worldview?" last modified 21 March 2001, http://web.engr.oregonstate.edu/~funkk/Personal/worldview.html
41 Aerts, et al., *Worldviews, From Fragmentation to Integration*, 18.
42 David K. Naugle, *Worldview: The History of a Concept* (Grand Rapids: William B. Eerdmans, 2002), 56.
43 Ibid., 66–67.
44 Aerts, et al., *Worldviews, From Fragmentation to Integration*, 25.
45 Vidal, "Wat is een Wereldbeeld?," 4.
46 Berghout, "Toward an Islamic Framework for Worldview Studies: Preliminary Theorization," 27.
47 Ibid., 28.
48 Ismāʿīl Rājī al-Fārūqī, *Islamization of Knowledge: General Principles and Work Plan* (Herndon, VA: International Institute of Islamic Thought, 1981).
49 Ismāʿīl Rājī al-Fārūqī, *Tawḥīd: Its Implication for Thought and Life* (Herndon, VA: International Institute of Islamic Thought, 1992).
50 Fatḥī Malkāwī followed in his footsteps and wrote a book entitled *Manẓūmat al-Qiyam al-ʿUlyā: al-Tawḥīd wa-l-Tazkiya wa-l-ʿUmrān*. It is a development of al-ʿUlwānī's treatise with focus on the issue of epistemological integration necessitated by this tripartite system. See Fatḥī Malkāwī, *Manẓūmat al-Qiyam al-ʿUlyā: al-Tawḥīd wa-l-Tazkiya wa-l-ʿUmrān* [The Higher Value System: Monotheism, Purification and Civilisation] (Herndon, VA: International Institute of Islamic Thought, 2013).
51 Ṭāhā Jābir al-ʿUlwānī, *Al-Tawḥīd wa-l-Tazkiya wa-l-ʿUmrān: Muḥāwala fī l-Kashf ʿan al-Qiyam wa-l-Maqāṣid al-Qurʾāniyya al-Ḥākima* [Monotheism, Purification, and Civilisation: Attempts to Reveal the Ruling Qurʾanic Values and Objectives] (Beirut: Dār al-Hidāya, 2003).

52 ʿAbd al-Ḥamīd Abū Sulaymān, *The Qurʾanic Worldview: A Springboard for Cultural Reform* (London: International Institute of Islamic Thought, 2011).
53 For some researchers the aforementioned approach, i.e., "Islamisation of knowledge" and Ṭāhā ʿAbd al-Rahmān's approach fall under the same category, that of "knowledge integration" with slight differences. See: Shākir Aḥmad al-Suhmūdī, *Minhāj al-Fikr al-ʿArabī al-Muʿāṣir* [The Methodology of Contemporary Arab Thought] (Jeddah: Markaz Taʾṣīl, 2015), 197.
54 Ṭāhā ʿAbd al-Raḥmān, *Buʾs al-Dahrāniyya al-Naqd al-Iʾtimānī li-Faṣl al-Akhlāq ʿan al-Dīn* [The Misery of Secularism: The Trustful Critique of Separating Ethics and Religion] (Beirut: Arab Network, 2014), 93. For the translation of the concept of "*Iʾtimāniyya*" into "trusteeship paradigm" see: Mohammed Hashas, "Taha Abderrahmane's Trusteeship Paradigm," *Oriente Moderno* 95, no. 1/2 (2015), 67–105.
55 Ṭāhā ʿAbd al-Raḥmān, *Rūḥ al-Dīn min Ḍīq al-ʿIlmāniyya ilā Saʿati al-Iʾtimāniyya* [The Spirit of Religion, from the Narrowness of Secularism to the Broadness of Trusteeship] (Beirut and Casablanca: al-Markaz al-Thaqāfī al-ʿArabī, 2012), 474.
56 Ibid.
57 Ibid., 93–108.
58 Ṭāhā ʿAbd al-Raḥmān, *Dīn al-Ḥayāʾ: Min al-Fiqh al-Iʾtimārī ilā al-Fiqh al-Iʾtimānī, Uṣūl al-Naẓar al-Iʾtimānī* [The Religion of Modesty: From Injunctive Jurisprudence to Trusteeship Jurisprudence, the Foundations of the Trusteeship Approach] (Beirut: al-Muʾassasa al-ʿArabiyya li-l-Fikr wa-l-Ibdāʿ, 2017).
59 See for instance: Ṭāhā ʿAbd al-Raḥmān, *Rūḥ al-Ḥadātha: Naḥwa al-Taʾsīs li- Ḥadātha Islāmiyya* [The Spirit of Modernity: An Introduction to Founding an Islamic Modernity] (Beirut and Casablanca: al-Markaz al-Thaqāfī al-ʿArabī, 2006).

## Bibliography

ʿAbd al-Ḥamīd, Muḥsin. *Al-Madhdhabiyya al-Islāmiyya wa-l-Taghayyur al-Ḥaḍārī [Islamic Doctrines and Civilizational Change]*. Doha: Qatar's Ministry of Endowments and Islamic Affairs, 1985.

ʿAbd al-Raḥmān, Ṭāhā. *Rūḥ al-Ḥadātha: Naḥwa al-Taʾsīs li-Ḥadātha Islāmiyya [The Spirit of Modernity: an Introduction to Founding an Islamic Modernity]*. Beirut and Casablanca: al- al-Markaz al-Thaqāfī al-ʿArabī, 2006.

ʿAbd al-Raḥmān, Ṭāhā. *Rūḥ al-Dīn min Ḍīq al-ʿIlmāniyya ilā Saʿati al-Iʾtimāniyya [The Spirit of Religion, from the Narrowness of Secularism to the Broadness of Trusteeship]*. Beirut and Casablanca: al-Markaz al-Thaqāfī al-ʿArabī, 2012.

ʿAbd al-Raḥmān, Ṭāhā. *Buʾs al-Dahrāniyya al-Naqd al-Iʾtimānī li-Faṣl al-Akhlāq an al-Dīn [The Misery of Secularism: the Trustful Critique of Separating Ethics and Religion]*. Beirut: Arab Network, 2014.

ʿAbd al-Raḥmān, Ṭāhā. *Dīn al-Ḥayāʾ: Min al-Fiqh al-Iʾtimārī ilā al-Fiqh al-Iʾtimānī, Uṣūl al-Naẓar al-Iʾtimānī [The Religion of Modesty: from Injunctive Jurisprudence to Trusteeship Jurisprudence, the Foundations of the Trusteeship Approach]*. Beirut: al-Muʾassasa al-ʿArabiyya li-l-Fikr wa-l-Ibdāʿ, 2017.

Abū Sulaymān, ʿAbd al-Ḥamīd. *The Qurʾanic Worldview: A Springboard for Cultural Reform*. London: The International Institute of Islamic Thought, 2011.

Adam, Fadzli Bin. "The concept of Khilāfah according to selected Sunni and Shīʿī Qurʾanic Commentaries." PhD diss. University of Leeds, 2001.

Aerts, Diederik et al. *Worldviews, From Fragmentation to Integration*. Brussels: VUB Press, 1994.

Alajmi, Abdulhadi. "'Ulama and Caliphs New Understanding of the 'God's Caliph' Term." *Journal of Islamic Law and Culture* 13, no. 1 (2011): 102–12.

Ibn ʿĀshūr, Muḥammad al-Ṭāhir. *Maqāṣid al-Sharīʿa al-Islāmiyya [The Objectives of Sharīʿa]*. Edited by Muḥammad al-Ṭāhir al-Misāwī. Jordan: Dār al-Nafāʾis, 2nd ed. 2001.

Al-Attas, Syed Muḥammad Naquib. *Prolegomena to the Metaphysics of Islam: An Exposition of the Fundamental Elements of the Worldview of Islam*. Kuala Lumpur: International Institute of Islamic Thought and Civilization (ISTAC), 1995.

Bayhī, Saʿīd. *Al-Taʾṣīl al-Sharʿī li-Mafhūm Fiqh al-Wāqiʿ [The Legal Foundation of the Notion of Fiqh al-waqi']*. Alexandria: al-Dār al-ʿĀlamiyya, 2nd ed., 2005.

Bennabi, Malek. *Vocation De L'Islam*. Beirut: Dar Albouraq, 2006.

Berghout, Abdelaziz. "Toward an Islamic Framework for Worldview Studies: Preliminary Theorization." *The American Journal of Islamic Social Sciences* vol. 24, no. 2 (2007): 22–43.

Chittick, William C. *Science of the Cosmos, Science of the Soul the Pertinence of Islamic Cosmology in the Modern World*. Oxford: Oneworld Publications, 2007.

Crone, Patricia, and Martin Hinds. *God's Caliph: Religious Authority in the First Centuries of Islam*. Cambridge: Cambridge University Press, 1986.

Darling, Linda T. "'The Vicegerent of God, from Him We Expect Rain': The Incorporation of the Pre-Islamic State in Early Islamic Political Culture." *Journal of the American Oriental Society* 134, no. 3 (2014): 407–29.

Drāz, Muḥammad ʿAbd Allāh. *The Moral World of the Qurʾan*. London: I.B. Tauris, 2008.

Al-Fārūqī, Ismāʿīl Rājī. *Islamization of Knowledge: General Principles and Work Plan*. Herndon, Virginia: International Institute of Islamic Thought, 1981.

Al-Fārūqī, Ismāʿīl Rājī. *Tawḥīd: Its Implication for Thought and Life*. Herndon, Virginia: International Institute of Islamic Thought, 1992.

Gardell, Mattias. "'Every Man and Woman is God's Caliph': The Rise of the Islamic Democratic Mainstream." In *Fundamentalism in the Modern World*, vol. 1. Edited by Ulrika Mårtensson, Jennifer Bailey, Priscilla Ringrose and Asbjorn Dyrendal. New York: I.B. Tauris, 2011, 240–265.

Al-Ghazālī, Muḥammad. *Al-Mahāwir al-Khamsa li-l-Qurʾān [The five Axes of the Qurʾan]*. Cairo: Dār al Shurūq, 2000.

Hallaq, Wael B. "Caliphs, Jurists and the Saljūks in the Political Thought of al-Juwaynī." *The Muslim World* 74, no. 1 (1984): 26–41.

Hamid, Abdul Wahid. *Islam: The Natural Way*. London: Muslim Education and Library Services, 2004.

Hamidullah, Muhammad. *Introduction to Islam*. Kuwait: International Islamic Federation of Student Organisations, 1970.

Hanne, Eric J. *Putting the Caliph in His Place: Power, Authority, and the Late Abbasid Caliphate*. Madison: Fairleigh Dickinson University Press, 2007.

Hashas, Mohammed. "Taha Abderrahmane's Trusteeship Paradigm." *Oriente Moderno* 95, no. 1/2 (2015): 67–105.

Al-Ḥusayn, Walīd. *Iʿtibār Maʾālāt al-Afʿāl wa-Atharuhu al-Fiqhī [The Consideration of the Consequences of Actions and their Jurisprudential Impact]*. Riyadh: Dār al-Tadmūriyya, 1st ed., 2008.

Iqbāl, Muḥammad. *The Reconstruction of Religious Thought in Islam*. London: Dodo Press, 2009.

ʿĪsāwī, ʿĀdil. *Fiqh al-Sunan al-Ilāhiyya wa-Dawruhā fī al-Binā al-Ḥaḍārī [Divine Norms and their Role in Civilizational Construction]*. Doha: Qatar's Ministry of Endowments and Islamic Affairs, 1st ed., 2012.
Jayyād, ʿAbd al-Riḍā Ḥasan. "Mafhūm al-Khilāfa al-Ilāhiyya li-l-Insān fī l-Qurʾān al-Karīm wa-Kitābāt al-ʿUlamāʾ al-Muslimīn [The Concept of Man's Vicegerency of God in the Noble Qurʾan and in Islamic Scholarship]". *Adab al-Kūfa Journal*, 1, no. 2 (2008): 133–155.
Al-Jīzānī, Muḥammad. *Fiqh al-Nawāzil [Methodology for Resolving New Legal Incidences]*. Cairo: Dār ibn Ḥazm, 2nd ed., 2006.
Johnston, David L. "The Human Khilāfa: A Growing Overlap of Reformism and Islamism on Human Rights Discourse?" *Islamochristiana* 28 (2002): 35–53.
Kant, Immanuel. *Critique of the Power of Judgment*. Edited by Paul Guyer. New York: Cambridge University Press, 2000.
Khan, Maulana Wahiduddin. *Islam Rediscovered: Discovering Islam from Its Original Sources*. New Delhi: Goodword, 2001.
Liebl, Vernie. "The Caliphate." *Middle Eastern Studies* 45, no. 3 (2009): 373–391.
Liew, Han Hsien. "The Caliphate of Adam: Theological Politics of the Qurʾānic Term Ḫalīfa." *Arabica*, 63 (2016): 1–29.
Malik, Fazlur Rahman. *Major Themes of the Qurʾan*. Chicago: University of Chicago Press, 2nd ed., 2009.
Malkāwī, Fatḥī Ḥasan. *Minhājiyyat al-Takāmul al-Maʿrifī [Methodology of Knowledge Integration]*. Beirut: International Institute of Islamic Thought, 1st ed., 2011.
Malkāwī, Fatḥī Ḥasan. *Manẓūmat al-Qiyam al-ʿUlyā: al-Tawḥīd wa-l-Tazkiya wa-l-ʿUmrān [The Higher Value System: Monotheism, Purification and Civilization]*. Virginia: International Institute of Islamic Thought, 2013.
Ibn Manẓūr, Muḥammad ibn Mukram. *Lisān al-ʿArab [The Tongue of the Arabs]*. Beirut: Dār Ṣādir, 3rd ed., 1993.
Al-Miʿmārī, Aḥmad. *Fiqh al-Tanzīl [Methods of Applied Fiqh]*. Beirut: Markaz Namāʾ, 1st ed., 2015.
Muṭahharī, Murtaḍā. *Fundamentals of Islamic Thought: God, Man and the Universe*. Berkeley: Mizan Press, 1985.
Al-Najjār, ʿAbd al-Majīd. *Fiqh al-Taḥaḍḍur al-Islāmī [The Jurisprudence of Islamic Civilization]*. Beirut: Dār al-Gharb al-Islāmī, 1st ed., 1999.
Al-Najjār, ʿAbd al-Majīd. *Khilāfat al-Insān bayna al-Waḥy wa-l-ʿAql [The Vicegerency of Man, Between Revelation and Reason: A Critique of the Dialectic of the Text, Reason, and Reality]*. Herndon, Virginia: International Institute of Islamic Thought, 3rd ed., 2005.
Nasr, Seyyed Hossein. *Ideals and Realities of Islam*. Chicago: ABC International, 2000.
Naugle, David K. *Worldview: the History of a Concept*. Cambridge: William B. Eerdmans, 2002.
Al-Nūrsī, Badīʿ al-Zamān Saʿīd. *The Words, On the Nature and Purposes of Man, Life, and All Things*. Translated by Şükran Vahide. Istanbul: Sözler, 2008.
Paret, Rudi. "Signification coranique de ḫalīfa et d'autres dérivés de la racine ḫalafa." *Studia Islamica*, 31 (1970): 211–217.
Al-Qāḍī, Wadād. "The Term "Khalīfa" in Early Exegetical Literature." *Die Welt des Islams*, 28/1 (1988): 392–411.
Al-Qaraḍāwī, Yūsuf. *Al-Khaṣāʾiṣ al-ʿĀmma li-l-Islām [The General Characteristics of Islam]*. Beirut: Muʾassasat al-Risāla, 2nd ed., 1983.

Al-Qaraḍāwī, Yūsuf. *Fī Fiqh al-Awlawiyyāt [Understanding Priorities]*. Cairo: Maktabat Wahba, 1996.

Quṭb, Sayyid. *Khaṣā'iṣ al-Taṣawwur al-Islāmī wa-Muqawwamātuh [Islamic Perception: its Characteristics and Key Elements]*. Beirut: Dār al-Shurūq, 1997.

Riḍā, Muḥammad Rashīd. *Tafsīr al-Manār [Interpretation of the Illuminator]*. Cairo: al-Hay'a al-Miṣriyya, 1990.

Rubin, Uri. "Prophets and Caliphs: The Biblical Foundations of the Umayyad Authority." In *Method and Theology in the Study of Islamic Origins*, edited by Herbert Berg, 73–99. Leiden: Brill, 2003.

Al-Ṣadr, Muḥammad Bāqir. *Our Philosophy*. Ahlulbayt Organization, 2014.

Al-Sawsawa, 'Abd al-Majīd. *Fiqh al-Muwāzanāt fī l-Sharī'a al-Islamiyya [The Balance between Benefits and Harms in Islamic Legislation]*. Dubai: Dār al-Qalam, 1st ed., 2004.

Searcy, Kim. "The Khalīfa and the Routinization of Charismatic Authority." *International Journal of African Historical Studies* 43, no. 3 (2010): 429–442.

Siddiqi, Abdul Hameed and Muḥammad Saeed Siddiqi. *The Islamic Concept of Religion and Its Revival*. Lahore: Kazi Publications, 1st ed., 1980.

Al-Suhmūdī, Shākir Aḥmad. *Minhāj al-Fikr al-'Arabī al-Mu'āṣir [The Methodology of Contemporary Arab Thought]*. Jeddah: Markaz Ta'ṣīl, 2015.

Al-'Ulwānī, Ṭāhā Jābir. *Al-Tawḥīd wa-l-Tazkiya wa-l-'Umrān: Muḥāwala fī l-Kashf 'an al-Qiyam wa-l-Maqāṣid al-Qur'āniyya al-Ḥākima [Monotheism, Purification, and Civilization: Attempts to Reveal the Ruling Qur'anic Values and Objectives]*. Beirut: Dār al-Hidāya, 2003.

Al-'Ulwānī, Zaynab. *Murāja'āt fī Taṭawwur al-Minhāj al-Maqāṣidī 'inda al-Mu'āṣirīn [Review of the Evolution of the Contemporary Maqāṣidī Approach]*. Virginia, Herndon: International Institute of Islamic Thought, 2012.

Vidal, Clément. "Wat is een wereldbeeld? (What is a worldview?)." in *Nieuwheid denken. De wetenschappen en het creatieve aspect van de werkelijkheid*. Edited by Van Belle, H. and Van der Veken, J. Leuven: Acco press, 2008.

Watt, William Montgomery. "God's Caliph: Qur'ānic Interpretation and Umayyad Claims." In *Iran and Islam, in Memory of the Late Vladimir Minorsky*. Edited by Clifford Edmund Bosworth, 565–74. Edinburgh: Edinburgh University Press, 1971.

# 2 Islamic Worldview in the Context of Modern Reformism

## 2.1 The Crisis of Islamic Thought in the Context of Modernity

The Algerian sociologist Mālik Bin-Nabī (d. 1973) noted that the first blow to the Islamic world from European modernity came in the early nineteenth century through the Western colonisation of most Muslim-majority countries. Although Muslims had been in contact with the West before, the peculiarity of this stage provided Muslims with "a new consciousness of their actual social situation" and turned their reality upside down. After awakening from a state of intellectual lethargy, they "found themselves in a new context which was not of their own making," and were thus compelled to "look for a way of living that conformed to the new reality, in both the ethical and the social spheres." It was this quest that gave birth to "the movements that would constitute the actual configuration of the Islamic world."[1]

As a result of the impact of modernity, Muslims had to deal with a tremendous gap between the reality of life on one hand, which they had abandoned for centuries at the levels of knowledge production, political and social influence, and material development, and their religious intellectual production on the other. Hence they failed to keep pace with the developments of modern life. In addition to the fact that they did not create or immediately influence the reality of the new world, Muslims did not have satisfactory solutions or answers for the world's new developments and challenges. They did not have a political, social, economic, administrative and epistemological alternative to the predominant ones in the world. Besides the fact that they did not contribute to the elaboration of the modern world, they did not even have a clear ethical standpoint from which they could face the new scientific and technological breakthroughs, despite their claims that Islam guides all aspects of human life.

The reason for the decline of Islamic civilisation and sciences was not Western colonialism. Before the modern age, Islamic sciences had lost their connection with Revelation and reality and had become fragmented and introverted, reiterating the legacies of the predecessors without adding any significant value to them. They were no longer governed by a comprehensive conception or overall intellectual patterns, and they did not address issues of public concern, among other things. However, this stagnant situation neither led to social nor religious unrest.

DOI: 10.4324/9781003335948-2

Despite all of their flaws, Islamic sciences did not lose their value in responding to the issues that remained within their scope, although such a response did not meet expectations in fulfilling their ontological function. However, adherence to them was worthwhile in order to experience the reality of the pre-modern era, albeit this adherence was not efficient in fulfilling all the teachings of Islam. The pre-modern flaws of Islamic sciences were of an intellectual order that did not culminate in social upheaval. Nevertheless, with the rise of modernity, the flaws evolved into social ones that led to scepticism towards religion and its usefulness in modern times. Commenting on this, Muḥammad al-Fāḍil ibn ʿĀshūr (d. 1970) said:

> No disruption or compulsion affected their life matters the way we are affected today. Instead, this sufficiency was due to the fact that the same conditions of individual and social life have, since the emergence of absolute *ijtihād* up to the emergence of the modern reform movement in the early years of the present century, continued exactly as they were, or at least in a very similar way in all their general constituents. [...] Therefore, the disruption of absolute *ijtihād* and its subsequent decline happened before the 13th century [19th] but as a matter of epistemic deficiency, which never resulted in any social distortion. However, during the past two centuries, the situation has been completely reversed, since the matters that were recorded in the books of jurisprudence have become unparalleled in present-day practical reality, and it is this hiatus that has made the question of *ijtihād* perceived in the modern world in a way that was never imagined or could ever be so in the past centuries. This reflects an instance of the rift between religion and practical life [...]. If the Islamic state was able to develop personal status laws derived from the various Islamic doctrinal schools (*madhāhib*), at the textual or exegetical levels, the question is: what kind of attitude does it hold vis-à-vis the rest of the general and particular laws? Where are *Sharīʿa* scholars, researchers in its provisions, and advocates of *ijtihād* with regards to the number of social, economic, and legal studies inundating Muslim countries with all types of alien systems permeating their faith and religion? As pointed out, all the attempts in this area relate to fragmented issues, most of which rank far lower than absolute *ijtihād*, whose discontinuity, as I have already pointed out, has been ascertained.[2]

Colonialism, through which Muslims were forcibly brought into contact with modernity, and the subsequent fall of the Ottoman Caliphate (1924), have brought about changes in the consciousness and reality of Muslims. This situation has led Islamic sciences and thought to a dead end whose exit still seems far away. One of the early initiatives to redress backwardness was through administrative reforms carried out within the Ottoman Empire, known as the *Tanẓīmāt* (organisations/regulations), which began in 1839 and ended in 1876, and which the French historian Catherine Mayeur-Jaouen considered an attempt to "restore Ottoman grandeur and Islam to their first stages of greatness"[3] in the face of the challenges of European modernity. These reforms, however, have only exacerbated the crisis of Islamic sciences, or perhaps exhibited the manifestations of this crisis in the modern epoch, in many respects, some of which have been touched upon by the modernist Pakistani thinker Fazlur Rahman (d. 1988).[4] Among the problems pointed out by Fazlur Rahman is that the Ottoman reforms were carried out under the supervision of secularists who were heavily influenced by Western thought, especially French thought, and who were far from traditional knowledge. This led to further marginalisation of religious thought from its role in public life at the level of legislation, politics and education. At the legislative level, the Ottoman endeavours to strengthen administrative centralisation and direct control over all the empire's citizens and get rid of the system of "*al-milla*," which granted each religious group the right to rule by its own laws, resulted in several reforms. Among these, one can cite the drafting of an Ottoman constitution, the establishment of a legislative authority within a non-religious public institution, i.e., the Ottoman parliament, and the adoption of a concept of citizenship, which includes state members of all religions. Politically, the state separated religion and government, thus creating separate governmental and religious functions. At the educational level, it established modern non-religious schools and universities and paid no attention to the reform of traditional education. All of this contributed to the marginalisation of Islamic sciences and scholars. These reforms excluded Muslim jurists from the legislative process and the government, leading to the distortion of numerous patterns and systems that typified the reality of the pre-modern Islamic era. This also affected doctrinal provisions laid out in jurisprudential scholarship.

The *Tanẓīmāt*'s educational system that ran parallel to the traditional one further excluded Islamic sciences from application and integration into modernity.[5] Remarkably, as Fazlur Rahman notes, religious scholars did not feel bothered by this practice, for this was in line with one of the epistemological distortions that have affected Islamic thought, i.e., the worldly life/Hereafter dichotomy.[6] This presented an opportunity for modern reformers to establish these programmes for strategic reasons that pushed them away from the religious programmes, which remained intact to satisfy the religious scholars. Theologians considered Western sciences, which yielded "practical arts" and "useful skills" efficacious in the "affairs of the world," while those sciences that educate the Islamic mind and soul, i.e., "religious sciences" concerned with "the affairs of the Hereafter," appertain to the realm and authority of traditional schools. Thus, the *Tanẓīmāt* contributed significantly to the widening of the gap between the traditional and the modern in all fields, especially the fields of education and science, thus resulting in "schizophrenia" at the social level and the level of a Muslim's personality, to use Fazlur Rahman's term.[7]

In addition to the fall of the Ottoman Empire (1924) and the European colonisation of most Muslim countries, the situation was exacerbated by the independence of Muslim countries and their ensuing division into a large number of nation-states during the 1960s. All these factors changed the political, legal, intellectual and epistemic patterns of life, as well as public affairs, societies and their operators, and those working in the field of social affairs. The elites were no longer divided into politicians and clerics, as was the case in pre-modern times;

many experts cropped up in various fields, such as science, economics, sociology, psychology, media and others, and the role of clerics was marginalised. The state was no longer the guarantor and "guardian of world and religion," as it claimed to be in pre-modern times.

All of these issues raised questions, challenges, and problems for Islamic thought, which required new forms of *ijtihād*. This situation, at times, led to the reconsideration of what was previously considered part of the domain of religion, but had been invalidated by scientific progress or questioned by new perceptions of man and life, became unacceptable, or whose exclusive historical nature unfolded after modernity broke some of the barriers that prevented its dissociation from religion. However, this new *ijtihād* would require of the Islamic mind what was never required in ancient times. The problematics posed for the Islamic mind in pre-modern times, after the consolidation of imitation (*taqlīd*), were of the atomistic or partial (*juzʾī*) type, which fitted well with the jurisprudential tradition and the systematic paradigms devised to deal with it. The treatment of these problematics only required the lowest ranks of *ijtihād*, i.e., extrapolation from the canons of jurisprudence, as ibn ʿĀshūr argued in the context of the discussion mentioned above. The problematics and changes brought about by European modernity (and, later, post-modernity) are but complete (and often global) changes in patterns, systems, perceptions and postulates; they are not partial or exclusively atomistic practices within the same pattern in which Islamic knowledge was produced, as was the case in the past. Hence, the non-adapted traditional methodological apparatus and epistemological model, as well as the actors operating in the field of Islamic sciences, proved deficient in meeting the challenges of modernity.

Added to the shift from slow atomistic changes to radical changes in patterns was the fact that the new world order, with all its systems, conditions, sciences, creations and innovations, is not the direct product of Muslims. As previously mentioned, it was not created within the Muslim pattern. More than ever before, this means, among other things, that the process of *ijtihād* to keep up with contemporary reality could not ignore the necessity of borrowing many of these new values and achievements and integrating them within the framework of the comprehensive Islamic system. In the past, most of the values and practices of reality were not alienated from the Islamic value system, thus facilitating the task of orienting reality to the values of Islam once the extrapolation process was set in motion. However, contemporary scholars dealt with modern reality through the inherited atomistic change-oriented methodological apparatus, which is inappropriate for that development, and they ended up concocting old and modern elements without attempting to integrate them into a coherent system and a clear vision and plan. Consequently, this process cannot be regarded as an act of *ijtihād* in the holistic sense of the word, which involves the treatment of specific practical issues within a governing overall ethical framework. It is, therefore, only a process of tinkering, concocting and accumulating that ultimately leads to adaptation with reality in order to maintain a minimum level of religiosity. This problem was raised, in more or less detail, by both Mālik Bin-Nabī (d. 1973)[8] and Ismāʿīl al-Fārūqī (d. 1986).[9]

Thus, the shock of Western modernity caused Islamic sciences to choke out their last breath, revealing their structural failure to address the issues of the modern times. If the majority of pre-modern Muslim scholars accepted Islamic sciences as they had inherited them, the change brought about by Western modernity has triggered among many modern Muslim reformists the conviction of the inefficiency of these sciences and has highlighted their flaws at many levels. The changes introduced by modernity have reopened old wounds in the body of Islamic sciences that the whole of pre-modern Islamic thought had overlooked. These old wounds included: The prohibition to take recourse directly to the texts of Revelation,[10] the separation of public affairs from the realm of religion,[11] the reduction of the field of interest of Islamic sciences into partial matters, the reduction of the core concern of religion to the matters of the Hereafter,[12] the dichotomy of reason and Revelation, and the lack of elaboration of a Qur'anic epistemology.[13] If these flaws had been forgotten, and most scholars in the age of stagnation of Islamic sciences had accepted the latter as they reached them without a strong need to question them, now these wounds were opened in such a way that they could not be overlooked by those whose concern was to integrate Islam within the fabric of modern reality. These afflictions appeared in various manifestations, including many epistemological questions posed by modernity – such as the nature of the relationship between Islamic sciences and modern sciences – with the traditional sciences being unable to answer them adequately. Furthermore, the abandonment of the Qur'an and the absence of theorisation about Qur'anic epistemology in Islamic thought pointed out by ibn Taymiyya (d. 728/1327)[14] have persisted, and are, in fact, exacerbated by modernity, as can be seen in the work of many researchers. While many of the early scholars had subjected the Qur'an to hybrid or extraneous epistemologies, as pointed out by ibn Taymiyya, many modernists have subjected it to the perceptions of modernity, as Fazlur Rahman notes.[15] The loss of Qur'anic epistemology has left them much room to repeat mistakes, or even commit bigger ones than those committed in the past, while traditional theologians' reactions could only materialise in the form of simple calls for adherence to tradition. Another one of these manifestations is what ibn ʿĀshūr pointed to in his arguments mentioned above, namely the inability of religious scholars in the modern era to use *ijtihād* in the context of the significant issues raised by the modern epoch in the political, economic and social fields, as well as other fields. Another problem is that of the lack of communication and integration between modern sciences and Islamic sciences.

Hence, the neo-reformists and neo-modernists were not pleased with the patchwork endeavours of the revivalist shaykhs[16] and others, as these did not go far beyond the patterns of thinking established by Islamic sciences before the era of modernity, and were therefore unable to compete with the posed challenge. The first of these "patchy" attempts emerged after the Ottoman reformists put in place *Majallat al-Aḥkām al-ʿAdliyya* (Mecelle). It was an attempt to codify Ḥanafī jurisprudence in the form of a civil code in order to facilitate the work of judges and jurists who are not well versed in Islamic jurisprudence. This happened after the Ottoman regular courts were separated from the *Sharīʿa* courts.[17] It soon became apparent that the inability of this attempt to solve the problem was due to the Ḥanafī school's inability to cope alone with the new concerns and social needs, which resulted from the "economic, political and cultural connection between the New East and the West."[18] Accordingly, the state resorted to abrogating some parts of the Mecelle, imbuing them with positive laws and modifying them to suit the new reality. Thereby the Mecelle was either wholly or partly abandoned in some Arab countries under the umbrella of the Ottomans.[19] Consequently, "the idea of concoction (*talfīq*) appeared, first within one doctrine, and then among the various doctrines of jurisprudential schools in the era of the nation-state."[20] This idea gave rise to the formation of cross-doctrinal *fiqh* councils.[21]

Another manifestation of the patchwork endeavours, which many reformists did not consider sufficient in fulfilling the requirements, was the attempt to simplify school curricula for students of Islamic sciences and to remove any unnecessary content from them. In addition to this, there was an attempt to filter the heritage from views that were not in line with the spirit of the age,[22] but without a new reading of the texts of Revelation that is based on a methodologically and epistemologically ingrained approach that would lead to the sanitisation of heritage on solid foundations and thus offer an alternative modern reading. At the level of education, the patchwork endeavours appeared through the introduction of "modern" subjects in the *Sharīʿa* curriculum[23] and in the growing interest in comparative jurisprudence.[24] At the level of *ijtihād*, there was a call for collective *ijtihād* and the involvement of experts from other sciences, such as medicine, astronomy and biology.[25]

Despite the fact that these efforts, which were triggered by the challenges of modernity, led to the "decline and then disappearance of the tenants of doctrinal imitation," and "to a high keenness for *ijtihād* in jurisprudential issues,"[26] these attempts did not rise to the level of dressing the wounds which were reopened by European modernity. This prompted a scholar like al-Fāḍil ibn ʿĀshūr to criticise this approach by arguing that, as quoted before, "if the Islamic state was able to develop personal status laws derived from the various Islamic doctrinal schools (*madhāhib*), at the textual or exegetical levels, the question is: what kind of attitude does it hold vis-à-vis the rest of the general and particular laws?"[27]

These patchwork approaches did not stand out from the pattern of the atomistic approach on which traditional jurisprudence settled. This variegated atomistic *ijtihād* "quickly revealed its inadequacy in many respects, as it required a new vision or visions about Islam, the Qurʾan, and its functions and roles."[28] Consequently, outside the doctrinal thinking pattern, many theses appeared to transcend the atomistic approach and embrace larger issues. The first to undertake this course was Imām Muḥammad ʿAbduh (d. 1905), who wrote on the relationship between religion and the state, and the relationship between religion and science.[29] Other books then appeared on various topics, such as democracy, economics, capitalism and other aspects of modernity: "Therefore, we can hardly find an issue of daily or public life not dealt with within the literature produced by *ijtihād* advocates."[30] However, these *ijtihād*-inspired efforts "did not follow clear principles,"[31] and did not change anything about the concept of jurisprudence and the pattern of jurisprudential thinking. On the other hand, these efforts did not create a new approach that would introduce a new concept of *ijtihād* and a new approach to it. They did not lead to the epistemological questioning of traditional Islamic sciences. Rather, they were only reactions to issues of reality without presenting a new epistemological vision and methodology in dealing with Revelation and reality. The objectives of the thinkers behind these theses were not clear enough, as Fazlur Rahman points out. Neither were they successful in proposing a new model; rather they were adapting a defensive attitude when criticising the West, as attempts "to save the minds of Muslims from being spoiled or even destroyed under the impact of Western ideas" or by the use of selections from the "new" Western ideas and mixing them with the "old" Islamic thought "so that the potion resulting from this chemistry will be healthful."[32]

Fazlur Rahman attributed the shortcomings in reforming Islamic thought to the absence of an Islamic worldview in these writers' approaches. He said that they

> dealt with social and political matters issue-by-issue, instead of approaching it as a social or political philosophy. Democracy is Islamic, but concepts like human rights and social justice (which are certainly declared to be Islamic) are not discussed in detail; egalitarianism is emphasized, but its nature and limits, if any, do not come up as problems; Islam has granted women rights, but why and what kinds of rights and by what rationale, is not clear. Most modernists are very reticent about theology, philosophy, or a worldview.[33]

It becomes apparent from Fazlur Rahman's arguments that these scholars had merely added Islamic traits to the concepts developed by Western modernity and confined themselves by considering sub-issues without questioning the concepts' philosophical foundations. This is one of the implications of the absence of this theology, philosophy, worldview or epistemological system from which the thinking on these major issues could emanate and which govern the cohesion of its constituents and approaches. This absence has led many of these thinkers to succumb to prevailing epistemologies and philosophies without questioning them. Hence, some writings and statements in favour of modern systems or perceptions emerged as if they were an inherent part of what Revelation advocates, such as "Islamic Capitalism," "Islamic Communism," "Islamic Democracy," among other slogans, even though many Muslim thinkers have addressed these advocacies and claims as extraneous subjects imposed on Revelation. However,

> as a result of the absence of this methodology so that we can benefit from Western development, the call to benefit from this Western knowledge has resulted in the mere reproduction of Western science, industry, systems, and hierarchies without much awareness [...] especially in relation to the cultural field and social systems.

Thus, many reformists in the modern era appeared to be

> inclined to reproduce the manifestations of Western development without any critical consideration through a prior methodology. This inclination was coupled with a crude compromise between what was reproduced and the Islamic principles in order to legitimise it in what resembles the raw reconciliation of Greek philosophy and Islamic principles made by Islamic peripatetic philosophers. [...] That took on such proportions that some called to interpret the Noble Qur'an so that it could conform to Western principles and values, as al-Thaʿālibī (d. 1944) did. The latter called for[34] a true, genuine, human and social interpretation of the Qur'an, that is, in short, an interpretation that conforms to the principles of the French revolution, which are the same principles as the Qur'an's.[35]

This fondness for Western progress among Muslim reformers at the beginning of the nineteenth century was within the framework of faith in religion and its usefulness in modern times. It was not intended to marginalise religion or challenge its usefulness; "however, it was from this standpoint [i.e., fascination by Western progress] that the secularist tendency [in the Muslim world], which does not see any place for religion in public life, emerged."[36]

The problematic of the absence of an Islamic worldview, and the concomitant comprehensive methodology in *ijtihād* it requires, manifested itself among the later generation of revivalists in the fact that their applied *ijtihād* was no more than an *a posteriori* process whose purpose was to describe the existing human reality and peoples' actions from a narrow point of view, and to end up judging them either favourably or negatively (*ḥalāl* or *ḥarām*). Hence, most of the teachings of religion (subsumed in its creedal system, its objectives, its spiritual teachings and comprehensive principles) remain inoperative due to the fact that *ijtihād* does not consider the general teachings of religion and because of its lack of practical means for its realistic articulations. This reflects the predominant attitude of contemporary religio-legal and religio-ethical thinking towards modern reality; it hardly looks at *ijtihād* but as an *a posteriori* process that deals with the existing fragmented facts through partial and narrow evaluation, judging them either favourably or negatively, and, at times, dealing with them through formal adjustments. This is, in fact, the path pursued by most workers in the field of contemporary applied *ijtihād*, i.e., *fatwā* institutions and jurisprudential councils all over the world.[37]

## 2.2 Islamic Worldview as Promising Horizon

It follows from the above-described manifestations of the crisis in Islamic sciences, in addition to the efforts undertaken by many reformists to address them, that the common challenge in all the aspects of distortion in Islamic sciences is the problem of fragmentation and the lack of integration of knowledge. As highlighted in the introduction, the most critical concern of the modern Islamic reformist movement since its inception has been the difficulty of transcending the tendency of a fragmented understanding of the texts of Revelation, and, thereby, the inability to address the problems facing Muslims from a holistic viewpoint. Nevertheless, as previously highlighted, these attempts were not able to make a breakthrough in contemporary *ijtihād*, albeit they enabled it to overcome some aspects of fragmentation. Noting the problematic of fragmentation in Islamic sciences does not necessarily translate to the identification of all the flaws that we have mentioned, the details of which depend on the criteria used in the diagnosis. These criteria remain unclear in most works that have dealt with the evaluation of Islamic sciences.[38]

The idea of *maqāṣid al-Sharīʿa* (*Sharīʿa* objectives) was rediscovered by the reformists of the twentieth century. They attached great importance to it as a promising feature in keeping with Western modernity and borrowing from it, and as an essential entry point to solve the problem of fragmentation and the lack of knowledge integration. Yet, this avenue came to a halt after the attempt of Muḥammad al-Ṭāhir ibn ʿĀshūr (d. 1973) to come up with approaches that do not embrace a holistic meaning of *ijtihād*, and others that were employed to adapt the Qurʾanic discourse to the standards of Western modernity.[39] The general failure to incorporate the higher objectives of *Sharīʿa* into an overall Qurʾanic worldview is at the centre of this crisis in contemporary scholarship in the field of *maqāṣid*, as we have demonstrated in a previous study.[40]

Hence, many studies have emerged, especially within the framework of the project of *Islamisation of Knowledge*, criticising the traditional methods of *ijtihād* and contemporary patchwork attempts. They believed that the latter have not been liberated from the classical paradigm of *ijtihād* in its reductionist model and fragmentised disciplines. The emphasis was put on the need to complement or replace the latter with a comprehensive methodology in order to pull out the Islamic intellectual output from fragmentation and legal formalism. These studies attempted to offer some suggestions on how to overcome the diagnosed structural and methodological deficiencies. The most important basis for the launching of such systematic reforms was the establishment of an Islamic methodology and epistemology based on the general philosophy that governs the teachings of Islam. This general philosophy has been addressed through different names, such as Islamic worldview, universal Islamic vision, Islamic frame of reference, Islamic cosmology, governing principles, overall representation, general philosophy, comprehensive interpretation, interpretive model or ideology, etc.[41] Many reformists, and most of those working in the field of traditional Islamic scholarship today, are not aware of the epistemological foundations that hinder Islamic sciences from attaining the level of actual effectiveness in the modern era. This is evident from the many studies presented in this area, and in which the thinking pattern does not seem to transcend the ideas that were established in Islamic scholarship during the eras of Islamic sciences stagnation. However, there exists a group of reformist thinkers, mostly non-specialists in the field of classical Islamic sciences, who were aware that the problematic in Islamic sciences, which is primarily epistemological and systematic, is due to the loss of a philosophical cohesion and the absence of a clear cosmology (worldview) in the foundation of these sciences. Some of these scholars shared ibn Taymiyya's view with regard to the absence of theorisation of a Qur'anic epistemology and the deviation of Ashʿarī epistemology from the Islamic frame of reference.[42] Fazlur Rahman even believed that all classical schools of *kalām* (speculative theology) contravened the worldview of the Qur'an, and that "it is to the credit of pre-modernist revivalism and modernism that they tried to undermine this thousand-year-old sacred folly and invite Muslims back to the refreshing fountain of the Qur'an."[43] However, he also believed that these pre-modern revivalist theologians did not build any new edifice instead; neither did the revivalists who came after them. Hence, Fazlur Rahman, along with other contemporary reformists, argued that the starting point in the reform of Islamic sciences and education, and its greatest necessity, is to develop an Islamic worldview, and that "unless such a system is attempted, there is little that can be ministered through education."[44]

A group of proponents of the *Knowledge Integration Project* argued that the biggest flaw that contributed to the fragmentation of Islamic thought and sciences, and to the decline of Islamic sciences and civilisation, was the distortion of the Islamic worldview. For instance, ʿAbd al-Ḥamīd Abū Sulaymān wrote:

> There is, in the Muslim community, a lack of enlightened awareness and a lack of concern to make a thorough, studied examination of the Islamic worldview. This lack of awareness and concern is among the primary causes behind the perplexity, passivity, decline, disintegration, and backwardness which the Muslim community, both communally and individually, has suffered from increasingly over the last few centuries.[45]

Abū Sulaymān argued that the reason that contemporary Muslim intellectuals have abandoned the Islamic worldview and instead adopted the methodology of Western thought, which is based on a non-Islamic vision, is their fascination with the Western model, besides the inherently stagnant Islamic thought. He believed that the only way for Muslim intellectuals to remedy this backwardness is by confronting it and reversing the deteriorating state of the *umma*, adding that "it is important for such thinkers to realize that the first issue to which attention must be given is that of the primacy of the Islamic worldview."[46]

Since its inception, contemporary Islamic reformism, as emphasised throughout this study, has been concerned with the problem of fragmentation and the issue of integration. Still in this respect, Abū Sulaymān states that

> the questions, then, which we need to address have to do, first, with the nature of the worldview appropriate for the Muslim community and its cultural system and, second, with the reasons for this worldview's distortion and marginalisation by Muslims, and the ways in which this distortion and marginalisation have taken place.[47]

After the "failed" reform attempts that lasted for centuries, it became clear, in the eyes of Abū Sulaymān

> that no matter how available the means may be or how intense the suffering, nothing will change unless Muslims develop a worldview that can give them a genuine sense of the meaning and purpose of their existence and, in this way, serve as a force for positive, constructive action and reform. In other words, without a positive worldview, which provides a sense of purposefulness and motivation, the Muslim community will remain static.[48]

Abū Sulaymān also claimed that the Islamic worldview had been distorted throughout history as a result of several factors. The first of these factors, in his view, is the demise of the "Companions," the generation educated by the Prophet (ﷺ) and inculcated with the Islamic worldview. Then the "Bedouin Arabs" took over and dominated the political life of the emerging *umma*. The Arab Bedouin tribes' command of Islam was incomplete at that time because of their recent introduction to it and on account of the harsh Bedouin life. They did not completely dispose of the pre-Islamic (*jāhiliyya*) worldview. Hence, the political realm prevailed over the religious, and it was utilised for personal interest, inevitably resulting in tyranny and corruption. The most important repercussion of that situation was its fundamental impact on intellectual life and the Islamic worldview.[49] Abū Sulaymān argued further that "the Bedouin tribes' negative influence on Islamic political life began with the collapse of the rightly guided caliphate and the establishment of the ruthless Umayyad dynasty. The lingering effects of their primitive ways of thinking and racist approach to human relationships further obscured the Qur'anic worldview."[50] The blurring and distortion of the Islamic worldview was exacerbated as many peoples and ethnicities joined the Islamic *umma* and intruded their cultures and their worldviews into Islamic thought, using, in particular, Greek formal logic and its mythically oriented doctrines.[51] Thus,

> the inclusion of pre-Islamic tribal ethnic heritage in Islamic thought, as well as *Isrāʾīlīyyāt* (narratives of Jewish origin), gnostic and mythological beliefs, and formal logic in its various forms, was, in fact, a kind of intellectual apostasy, a creedal blur, and a backward movement, which necessarily led to the deviation of thought, the depletion of creative energies, the blurring of the Islamic worldview, and the baffling of the civilizational progress of the *umma*.[52]
>
> Those blurs, distortions, and deviations prevailed over the centuries and obscured many of the guiding principles as reflected in the overall civilizational Qur'anic worldview, which was abandoned in fact, so much so that the Noble Qur'an became a mere source of invoking blessings and for supplication through recitation and memorization, thus resulting in the absence of *ijtihād* and the prevalence of exaggerated demands for texts of historical applications.[53]

Abū Sulaymān is convinced that the blurring of the Islamic worldview caused by these factors ultimately led to the focus of the majority of scholars of the *umma* on worship, civil and family

> laws and regulations governing mundane transactions such as sales agreements and the like. As a consequence, there was no time nor energy left for writing books that deal with the public sphere, that is, the management of government affairs and public interests. The only books that did touch upon such themes restricted themselves to nebulous exhortations to justice. Unfortunately, those books were dedicated to the wielders of dictatorial powers, who would never have heeded such exhortations, to begin with. The nearly-complete loss of the Islamic worldview with its balanced emphasis on the public and private spheres resulted in an overreliance on the rhetoric of threat and intimidation.[54]

Abū Sulaymān argued that the failure of Muslims to build Islamic social sciences throughout history was due to the lack of "commitment on their part, in the aftermath of the generation of the Prophet's 'Companions' to the worldview of the Qur'an." This was also considered by Abū Sulaymān as one of the reasons behind the division of Muslims into disparate groups and parties in the past, as in the present.[55] Although the examination of the historical context in which the Islamic worldview evolved lies outside the scope of my study, I must point out here that I do not share many of Abū Sulaymān's criticisms on the development of medieval Islam.

In line with Abū Sulaymān's arguments, a group of Muslim scholars emphasised the necessity of adopting the Islamic worldview as a solution for reforming contemporary Islamic thought and for engaging in current intellectual and scientific issues. Several attempts were made in this area in the second half of the twentieth century, some of which were mentioned in the introduction to this study. As previously stated, these attempts constitute, in sum, an important asset in the development of the Islamic worldview. Although these contributions provide many answers to the questions of the worldview from an Islamic perspective, there is no field of study or unique branch in the context of contemporary Islamic thought that is devoted to this subject and its ramifications so far, as pointed out earlier in this study.

Further, I argue that most of the works in this regard do not deal with the issues that make up the worldview as an entity and a coherent system, but most frequently they are somewhat concerned with some partial aspects of the Islamic worldview in a scattered manner. For example, many of these attempts begin by trying to build an Islamic worldview by citing the major concepts and principles that they consider its most important constituents. Yet they neither draw a clear link between them nor make a sufficient investigation of what they mean; they do not illustrate how they communicate with all the teachings of Revelation, their ontological purpose and roots, or their position in the overall Islamic system. These principles were not addressed in an ontological, epistemological, methodological or integrative manner that would justify their unique selection; hence they were not organised into a coherent and comprehensive system. The comments made by studies on the great principles as features of the Islamic worldview hardly exceed the level of emphasis on their importance as great principles, and they hardly depart from what the Qur'an manifestly dealt with concerning these principles. As an act in itself, the enumeration of major principles "constituting the Islamic worldview" cannot be taken as a theory or system. The lack of an in-depth study of the impact and requirements of the Islamic worldview in the field of Islamic sciences and *ijtihād* is another example of the deficiency of those studies.[56] Despite placing great emphasis on its importance and calling for its adoption, one can only note that, to the present day, the Islamic worldview has not been translated into a coherent, integrated theory.

An important question that needs to be answered in this regard is that of the function of this worldview as such. Apparently, the proponents of the Islamic worldview did not agree on the purpose of this endeavour, given the ambiguity surrounding the function of Islamic sciences in their perceptions, as can be noted from their works. If many scholars in the field of Islamic thought were to agree to diagnose the problem of fragmentation as a general defect in Islamic sciences, and if some of them consider that one of the most important approaches to address this problem is to formulate a philosophical vision governing those sciences, there would remain an ambiguity in their perception of the function of those sciences and, therefore, in their perception of the type of reform intended for them and, as a result, in the role the worldview plays in the reform of these sciences and, consequently, in the very elaboration of that worldview.

Though a staunch advocate of the Islamic worldview as an approach to reform in Islamic education and its sciences and disciplines, Fazlur Rahman, for example, has a purpose in developing an Islamic worldview that hardly goes beyond the review of certain legal provisions and principles of the Islamic tradition and the Qur'an in line with the spirit of the age. This is shown through the models of reform that he advocated by adopting that vision, such as a review of the prohibition of usury (*ribā*), the inheritance of women, and the *ḥadd* (legally prescribed penalty) of stoning, for instance. It seems as if his sole purpose is to rid Islam of what he considers historical views, as if the only crisis of Islamic sciences lies in their inclusion of historical elements extraneous to the teachings of the Qur'an. The role of the worldview, therefore, is reduced to the correction of "misunderstandings" through a holistic approach to the Qur'an and its history. Fazlur Rahman indeed called for better communication between Islamic sciences and modern sciences, but he did not specify the meaning of such communication, and whether it means merely freeing Islamic sciences of what is contrary to modern sciences, or more than that.

On the other hand, it appears, through his definition of *ijtihād*, that Fazlur Rahman's use of this new approach is not intended to restore the status of Islamic sciences and *ijtihād* to their ontological function. After explaining the need to start from the Qur'anic worldview in order to address the diagnosed modern reality, he proceeds to define this intellectual effort as *ijtihād*,

> which means the effort to understand the meaning of a relevant text or precedent in the past, containing a rule, and to alter that rule by extending or restricting or otherwise modifying it in such a manner that a new situation can be subsumed under it by a new solution.[57]

This definition, in fact, hardly stands out from the classical atomistic approach to *ijtihād*, which is confirmed by the examples given by Fazlur Rahman, and which hardly transcends the mere review of jurisprudential provisions that all scholars agreed upon. The problematic that persists is that, despite the identification of the flaw (fragmentation), the way of its treatment (integration) and its first step (the worldview), the question remains regarding the criterion on which the assessment of Islamic sciences, thought and reform lies in modern reality. While some reformists have reckoned with the importance of elaborating the Islamic worldview, the loss of or disruption in the criterion on which they evaluated Islamic sciences and contemporary reform has led them to the loss of clarity or confusion in the use of that vision in the reform of Islamic thought. I suppose that the absence of clarity in the criterion on which Islamic sciences and thought were evaluated not only resulted in a blurred and distorted implementation of the worldview, but also inevitably led to the blurring and distorting of its very elaboration. Hence, one of the main concerns of this study will be the need to raise the question of the foundations, standards and approaches that makes that worldview a Qur'anic one.

Clearly, one of the conditions for the consistency and harmony of this worldview is that it should not be addressed in isolation from the ontological and teleological purposes of Islamic sciences and thought,[58] which are supposed to be framed by that worldview. However, the problem in many of the studies dealing with the Islamic worldview and the problem of knowledge integration lies in the fact that they are outward and not inward oriented. In other words, they try to elaborate a worldview in order to respond accurately to the current issues of the age, and not to handle Islamic sciences and thought from within. These studies deal with knowledge integration between modern and traditional sciences in particular, but they hardly pay attention to knowledge integration within Islamic sciences in order to address the problem of fragmentation. To confirm this fact, it suffices to refer to the 34 research papers presented at the conference on "Knowledge Integration and Its Role in Enabling Higher Education to Contribute to the Advancement of Civilization in the Islamic World," organised by the International Institute of Islamic Thought in 2010. Not one of these papers addressed the problem of the internal integration of Islamic sciences, and they barely go beyond knowledge integration in the sense of external integration, i.e., between Islamic sciences and modern sciences. Some of the research papers referred to knowledge integration in the context of Islamic heritage, in the sense that some classical scholars, who are familiar with different kinds of knowledge, called for the consideration of all sciences given the existence of a degree of integration and communication between the traditional sciences. Yet, this does not amount to the level of integration required to overcome the problem of fragmentation in Islamic thought. Consequently, it is only a case of low-level integration.[59] This is the predominant trend in the *Knowledge Integration Project*. It should also be borne in mind that the project was originally called *Islamisation of Knowledge*; thus, it emerged inherently oriented towards modern knowledge. The primary goal of this project was to eliminate the dichotomy of religious and secular education, which was prevalent in the Islamic world, and replace it with a unified system in which Islamic sciences are integrated with modern sciences.[60] Hence, it automatically turned to external integration. This also applies to the remaining studies mentioned in the introduction of the present work, which are concerned with the construction of the Qur'anic philosophy or the Islamic worldview. Despite their importance in framing Islamic thought, these studies do not seek to develop a philosophical or epistemological framework for Islamic sciences, and there is to the best of my knowledge no single study dedicated to this purpose.

The action plan underlying the Islamisation of Knowledge Project indeed includes a "critical evaluation of Islamic heritage" based on the "Islamic worldview";[61] hence, some of its theses include a critique and a revision of Islamic sciences. However, they are few in number and do not tend to rebuild Islamic sciences epistemologically and methodologically, and they do not fulfil the promise of revision on the basis of the Islamic worldview. Perhaps one of the reasons behind this situation, besides the lack of the elaboration of a system or theory of an Islamic worldview based on a clear epistemological and methodological vision until now, is the shortage of specialists in classical Islamic sciences among the proponents of this project who contributed to the elaboration of its theses. Many of its proponents hail from a social sciences background, and their concern focuses on "the building of generations of specialists trained in social sciences to deal with life matters who are prepared to interact with the Islamic faith and its objectives (*maqāṣid*), as well as with its texts, to generate a realistic Islamic thought."[62] As previously mentioned, the fact that these studies were not much concerned with the internal integration of Islamic sciences is due to the intrinsic nature of the project itself, which, in origin, is externally oriented.

It should be stressed here again, that the Islamic worldview cannot be geared towards the outside without, first and foremost, having an internal basis from which it emerges. Indeed, the crisis of Islamic thought and sciences lies, above all, in its internal fragmentation and epistemological distortion. Therefore, it is impossible to evaluate modern knowledge epistemologically or integrate it with Islamic sciences without undertaking a prior internal reform. The very elaboration of a worldview depends on this reform. Moreover, the process of external knowledge integration is pointless if the sciences that are meant to be integrated with modern sciences and disciplines are epistemologically and systematically dysfunctional. However, the value of the interest in modern knowledge in the epistemological and systematic evaluation of Islamic sciences cannot be denied.

It has become clear from the discussion in this chapter that the emphasis on the Islamic worldview emerged with the modern Islamic reformist movement as an answer to the issues of fragmentation in Islamic sciences and thought revealed with the rise of Western modernity. The attempts at elaborating that worldview, even though they paid attention to the issue of fragmentation of Islamic sciences, were often hasty reactions to modern patterns of thinking, not departing from an original, consistent and clearly defined Islamic epistemology or methodology, as will become clear throughout this study. Moreover, the purpose was often the integration of Islamic thought with modern knowledge without any consideration of the internal integration of Islamic sciences, which is one of the reasons for the failure to build an integral Islamic worldview to this day.

While the scope of this study is not wide enough to pose the problematic of the Islamic worldview in all its aspects, nor that of knowledge integration in Islamic sciences, it will focus, as previously mentioned, on one of the most important elements of that worldview, namely the function of *istikhlāf* (vicegerency). This concept is susceptible to serve as a basis for knowledge integration in Islamic sciences by virtue of the convergence of all areas of Islamic knowledge and scholarship to this end. However, as will be demonstrated later, this component, in turn, has not received the attention it deserves within the attempts to build an Islamic worldview.

## Notes

1 Mālik Bin-Nabī, *Wijhat al-ʿĀlam al-Islāmī* [Vocation of Islam] (Damascus: Dār al-Fikr, 2002), 48.
2 Muḥammad al-Fāḍil ibn ʿĀshūr, *Wamaḍāt Fikr* [Glances of Thought] (Tunis: al-Dār al-ʿArabiyya li-l-Kutub, 1982), 38–41.
3 A.-L. Dupont, C. Mayeur-Jaouen, C. Verdeil, *Histoire du Moyen-Orient du XIXe siècle à nos jours* (Paris: Armand Colin, 2016), 59.
4 Fazlur Rahman Malik, *Islam and Modernity: Transformation of an Intellectual Tradition* (Chicago: University of Chicago Press, 1982), 46–49.
5 It is worth mentioning that the first one to create these parallels before the Ottoman *Tanẓīmāt* was Muḥammad ʿAlī Bāshā (d. 1849), the Ottoman governor of Egypt between 1805 and 1848. He created separate modern schools in order to teach modern sciences, thereby leaving al-Azhar with the focus on religious education and language. As was the case with religious scholars after the separation of "religious" and "secular" education as a result of the Ottoman reforms, al-Azhar scholars did not protest either. See: Zakariyyā Fāyid, *al-ʿIlmāniyya: al-Nashʾa wa-l-Athar fī l-Sharq wa-l-Gharb* [Secularism: Origin and Influence in the East and the West] (Cairo: al-Zahrāʾ li-l-Iʿlām al-ʿArabī, 1988), 10.
6 The Ashʿarī theory of intellectual identification of good and evil (*al-taḥsīn wa-l-taqbīḥ al-ʿaqlīyayn*), and theodicy, led to the introduction of several dichotomies that are foreign to the Islamic epistemology, and that most scholars of the fundamentals of Islamic jurisprudence had acknowledged. One such dichotomy is the reason-Revelation dichotomy. Since, in their understanding, Revelation is not subject to the logic of human reason, they can contradict each other, and, consequently, Revelation should be protected from reason. Therefore, reason was often approached with caution and suspicion. In fact, its role was seen as secondary. Al-Shāṭibī writes, "The implementation of reason should stay within the confines of Revelation for several

reasons." One of them is "the fact that reason is incapable of identifying good and evil, as is established in both theology and the fundamentals of jurisprudence." Abū Isḥāq al-Shāṭibī, *al-Muwāfaqāt* [The Reconciliation], annotated by Mashūr ibn Ḥasan (Cairo: Dār ibn ʿAffān, 1997), vol. 1, 125. Another dichotomy is the dichotomy of worldly and otherworldly interests. Since interests (*maṣlaḥa*) have no independent objective reality, the entire content of Revelation is a matter of abstract worship. Any short-term benefits that people may get from abiding by its teachings are not the original purpose of Revelation. The only viable purpose is the reward in the afterlife, which is attained after the realisation of that worship. Consequently, if there is a conflict between worldly interests and interests of the afterlife, which they consider to be religious interests (a conflict that is only imaginary and has no foundations in Revelation), otherworldly interests take priority. This prevailing conflict gave rise to the worship-interests dichotomy. There are no worldly interests in worship since it is intended initially only for adoration and reward in the afterlife. God did not command people to worship Him in ways that fulfil their natural needs, nor is there a natural aspiration to worship in the human being. As al-Shāṭibī comments, acts of worship belong to the category of actions "where there is no natural or instinctive drive that motivates people to perform it. Rather, natural human inclination may conflict with it or compete with it, as is the case for acts of worship as they are mere commandments." Ibid., vol. 3, 386–88. The same applies to religious beliefs (*ʿaqāʾid*) because, just like acts of worship, they are mere commandments that one should abide by for the purpose of adoration and reward in the afterlife. Therefore, they have classified articles of creed and beliefs with the category of "abstract adoration." See: Muḥammad ibn Aḥmad al-Sarakhsī, *Uṣūl al-Sarakhsī* [The Fundamentals of *al-Sarakhsī*] (Beirut: Dār al-Maʿrifa, n.d., vol. 2), 290. The only role faith plays in human life is adoring God to avoid punishment in the afterlife and to gain the reward of paradise. Any worldly gains that one can obtain from faith (if any) are secondary matters. Consequently, Muslim scholars did not focus on the worldly benefits of faith.

7 Fazlur Rahman, *Islam and Modernity: Transformation of an Intellectual Tradition*, 47–48.

8 Bin-Nabī, *Wijhat al-ʿĀlam al-Islāmī*, 77–83.

9 Ismāʿīl Rājī al-Fārūqī and Lamya Lois, *The Cultural Atlas of Islam* (Riyadh: Obeikan Library, 1998), 134–35.

10 Starting from the fourth century AH, tenth century CE, we see a growing consensus among scholars, apart from the Ḥanbalis (even though most of the latter were also imitators (*muqallidūn*) in fact), that absolute *ijtihād* (direct return to the texts of Revelation to deduce rulings or methodology) became prohibited, that its gate was closed and that no scholar could have its required skills, as we see clearly in their statements. For example, al-Qaffāl (d. 417/1026) claims that "two kinds of scholars can issue edicts (*fatāwī*). The first includes those who meet all the qualifying criteria for *ijtihād*, and there are today no more scholars left with that criteria. The other kind includes those who follow the school of one of the Imams, such as al-Shāfiʿī." Zayn al-Dīn al-Munāwī, *Fayḍ al-Qadīr Sharḥ al-Jāmiʿ al-Ṣaghīr* [The Blessings of the Mighty in the Explanation of the Small Treatise] (Cairo: Al-Maktaba al-Tijāriyya al-Kubrā, 1937), vol. 1, 9.

11 Due to political reasons, early in Islamic history a separation occurred between the worlds of governance and scholarship, which made many scholars abstain from public life and led to the progressive removal of public affairs from the domain and scope of religion in the subsequent eras. This gradual withdrawal of religious scholarship from public reality played a role in the fact that Islamic sciences became too abstract and often preoccupied with mere theoretical issues that are irrelevant to real life matters until they eventually turned into textbooks with limited reiterations, recapitulations and commentaries on the works of the pioneers. The impacts of this rupture also included the seclusion of scholars and their persecution by rulers, thus leading some of them to

excoriate worldly matters and remove them from the scope of religion to the extent that religion became, for many of them, an individual matter. It was concerned with nothing more than salvation from Hell and the achievement of Heaven. What Muslim scholars have termed "otherworldly interests" or "subsequent interests" (*maṣāliḥ ʾājila*) became the core of religion and its primary purpose, whereas what they termed "worldly interests" or "instant interests" (*maṣāliḥ ʿājila*) were only secondary and incidental issues that did not constitute the actual *raison d'être* of religion. See for instance:

- Ibn Qayyim al-Jawziyya, *Iʿlām al-Mawqqiʿīn ʿan Rabb al-ʿĀlamīn* [Information for Those Who Write on Behalf of the Lord of the Worlds], ed. Muḥammad ʿAbd al-Salām Ibrāhīm, (Beirut: Dār al-Kitāb, 1991) vol. 4, 283–84
- Jamāl al-Dīn al-Afghānī and Muḥammad ʿAbduh, *Al-ʿUrwa al-Wuthqā* [The Firmest Bond], (Cairo: Hindāwī Foundation, 2012), 64
- Khayr al-Dīn al-Tūnisī, *Aqwam al-Masālik fī Maʿrifat Aḥwāl al-Mamālik* [The Surest Path to Knowledge Regarding the Condition of Countries], (Beirut: Dār al-Kitāb al-Lubnānī, 2012), 61–62
- Ḥasan al-Turābī, *Qaḍāyā al-Tajdīd: Naḥwa Minhaj Uṣūlī* [The Questions of Reform: Towards a Fundamental Methodology], (Khartoum: Maʿhad al-Buḥūth wa-l-Dirāsāt al-Ijtimāʿiyya, 1990), 197–99
- Al-Fārūqī, *Islamization of Knowledge: General Principles and Work Plan*, 28–30

12 Because of the rift between public life and scholarship, inter alia, many scholars juxtaposed the secular quest and the pursuit of the Hereafter by condemning the former and commending the latter. While this dichotomy led many Muslims to abandon worldly life and embrace asceticism and Sufism at the social level, it resulted in an epistemological distortion at the intellectual level. This is reflected in their division of Revelation in terms of religious teachings and worldly teachings, claiming that the interests of the Hereafter have precedence over the interest of the worldly affairs. "Religious interests," including creed and worship, as such are therefore interests of the Hereafter, and "worldly interests" stated in Revelation are secondary interests that were not intended to have priority and do not constitute the objective of religion. See, for example, Al-Shāṭibī, *Al-Muwāfaqāt*, vol. 2, 358–72. Hence, it became no longer important for religion to frame and orient worldly life in an ethical manner, because engaging in reality to achieve its interests became a secondary matter, which is not the primary purpose of Revelation. Therefore, it is satisfactory that those who are ignorant about religion or who care less about it indulge in reality the way they wish, as long as they do not violate the teachings of the "Hereafter" or violate the particular rulings of Revelation. Thus, the rupture between knowledge/religion and governance/practice contributed to the development of the epistemological and methodological theories that reinforce it and justify it methodologically. Indeed, the worldly life/hereafter dichotomy got justified at the epistemological and methodological levels by the Ashʿarite's moral relativist approach, which durably influenced the discipline of *uṣūl al-fiqh*. To appreciate the impact of this issue, one only needs to take a look at the thesis of al-Shāṭibī (d. 790/1388), which is considered the most comprehensive and sophisticated treatise on the fundamentals of jurisprudence. In this treatise, which is saturated with Ashʿarite epistemology, he writes that "All things are inherently (ontologically) equal, the intellect cannot judge if they are good or evil. Thus, the portrayal of an interest (*maṣlaḥa*) as such depends on God in ways that human intellect can accept and feel comfortable with. Hence, qualifying things as interests belong to the realm of worship, and anything based on worship is also worship." Ibid., vol. 2, 535. On this basis, Revelation is not intended to serve any human interests other than worshipping God, which in turn qualifies people for reward in the afterlife. Worldly interests in Revelation, if any, are not initial objectives. Instead, they are mere secondary matters that can be best described as "favours that God has bestowed upon people." Ibid., vol. 2, 328. This clarifies why Ashʿarites believe that true worship and religiosity mean abiding by the commands of Revelation without seeking any worldly interests, objectives or benefits. Ibid., vol. 3,

99–100. Muḥammad Rashīd Riḍā (d. 1935) said: "Then, Muslim scholars themselves considered the involvement in sciences and arts, upon which the interests of the world depends, a deviation from religion, and some of them went as far as to argue that it is harmful to religious belief and could lead to its desertion, [...] that attitude is clearly a deviation from the guidance of the Qur'an!" Muḥammad Rashīd Riḍā, *Tafsīr al-Manār* [Interpretation of the Illuminator] (Cairo: Al-Hay'a al-Miṣriyya, 1990), vol. 2, 274.

13 We have investigated all of these issues in detail in our forthcoming book, *The Contemporary Epistemological Challenges of Religio-Ethical Reasoning (Ijtihād) and Islamic Sciences: Towards a Benchmark for Reappraisal.*

14 Ibn Taymiyya considered that rational knowledge (especially Greek philosophy and logic) influenced Islamic theology in a way that led to its deviation from its original foundation, which prevented Muslims from understanding the Qur'an in all its aspects and from articulating its epistemological system. It created divergence among Muslims around the Qur'an and divided them into three major groups: one group which put the creed, as determined by Revelation, behind itself, favouring philosophy instead; a second group that mixed creed and philosophy to the extent of formulating a hybrid referentiality that accommodates Revelation and philosophy; and a third group that refused to follow either group, but whose approach to creed did not transcend the level of reaction and the mere reaffirmation of what is already stated in the texts. The latter group did not take the texts as frames of reference that canalise thought and produce evidence. The two first groups, according to ibn Taymiyya, subjugated the Qur'an to non-Qur'anic epistemologies; as for the third one, it did not develop a Qur'anic epistemology, leaving room for the other groups to carry on their enterprise. See, for instance: Taqī al-Dīn ibn Taymiyya, *Majmū' al-Fatāwā* [The Compilation of Fatwas] (Medina: King Fahd Complex for the Printing of the Holy Quran, 1995), vol. 19, 160–63.

15 Fazlur Rahman, *Islam and Modernity: Transformation of an Intellectual Tradition*, 4.

16 A number of scholars have distinguished between the first generation of modern Muslim reformers, such as Jamāl al-Dīn al-Afghānī (d. 1897), his disciple Muḥammad 'Abduh (d. 1905), the latter's disciples and their contemporaries, who admired Western modernity and were more open to its acceptance and achievements, and those who came after the fall of the Ottoman Caliphate in the context of the division of the Islamic countries and the tyranny of Western colonialism, and who fought for Islamic identity and character in the face of the West and the secularism that replaced the Islamic State. Among this latter group, we find Ḥasan al-Bannā (d. 1949), Sayyid Quṭb (d. 1966) and Abū al-A'lā al-Mawdūdī (d. 1979). Fazlur Rahman called the first group "modernists" and the second "neo-revivalists" or "neo-fundamentalists," while "traditional revivalists" were pre-modern reformers, such as the Wahhābīs (Ibid., 136). Raḍwān al-Sayyid, on the other hand, called the first group "reformists" and the second "revivalists." What I mean by reformists and neo-modernists here are those latter-day reformers who have transcended the conservative course of revivalists.

17 Muṣṭafā al-Zarqā, *al-Madkhal al-Fiqhī al-'Āmm* [The General Introduction to *Fiqh*] (Damascus: Dār al-Qalam, 3rd ed., 2012), vol. 1, 225–26; 238–39.

18 Ibid., vol. 1, 243.

19 Ibid., vol. 1, 243–46.

20 Raḍwān al-Sayyid, *al-Ṣirā' 'alā al-Islām* [The Fight for Islam] (Beirut: Dār al-Kitāb al-'Arabī, 2004), 236.

21 Al-Zarqā, *al-Madkhal al-Fiqhī al-'Āmm*, vol. 1, 248–49.

22 Al-Sayyid, *al-Ṣirā' 'alā al-Islām*, 220.

23 Ibid., 226; see also: Zarqā, *al-Madkhal al-Fiqhī al-'Āmm*, vol. 1, 253.

24 Al-Zarqā, *al-Madkhal al-Fiqhī al-'Āmm*, vol. 1, 252

25 Ibid., vol. 1, 251.

26 Al-Sayyid, *al-Ṣirā' 'alā al-Islām*, 238.

27 Ibn 'Āshūr, *Wamaḍāt Fikr*, 41.

28 Al-Sayyid, *al-Ṣirāʿ ʿalā al-Islām*, 238.
29 Ibid.
30 Ibid., 238–39.
31 Ibid., 239.
32 Fazlur Rahman, *Islam and Modernity: Transformation of an Intellectual Tradition,* 86–87.
33 Ibid., 152–53.
34 ʿAbd al-Majīd al-Najjār, *Mashārīʿ al-Ishhād al-Ḥaḍārī* [The Projects of Civilizational Reform] (Beirut: Dār al-Gharb al-Islāmī, 1999, vol. 1), 169–70.
35 ʿAbd al-ʿAzīz al-Thaʿālibī, *Rūḥ al-Taḥarrur fī l-Qurʾān* [The Spirit of Liberation in the Qurʾan] (Beirut: Dār al-Gharb al-Islāmī, 1985), 118.
36 Al-Najjār, *Mashārīʿ al-Ishhād al-Ḥaḍārī*, 171.
37 Chauki Lazhar, *Mūjibāt Tajdīd Uṣūl al-Fiqh fī l-ʿAṣr al-Ḥadīth* [The Need for Reform in *Uṣūl al-Fiqh* in Modern Times] (Beirut: Dār al-Mashriq, 2016), 120–38.
38 This is visible, for instance, in the many research papers published among the proceedings of the symposium on the reappraisal of Islamic sciences organised in Morocco in 2010. See: ʿAbd al-Salām Ṭawīl, ed., *al-ʿUlūm al-Islāmiyya: Azmat Manhaj am Azmat Tanzīl?* [Islamic Sciences: Crisis of Methodology or Application?] (Beirut: Dār Madārik, 2011).
39 Chauki Lazhar, "Taṭawwur al-Tandhīr al-Maqāṣidī fī l-ʿAṣr al-Ḥadīth" [The Development of Contemporary Theorizations of *Sharīʿa* Objectives], *Majallat Islāmiyyat al-Maʿrifa* 90 (Fall 2017).
40 Ibid.
41 See Malkāwī, *Minhājiyyat al-Takāmul al-Maʿrifī*, 98.
42 Fazlur Rahman is counted among those who considered the Ashʿarī doctrine as "an almost total distortion of Islam." Fazlur Rahman, *Islam and Modernity: Transformation of an Intellectual Tradition,* 133.
43 Ibid., 152.
44 Ibid., 86.
45 Abū Sulaymān, *The Qurʾanic Worldview: A Springboard for Cultural Reform* (London: International Institute of Islamic Thought, 2011), 2.
46 Ibid., 3.
47 Ibid.
48 Ibid., xx.
49 Ibid., 8–30.
50 Ibid., 11.
51 Ibid., 12.
52 This paragraph comes from the Arabic version of the book and was not included in the later English translation. Abū Sulaymān, *al-Ruʾya al-Kawniyya al-Ḥaḍāriyya al-Qurʾāniyya, al-Munṭalaq al-Asās li-l-Iṣlāḥ al-Insānī* [The Qurʾanic Civilisational Worldview: The Main Entry for Human Reform] (Cairo: Dār al-Salām, 2009) 41.
53 Ibid., 48.
54 Abū Sulaymān, *The Qurʾanic Worldview: A Springboard for Cultural Reform*, 28.
55 Abū Sulaymān, *al-Ruʾya al-Kawniyya al-Ḥaḍāriyya al-Qurʾāniyya*, 47; and see: Abū Sulaymān, *The Qurʾanic Worldview: A Springboard for Cultural Reform*, 21–22.
56 In support of these arguments, it suffices to review the attempt of one of the pioneers of the *Knowledge Integration Project*, ʿAbd al-Ḥamīd Abū Sulaymān, whose book *The Qurʾanic Worldview: A Springboard for Cultural Reform* is one of the latest attempts in this regard. In its introduction, he points out that the book is the sum total of his life experience in the field of education and thought reform. All of the observations I have made here apply to this work.
57 Fazlur Rahman, *Islam and Modernity: Transformation of an Intellectual Tradition*, 8.
58 What is meant here by the ontological and teleological purposes of Islamic sciences, are the original functions and intended outcomes of these sciences as defined by their

initial epistemological framework, i.e., Revelation. These can only emerge by a genealogical examination of these sciences that sheds light on the way Revelation requires their existence, how they function within its framework, how they realise its objectives, and their interdependence within that context. Only this degree of investigation can allow the development of a constant universal standard for the evaluation and appraisal of Islamic sciences in their historical and contemporary movements, an enterprise that we attempted in our manuscript in preparation, *The Contemporary Epistemological Challenges of Religio-Ethical Reasoning (Ijtihād) and Islamic Sciences: Towards a Benchmark for Reappraisal.*

59 See these papers in: Rāʾid ʿUkkāsha, ed., *al-Takāmul al-Maʿrifī: Atharuhu fī l-Taʿlīm al-Jāmiʿī wa-Ḍarūratuhu al-Ḥaḍāriyya* [Knowledge Integration: Its Role in Higher Education and Its Civilizational Imperative] (Herndon, VA: International Institute of Islamic Thought, 2012, vol. 1). Similarly, studies that did deal with the issue of knowledge integration within Islamic sciences did not provide a critical epistemological review of Islamic sciences, and they only limited themselves to an often apologetic presentation of the degree of integration that existed in traditional Islamic knowledge. See, for example, the research papers presented at the symposium organised in 2009 by Dār al-Ḥadīth al-Ḥasaniyya on the theme of knowledge integration between Islamic sciences: *al-Takāmul al-Maʿrifī bayna al-ʿUlūm al-Islāmiyya: al-Usus al-Naẓariyya wa-l-Shurūṭ al-Taṭbīqiyya* [Knowledge Integration between Islamic Sciences: Theoretical Foundations and Practical Requirements] (Rabat: Dār al-Ḥadīth al-Ḥasaniyya, 2010). See also: Ṭāhā ʿAbd al-Raḥmān, *Tajdīd al-Manhaj fī Taqwīm al-Turāth* [The Reform of the Methodology of Appraising Heritage] (Casablanca: al-Markaz al-Thaqāfī al-ʿArabī, 2nd ed., 2007), 75 ff; and Ṣalḥa Hāj Yaʿqūb, "Al-Takāmul al-Maʿrifī fī l-Turāth al-ʿArabī al-Islāmī: Dirāsa Taḥlīliyya wa-Naqiyya" [Knowledge Integration in Arabo-Islamic Heritage], *The Journal of Arabic Language for Specialized Research* 2.1 (April 2015).

60 Al-Fārūqī, *Islamization of Knowledge: General Principles and Work Plan*, 22.

61 Ibid., 76–77.

62 Abū Sulaymān, *al-Ruʾya al-Kawniyya al-Ḥaḍāriyya al-Qurʾāniyya*, 12.

## Bibliography

ʿAbd al-Raḥmān, Ṭāhā. *Tajdīd al-Manhaj fī Taqwīm al-Turāth [The Reform of the Methodology of Appraising Heritage]*. Casablanca: al-Markaz al-Thaqāfī al-ʿArabī, 2nd ed., 2007.

Abū Sulaymān, ʿAbd al-Ḥamīd. *The Qurʾanic Worldview: A Springboard for Cultural Reform*. London: The International Institute of Islamic Thought, 2011.

Abū Sulaymān, ʿAbd al-Ḥamīd. *Al-Ruʾya al-Kawniyya al-Ḥaḍāriyya al-Qurʾāniyya, al-Munṭalaq al-Asās li-l-Iṣlāḥ al-Insānī [The Qurʾanic Civilizational Worldview: the Main Entry for Human Reform]*. Cairo: Dār al-Salām, 2009.

Al-Afghānī, Jamāl al-Dīn and Muḥammad ʿAbduh. *Al-ʿUrwa al-Wuthqā [The Firmest Bond]*. Cairo: Hindāwī Foundation, 2012.

Ibn ʿĀshūr, Muḥammad al-Fāḍil. *Wamaḍāt Fikr [Glances of Thought]*. Tunis: al-Dār al-ʿArabiyya li-l-Kutub, 1982.

Bin-Nabī, Mālik. *Wijhat al-ʿĀlam al-Islāmī [Vocation of Islam]*. Damascus: Dār al-Fikr, 2002.

Dār al-Ḥadīth al-Ḥasaniyya. *Al-Takāmul al-Maʿrifī bayna al-ʿUlūm al-Islāmiyya: al-Usus al-Naẓariyya wa-l-Shurūṭ al-Taṭbīqiyya [Knowledge Integration Between Islamic Sciences: Theoretical Foundations and Practical Requirements]*. Rabat: Dār al-Ḥadīth al-Ḥasaniyya, 2010.

Dupont, Anne-Laure, Catherine Mayeur-Jaouen, and Chantal Verdeil. *Histoire Du Moyen-Orient: Du XIXe siècle à Nos Jours*. Paris: Armand Colin, 2016.

Al-Fārūqī, Ismāʿīl Rājī. *Islamization of Knowledge: General Principles and Work Plan*. Herndon, Virginia: International Institute of Islamic Thought, 1981.

Al-Fārūqī, Ismāʿīl Rājī and Lamya Lois. *The Cultural Atlas of Islam*. Riyadh: Obeikan Library, 1998.

Fāyid, Zakarīyyā. *Al-ʿIlmāniyya: al-Nashʾa wa-l-Athar fī l-Sharq wa-l-Gharb [Secularism: Origin and Influence in the East and the West]*. Cairo: al-Zahrāʾ lil-Iʿlām al-ʿArabī, 1988.

Ḥājj Yaʿqūb, Ṣalḥa. "Al-Takāmul al-Maʿrifī fī l-Turāth al-ʿArabī al-Islāmī: Dirāsa Taḥlīliyya wa-Naqdiyya [Knowledge Integration in Arabo-Islamic heritage]." *The Journal of Arabic Language for Specialized Research* 2, no. 1 (April 2015): 54–76.

Lazhar, Chauki. "Taṭawwur al-Tandhīr al-Maqāṣidī fī l-ʿAṣr al-Ḥadīth [The Development of Contemporary Theorizations of *Sharīʿa* Objectives]". *Majallat Islāmiyyat al-Maʿrifa* 90 (Fall 2017): 17–53.

Lazhar, Chauki. *Mūjibāt Tajdīd Uṣūl al-Fiqh fī l-ʿAṣr al-Ḥadīth [The Need for Reform in Uṣūl al-Fiqh in Modern Times]*. Beirut: Dār al-Mashriq, 2016.

Malik, Fazlur Rahman. *Islam and Modernity: Transformation of an Intellectual Tradition*. University of Chicago Press, 1982.

Al-Munāwī, Zayn al-Dīn. *Fayḍ al-Qadīr Sharḥ al-Jāmiʿ al-Ṣaghīr [The Blessings of the Mighty in the Explanation of the Small Treatise]*. Cairo: al-Maktaba al-Tijāriyya al-Kubrā, 1937.

Al-Najjār, ʿAbd al-Majīd. *Mashārīʿ al-Ishhād al-ḥaḍārī [The Projects of Civilizational Reform]*. Beirut: Dār al-Gharb al-Islāmī, 1st ed., 1999.

Ibn Qayyim al-Jawziyya, Shams al-Dīn. *Iʿlām al-Mawqqiʿīn ʿan Rabb al-ʿĀlamīn [Information for Those Who Write on Behalf of the Lord of the Worlds]*. Edited by Muḥammad ʿAbd al-Salām Ibrāhīm. Beirut: Dār al-Kitāb, 1991.

Riḍā, Muḥammad Rashīd. *Tafsīr al-Manār [Interpretation of the Illuminator]*. Cairo: al-Hayʾa al-Miṣriyya, 1990.

Al-Sarakhsī, Muḥammad ibn Aḥmad. *Uṣūl al-Sarakhsī [The Fundamentals of al-Sarakhsī]*. Beirut: Dār al-Maʿrifa, n.d.

Al-Sayyid, Raḍwān. *Al-Ṣirāʿ ʿalā al-Islām [The Fight for Islam]*. Beirut: Dār al-Kitāb al-ʿArabī, 2004.

Al-Shāṭibī, Abū Isḥāq. *Al-Muwāfaqāt [The Reconciliation]*. Annotated by Mashūr ibn Ḥasan. Cairo: Dār ibn ʿAffān, 1997.

Ṭawīl, ʿAbd al-Salām, ed. *Al-ʿUlūm al-Islāmiyya: Azmat Manhaj am Azmat Tanzīl? [Islamic Sciences: Crisis of Methodology or Application?]*. Beirut: Dār Madārik, 2011.

Ibn Taymiyya, Taqī al-Dīn. *Majmūʿ al-Fatāwā [The Compilation of Fatwas]*. Medina: King Fahd Complex for the Printing of the Holy Quran, 1995.

Al-Thaʿālibī, ʿAbd al-ʿAzīz. *Rūḥ al-Taḥarur fī l-Qurʾān [The Spirit of Liberation in the Qurʾan]*. Beirut: Dār al-Gharb al-Islāmī, 1985.

Al-Tūnisī, Khayr al-Dīn. *Aqwam al-Masālik fī Maʿrifat Aḥwāl al-Mamālik [The Surest Path to Knowledge Regarding the Condition of Countries]*. Beirut: Dār al-Kitāb al-Lubnānī, 2012.

Al-Turābī, Ḥasan. *Qaḍāyā al-Tajdīd: Naḥwa Minhaj Uṣūlī [The Questions of Reform: Towards a Fundamental Methodology]*. Khartoum: Maʿhad al-Buḥūth wa-l-Dirāsāt al-Ijtimāʿiyya, 1990.

ʿUkkāsha, Rāʾid, ed. *Al-Takāmul al-Maʿrifī: Atharuhu fī l-Taʿlīm al-Jāmiʿī wa-Ḍarūratuhu al-Ḥaḍāriyya [Knowledge Integration: its Role in Higher Education and its Civilizational Imperative]*. Virginia: International Institute of Islamic Thought, 2012.

Al-Zarqā, Muṣṭafā. *Al-Madkhal al-Fiqhī al-ʿĀmm [The General Introduction to Fiqh]*. Damascus: Dār al-Qalam, 3rd ed., 2012.

# 3 The Concept of *Istikhlāf* in Islamic Heritage

Before proceeding to analyse the contemporary discourse on vicegerency as a human existential function and discussing the outlines of a Qur'anic theory of vicegerency, it is indispensable to sketch a picture of the conception of *istikhlāf* in classical Islamic scholarship. In the introduction to this study, I stated that classical scholars did not pay much attention to the concept of *khilāfa* (vicegerency) or *istikhlāf* as an existential function, nor did they study it exclusively as an independent subject matter. The word *khilāfa* was mostly used with reference to a political function or institution. Since my approach focuses on *istikhlāf* as a human responsibility, the scope of attention will be limited to the traditional interpretations of the most obvious Qur'anic verses in introducing the concept of *istikhlāf* as a human function, which is articulated in the Qur'anic verse: "When your Lord said to the angels, 'Indeed, I am going to set a *khalīfa* on earth.'" (Q 2:30). Since the first century of the Muslim era, Muslims have held different interpretations of this verse. This chapter is mainly concerned with the most significant differences and their context, which are related to the identity of the one who is deputised by the vicegerent (*mustakhlaf 'anhu*), the vicegerent himself (*khalīfa*) and the nature of that which is delegated to the responsibility of the vicegerent, i.e., the object of vicegerency (*mustakhlaf fīhi*). Furthermore, attention will be given to the way human existential function and vicegerency were conceived in the light of classical epistemological patterns.

## 3.1 Who is Man the Deputy of?

At the heart of the most important issues regarding these divergences lies the identification of the one of whom the vicegerent is a deputy, a debate which goes back to the era of the companions. Al-Ṭabarī (d. 310/922) said:

> *Al-khalīfa* is derived from the statement: So-and-so deputises for so-and-so in this matter when he takes up his position after him. [...] If someone said: Who/what populated the earth before human beings so that Adam could replace him and become his successor? The answer is that exegetes have differed in this regard.

DOI: 10.4324/9781003335948-3

Al-Ṭabarī then quotes the opinion of ibn ʿAbbās (d. 68/687) that Adam (the human being) was a successor to the jinn who had inhabited the land before him, a view emanating from the *Isrāʾīlīyyāt* (narratives imported from Judeo-Christian sources).[1] Moreover, al-Ṭabarī cites another opinion by al-Ḥasan al-Baṣrī (d. 110/728) that *istikhlāf* conveys the succession of human generations. He then quotes a third narrative attributed to ibn ʿAbbās and ibn Masʿūd (d. 32/652), among other companions, and then says:

> The interpretation of the verse based on this narrative that we have mentioned on the authority of ibn Masʿūd and ibn ʿAbbās is: 'I will establish a vicegerent on earth who will deputise Me in ruling among My creatures,' and the designated *khalīfa* is Adam and whoever takes up a similar position in God's obedience and establishment of justice among His creatures.[2]

It seems that this opinion, i.e., vicegerency on behalf of God, is the opinion of al-Ṭabarī himself, as it is difficult to understand this idea from the initial narration of ibn ʿAbbās and ibn Masʿūd.

Al-Ṭabarī has been cited by a large number of exegetes who have examined this difference in interpretation. Mainstream scholars had forbidden the attribution of the title "*khalīfa* of Allah" to the ruler, as reported by al-Māwardī (d. 450/1058)[3] and ibn Khaldūn (d. 808/1405)[4] because, in his political position, he succeeds his human predecessor and is not a vicegerent of God in this regard. A group of exegetes from various doctrinal schools interpreted the concept of *khalīfa* in this verse as a vicegerent of God. The Atharī (Salafī) scholar al-Samʿānī (d. 489/1095) said:

> God calls him a *khalīfa* because he succeeds others and he is also called *khalīfa* because others succeed him. It is also said that he is called a *khalīfa* because he is the vicegerent of God on earth, who establishes His laws and implements His teachings, and this is the correct interpretation.[5]

Similarly, al-Baghawī (d. 516/1122) said: "It is said so because others succeed him, but the correct meaning is that he is the vicegerent of God on earth where he establishes His laws and implements His teachings."[6]

It should be pointed out that these statements have been circulating in the books of *tafsīr* (exegesis) without raising controversy among their authors. Most of the exegetes have cited the three opinions documented by al-Ṭabarī without making one dominate over the others. However, it was Shaykh al-Islām ibn Taymiyya (d. 728/1327) who first contested the idea that man is a vicegerent of God on Earth. He problematised the concept at the creedal level and cited evidence that refutes it and considers it as an act of *shirk* (polytheism).[7] The large corpus of recent studies that deal with the differences among scholars' interpretations regarding the permissibility of saying that 'man is a vicegerent of God' is in consensus with the idea that ibn Taymiyya prohibited it altogether. Although ibn Taymiyya's language is explicit and rigid in vilifying and prohibiting this title, I do not share the opinion stated in these studies that ibn Taymiyya meant absolute prohibition. This is because ibn Taymiyya's opinion was not formulated within the context of the discussion of those who espoused that viewpoint among the scholars of exegesis and others who followed it. Instead, ibn Taymiyya's vilification of the concept developed in the context of his reaction to those who employed the title in order to serve intellectual patterns that are considered to be contrary to the Islamic creed, foremost of which were the doctrine of 'incarnation' and 'pantheism,' i.e., *waḥdat al-wujūd* (oneness of existence), which utilised this view for claiming that man is God embodied in his creation. Ibn Taymiyya's refutation of the statement that a human being could act as a vicegerent of God came only in this context, i.e., in response to the radical views of Sufism, but it never occurred in the context of the discussion of those who advocated it among exegetes and other scholars. In his interpretation of the verse of *khilāfa* in *sūrat al-Baqara* and elsewhere, ibn Taymiyya said:

> That is, a "*khalīfa* succeeding those who preceded you among human beings," and it is not intended that he is a vicegerent of God, and that he is for God as the pupil of the eye,[8] as some pagans who believe in incarnation and pantheism said, such as the author of *al-Futūḥāt al-Makiyya* [The Meccan Revelations], and that he is the embodiment of God's names, interpreting accordingly God Almighty's saying: "And He taught Adam the Names, all of them" (Q 2:31, Arberry), and likening man to God though it is prescribed to draw this kind of likeness, as the Qur'anic verse says: "Nothing is like Him" (Q 40:11, Ali Qarai), among other similar statements which aim to distort Texts and corrupt reason.[9]

Moreover, he said:

> God's words: "Indeed, I am going to set a *khalīfa* on earth" (Q 2:30) conveys the meaning of succession in the line of creation on Earth that existed before that, as exegetes and scholars have stated. Regarding the opinion of some advocates of pantheism who believe that man is God's vicegerent, it is a reflection of their ignorance and delusion.[10]

Some scholars considered that ibn Taymiyya prohibits the use of such a title in a categorical manner, arguing that some of his statements are unrestrictive and absolute, such as: "It is not permitted to ascribe a *khalīfa* to God."[11] The other citations of ibn Taymiyya, which suggest a categorical prohibition, include "Whoever ascribes a *khalīfa* to God is said to be committing an act of polytheism"[12] and "God Almighty has no successor at all,"[13] among other statements. However, all these statements came, without exception whatsoever, in the context of ibn Taymiyya's response to those who advocated pantheism and anthropomorphism.[14] Hence, they should be perceived in relation to this backdrop and within the confines of the intended meaning. Ibn Taymiyya, nonetheless, did not accuse the exegetes who held these views of making polytheistic pronouncements.

It is clear that ibn Taymiyya's discussion is aimed at those who use this opinion to prove the doctrine of pantheism, which does not distinguish between vice and virtue, and argues that since the entire universe is God, it can only be good. Ibn Taymiyya's argument in this regard is clear:

> It has been shown that these claims about *khilāfa* and the like emanate from those known for vanity, oppression, and polytheism and who seek to become tyrants in this world, the like of the Pharaoh, the pantheists and their acolytes who claim a status comparable to that of God Almighty, and that He needs his servants just as the latter need Him. Immaculate is He, and He is greatly exalted above what they say. [...] How can a Muslim permit himself to make such a claim, that he is a vicegerent of God, and that he deputises for Him? This is equivalent to saying that the Pharaoh, Nimrod and the like were vicegerents of God who deputised for Him. The apologists apply this meaning constantly to the extent that every human being becomes a vicegerent of God because he belongs to the species sent down to manage and rule over others, such as animals, and they do not differentiate between those who obeyed God and those who disobeyed Him. Rather, they liken the believers who do righteous deeds to the wicked spoilers on earth and God-fearing people to ungodly ones. They do so by associating that which God has set apart. It is in this context that pantheists have legitimated every type of polytheism in the world, which is tantamount to making the servants vicegerents who deputise for God in roles that are similar to what is practised among caliphs and representatives of kings. Many of the polytheists draw these types of concordance between the question of God and His worship to that of kings.[15]

Ibn Taymiyya, however, stated that it is permissible to argue for this opinion if it is stripped of these beliefs:

> Whoever claims that he or someone else deputises for God or he is His vicegerent but does not follow God's commands as directed through His messengers lied to God and is a haughty person who commits acts of injustice. [...] If by saying that he is a "deputy" he means the messenger, conveyer and the implementer, then it is right to say so, but if he meant it in the sense of acting on God's behalf in what He does not do or cannot control, then it is a lie which is championed by the Qadarites (determinists) who believe in independent actions and in the idea that God did not create human actions, which is an invalid argument.[16]

Hence, it is erroneous to classify ibn Taymiyya among those who argued for the prohibition of the statement that man can act as a vicegerent of God, because his argument came in a specific context rather than that of the opinions of exegetes, such as al-Ṭabarī, al-Samʿānī, al-Baghawī, and al-Iṣfahānī (d. 502/1108) among many others who adopted the same position. In other words, ibn Taymiyya's statement came in the context of his refutation of the concept of the *khilāfa* of man as a vicegerent of God within the pantheistic intellectual model, not within the intellectual model of exegetes and those who shared their views, for he said that it was a palatable idea, as quoted above. This is equally evidenced by the fact that ibn Qayyim al-Jawziyya (d. 751/1350), the disciple of ibn Taymiyya, addressed the issue of the *khilāfa* of man as a vicegerent of God, but he did not vilify those who advocated this position or consider their practice the result of ignorance, delusion or polytheism, as did his mentor. The most striking thing he ever said about *khilāfa* in the sense that man is a vicegerent of God was: "The party forbidding its use is right."[17] This was not because ibn al-Qayyim "verged towards leniency and moderation in comparison with his mentor,"[18] as some scholars argued. Rather, the reason is that ibn al-Qayyim's discussion of this opinion was not in the context of his response to those who employed it within pantheist patterns, but rather he used it in the context of the apologists among the exegetes, which is why he did not reject this opinion at the creedal level but only comments on a few linguistic arguments.[19]

What is striking in this context is that several contemporary researchers have tried to challenge the vicegerency claim and exonerate the Islamic heritage from it by illusively arguing that it is an innovation and by putting forward some hasty statements that can be easily invalidated. Among these is the author of the following statement: "I did not find anybody who stated that *khilāfa* refers to vicegerency on behalf of (*ʻan*) God except among the latter-day exegetes, such as al-Ālūsī (d. 1854), al-Ṭāhir ibn ʿĀshūr (d. 1973) and among the subsequent generations."[20] It would suffice to quote ibn al-Jawzī's words (d. 597/1200) in response to this claim. The latter asserted that one of the common opinions among scholars is that *istikhlāf* means "vicegerency on behalf of (*ʻan*) God almighty, because believers are God's vicegerents on earth."[21] He also said: "There are two opinions about the meaning of the *khilāfa* of Adam: First, it is used in the sense that he is a vicegerent on behalf of (*ʻan*) God Almighty on earth."[22] Abū Ḥayyān (d. 745/1344) said: "The *khalīfa*, it is said, is Adam because he is the successor of the angels [...] or the vicegerent on behalf of (*ʻan*) God Almighty."[23] From the perspective of this contemporary researcher, "Imām al-Ṭabarī's statement is in reference to *khalīfa* as a creation of God (*khalīfa minnī*) not as a vicegerent on behalf of God (*khalīfa ʿannī*)."[24] The invalidity of his viewpoint is evidenced by al-Ṭabarī's statement, which is mentioned above, "I will establish a vicegerent on earth who will deputise Me (*yakhlufunī*) in ruling among My creatures." The word "*yakhlufunī*" is explicit in that it refers to humans as *khalīfa* on behalf of God, which the researcher left out from his quotation of al-Ṭabarī for some reason. Furthermore, "*yakhlufunī*" can only mean "deputise Me," since the other senses of the word, such as succeed or replace, are not applicable to God.

In the same context, some argue that the idea of *khilāfa* of God is a modern invention unknown to the ancients, especially among the *salaf* (three first Muslim generations). Shaykh ʿAbd al-Raḥmān Ḥabanka al-Maydānī (d. 2004) said, for instance, that this opinion is "one of the fallacies committed by some contemporary Islamic thinkers."[25] Al-Maydānī considered that Muḥammad Rashīd Riḍā (d. 1935) was the first to put forward such an opinion. He continued: "The idea of man's *khilāfa* of God is a modern innovation in Islamic thought, as none of the *salaf* ever advocated it, nor does it have any legal textual basis, in addition to the fact that textual and logical Islamic doctrinal rules reject it."[26] Another researcher said:

> I completely agree with Shaykh al-Maydānī that it was never proven that any of the companions said that Adam (peace be upon him), a human being in general or the Prophet (ﷺ) was a *khalīfa* of God or acted on behalf of God; rather, this was apparently rejected (*marfūḍ*) and was not known (*ghayr ma'rūf*).[27]

We may, then, wonder how an unknown idea was rejected. Another researcher said: "It is not mentioned in any authentic sayings of the Prophet, that anyone is a *khalīfa* of God."[28] He added: "The claim that it is a man who is the *khalīfa* of God perhaps finds its first and clearest expression in Muḥammad 'Abduh's writings (d. 1905),"[29] and continued: "it is an entirely new interpretation."[30]

In any case, the invalidity of these statements is evidenced by a set of transmitted narratives going back to the Prophet (ﷺ), the companions and their successors. Likewise, it is further refuted by a significant set of proofs that confirm that the idea that the human being is the vicegerent of God (whether the vicegerent is Adam, all prophets, prophets and righteous people, or humanity as a whole) was commonly found in Islamic heritage across the eras and the doctrinal tendencies, as will be shown below.

As for the literature that confirms the existence of the idea that a human being may act as the vicegerent of God among the *salaf*, we can cite the following examples:

- The Prophet (ﷺ) said: "If you see him, pledge allegiance to him even if you have to crawl on ice because he is al-Mahdī, the *khalīfa* of God."[31]
- The Prophet (ﷺ) said: "If one day you see the *khalīfa* of God on earth, then follow him."[32]
- Describing the turmoil of the end of times, the Prophet (ﷺ) said: "If Allah has [at that time] a *khalīfa* on earth who flays your back and takes your property, obey him, otherwise die holding onto the stump of a tree."[33]
- It is narrated that the Prophet (ﷺ) said: "Adam and Moses had an argument; thereupon, Moses said: 'You are the *khalīfa* of God.'"[34]
- Ibn 'Umar (d. 73/693) related that, in the wake of the rebellion against the central authority of Medina after the demise of the Prophet (ﷺ), the Prophet's successor, Abu Bakr (d. 13/634) ascended the pulpit and addressed the people saying "I swear by God, I will continue establishing God's commands and strive in God's cause until God fulfils His promise and covenant for us, so that those of us who get killed as martyrs will be in Paradise, and those of us who remain will remain as God's *khalīfa* on his land and inheritors of the worship of the Truth. That is because God almighty said, and He never breaks his word, 'Allah has promised those who have believed among you and done

righteous deeds that He will surely grant them *khilāfa* upon the earth'" (Q 24:55, b.o. Sahih Intl).[35]

- It is reported that ʿAlī (d. 40/660) said: "Those are the vicegerents (*khulafāʾ*) of God, the Almighty and Exalted, on earth, they make the call to His religion."[36]
- Abū Ḥabīb al-Sulaymī (d. 74/693) said: "I read in conventional wisdom that one should 'listen to the questioner until he finishes and then reply with mercy and kindness, be like a merciful father to the orphan and be just towards the oppressed so that you may become a vicegerent (*khalīfa*) of God on earth.'"[37]
- ʿAbd Allāh ibn Jaʿfar (d. 80/699) is reported to have said: "Abū Bakr was designated a caliph over us, and he was a vicegerent of God par excellence. He was merciful and compassionate towards us."[38]
- It is reported that al-Ḥasan al-Baṣrī (d. 110/728) used to say, after reciting Q 41:33 ("And who is better in speech than one who invites to Allah and does righteousness and says, 'Indeed, I am of the Muslims.'" Sahih Intl): "This [person described by the verse] is God's beloved, God's close friend, God's chosen one, God's elect, the most loved by God on earth; he replied to God's call, he called the people to that which he replied to, he did a good deed when replying and said 'Indeed, I am of the Muslims,' this is the *khalīfa* of Allah!"[39]
- Al-Ḥasan al-Baṣrī also said: "God will always have advisors, they advise for God among His people and advice for God's servants about God, they work for God on earth with advice; those are the vicegerents of God on earth."[40]
- It is narrated that ʿAbd Allāh ibn Naʿīm al-Maʿāfirī (d. 137/754) said: "I heard the Shaykhs say: 'He who commands virtue and forbids vice is a vicegerent of God on earth, of His book and of the Messenger of God (ﷺ).'"[41]

The above are a few selected samples of sources that support the thesis that the idea that man may act as the vicegerent of God was not uncommon among the *salaf*. In fact, I could not find any scholar who prescribed the reference to these texts. This raises the question of how it could be asserted that none of the *salaf* generations ever approved the saying that one is "God's vicegerent" and that this was "unacceptable and unknown."[42]

Moreover, some of these researchers confuse the prohibition of scholars attributing the title "vicegerent of God" to rulers and the absolute prohibition of its use. Therefore, they applied the prohibition to attribute that title to the human being in a categorical manner, and some of them rushed in asserting that "*istikhlāf* refers to the succession of preceding nations or individuals. This is the position of the majority of exegetes."[43] However, as previously mentioned, most of the exegetes conveyed the controversy on the issue without making one opinion predominate over another and without expatiating on it. None of them said that this is the opinion of most scholars, except ibn al-Qayyim.[44] However, there is no evidence that this reflects the opinion of the majority of the exegetes, as mentioned above, and no scholar before ibn al-Qayyim has reported that this was the opinion of most scholars. Some of them, however, reported that most scholars were of the opinion that the attribution of the title "vicegerent of God" to rulers is prohibited; so, ibn al-Qayyim may have tried to generalise that consensus. Ibn Khaldūn's words on the position of the majority of the scholars in this regard are explicit:

> Having shown the reality of this position and the fact that man acts on behalf of the Legislator in the preservation of religion and the policies of the world are called *khilāfa* and imamate and the undertaker of the task is a *khalīfa* and imām. He is called an imām in comparison with the imam who leads people in prayer in the sense that he is followed by people, which is why the notion of "grand Imamate" is used in this regard, whereas the *khalīfa* title refers to the fact that he succeeds the Prophet in handling the affairs of his *umma*, and he is therefore called *khalīfa* in the absolute sense and the *khalīfa* of the Messenger of God. People have differed regarding his designation as *khalīfa* of God. Some have approved this designation based on the general use of *khilāfa* as attributed to human beings, as in God Almighty's words: "I will set a *khalīfa* on earth" (Q 2:30) and "He has made you *khalāʾif* on earth" (Q 6:165). Nevertheless, the majority of scholars have prohibited its use because he [the ruler] is not included in the meaning of the verse and Abū Bakr forbade it.[45]

Ibn Khaldūn thus clarifies that the opinion articulated by the majority of scholars regarding the prohibition concerns the attribution of the title vicegerent of God to rulers, while it seems clear that those who have permitted it have relied on an analogy in using "the general use of *khilāfa* as attributed to human beings." The majority of scholars, however, have prohibited such use in the case of rulers "because he [the ruler] is not included in the meaning of the verse"; so, it is understood that they believed that the meaning of the verse concerns the ordinary human (as vicegerent of God).

Moreover, these researchers have jumped to the conclusion that vicegerency is a religious innovation, a creedal deviation, and an act of polytheism; in doing so, they were imitating ibn Taymiyya and confining themselves to his arguments. For instance, one of them said: "What does the existence of a *khalīfa* besides God mean? Isn't this outright polytheism as perceived by ibn Taymiyya? Furthermore, how would polytheism be defined other than in this sense?"[46] Another one said: "I followed this opinion for a long time [i.e., that man is the *khalīfa* of God] until a reading of ibn Taymiyya on the subject led me to have second thoughts."[47]

This overhasty decision of imitating ibn Taymiyya does not take into account the context in which he dealt with the issue, nor the fact that ibn Taymiyya himself had permitted the use of the attributive title of vicegerent of God outside of that pantheistic intellectual pattern, as I have explained. This applies to ibn al-Qayyim as well, as I will highlight below.

This hasty acceptance of the idea that ibn Taymiyya prohibited the use of the term "vicegerent of God" without paying attention to what he meant, also applies to all those contemporaries who opposed ibn Taymiyya's view and who advocated the concept of vicegerency of God. They disagreed with ibn Taymiyya and challenged his opinion from the same perspective. One of them, for instance, has said:

> His [ibn Taymiyya's] doctrine about the interpretation of *istikhlāf* and his judgement about those who advocate vicegerency as having committed acts of polytheism is an error, and it is more detrimental when it emanates from a scholar in his calibre because the Prophet (ﷺ) has warned against such errors. [...] The gravity of the error of Shaykh al-Islām ibn Taymiyya (May God Have Mercy on Him) has a degree proportionate to his scholarly status. The gravity of Shaykh al-Islām's doctrine regarding *istikhlāf* lies in his ruling that the advocate of man's vicegerency of God on earth is committing an act of polytheism, a ruling which has averted many Muslims from accepting this interpretation.[48]

Yet another critic of ibn Taymiyya's position said:

> There is no doubt that ibn Taymiyya's position is subject to critique, because those who have permitted man's "vicegerency of God" did not do so based on the death, absence or incapacity of the *mustakhlaf* (succeeded/deputised), but rather on the basis of another meaning, that is mentioned by al-Rāghib al-Iṣfahānī (d. 502/1108). The latter stipulates that in the same way that *khilāfa* takes place upon the absence, death, or incapacity of the *mustakhlaf*, it can take place with the *mustakhlaf* to honour the *mustakhlif* (deputy). Accordingly, ibn Taymiyya's viewpoint in prohibiting it is right with respect to the meanings mentioned. However, what others have stated in terms of permissibility comes in the context of the other meaning, i.e., the honorific one.[49]

So, this objection to ibn Taymiyya arose in the context of the endeavour to clarify the view of "those who have permitted the use of the *khilāfa* of God" without realising that ibn Taymiyya was not discussing the arguments of those who permitted the use of this term, and whose views the researcher explained, such as al-Iṣfahānī, but rather he was discussing the views of others "who have permitted the use of the *khilāfa* of God" and who had different thought patterns.

In confirmation of the above, and in addition to ibn Taymiyya's explicit permissibility of the use of the term *khilāfa* of God if it is free from the context of pantheism, ibn Taymiyya himself used the phrase "*khalīfat Allāh*" (vicegerent of God) outside the context of its rejection when debating the advocates of pantheism and the oneness of existence. This proves that the seriousness of his opposition towards the use of this phrase was only towards that specific context. He said, for example: "ʿUmar ibn ʿAbd al-ʿAzīz (d. 101/720), may God be pleased with him, who was a vicegerent of God on earth, had entrusted agents to stop incomers from kissing the ground, and he punished those who did so."[50] Even his disciple, ibn al-Qayyim, who suggested that the meaning of *khilāfa* may convey the idea of human succession from one generation to the other rather than man's vicegerency of God on Earth, was found to have permitted, in another book, saying that man is God's vicegerent and agent on Earth if the meaning as such is devoid of aspects of pantheism. Ibn al-Qayyim said:

> As for the Lord's entrustment of his servant as vicegerent, [...] is it correct to say that someone can be God's *wakīl* (agent)? In my view, no, because the agent is the one who acts on behalf of his delegator by way of delegacy, and God Almighty does not have a deputy and is succeeded by no one. Rather, it is He who confers vicegerency upon His servant, as the Prophet (ﷺ) said: "O Allah! You are my companion in the journey and the *khalīfa* of my family." This being said, the use of the expression should not be prohibited if what is meant is that he [man] is entrusted to preserve, care for and undertake what he has been entrusted with.[51]

In sum, these researchers have made this difference in opinion a creedal matter, thinking that they are following in the footsteps of ibn Taymiyya, but without realising that ibn Taymiyya was deconstructing intellectual and epistemological patterns. His purpose was not to discuss and evaluate abstract opinions, whether it was one opinion or the other. Ibn Taymiyya was not problematising many of these opinions, including those borrowed from Greek philosophy, outside of their epistemological framework. In addition to the plain fact that he did not problematise the saying that man can be a deputy of God if stripped of the pantheistic pattern, other examples include the fact that ibn Taymiyya accepted the philosophers' conception, which argues that man is a microcosm (*al-ʻālam al-ṣaghīr*), and he did not shy away from it[52] outside that pattern, even though it is a statement that is rooted in a pantheistic epistemology and based on the belief that "existence is God's self-expression."[53] This perception relates to man's vicegerency of God on Earth in the pantheistic pattern, whereby the microcosm is considered a manifestation of God on Earth that represents Him thereon. This is one of the bases of ibn Taymiyya's objections to man's vicegerency of God on Earth. They meant that this microcosm stands in for God or is an embodiment of God, which made him say: "As for the claim that a human being is a vicegerent whom God has deputised to act on His behalf in managing the kingdom, for he is in His image in this respect, this includes the meaning of kingship and of him being an image of the world. However, its falsehood comes from the claim that man deputises for God Almighty, for nothing at all can substitute God."[54] Nevertheless, ibn Taymiyya said that man is the microcosm, that he is created in the image of God and explicitly described some individuals as being vicegerents of God. He permitted the use, in other contexts, of the statement that man is a deputy of God, as I have shown, which indicates that he does not discuss these opinions in an isolated manner when criticising them. Ibn Taymiyya himself explained his approach arguing that he does not discuss isolated opinions when discussing the authors of those epistemic theories, but rather he discusses them to the extent that they operate within distorted patterns.[55]

Accordingly, it seems that the claim of a group of contemporary researchers that the idea of man as God's vicegerent is a modern innovation that is unknown in Islamic heritage, is refutable. It rather applies to their own claim and not to those they have falsely accused of invention. Indeed, the absolute rejection of the saying that a person is God's vicegerent based on the assumption that it is an act of polytheism is a modern unprecedented opinion, and even ibn Taymiyya himself did not pass such a judgement. Hence, it is pointless to engage in further discussion about the evidence put forward by the detractors of that saying for three reasons. Firstly, it has become clear that the differences among ancient exegetes and all other Sunni scholars about this issue were not of a creedal nature, but they became so for some contemporaries who thought they were emulating ibn Taymiyya, without reckoning the context of his objection. Therefore, it is needless to engage in the polemics of *istikhlāf* outside of the intellectual pattern wherein it was approached by the contemporaries who advocated it. Secondly, researchers have already responded to the creedal and other objections in significant detail.[56] Thirdly, the discussion in the coming chapters about this concept and its intended meaning will suffice to refute any further objection.

## 3.2 Who is the *Khalīfa?*

Classical Islamic scholars have differed on the identity of the *khalīfa* (vicegerent) designated by God for *istikhlāf* (vicegerency). The following people have been suggested:

1. Adam[57]
2. "Adam and whoever takes up a similar position in God's obedience and establishment of justice among His creatures,"[58] or, in other words: "Whoever has been entrusted with the management of the affairs and interests of people on earth"[59]
3. God has only made Adam and David vicegerents[60]
4. All prophets[61]
5. Humanity

Those who argue for the last position are divided into two groups. The first one consists of the advocates of the general meaning of *khilāfa* in the sense that humans are successors of the jinn who populated the earth prior to them or humans succeeding over each other across the generations. Therefore, the *khalīfa* would be "Adam and his descendants," i.e., the human species.[62]

The second group consists of those who argue that *khilāfa* is man's vicegerency on behalf of God but without limiting the *khilāfa* to Adam, the prophets or those who stand in for them. Referring to this group, as cited earlier, ibn Khaldūn said with regard to the ruler: "People have differed regarding his designation as *khalīfa* of God. Some have approved this designation based on the general use of *khilāfa* as attributed to human beings, as in God Almighty's words: 'I will set a *khalīfa* on earth' (2:30) and 'He has made you *khalā'if* on earth' (6:165). Nevertheless, the majority of scholars have prohibited its use because he [the ruler] is not included in the meaning of the verse."[63] If the intended meaning of this view of *khilāfa* for human beings in general, which some applied to rulers analogically, had meant the succession of one generation over another, the ruler would have been included as well and without controversy just like all other human beings. By denying the inclusion of the ruler, the majority of scholars indicate that the intended meaning is that human species are God's vicegerents, and therefore the human being in his role as a ruler is excluded, because in his political position, he deputises for his predecessor, not for God.

This is further confirmed by the fact that ibn Khaldūn himself is an advocate of the idea that *istikhlāf* includes the human species. He said, for example: "The human being is a leader by nature as required by *istikhlāf* for which he has been created,"[64] adding: "The hand of the human being is spread out over the realms of the world by virtue of *istikhlāf* that God has conferred upon him."[65] If ibn Khaldūn had thought that *istikhlāf* meant succession over ancient generations, he would not have made it a purpose for human creation in harmony with human *fiṭra*.

When addressing Q 6:165 ("He has made you *khalāʾif* on earth"), many exegeses, from different doctrinal affiliations, explained that this verse has three plausible meanings. The first: He made the community of Muḥammad (ﷺ) the successors of all the previous communities; the second: He made human generations succeed each other; the third: He made all humans "God's vicegerents on earth, possessing and managing it."[66]

The opinion that all humans must act as God's vicegerents is also clearly expressed by al-Shāṭibī (d. 790/1388) who argues that when the human being preserves the Divine intent, he fulfils the mission assigned to him and "acts as a vicegerent of God. [...] What is required from him [the vicegerent] is to assume the position of the One Who deputised him in running His rules and objectives to their right course, which is clear."[67] Also, the *Ḥadith* commentator Sharaf al-Dīn al-Ṭībī (d. 743/1342) is categorical that "The human being is nothing but God's *khalīfa* on His land."[68] Likewise, the East African Ḥanafī Jurist Fakhr al-Dīn al-Zaylaʿī (d. 743/1342) wrote, "The human was created as an honoured being in order to bear [the religious] assignments, to engage in obedience and to be God almighty's *khalīfa* on earth."[69] Similarly, the Andalusian Qurʾan Scholar al-Ḥarālī (d. 638/1240) wrote, "Since the Qurʾan came down in accordance with human behaviour through time, the consistency of its message is fluctuating between a message on religion received from God, an establishment of rulings where the human being is God's vicegerent in the execution of his commandments and an expenditure where he is vicegerent in the conveyance of His favours, because courage and generosity are vicegerency while cowardice and stinginess are alienation from it."[70]

This opinion is also found in the previously cited work of ibn al-Qayyim: "God Almighty entrusts the servant as guardian in the preservation of all that he has been entrusted with. [...] God Almighty does not have a deputy and is succeeded by no one. [...] This being said, the use of the expression should not be prohibited if what is meant is that he [man] is entrusted to preserve, care for and undertake what he has been entrusted with."[71] Based on this, every person (ibn al-Qayyim did not specify but said "the servant") is a vicegerent of God, given that the human being is commanded to undertake, care for and preserve the individual and collective affairs that he has been entrusted with.[72]

Ibn al-Jawzī (d. 597/1200) asserts that scholars commonly hold two opinions about the *istikhlāf* that is promised to the believers in Q 7:129, "the first: that it is the succession of Pharaoh and his people. The second: that it is vicegerency on behalf of (*ʿan*) God almighty, because believers are God's vicegerents on earth."[73] In the same vein, al-Rāzī (d. 606/1209) commented on Q 24:55 ("Allah has promised those who have believed among you and done righteous deeds that He will surely grant them succession/vicegerency upon the earth," b.o. Sahih Intl), saying: "that means that (He promised them that) they (the believers) would become the vicegerents of God on earth."[74] Commenting on the latter verse, the Atharī (Salafī) *Ḥadith* scholar Aḥmad al-Qaṣṣāb (d. 360/971) writes, "*Istikhlāf* is a noun that indicates a meaning, and everyone who partakes in that meaning deserves it [that name], even if he does not have the merit of prophethood. [...] The meaning of *istikhlāf* is that the *mustakhlaf* (deputy) takes the position of the *mustakhlif* (deputised). Since God placed Adam and David, blessings on them, in His position on earth in judging between His servants, they deserved that title thereby. Also, Allah has promised the believers who work in obedience [to Him] to grant them *khīlāfa* like He did to others. Hence, they are His vicegerents in that, although they are not His prophets."[75]

The view that the designated vicegerent is the human being, in general, was also articulated by al-Rāghib al-Iṣfahānī (d. 502/1108) and al-Ghazzālī (d. 505/1111) after him.[76] In his Qurʾan exegesis, al-Iṣfahānī said: "It is the right of all people to be the vicegerents of God."[77] Also, in the chapter entitled "Mā li-ajlihi ʾawjad al-insān" (The Purpose of Existence of the Human Being) in his book, *al-Dharīʿa ilā Makārim al-Sharīʿa* (The Book of Means to the Noble Qualities of Sharīʿa), al-Iṣfahānī said: "Human beings as such are like each other [...] and their honour lies in that they are integrally meant for the purpose which they are created for. [...] The function that is related to the human being consists of three things: (1) Building and populating the earth (*ʿimārat al-arḍ*), [...], (2) worshipping God [...] and (3) deputising Him [...]; this is reflected in the emulation of God the Highest to the degree of human ability."[78] Al-Iṣfahānī has made man's vicegerency of God a human mission, albeit not required but desirable, as will be shown.

The above positions[79] refute a new set of those countless groundless statements around our subject matter, such as the claim that "the earliest exegetes naturally took [*khilāfa*] to mean 'successor of an earlier creation that once dominated the earth.'" And that "This usage suggests that the modern translation of the 'caliph' as 'deputy' or 'vicegerent' is imprecise, as is the idea popularised in the twentieth century that the humans are metaphysical 'vicegerents of God.'"[80] Similarly, they refute the claim that the opinion that all humans are vicegerents of God is a "modern innovation,"[81] or a modern Islamist theory. Andrew March, for instance, writes: "The notion that all of mankind (but particularly the Muslim *umma*) have been deputized as God's vicegerent on earth was put into circulation by the Pakistani Islamist theorist of Divine sovereignty (*ḥākimiyya*), Mawdūdī (1903–1979), and picked up forcefully by Quṭb."[82] He adds, in another study, that "It is widely asserted that the interpretation by which God has deputized all of mankind as His representative, whether this means as stewards over the earth or with some kind of political authority among humans, is a strictly modern invention."[83] The invalidity of these claims and the fact that the deputisation of humankind as vicegerents of God was a widespread idea in Islamic heritage will be further disclosed through some of what follows below.

## 3.3 What is Man Deputised For?

The classical scholars also disagreed about the object of vicegerency (*al-mustakhlaf fīhi*), i.e., the matters assigned to the human being that he should handle as vicegerent of God. Abū Ḥayyān (d. 745/1344) said: "Adam is entrusted with two things: the first is ruling with truth and justice and the second is building and populating the earth, through ploughing, harvesting and irrigating the land," adding: "It is said that the *khalīfa* is a title ascribed to anyone who has been entrusted with the task of managing the lives and affairs of human beings."[84] Al-Sam'ānī (d. 489/1095) said: "He is called a *khalīfa* because he is the vicegerent of God on earth, where he establishes His laws and implements His teachings, and this is the correct definition."[85] Al-Baghawī (d. 516/1122) also said: "The correct view is that he is the vicegerent of God on earth to establish His laws and implement His teachings."[86]

Al-Bayḍāwī (d. 685/1286) wrote:

> It is Adam (Peace and Blessings be Upon Him) because he was the vicegerent of God on earth, and this is also the case of every prophet that God has entrusted to build and populate the earth, implement policies, make people fulfil their wishes and execute the commands of God among them. This is by no means out of the Almighty's need for someone to deputise for Him, but rather on account of the limitations of the scene of vicegerency (*mustakhlaf 'alayhi*, i.e., the world) in receiving His bounties and commands without a medium.[87]

Even though al-Bayḍāwī states that the vicegerent is Adam and all the prophets, his arguments imply that he is of the opinion that all humans are also included: "They said that 'will You create on it those who will cause corruption in it and shed blood?' (Q 2:30) expresses the surprise that the building and populating of the earth will be entrusted to those who will spoil it," even though the prophets are infallible. Al-Bayḍāwī continues his arguments which imply that *istikhlāf* concerns all human beings, indicating the reason why the angels were surprised when God declared the establishment of the vicegerent, a human who is subject to error. He commented on the angels' surprise by saying that they did not reckon the intellectual and ethical faculties of man and the fact that his strength also lies in his solidarity with his fellow human beings. He said:

> They neglected the virtue of each of the two powers when it is tamed and responsive to the mind, trained to do good through chastity, courage, resistance

> to impulses and dedication to fairness. They did not know that unity fulfils what individuality falls short of achieving, such as dealing with partial matters, eliciting creativeness and transforming the benefits of creatures from power to action, which is intended by *istikhlāf.* It is to this that God Almighty refers to in general when He said: "Indeed I know what you do not know."[88]

Al-Ālūsī (d. 1854), referring to some Sufi scholars' opinion about the object of vicegerency, said about the meaning of the last part of verse 2:30, when God said to the angels: "I know what you do not know":

> It was said: the best explanation to that what was unknown [to the angels] is God Almighty's words: "I know the unknown of the heavens and the earth." It is understood from the folk's [Sufis] terms, may God Almighty sanctify their secrets, that what is meant by the verse is to express the wisdom behind vicegerency in the most precise and complete way. It [the latter verse] is as if He Almighty said "I want to appear with my names and attributes but that is not realised through your [the angels] creation, for I know what you don't know because of the limits of your aptitudes and the insufficiency of your abilities, thus you are not suitable to manifest in you all the Names and Attributes. Hence, the knowledge of Me does not complete with you and my treasure does not appear in you, it is thus necessary to create he who has those aptitudes, so that he becomes a reflection of Me, a mirror of My Names and Attributes, a manifestation of the dualities in Me, an appearance of what was hidden in Me, so that he hears through Me and sees through Me and so on and so on."[89]

Ibn Khaldūn wrote:

> Given that the senses considered in the world of beings are the regulated ones, while the irregulated ones are subordinate to the regulated ones, the actions of animals are incorporated into the latter and, hence, they [the animals] were subservient to human beings. The actions of humans have appropriated the world creatures and everything that it compasses, and all of it has become subordinate to the human being. This reflects the meaning of *istikhlāf* mentioned in the Qur'anic verse: "I will set a vicegerent on earth" (Q 2:30). Thought is a human characteristic that distinguishes man from other animals. The humanness of man is gauged by the extent to which the causes and effects are present in an organised manner in thought.[90]

Ibn Khaldūn further said, when discussing the reason for the presence of the element of water on Earth, that "God wanted to create animals on it and populate it with the human species that has vicegerency over it all."[91] He added: "The hand of the human being is spread out over the realms of the world as a result of the *istikhlāf* conferred upon him by God [...]; thus, human actions are indispensable in everything that can be possessed and monetized."[92]

On the other hand, ibn Taymiyya said: "Whoever claims for himself, or for others as well, that he deputises for God or that he is His vicegerent, but he does not command what God has enjoined through His messengers, he has lied to God and is arrogant and unjust. [...] If what is meant by vicegerent is conveyer, messenger and executer, then it is correct."[93] Al-Ṭabarī considered the object of vicegerency to be "obedience to God and the rule of justice among His Creation."[94] Moreover, ʿAbd Allāh ibn Naʿīm al-Maʿāfirī (d. 137/754) said: "I heard the Shaykhs say: 'He who commands virtue and forbids vice is God's vicegerent on earth and is the *khalīfa* of His Book and Prophet (Peace and Blessings be Upon Him).'"[95] Abū Ḥabīb al-Sulaymī (d. 74/693) said: "I read in conventional wisdom that one should 'listen to the questioner until he finishes and then reply with mercy and kindness, be like a merciful father to the orphan and be just towards the oppressed so that you may become a vicegerent of God on earth.'"[96] Al-Ḥasan al-Baṣrī (d. 110/728) said: "God will always have advisors, they advice for God among His people and advice for God's servants about God, they work for God on earth with advice; those are the vicegerents of God on earth."[97] Abū ʿUbayd al-Busrī (d. 238/853) said: "Didn't you know that people who love each other are the vicegerents of God on his earth?"[98] Furthermore, ibn Miskawayh (d. 421/1030) said: "The reformers (*al-muṣliḥūn*) are the real vicegerents of God in reforming (*iṣlāḥ*) the people and the land."[99]

Al-Shāṭibī (d. 790/1388) expressed his opinion on the object of vicegerency as follows:

> The intent of the Legislator is to preserve the necessities and the related needs and embellishments, which is exactly what was assigned to the human being; he is thus obliged to intend to do so, otherwise he would not be acting as a preserver; because deeds depend on intentions. The realisation of that is when the human being acts as a vicegerent of God in establishing these interests as per the best of his capacity. The lesser degree of that is to be a vicegerent in [taking care of] his own self, then his family and then all who have an interest in him. Therefore, the Prophet (ﷺ) said, "All of you are guardians and are responsible for your wards." And He said in the Qurʾan: "Believe in Allah and His Apostle, and spend out of what He has made you to be successors of" (Q 57:7, Shakir). And that is what is intended by His words: "I will set a vicegerent on earth." (Q 2:30). [...] What is required from him [the vicegerent] is to assume the position of the One Who deputised him in running His rules and objectives to their right course, which is clear.[100]

In his interpretation of the Qurʾanic verse "Believe in Allah and His Apostle, and spend out of what He has made you to be successors/vicegerents of (*mustakhlafīna fīh*)" (Q 57:7), al-Zamakhsharī (d. 538/1143) wrote: "*Mustakhlafīna fīh* means that your wealth is God's, for it is of His own creation and He has entrusted it to you and enabled you to enjoy having it, and He made you vicegerents in order to manage it. It is not really yours, and you are but in the position of an agent or deputy."[101] Al-Samarqandī (d. 373/983) said: "It is said that its meaning is that wealth and the whole world belong to God Almighty who entrusts His servants with His wealth and orders them to decide of it, as He has made them vicegerents over it."[102] Al-Rāzī (d. 606/1209) also wrote: "The one entrusted to dispose of this wealth is in a position similar to that of an agent, deputy or successor."[103] Al-Bayḍāwī said: "Spend out of that wherein He has made you successors, refers to the wealth over which God has made you vicegerents so that you can dispose of it because it is in fact His, not yours."[104] Undoubtedly, these views, which are cited by many exegetes, support the idea that man is God's vicegerent in disposing of His wealth. They do not mean that humans succeed each other in entrustment over wealth, since they distinguish between this latter view and the former one when citing them.

About his understanding of the object of vicegerency, al-Rāghib al-Iṣfahānī (d. 502/1108) wrote: "It is the emulation of God Almighty, to the extent of the capacity of human beings in running affairs and implementing the virtues of *Sharīʿa*, which consist of wisdom, justice among people, insight, charity and grace [...], while what is meant by running human affairs is twofold: one concerns the self, body and personal things, and the other relates to others like family and fellow countrymen."[105] He added: "Knowledge is a profession on the one hand, worship on another and the pursuit of the vicegerency of God Almighty on a nobler one because by entrusting the human being, God Almighty opens his heart to knowledge. This is an exclusive attribute of God Almighty and the store of the noblest treasures. He has ordered him to spend on everybody, the more he spends as required, whenever it is required and in the manner required, the higher his position near the Deputized becomes."[106] He further said: "Human life in this world is pursued in three manners. [...] Third, there are people who live the worldly life to its full extent and yet reckon what is required; with being an agent of God Almighty, they limit their use of it in order to meet the requirements of God. The rest is kept aside to spend as they have been commanded, and this is better, as previously mentioned, because in this case, man becomes a vicegerent of God Almighty."[107] In addition, as quoted in the previous section, many exegetes reported that one of the plausible meanings of Q 6:165 is that God made all human beings vicegerents of God in terms of possessing the earth and managing it.

It should be deduced from the above that what is entrusted by God to the human being as an object of his vicegerency on His behalf, as stated by classical scholars, may be one or more of the following:

1. Ruling with truth and justice
2. Building and reviving the land by ploughing, harvesting and planning[108]
3. Producing beneficial things for human beings and turning power into action
4. Using thought in organising the universe (world of action) and running it
5. Achieving human interest
6. Executing God's commands
7. Implementing God's rules and objectives as per the right course
8. Running people's affairs and achieving their wellbeing
9. Enjoining virtue and forbidding vice

10. Calling people to God
11. Being merciful, kind and just towards the weak and the oppressed
12. Being advisors
13. Loving one another
14. Reforming the people and the land
15. Possessing the earth and managing it
16. Managing wealth
17. Managing material and moral affairs of self, family and society
18. Learning and education
19. Manifesting God's Names and Attributes in His creation

These different opinions around the object of *khilāfa* (which are non-exhaustive) demonstrate, once again, that the view that all human beings are God's vicegerents on Earth was widespread among classical scholars. Indeed, most of the above-listed duties (which, according to their authors, the human being is supposed to perform as a vicegerent of God) are not specific to prophets or rulers but, rather, incumbent on everyone.

## 3.4 Vicegerency and Human Existential Function

All that has been stated so far highlights the fact that the concept of *istikhlāf* (vicegerency) as a human existential mission was a common idea among classical Muslim scholars.[109] However, it did not receive significant theoretical attention and there are only some traces of it that take the form of passing comments in the books of exegesis and others. Among the rare scholars who have dealt with the concept as a human function in more than a brief commentary is Imām al-Rāghib al-Iṣfahānī (d. 502/1108), but he did not consider it the most primordial function for which man was created, nor did he consider *khilāfa* obligatory for all people. In his view, it is no more than a supererogatory recommended task attained only by a select group of people,[110] as will be shown later.

Ibn ʿArabī (d. 638/1240), on the other hand, used the concept of *istikhlāf* within the pantheistic/anthropomorphistic pattern, not as a function, responsibility or existential goal of the human being, but rather as an existential fact in the human creation. The purpose for which God has created man is but God's desire to see Himself outside of Himself in an encompassing universe that contains all of His names.[111] Since man is the only being that is qualified to gather all Divine attributes in himself, that Divine purpose can only be achieved through man.[112] Man is also like the eye through which God looks at His Creation.[113] God establishes and protects the world through man, the perfect man, the vicegerent;[114] so, He "calls him a vicegerent for this reason, because He, the Almighty, is the One who maintains through him His Creation [...] and the world is still preserved as long as this perfect man lives in it."[115]

Ibn ʿArabī did not regard the perfect human being, who is God's vicegerent, as the (common) human species, as the ordinary human is not capable of embodying all the Divine attributes; this is rather reserved for the mystic who has attained this kind of knowledge by *kashf* (Divine knowledge unveiled to the heart). The hearts of others are too narrow to assimilate all of it;[116] so, they cannot be God's vicegerents. The vicegerent is

> the perfect human being who embodies the realities and the features of the world. The world is seen while the vicegerent is unseen (metaphysical) [...] and is the result of the combination of two images: the image of the world and the image of the Truth, and both are the "Hands of the Truth." Satan is part of the world, but he has not achieved this combination, which is why Adam was chosen as a vicegerent; so, if he does not appear in the image of the One who has entrusted him with the vicegerency, he would not be a *khalīfa*.[117]

According to ibn ʿArabī's doctrine of *waḥdat al-wujūd* (oneness of existence), one human being does not differ from another one, not even from other living beings or Satan; in terms of him/her being part of the world, he/she is an expression of some of God's attributes and a manifestation of God in the universe, because "the flow of truth in living beings through the image"[118] is equally among all living beings.[119] The human being, however, differs in terms of the ability to absorb all the Divine attributes in himself; yet, this can only be attained by the gnostic Sufis. The title of vicegerent, therefore, is only rightfully attributed to gnostic Sufis who are capable of seeing the manifestations of Divine attributes in all living beings.[120]

> Hence, vicegerency is only valid for the perfect man. He has created his outward image by the Truth of the world and its images and has created his inward image by the image of God Almighty [...], but no one possesses the totality of the attributes of the vicegerent whose success is granted by this totality. If it had not been for the flow of Truth in living things in the image form, the world would not have existed. Also, had it not been for these holistic and reasonable Truths, there would have been no status for physical creatures.[121]

The universe (physical creatures), as a physical manifestation of God (flow of Truth), was thus only created for the purpose of the existence of the vicegerent through whom God can see Himself (holistic and reasonable Truths), and is only sustained by the vicegerent.

As previously mentioned, the concept of *istikhlāf* as a purpose of human creation occurs quite frequently in the writings of ibn Khaldūn to the extent that one researcher said: "Ibn Khaldūn has made of the concept of *istikhlāf* the root from which the branches of the tree of thought, in general, and education, in particular, sprout."[122] Another one said: "The Khaldunian conception of human life and civilization is purely Islamic and is based on the Qurʾanic concept of *istikhlāf*, which is a basic concept in Islamic thought and is defined in a number of verses and their explanations."[123] However, if it is clear that ibn Khaldūn considers *istikhlāf* a purpose for which man was placed on Earth, the argument that he has based his thought on that concept is questionable. Furthermore, it cannot be said that ibn Khaldūn believes that *istikhlāf* is a human responsibility. Rather, it appears that he considers it an existential fact and not an existential task. This is what we could conclude by examining his definitions of the concept. He said for instance, as quoted before: "The actions of humans have appropriated the world's creatures and everything that it compasses, and all of it has become subordinate to the human being. This reflects the meaning of *istikhlāf* mentioned in the Qur'anic verse: 'I will set a vicegerent on earth' (Q 2:30)."[124] He added: "The hand of man is spread out over the realms of the world as a result of the *istikhlāf* that was given to him by God, all humans' hands are spread, and this is hence a common fact."[125] What emerges from this, and from other references to the concept in ibn Khaldūn's work, is that *istikhlāf* is not a responsibility but a *fait accompli* common to all human beings, which is the fact that all creatures were subjugated for man. This is clear from the terms he uses: "have appropriated," "has become subordinate," "is spread out," and "the *istikhlāf* that was given to him." All of these indicate that *istikhlāf* is not something that man should strive for, but is rather something that he already possesses. Hence, *istikhlāf* is not a function but the mere fact that God harnessed the creation for man, an idea that ibn Khaldūn explicitly states.[126]

Furthermore, ibn Khaldūn did not establish a theory of *istikhlāf* as such. It appears to me that within a comparative framework, ibn Khaldūn distinguished himself by referring to the concept while exposing his theses on human existence and civilisation; otherwise, the indication that *istikhlāf* is the purpose of human creation is not unique to ibn Khaldūn. On the other hand, ibn Khaldūn's references were merely superficially tackling the issue at hand. Except for a few words here and there, he did not elaborate on the matter and did not specify its meaning, nor did he indicate how the concept of *istikhlāf* controls the teachings of Islam, nor its place in the Islamic worldview. With the exception of occasional scanty references, he did not state whether or how all of the human, civilisational and scientific issues he discussed branch out of the concept of *istikhlāf*, nor did he attempt to draw links between them or specify the framework within which *istikhlāf* operates. Therefore, any endeavour to relate ibn Khaldūn's thought with the concept of *istikhlāf* comes not without a significant dose of interpretation and overstatement, as becomes clear by looking at the theses of researchers who tried to do this.[127]

Extensive research in the field reveals that, as an existential function or as the purpose for which man was created, the concept of *istikhlāf* has not received much theoretical attention in Islamic heritage, and it has not been studied in the books of creed, theology, Sufism, etc. as a separate issue or an independent chapter, let alone a dedicated book. Al-Iṣfahānī's attempt in his book *al-Dharīʿa ilā Makārim al-Sharīʿa* (The Book of Means to the Noble Qualities of *Sharīʿa*) stands as an exception to these generalisations. The first chapter entitled "The Conditions of Man, His Powers, Virtues, and Morals" contains three titles that deal with the concept of *istikhlāf*: "The reason for man's existence," "The means to achieve the vicegerency of God" and "The purification of the Soul as a condition for the validity of the vicegerency and perfect worship of God Almighty."

In the introduction, al-Iṣfahānī explains that he wrote the book to show "how a human being can attain the status of *al-ʿubūdiyya* (total devotion to and worship of God), an honour which God Almighty confers upon the pious, and from which man can be elevated higher to embrace the status of *khilāfa* that God Almighty has reserved for the truthful and the martyrs."[128]

The pressing question here concerns the reason behind the marginal theoretical status of the concept of *istikhlāf* as an existential function in Islamic intellectual heritage. In seeking a response, we may formulate a more general question: Why was the question of man's existential function (in general) underrated in Islamic intellectual heritage? The subject of human existential function has not been accorded a status commensurate with its importance, as it was not an issue of Islamic theology, Sufism or other Islamic sciences. When treated in the books of Islamic heritage, the function of man is often incidental, digressive in nature or raised in the context of other matters.

The hypothesis that emerges from the analysis of the classical heritage on the human existential function is that the issue did not receive significant theoretical attention for two reasons, which I will put forward here in an attempt to prove my own hypothesis. The first is that the issues which Islamic sciences have dealt with extensively during their peak, before being transformed into scholastic issues reported in a truncated manner out of context and without any significant addition, were only realistic issues. That is, they were addressed in response to problematics that were posed by intellectual or social reality.[129] It seems that the issue of defining the human existential function did not present itself as a problematic during the classical ages, especially if we take into account the Qur'anic verse that explicitly states this mission: "And in no way did I create the jinn and humankind except to worship Me" (Q 51:56, Ghali). It is true that opinions diverged about the interpretation of this verse and the question of whether worship is an existential function of man, as will be shown later. This is a difference that arose from the epistemological backgrounds of the exegetes. However, outside the context of this disagreement, opinions did not differ in determining the meaning of worship in a significant way.[130] Those who said that it is an existential function were not in need of framing the concept of worship theoretically, nor defending their definition of it, for it was clear to everyone that the worship of God is represented in the submission to Him alone, abiding by all that God likes and commands and avoiding all that He dislikes and forbids.[131] There was no reason to theorise the concept of worship as an existential function or to delve into its discussion further than what was already elaborated in Islamic sciences books on the details of adherence to God's laws at the creedal, spiritual and practical levels. Thus, all scholars agree that the human being was created to worship God, and about the general meaning of worship. However, they disagree on whether that is a function or a mere predestination. Hence, the question of what man was created for was not an issue, as the meaning of worship was clear to everybody. Consequently, we found that the rare minority of scholars who conducted investigations into the question of the human existential mission, chief among whom is al-Iṣfahānī, barely elaborated on the concept of worship. While acknowledging it as the mission for which man is created, they could hardly add more to the fact that it means "complying with what the Almighty commands and forbids."[132] As an existential mission, the meaning of worship did not transcend mere adherence to the explicit teachings of Revelation in order to embrace a conceptual system that constitutes a philosophy of man in life, unlike the concept of *istikhlāf* whose worldly merits al-Iṣfahānī tried to reveal and justify at the philosophical level. This leads us to the second reason for the lack of theoretical interest in the existential mission of man in Islamic heritage.

The second reason is epistemological and relates to the ideological disputes between the different schools of theology and the resulting epistemological deviation in beliefs and concepts. In line with their epistemological systems, many intellectual trends in Islamic heritage did not believe that man was created to accomplish a specific goal or function in the world. Sufis and some philosophers argued that man's knowledge and work should not have an aim, nor should they be intended to address problems and seek specific worldly goals. Rather, knowledge should be for the sake of knowledge, and it is not possible for a man to be wise if he were to seek knowledge other than for the love of wisdom. The ultimate goal of the human being should be geared towards self-accomplishment through annihilation (*fanā'*) for the sake of God so that the difference between man and knowledge and between the subject matter and the learner dissolves. Islamic sciences, i.e., the sciences of Revelation, are only a means to rational sciences, i.e., philosophy and mysticism, which are not acquired by accumulation and transmission. The latter sciences are the goal of science because they are the only ones that enable annihilation.[133] The transmitted sciences, however, are not capable of leading one to the truth.

On the other hand, Ash'arites, Maturidis and some Sufis argue that the purpose of Revelation is to test people and not to achieve worldly purposes. Whatever worldly purpose or interest achieved is but a bounty from God and it is not the primary intention. In their view, God's perfection requires that He is devoid of purposes and does not act for the sake of wisdom, motive or interest necessitating that action. Hence, the meaning of the "*lām*" (to) in the Qur'anic word "*li-ya'budūn*" (to worship Me) does not indicate reason or purpose, but rather it is a "*lām*" that conveys outcome and process. In other words, it does not mean that worship is the motive, wisdom or purpose for which man was created, but it is merely God's destiny and will, not for anything else but for His own Will, which does not relate to man's appreciation of what is bad or good or of what is an interest or a corruption. Based on their claim that denies worship a sense of purpose, many of these scholars think that worship is but a destiny that God has decreed for worshippers and it is not required of all human beings. So, "the verse is specific to those who worship Him; that is, the believers among the jinn and mankind and is not as general as to include all His Creation." Hence, the verse can be paraphrased as: "I want them to worship Me, which is why I created them, and every human being follows what he has been created for; so, whoever has been made for worship and created for it, its path is smoothened for him, and whoever is made for the world and created for it, its path is smoothened for him,"[134] as Abū Ṭālib al-Makkī (d.

386/996) argues. Moreover, Abū al-Ḥasan al-Ashʿarī (d. 324/935), the founder of the Ashʿarī school, said: "If they inquire about the meaning of the Qurʾanic verse: 'And in no way did I create the jinn and humankind except to worship Me,' (Q 51:56) the answer is that God Almighty has assigned this to the believers only, not the unbelievers because He tells us that He has created for hell many of the jinn and humans. God has full cognizance of them, has counted them and recorded their names and the names of their parents."[135] If the letter "*lām*" (for/to/so that) does not convey reason, wisdom or purpose, the purpose of the human being is not to realise worship, but this latter rather is merely the inevitable destiny of the believers. Consequently, there is no justification for the epistemic theorisation of man's existential function.

Ibn Taymiyya eloquently outlined the different intellectual approaches on the issue of existential purpose on the basis of their epistemological pattern. He said: "When people talked about the reason and wisdom behind creation, each and every one spoke from the perspective of their own knowledge, and they attained one side of the truth, but the other sides remained hidden." He then summarised the interpretations of Muslim scholars around the meaning of the previously stated verse (Q 51:56), according to their views of worship as a human purpose and their intellectual patterns. We can recognise a dozen groups from his division.[136]

Ibn Taymiyya's summary of the views of Islamic groups on the purpose of human creation reflects in a significant way the interference of the ideological disputes in the perception of that purpose. The opinion of half of these groups, as demonstrated by ibn Taymiyya, is a consequence of an epistemological model that has deviated from the model of Revelation, such as the denial of destiny, human free will, justification of God's actions, wisdom or purpose and causality. In order to react to one of the latter groups, five of the 12 groups mentioned by ibn Taymiyya adopted a far-fetched interpretation of the Qurʾanic verse. They felt forced to deny the creation of man for the purpose of worship, just to avoid embracing the patterns of speculative theologians. As for the only Sunnite group who did affirm that worship is the purpose behind human creation, they have not developed the concept theoretically. It is highly probable that this goes back to the criticism levelled at them by ibn Taymiyya, as I pointed out before, i.e., their abstention from developing a Qurʾanic epistemology. They thus contented themselves with the overt meaning of the Qurʾanic verse, while asserting that worship is a purpose, without rationalising the concept or expatiating upon its logic or philosophy. This may have led some groups to argue that Islamic sciences do not lead to the truth or that they do not provide "conclusive formal evidence-based reasoning (*burhān*)."[137]

The Ashʿarī school, which prevailed in the Islamic world after the fifth *hijrī* century,[138] did not believe that Revelation came down in order to achieve worldly interests in the first place, as per its epistemological model based on the denial of purpose and causality. They argued that there is no real interest in Revelation for the human being except worship, through which the human being achieves a reward in the Hereafter, whereas worldly interests, if any, are only bounties conferred by God and are neither intended nor always resultant from Revelation, for they are only secondary matters. The human being has no intended worldly interest in prayer in the first place; rather, what is meant by it is only worship and reward in the Hereafter. The peak of religiosity for the human being is to abide by the Divine commands regardless of any interest, objective or benefit.[139] Since the interest (*maṣlaḥa*) does not assume an objective truth, all that Revelation has come down with is mere worship, and whatever includes a worldly benefit for the human being is not originally intended by Revelation.[140] Therefore, the only purpose is the reward in the Hereafter for what man has achieved through worship.[141] If the only meaning of worship is the commitment to Revelation and obedience to God in order to attain the reward in the Hereafter, then no justification remains for elaborating on the existential purpose for which man is created, or developing its rationale and philosophy.

Given that most of the Islamic groups do not see in worship a purpose for human existence, according to their epistemological patterns or in reaction to other groups, it is only normal that they do not focus on the issue of existential human purpose and they do not examine it as an aspect of creed, theology or Sufism. This particularly applies to the concept of *istikhlāf*, because the creation of man for this purpose is less explicit in the Qur'an than the creation of man for the purpose of worship. Even those who have espoused the position that vicegerency is a purpose of the existence of man have not gone beyond its simple diagnosis as an existential purpose and the determination of its meaning through the use of a few expressions. Moreover, they did not clarify the relationship between vicegerency and worship; thus, the concept has remained ambivalent.

It should be noted that al-Rāghib al-Iṣfahānī is the only one who has attempted to clarify the relationship between worship and vicegerency. After emphasising the function of the human being in building and populating the earth (*ʿimārat al-arḍ*), worship and vicegerency, he points out how vicegerency is achieved through the use of the virtues of *Sharīʿa*, and that the vicegerent is the one who embodies virtues, i.e., supreme Islamic morality. Then he devotes a section under the title: "The difference between the virtues of *Sharīʿa*, worship, and *ʿimārat al-arḍ* (building and populating the earth)."[142] He says:

> You should know that worship is more general than virtue because every virtue is a kind of worship but not every worship is a virtue. The difference between them is that worship has known and determined requirements and boundaries, and the one who abandons it becomes an unjust transgressor, but virtues are different. Man has not fulfilled the virtues of *Sharīʿa* unless he performs the functions of worship. So, observing worship is a matter of justice, and performing virtues is a matter of grace and thus, a supererogatory act. Supererogatory acts are not accepted by those who neglect the obligatory, nor is an act of grace accepted from those who abandon justice. In fact, engaging in acts of grace is accepted only after engaging in justice. Justice is required while grace is complementary. So, how imaginable is it that something that does not exist as such can be complemented? This is why it is said that he who has abandoned the fundamentals cannot attain anything.

> However, whoever is preoccupied with performing the obligatory is forgiven if he cannot do acts of grace, but whoever is doing the opposite is vain. God Almighty points to justice in terms of rulings and to kindness in terms of virtues: "Indeed Allah enjoins justice and kindness" (Q 16: 90). He also says: "O you who have faith! Bow down and prostrate yourselves, and worship your Lord, and do good so that you may be felicitous" (Q 22:77). Hence, good acts are something additional to worship.[143]

Though the doctrinal affiliation of al-Rāghib al-Iṣfahānī is not clear, as he is hardly mentioned in biographical works, it appears evident from his position on worship here that it is based on the Ashʿarī epistemology. This appears in several respects, including his differentiation between, on the one hand, morality and acts of goodness (virtues of *Sharīʿa*), through which the human being becomes a *khalīfa,* and on the other hand, worship. It is as if worship does not automatically lead to morality. In his view, not all acts of worship are acts of virtue or from which virtue results. He also distinguishes between grace and obligation. He regards kindness, good manners and acts of goodness that make a person a *khalīfa* supererogatory rather than obligatory. What may result from worship in terms of acts of goodness or virtues, if they ever do so, is an act of grace and not the primary intended outcome; rather, the primary intended outcome and the duty is only worship. Therefore, virtues should not divert man's focus from worship.

The book's editor could not refrain from commenting on the above statements, trying to find the evidence that could not be found in al-Iṣfahānī's work, to prove that he did not differentiate between worship and morality. He says: "Al-Iṣfahānī's citations show that there is no separation between worship and virtue, for the latter relates to the former in terms of causality and effect. Prayer is a form of worship, but it forbids vice, and *zakāt* is an act of worship, but it serves to purify. Thus, virtues are acts of grace based on worship, and the latter requires them by virtue of an inherent wisdom."[144] However, this is not the Ashʿarī position, and it is not al-Iṣfahānī's position either. It is difficult to attribute it to the latter since he, contrary to what the editor said, did differentiate between worship and virtue in a way that leaves no room for interpretation. For example, he said that virtue is "additional to worship," and that the latter is required while the former is complementary, which stipulates that worship is not a virtue per se, and that virtue does not automatically result from worship, but rather it is something extra. He also said: "whoever is preoccupied with grace at the expense of obligation," showing that he considers them two different things. Furthermore, he said that worship is a form of justice and that acts of virtue are supererogatory. Moreover, he denied that all forms of worship are considered acts of virtue. All of these statements are in line with Ashʿarī and even Māturīdī[145] patterns, in the sense that the good acts that may result from worship are not the primary intent, but are only acts of grace, for the primary intent should only be worship. Any act of goodness that may (or may not) result from the act of worship is but a favour from God bestowed upon His servants. In any case, grace is not the primary intent and, as explained above, it is not necessarily inherent in worship.

Indeed, al-Iṣfahānī confirmed afterwards that worship purifies the soul, but he had stressed earlier that this is not constant in worship and that not every act of worship is a virtue. It appears from his overall thesis that the morality and purification of the soul that may result from worship are not automatic and that this is not the primary purpose nor is it obligatory, but rather a supererogation and a grace. Even though it is one of the missions of man, the achievement of virtues as attributes of the soul that enables it to attain *istikhlāf* is supererogatory and of a secondary nature, and it is not the first intent of worship. This is again in line with the Ashʿarī school of thought in the sense that the purpose of worship is, above all, hereafter-oriented, and the other results are not intended for their own sake. This again goes back to the denial of purpose, causality and wisdom; if God would have commanded the human being to worship Him with the aim of achieving worldly purposes as goodness and ethics, that would mean that God does things under the constraint of external purposes or forces, which goes against monotheism according to Ashʿarī epistemology. Furthermore, that would mean that Revelation responds to an objective rationale of good and evil, while good and evil do not exist objectively but are only attributed to things by God through Revelation without responding to an objective rationale. Hence, al-Iṣfahānī emphasised that worship "is the *raison d'être* of the Hereafter just as water, which is needed to purify the body, is the *raison d'être* of worldly life."[146]

Just as most Ashʿarites deny that the human being is created for worship as an existential objective in accordance with their pattern of denying causality and worldly oriented benefits for worship, while considering that the worldly causes and interests contained in Revelation are only secondary acts of grace, al-Iṣfahānī followed the same path. He reduced the concept of worship stated in the Qurʾanic verse "*illa li-yaʿbudūn*" (except to worship Me) into the acts of abstract ritual adoration, making them obligatory and important tasks, while other benefits and worldly matters in Revelation, such as acts of goodness and morals that concern the wellbeing of humans, are only acts of grace and supererogation, as he clearly stated. This seems to be the reason that compelled al-Iṣfahānī to argue that *istikhlāf* is a supererogatory matter, not a required one, in line with the logic that what results in worldly achievements is not intended in itself, which is an Ashʿarī doctrinal view as well.[147] Thus, the primary, original and obligatory mission of the human being or what is preordained for him (according to those who argue that the Arabic letter "*lām*" in the Qurʾanic word conveys consequence and process, while al-Iṣfahānī did not clarify its intended reference) remains abstract adoration for the sake of salvation in the Hereafter.

In responding to al-Iṣfahānī's separation of ethics and worship, some contemporary scholars have omitted to reckon with the Ashʿarī epistemic pattern that al-Iṣfahānī was following. One such scholar says:

> Here, we reproach our Imām al-Iṣfahānī for an important matter. He distinguishes between the provisions and the virtues of *Sharīʿa*, and he considers worship to be more general than virtue. [...] This is what the Imām explicitly states in his book. [...] However, we cannot agree with him that all the virtues

are included under the banner of grace and supererogation because their foundations are dictated in the Qur'an and the Sunna as spiritual acts whose inviolability constitutes the essence of salvation on the Day of Resurrection. [...] The Qur'anic verses and the *Ḥadīths* are clear on the importance of these ethical values that must exist and be maintained.

The same scholar goes on to provide Qur'anic evidence that refutes al-Iṣfahānī's position and then says:

There is no doubt that many of the virtues of *Sharī'a* are part of the fundamentals of religion, and they are not mere acts of "grace" or "supererogation." The Qur'anic verse he cites, "Indeed Allah enjoins justice and kindness" (Q 16:90), can be used as an argument against him. Al-Iṣfahānī considers justice "an obligation" and kindness a "supererogation." How can this be correct when we know that they are both commanded in the Holy Qur'an? Fundamentally, what is commanded in the Qur'an should be an obligation. [...] In his comments on the verse in *sūrat al-Ḥajj* "and do good so that you may be felicitous" (Q 22: 77), al-Iṣfahānī said: "The act of goodness is an addition to worship." In my view, however, this addition is not a supererogation; rather, it is an obligation commanded by God, as he has commanded that He be worshipped and prayed to. All of this is associated with acts of goodness in the same Qur'anic verse, and God has made of success an outcome of all of this: "O you who have faith! Bow down and prostrate yourselves, and worship your Lord, and do good so that you may be felicitous" (Q 22:77).[148]

Thus, this scholar has commented exhaustively on al-Iṣfahānī's interpretation, but he does not indicate that this position is that of Ash'arites. The problematic is too profound to be answered in the form of a reaction to an abstract opinion. It should rather be addressed from within the epistemological pattern in which it was created.

In conclusion, the concept of *istikhlāf* as an existential human function is common Islamic heritage, but it has not received significant theoretical attention, which explains why it has remained a vague concept. The few scholars who gave it more consideration, such as al-Rāghib al-Iṣfahānī and ibn 'Arabī, have done so within an epistemological framework that deviates from the epistemology of Revelation. The indispensable return to heritage in order to resume the examination of the concept of *istikhlāf* and establish it in the modern context cannot be confined to the examination of abstract opinions, without considering the epistemological paradigm in which they arose and other factors of influence. If it does not reckon along with the epistemological question, the critique of the opinions of ancient or contemporary scholars regarding the concept of *istikhlāf*, the building on relevant unfolding research developments in Islamic heritage or the comparison of the opinions of contemporary and classical scholars regarding the concept will remain evidently short-sighted. This brings me back to my argument in the second chapter of this study regarding the establishment of solid criteria for the assessment of Islamic sciences as essential; otherwise, the assessment will be made on the basis of criteria that are themselves subject to opposition and appraisal. The question that should be posed here is: Since the concept of *istikhlāf* has gained significant popularity in the modern era, what part did modern studies play in the appraisal of that concept?

## Notes

1 Indeed, despite the fact that many (ancient and modern) Muslim scholars claimed that the jinn lived on Earth before the human being, this opinion does not have any grounds in Islamic texts (Qur'an and Sunna). Some argued that this is indicated by the fact that the jinn, as stated in the Qur'an, were created before the human being. However, this does not mean that they were on Earth. Instead, as is clear from the Qur'an, Iblīs (Satan), the father of the jinn, settled on Earth together with Adam and Eve, and not before.

2 Muḥammad ibn Jarīr al-Ṭabarī, *Jāmi' al-Bayān 'an Ta'wīl Āyī al-Qur'ān* [The Comprehensive Exposition of the Interpretation of the Verses of the Qur'an], ed. Aḥmad Muḥammad Shākir (Beirut: Mu'assasat al-Risāla, 2000), 449–52.

3 'Alī Abū al-Ḥasan al-Māwardī, *al-Aḥkām al-Sulṭāniyya* [The Ordinances of Governance] (Cairo: Dār al-Ḥadīth, n.d.), 39.

4 'Abd al-Raḥmān ibn Khaldūn, *Dīwān al-Mubtada' wa-l-Khabar fī Tārīkh al-'Arab wa-l-Barbar wa-Man 'Āṣarahum min Dhawī al-Sha'n al-Akbar* [Book of Lessons, Recordings of the Beginnings and Events in the History of the Arabs, the Berbers and Their Powerful Contemporaries] (Beirut: Dār al-Fikr, 1988), 239.

5 Abū al-Muẓaffar Manṣūr al-Sam'ānī, *Tafsīr al-Qur'ān* [The Interpretation of the Qur'an], ed. Yāsir ibn Ibrāhīm and Ghunaym ibn 'Abbās (Riyadh: Dār al-Waṭan, 1997), vol. 1, 64.

6 Al-Ḥusayn al-Baghawī, *Ma'ālim al-Tanzīl fī Tafsīr al-Qur'ān* [Qur'anic Exegesis], ed. 'Abd al-Razzāq al-Mahdī (Beirut: Dār Iḥyā' al-Turāth al-'Arabī, 1999), vol. 1, 102.

7 Some scholars before Ibn Taymiyya, including al-Nawawī (d. 676/1277), prohibited the use of the title "*khalīfa* of God" in reference to the ruler. Al-Māwardī said that this is the opinion of mainstream scholars, as I mentioned before, but based on my research, none of the scholars preceding ibn Taymiyya openly and categorically prohibited its use for the human being in general or indulged in lengthy discussion about those advocating it.

8 As we will elaborate below, according to some Sufi views, a person in relation to God is like the pupil of the eye through which God sees His creation, for He needs man to deal with His creation, because man (as vicegerent) is the medium in which the Divine attributes have been fulfilled.

9 Taqī al-Dīn ibn Taymiyya, *Minhāj al-Sunna al-Nabawiyya fī Naqḍ Kalām al-Shī'a al-Qadariyya* [The Way of the Prophet's *Sunna*: A Critique of the Theological Discourse of al-Qadariyya Shiites], ed. Muḥammad Rashād Sālim (Riyadh: Imām Muḥammad ibn Sa'ūd Islamic University, 1986), vol. 1, 509–10. See also his detailed response to this opinion in which he discusses the views of the proponents of incarnation and pantheism in *Bayān Talbīs al-Jahmiyya fī Ta'sīs Bida'ihim al-Kalāmiyya* [Exposition of the Falsehoods of al-Jahmiyya in the Establishment of Their Theological Innovations] (Medina: King Fahd Complex for the Printing of the Holy Qur'an, 2005), vol. 6, 576–612.

10 Ibn Taymiyya, *Minhāj al-Sunna al-Nabawiyya*, vol. 7, 353.

11 Ibn Taymiyya, *al-Fatāwā al-Kubrā* [Major Fatwas] (Beirut: Dār al-Kutub al-'Ilmiyya, 1987), vol. 5, 122.

12 Ibid., vol. 5, 123.
13 Ibn Taymiyya, *Minhāj al-Sunna al-Nabawiyya*, vol. 6, 589.
14 Even though the advocates of these anthropomorphistic opinions (some gnostic Sufis) were Muslims, ibn Taymiyya did consider them to be indulging in a type of polytheism, for various reasons, among others: The fact they believed that the human soul is eternal, that he (the perfect man) is an incarnation of God on Earth, that God's creation is God, that worshipping any creature equals worshipping God, etc.
15 Ibid., vol. 6, 606–08.
16 Ibid., vol. 6, 602–03.
17 Ibn Qayyim al-Jawziyya, *Miftāḥ Dār al-Saʿāda wa-Manshūr Wilāyat al-ʿIlm wa-l-Irāda* [Key to the Blissful Abode] (Beirut: Dār al-Kutub al-ʿIlmiyya, n.d.), vol. 1, 152.
18 Yūsuf al-Qaraḍāwī, *Fatāwā Muʿāṣira* [Contemporary Fatwas] (Kuwait: Dār al-Qalam, 2005), vol. 2, 175.
19 Ibn al-Qayyim, *Miftāḥ Dār al-Saʿāda,* vol. 1, 151–53.
20 ʿAbd Allāh ibn Ibrāhīm al-Nāṣir, "The Principle of Vicegerency in the Islamic Economy: A Study in the Light of the Qurʾan," *Journal of Qurʾanic Studies* 7, no. 1 (2005), 145.
21 Jamāl al-Dīn ibn al-Jawzī, *Zād al-Masīr fī ʿIlm al-Tafsīr* [The Victuals of the Journey in the Exploration of the Science of Exegesis], ed. ʿAbd al-Razzāq al-Mahdī (Beirut: Dār al-Kitāb al-ʿArabī, 2001), vol. 2, 146.
22 Ibn al-Jawzī, *Zād al-Masīr fī ʿIlm al-Tafsīr*, vol. 1, 50.
23 Athīr al-Dīn Abū Ḥayyān, *al-Baḥr al-Muḥīṭ fī l-Tafsīr* [The Vast Expanse of Exegesis], ed. Sidqī Muḥammad Jamīl (Beirut: Dār al-Fikr, 1999), vol. 1, 227.
24 Al-Nāṣir, "The Principle of Vicegerency in the Islamic Economy," 145.
25 ʿAbd al-Raḥmān Ḥabanka al-Maydānī, "Hal al-Insān Khalīfa ʿan Allāh fī Arḍihi?" [Is Man the Vicegerent of God on Earth?], *Majallat Kuliyyat al-Daʿwa wa-Uṣūl al-Dīn bi-Makka al-Mukarrama*, no. 1 (1983), 31.
26 ʿAbd al-Raḥmān Ḥabanka al-Maydānī, *Lā Yaṣiḥ an Yuqāl al-Insān Khalīfa ʿan Allāh fī Arḍihi fa Hiyya Maqūla Bāṭila* [The Impropriety and Invalidity of the Belief that Man is the Vicegerent of God on Earth] (Mecca: Maktabat Iḥyāʾ al-Turāth al-Islāmī, 1991), 36.
27 Yūsuf al-Zayūt, "Madā Ṣiḥḥat al-Qawl bi-ʾanna al-Insān Khalīfat Allāh fī l-Arḍ" [The Extent of the Validity of the Statement that Man is the Vicegerent of God on Earth], *Majalat Jāmiʿat Dimashq* XVII, no. 2 (2001), 271.
28 Jaafar Sheikh Idris, "Is Man the Vicegerent of God?" *Journal of Islamic Studies* 1, no. 1 (1990), 103.
29 Ibid., 106.
30 Ibid., 108.
31 Transmitted by ibn Māja in his *Sunan* (no. 4084). Al-Buṣayrī said in *al-Zawāʾid* on the authority of ibn Māja: "The *Ḥadīth*'s chain of transmission is authentic, and its narrators are trustworthy." Al-Ḥākim also narrated it in *al-Mustadrak*, in which he said: "It is authentic on the conditional transmission chain of the *Shaykhayn.*" Al-Dhahabī said "it is an authentic *Ḥadīth* on the conditional transmission chain of al-Bukhārī and Muslim." Muḥammad ibn Māja, *Sunan ibn Māja*, ed. Muḥammad Fuʾād ʿAbd al-Bāqī (Cairo: Dār Iḥyāʾ al-Kutub al-ʿArabiyya, n.d.).
32 Transmitted by Aḥmad in his *Musnad* (no. 23425), ranked as *Ḥadīth ḥasan* by Shaykh Shuʿayb al-Arnaʾūṭ. Aḥmad ibn Ḥanbal, *Musnad al-Imām Aḥmad ibn Ḥanbal,* ed. Shuʿayb al-Arnaʾūṭ, ʿĀdil Murshid, et al. (Beirut: Muʾassasat al-Risāla, 2001).
33 Transmitted by Abū Dāwūd in his *Sunan* (no. 4244), ranked as *ṣaḥīḥ* by Shaykh Shuʿayb al-Arnaʾūṭ. Sulaymān Abū Dāwūd, *Sunan Abī Dāwūd*, ed. Shuʿayb al-Arnaʾūṭ and Muḥammad Kāmil (Beirut: Dār al-Risāla al-ʿIlmiyya, 2009).
34 Transmitted by ʿAbd ibn Ḥamīd (d. 259/863) in his *Musnad* (no. 949), from the companion Abū Saʿīd al-Khudrī (d. 74/693). Regardless of the authenticity of this *Ḥadīth*, it is enough to know that this saying was certainly in circulation among the first generations (*salaf*) of Muslims. ʿAbd ibn Ḥamīd al-Kassī, *al-Muntaghab min Musnad*

*ʿAbd ibn Ḥamīd* [Selections from Musnad ʿAbd ibn Ḥamīd], ed. Ṣubḥi al-Badrī and Mahmūd Khalīl (Cairo: Maktabat al-Sunna, 1988).

35 Indeed, would *khilāfa* merely refer to intergenerational succession, there would be no point promising its realisation to the righteous people, since it would be a *fait accompli* common to all people. This narrative is transmitted by al-Muttaqī al-Hindī in *Kanz al-ʿUmmāl* (no. 14164). Al-Muttaqī al-Hindī, *Kanz al-ʿUmmāl* [Treasures of the Doers of Good Deeds], ed. Bakrī Ḥayyānī and Ṣafwat al-Saqā (Beirut: Muʾassasat al-Risāla, 5th ed., 1981).

36 Transmitted by al-Shajarī in *Tartīb al-Amālī* (no. 332). Yaḥyā al-Shajarī, *Tartīb al-Amālī*, ed. Muḥammad Ḥasan (Beirut: Dār al-Kutub al-ʿIlmiyya, 2001).

37 Transmitted by Aḥmad in *al-Zuhd* (no. 544), and al-Dulābī in *al-Kunā wa-l-Asmāʾ* (no. 793). Aḥmad ibn Ḥanbal, *al-Zuhd* [Asceticism] (Beirut: Dār al-Kutub al-ʿIlmiyya, 1999); Muḥammad al-Dulābī, *Al-Kunā wa-l-Asmāʾ* [Nicknames and Names], ed. Muḥammad al-Fārayābī (Beirut: Dār ibn Ḥazm, 2000).

38 Transmitted by al-Ḥākim in *al-Mustadrak* (no. 4468). Al-Ḥākim al-Naysabūrī, *Al-Mustadrak ʿalā al-Ṣaḥīḥayn*, ed. Muṣṭafā ʿAbd al-Qādir (Beirut: Dār al-Kutub al-ʿIlmiyya, 1990).

39 Reported by ibn al-Mubārak (d. 181/797) in *al-Zuhd wa-l-Raqāʾiq* (n. 1446), and ʿAbd al-Razzāq (d. 211/827) in his *Tafsīr* (n. 2710). ʿAbd Allāh ibn al-Mubārak, *al-Zuhd wa-l-Raqāʾiq* [Asceticism and Spirituality], ed. Ḥabīb al-Raḥmān al-Aʿẓamī (Beirut: Dār al-Kutub al-ʿIlmiyya, n.d.); ʿAbd al-Razzāq al-Ṣanʿānī, *Tafsīr ʿAbd al-Razzāq*, ed. Maḥmūd ʿAbduh (Beirut: Dār al-Kutub al-ʿIlmiyya, 1419AH).

40 Ibn Baṭṭāl al-Qurṭubī, *Sharḥ Ṣaḥīḥ al-Bukhārī*, ed. Abū Tamīm Yāsir (Riyadh: Maktabat al-Rushd, 2nd ed. 2003), vol. 1, 130.

41 Transmitted by al-Marwazī in *Kitāb al-Fitan,* (no. 245). Naʿīm al-Marwazī, *Kitāb al-Fitan* [The Book of Tribulations and War], ed. Samīr al-Zuhayrī (Cairo: Maktabat al-Tawḥīd, 1992).

42 We found that ʿIzz al-Dīn ibn ʿAbd al-Salām (d. 660/1262) seemingly holds a similar view, i.e., that the *salaf* generations prohibited the saying "*khalīfa* of Allah." He said, "This was not acceptable to the *salaf*, they rejected the saying '*khalīfa* of Allah.'" ʿIzz al-Dīn ibn ʿAbd al-Salām, *Fawāʾid fī Mushkil al-Qurʾān* [Lessons about Problematic Qurʾanic Verses], ed. Sayyid Riḍwān ʿAlī al-Nadwī (Jeddah: Dār al-Shurūq, 1982), 67. Nevertheless, it seems that ibn ʿAbd al-Salām is not of the opinion that the *salaf* are generalising this to all human beings, since he says in his *tafsīr* that one plausible meaning of *khalīfa* in Q 2:30 is that God is saying, I will place "a *khalīfa* who will deputize Me in judging between creatures, that is Adam, peace be upon him, and all those who take his place among his offspring." ʿIzz al-Dīn ibn ʿAbd al-Salām, *Tafsīr al-Qurʾān*, ed. ʿAbd Allāh al-Wahbī (Beirut: Dār ibn Ḥazm, 1996), vol. 1, 114.

43 Al-Nāṣir, "The Principle of Vicegerency in the Islamic Economy," 162.

44 Ibn al-Qayyim, *Miftāḥ Dār al-Saʿāda,* vol. 1, 152.

45 Ibn Khaldūn, *Dīwān al-Mubtadaʾ wa-l-Khabar*, 239.

46 Al-Zayūt, "Madā Ṣiḥḥat al-Qawl bi-ʾanna al-Insān Khalīfat Allāh fī l-Arḍ," 280.

47 Idris, "Is Man the Vicegerent of God?" 99.

48 Fārūq Aḥmad al-Dasūqī, *al-Khilāfa al-Islāmiyya Uṣūluhā wa-Ḥaqīqatuhā wa-Ḥatmiyyat ʿAwdatihā* [The Islamic Caliphate: Its Origins, Truth and the Imperative of Its Return] (Cairo: 1998), 259–60.

49 Aḥmad Ḥasan Faraḥāt, *al-Khilāfa fī l-Arḍ* [Vicegerency on Earth] (Kuwait: Dār al-Arqam, 2003), 14–15.

50 Ibn Taymiyya, *Majmūʿal-Fatāwā,* vol. 27, 93.

51 Ibn Qayyim al-Jawziyya, *Madārij al-Sālikīn bayna Manāzil Iyyāka Naʿbud wa-Iyyāka Nastaʿīn* [The Wayfarers' Stages], ed. Muḥammad al-Muʿtaṣim Billāh (Beirut: Dār al-Kitāb al-ʿArabī, 1996), vol. 2, 126.

52 Ibn Taymiyya said: "God Almighty has revealed, out of His great will and wondrous wisdom, among the righteous descendants of Adam, prophets and God's protégés,

qualities unparalleled among angels, by making them encompass all the things that He placed separately among His other creatures. He created their bodies from clay and their spirit from heaven. It is therefore said that man is the microcosm and a reflection of the macrocosm (universe)." Ibn Taymiyya, *Majmū' al-Fatāwā*, vol. 11, 96.

53 Ibn Taymiyya, *al-Fatāwā al-Kubrā*, vol. 5, 122.

54 Ibn Taymiyya, *Minhāj al-Sunna al-Nabawiyya*, vol. 6, 589.

55 Ibn Taymiyya, *Bayān Talbīs al-Jahmiyya*, vol. 6, 577-81.

56 See, for instance, al-Dasūqī, *al-Khilāfa al-Islāmiyya*.

57 See: Muḥammad Shams al-Dīn al-Qurṭubī, *Al-Jāmi' li-Aḥkām al-Qur'ān* [The Compiler of the Rulings of the Qur'an], ed. Aḥmad al-Bardūnī and Ibrāhīm al-Aṭafīsh (Cairo: Dār al-Kutub al-Miṣriyya, 1964), vol. 1, 263, and Abū Ḥayyān, *al-Baḥr al-Muḥīṭ fī l-Tafsīr*, vol. 1, 227.

58 Al-Ṭabarī, *Jāmi' al-Bayān*, vol. 1, 227, and al-Māwardī, *al-Nukat wa-l-'Uyūn* [The Exegesis of al-Māwardī], ed. Sayyid ibn 'Abd al-Maqṣūd (Beirut: Dār al-Kutub al-'Ilmiyya, n.d.) vol. 1, 95.

59 Abū Ḥayyān, *al-Baḥr al-Muḥīṭ fī l-Tafsīr*, vol. 1, 227.

60 Al-Baghawī, *Sharḥ al-Sunna* [Explanation of the Sunna], ed. Shu'ayb al-Arna'ūṭ (Damascus: al-Maktab al-Islāmī, 1983), vol. 14, 75.

61 Abū Ḥayyān, *al-Baḥr al-Muḥīṭ fī l-Tafsīr*, vol. 1, 227.

62 Al-Ṭabarī, *Jāmi' al-Bayān*, vol. 1, 451; al-Māwardī, *al-Nukat wa-l-'Uyūn*, vol. 1, 95; and Maḥmūd ibn 'Amr al-Zamakhsharī, *al-Kashāf 'an Ḥaqā'iq Ghawāmiḍ al-Tanzīl* [The Discoverer of Revealed Truths] (Beirut: Dār al-Kitāb al-'Arabī, 1987), vol. 1, 124.

63 Ibn Khaldūn, *Dīwān al-Mubtada' wa-l-Khabar*, 239.

64 Ibid., 185.

65 Ibid., 477.

66 See for instance:

- Al-Zamakhsharī, *al-Kashāf*, vol. 2, 84
- Fakhr al-Dīn al-Rāzī, *al-Tafsīr al-Kabīr* [The Great Exegesis] (Beirut: Dār Iḥyā' al-Turāth al-'Arabī, 1999), vol. 14, 192
- Nāṣir al-Dīn al-Shirāzī al-Bayḍāwī, *Anwār al-Tanzīl wa-Asrār al-Ta'wīl* [The Lights of the Revelation and the Mysteries of Interpretation], ed. Muḥammad al-Mar'ashilī (Beirut: Dār Iḥyā' al-Turāth al-'Arabī, 1997), vol. 2, 192
- Abū Ḥayyān, *al-Baḥr al-Muḥīṭ fī l-Tafsīr*, vol. 9, 152
- Sirāj al-Dīn ibn 'Ādil al-Ḥanbalī, *al-Lubāb fī 'Ulūm al-Kitāb* [The Core Sciences of the Book], ed. 'Ādil Aḥmad and 'Alī Muḥammad (Beirut: Dār al-Kutub al-'Ilmiyya, 1998), vol. 8, 540

67 Al-Shāṭibī, *al-Muwāfaqāt*, vol. 3, 25.

68 Sharaf al-Dīn al-Ṭībī, *Sharḥ al-Ṭībī 'alā Mishkāt al-Maṣābīḥ* [The Explanation of al-Ṭībī on Mishkāt al-Maṣābīḥ], ed. 'Abd al-Ḥamīd Hindāwī (Mecca: Maktabat Nizār Muṣṭafā al-Bāz, 1997), vol. 6, 1841.

69 Fakhr al-Dīn al-Zayla'ī, *Ṭibyān al-Ḥaqā'iq Sharḥ Kanz al-Daqā'iq* [The Explanation of Kanz al-Daqā'iq] (Cairo: al-Maṭba'a al-Kubrā al-Amīriyya, 1313 AH), vol. 6, 98–99.

70 Abū al-Ḥasan al-Ḥarālī, *Turāth Abī al-Ḥasan al-Ḥarālī al-Marākishī fī l-Tafsīr* [The Tafsīr Legacy of Abū al-Ḥasan al-Ḥarālī], ed. Muḥammādī al-Khayyāṭī (Rabat: al-Markaz al-Jāmi'ī, 1997), 384.

71 Ibn al-Qayyim, *Madārij al-Sālikīn*, vol. 2, 125–26.

72 In some editions of ibn al-Qayyim's *Badā'i' al-Fawā'id*, one of its chapters is titled, "The human being is God's *khalīfa* on earth." Yet, it is unclear whether this sentence can be attributed to ibn al-Qayyim. See: Ibn Qayyim al-Jawziyya, Shams al-Dīn, *Badā'i' al-Fawā'id* [The Amazing Insights], ed. Hishām 'Aṭā, 'Ādil al-'Adawī and Ashraf Aḥmad (Mecca: Maktabat Nizār Muṣṭafā al-Bāz, 1996), vol. 3, 742.

73 Ibn al-Jawzī, *Zād al-Masīr fī 'Ilm al-Tafsīr*, vol. 2, 146.

74 Al-Rāzī, *al-Tafsīr al-Kabīr*, vol. 22, 39.

75 Aḥmad al-Qaṣṣāb, *al-Nukat al-Dālla ʿalā al-Bayān fī Anwāʿ al-ʿUlūm wa-l-Aḥkām* [Issues in Clarifying Different Types of Sciences and Rulings], ed. Ibrāhīm al-Junayd, (Dār al-Qiyam, 2003), vol. 2, 482–83.

76 Al-Ghazzālī cited al-Iṣfahānī's words in this regard without mentioning the author. See: Muḥammad Abū Ḥāmid al-Ghazzālī, *Mīzān al-ʿAmal* [The Balance of Work], ed. Sulaymān Dunyā (Egypt: Dār al-Maʿārif, 1964), 383–84.

77 Al-Iṣfahānī, *Tafsīr al-Rāghib al-Iṣfahānī* [The Exegesis of al-Rāghib al-Iṣfahānī], ed. ʿĀdil ibn ʿAlī al-Shādī (Riyadh: Dār al-Waṭan, 2003), vol. 2, 772.

78 Al-Rāghib al-Iṣfahānī, *al-Dharīʿa ilā Makārim al-Sharīʿa* [The Book of Means to the Noble Qualities of *Sharīʿa*], ed. Abū Zayd al-ʿAjamī (Cairo: Dār al-Salām, 2007), 82–83.

79 These are only some selected samples of classical opinions stating that mankind are God's vicegerents.

80 Ovamir Anjum, *Who Wants the Caliphate?* (Yaqeen Institute for Islamic Research, 2019), 18. Adding the icing on the cake of erroneous assertions around this issue, Anjum goes further to claim that the metaphysical meaning of *khilāfa* as mankind's deputisation on behalf of God, "is not merely a linguistic quibble; entire genres of literature both by Muslim authors and Orientalists have emerged based on this misunderstanding." "For the Orientalist literature, the confusion has been spread since Patricia Crone and Martin Hinds, *God's Caliph* (1986). For contemporary Muslim literature, an endless stream of literature is being generated that describes humans as God's vicegerents. Its earliest case may have been Abu al-Aʿla al-Mawdudi's popular Urdu exegesis of the Qur'an, *Tafhim al-Qur'an*." Ibid., 19.

81 Idris, "Is Man the Vicegerent of God?" 106–10.

82 Andrew F. March, "Modern Islamic Conceptions of Sovereignty in Comparative Perspective," in *The Oxford Handbook of Comparative Political Theory*, ed. Leigh K. Jenco, Murad Idris, and Megan C. Thomas (New York: Oxford University Press, 2020), 553.

83 Andrew F. March, *The Caliphate of Man*, 250. In support of this claim, March referred to some studies that themselves uncritically relied on some of the studies that we have criticised, see: Fritz Steppat, "God's Deputy: Materials on Islam's Image of Man," *Arabica* 36, no. 2 (1989): 163–72; Sarra Tlili, *Animals in the Qurʾan* (New York: Cambridge University Press, 2012), 117–22. March did discuss this issue from a (limited) number of classical sources, some of which we presented above. However, he does so while denying that these authors made the claim that vicegerency means that mankind are God's deputies on Earth. Indeed, he denied that early Muslim scholars attributed the vicegerency of God to the human being, claiming that they were rather of the opinion that mankind "as a present people is the successor of past ones, it is not God's vicegerent, although it may have certain divine charges as well as a general grant from God to 'inherit the earth' and all that that implies by way of the cultivation of the Earth and accepting it as a sacred trust. When all humans (or at least all Muslims) were taken to be God's *khulafāʾ*, this meant, in the first place, a universal charge to behave righteously." Ibid., 33. So, mankind, according to what March attributes to the early scholars, are not God's vicegerents in the sense that they are deputising for Him, but only in the sense that they carry a Divine responsibility or "a universal charge to behave righteously." As for those scholars who attributed vicegerency of God to man in the sense of deputisation, March thinks that they regarded the vicegerency of God in that sense as "an office, occupied by specific men, rather than a status enjoyed by the multitude. This is an association that was to last well into the nineteenth century, and even in the debates on the caliphate in the 1920s, despite the general universalization of the 'caliphate of Adam' in exegetical literature during this period." Ibid., 35. As for "The later exegetes," they, according to March, "do refer to the possibility of the caliphate as the collective inheritance of nations who are charged with the dual task of establishing truth (*iqāmat al-ḥaqq*) and cultivating the Earth (*ʿimārat al-arḍ*)."

But "this may refer to mankind enjoying certain of God's favors on Earth in addition to weighty obligations of obedience." Ibid. As for "Al-Rāghib's tripartite account of man's function – *ʿimāra, ʿibāda, khilāfa*" it "does not allow for cultivating and civilizing the Earth to be an explanation of what being God's *khalīfa* means. Instead, we should see the vicegerency of God (*khilāfat Allāh*) as an aspiration, something individual humans might lay claim to at the end of their struggle for self-purification and virtue. The concept preserves its traditional reference to the worldly ruler of Muslims – the caliph – but individual self-mastery becomes the primary qualification for the political ruler: "He who cannot rule over his own soul is not suitable for ruling others." Moreover, the status of God's caliph is generalised as an aspiration for all humans without being universalised as the inherent dignity or authority of all humans: "Only he who is pure of soul is suited for the vicegerency of God, because this vicegerency is the imitation of God according to man's capacity to strive for divine actions." Ibid., 36. Overall, March is not refuting the idea that pre-modern scholars believed that mankind could be God's vicegerents in the sense of having a responsibility from God, but he is refuting that they adopted the idea that humans could be His vicegerents in the sense of being His deputy on Earth, an idea that is clearly erroneous as we saw and as will be further demonstrated. Also, contrary to March's claim, the idea of "caliphate as the collective inheritance of nations who are charged with the dual task of establishing truth (*iqāmat al-ḥaqq*) and cultivating the Earth (*ʿimārat al-arḍ*)," cannot be correctly attributed to any classical or pre-modern scholar, as will be discussed.

84 Abū Ḥayyān, *al-Baḥr al-Muḥīṭ fī l-Tafsīr*, vol. 1, 227.

85 Al-Samʿānī, *Tafsīr al-Qurʾan*, vol. 1, 64.

86 Al-Baghawī, *Maʿālim al-Tanzīl*, vol. 1, 102.

87 Nāṣir al-Dīn al-Shirāzī al-Bayḍāwī, *Anwār al-Tanzīl wa-Asrār al-Taʾwīl*, vol. 1, 68.

88 Ibid.

89 Shihāb al-Dīn al-Ālūsī, *Rūḥ al-Maʿānī fī Tafsīr al-Qurʾān al-ʿAẓīm wa-l-Sabʿ al-Mathānī* [The Spirit of Meanings in the Interpretation of the Great Qurʾan and the Seven Verses], ed. ʿAlī ʿAbd al-Bārī (Beirut: Dār al-Kutub al-ʿIlmiyya, 1994), vol. 1, 225.

90 Ibn Khaldūn, *Dīwān al-Mubtadaʾ wa-l-Khabar*, 593.

91 Ibid., 57.

92 Ibid., 477.

93 Ibn Taymiyya, *Minhāj al-Sunna al-Nabawiyya*, vol. 6, 602–3.

94 Al-Ṭabarī, *Jāmiʿ al-Bayān*, vol. 1, 452, and al-Māwardī, *al-Nukat wa-l-ʿUyūn*, vol. 1, 95.

95 Al-Marwazī, *Kitāb al-Fitan* (no. 245).

96 Aḥmad, *al-Zuhd* (no. 544), and al-Dulābī, *al-Kunā wa-l-Asmāʾ* (no. 793).

97 Ibn Baṭṭāl, *Sharḥ Ṣaḥīḥ al-Bukhārī*, vol. 1, 130.

98 Abū Nuʿaym al-Iṣfahānī, *Ḥilyat al-Awliyāʾ* [The Adornment of the Saints] (Cairo: Dār al-Saʿāda, 1974), vol. 12, 167.

99 Abū ʿAlī ibn Miskawayh, *Tahdhīb al-Akhlāq wa Taṭhīr al-Aʿrāq* [Refinement of Morals and Purification of Provisions], ed. ibn Khaṭīb (Cairo: Maktabat al-Thaqāfa al-Dīniyya, n.d.), 135.

100 Al-Shāṭibī, *al-Muwāfaqāt*, vol. 3, 25.

101 Al-Zamakhsharī, *al-Kashāf*, vol. 4, 473.

102 Naṣr ibn Muḥammad al-Samarqandī, *Baḥr al-ʿUlūm* [The Vast Expanse of the Sciences of *Sharīʿa*], ed. ʿAlī Muḥammad Muʿawwaḍ (Beirut: Dār al-Kutub al-ʿIlmiyya, 1993), vol. 3, 323.

103 Al-Rāzī, *al-Tafsīr al-Kabīr*, vol. 29, 450.

104 Al-Bayḍāwī, *Anwār al-Tanzīl wa-Asrār al-Taʾwīl*, vol. 5, 186.

105 Al-Iṣfahānī, *al-Dharīʿa ilā Makārim al-Sharīʿa*, 83–84.

106 Ibid., 272.

107 Ibid., 279.

108 This invalidates the claim that the interpretation of the meaning of *khilāfa*, in the sense of material building and populating the earth, is a novel idea put forward by contemporary revivalists. See: Idris, "Is Man the Vicegerent of God?" 106–10.
109 As noted above, this idea was in circulation since the era of the companions without any objection until ibn Taymiyya, who, himself, accepts it outside the framework of *waḥdat al-wujūd*. We also saw in ibn Khaldūn's words that he considered this view to be the position of the majority of scholars.
110 Al-Iṣfahānī, *al-Dharīʿa ilā Makārim al-Sharīʿa*, 163–64.
111 Muḥyī al-Dīn ibn ʿArabī, *Fuṣūṣ al-Ḥikam* [The Ringstones of Wisdom] (Beirut: Dār al-Kitāb al-ʿArabī, n.d.), 48.
112 Ibid., 49.
113 Ibid., 50.
114 Ibid.
115 Ibid.
116 Ibid., 120.
117 Ibid., 54.
118 Ibid., 55.
119 See: Masataka Takeshita, "The Theory of the Perfect Man in ibn ʿArabī's Fuṣūṣ al-Ḥikam," *Orient* 19 (1983), 96.
120 Ibid., 97.
121 Ibn ʿArabī, *Fuṣūṣ al-Ḥikam*, 55.
122 Al-Jīlānī ibn al-Tūhāmī, *Falsafat al-Insān ʿinda ibn Khaldūn* [The Philosophy of the Human Being in the Work of ibn Khaldūn] (Beirut: Dār al-Kutub al-ʿIlmiyya, 2011), 81.
123 ʿAlī Umlīl, *al-Khiṭāb al-Tārīkhī: Dirāsa li-Minhajiyyat ibn Khaldūn* [Historical Discourse: A Study of ibn Khaldūn's Methodology] (Beirut: Dār al-Tanwīr, 1985), 198.
124 Ibn Khaldūn, *Dīwān al-Mubtadaʾ wa-l-Khabar*, 593.
125 Ibid., 477.
126 Ibid., 476–77.
127 This can be observed, for instance, in: ibn al-Tūhāmī, *Falsafat al-Insān ʿinda ibn Khaldūn*.
128 Al-Iṣfahānī, *al-Dharīʿa ilā Makārim al-Sharīʿa*, 60.
129 See, for instance: ʿAbd al-Majīd al-Najjār, *Fiqh al-Tadayyun Fahman wa-Tanzīlan* [The Jurisprudence of Religiosity: Understanding and Implementation] (Mohammedia, Algeria: Dār Qurṭuba, 3rd ed. 2006), 89–96.
130 After presenting the comments of exegetes on the meaning of worship, Abū Ḥayyān said: "They are all closely related in meaning." In another context, he said: "These are closely related sayings." Abū Ḥayyān, *al-Baḥr al-Muḥīṭ fī l-Tafsīr*, vol. 1, 44, 657.
131 Much of what has been said in the interpretation of "except that they may worship Me," does not deviate from this meaning, even if they have questioned whether it is a function and whether it addresses the totality of people. Some of the interpretations state that it means "except for affirming Unicity" or "except for knowing their Lord," and it has also been interpreted as "doing everything God has commanded," "to command them to obey and worship God," "to acknowledge their submission to Me," "to bring them to My path so that they can submit to Me" or "to acknowledge me as a Deity deserving of worship willingly or unwillingly."
132 Al-Iṣfahānī, *al-Dharīʿa ilā Makārim al-Sharīʿa*, 239.
133 See: William C. Chittick, *Science of the Cosmos, Science of the Soul*, 138.
134 Abū Ṭālib al-Makkī, *Qūt al-Qulūb fī Muʿāmalat al-Maḥbūb wa-Waṣf Ṭarīq al-Murīd ilā Maqām al-Tawḥīd* [The Sustenance of Hearts], ed. ʿAṣim Ibrāhīm al-Kayyālī (Beirut: Dār al-Kutub al-ʿIlmiyya, 2005), vol. 2, 50–51.
135 Abū al-Ḥasan al-Ashʿarī, *al-Ibāna ʿan Uṣūl al-Diyāna* [The Elucidation Concerning the Principles of Religion], ed. Fawqiyya Ḥusayn Maḥmūd (Cairo: Dār al-Anṣār, 1977), 191–92.

136 *The first group* (Ibn Taymiyya, *Majmū ʿ al-fatāwa*, vol. 8, 37) consists of al-Ashāʿira, Jahm ibn Ṣafwān (d. 128/745) and al-Jabriyya (determinists). They hold the opinion that God did not create man for a purpose, neither for worship nor for other things. Al-Ashāʿira developed this position on the basis of their intellectual pattern which includes the denial of wisdom, justification and *al-taḥsīn wa-l-taqbīḥ* (the intellectual inability to identify good and evil): "Originally, they are of the opinion that God does not create anything for any reason, and He does not create anyone neither for worship nor for other purposes. They also believe that there is no '*lām*' (for/so that/in order…) in the Qurʾan in the sense of 'reason,' but they accept that there may be a '*lām*' that conveys 'consequence' in the Qurʾan." Ibid., vol. 8, 44. Jahm ibn Ṣafwān also made this argument in line with his denial of Divine attributes, such as wisdom, whereas al-Jabriyya made it in line with their denial of human freedom in choosing their actions.

*The second group* is made up of philosophers who believe in natural determinism and whose "arguments go further than that; they say that the torment of man and other harmful things cannot be avoided. They say that harm is self-obligatory, and things happen as an intrinsic consequence of things." Ibid., vol. 8, 38. In other words: Everything happening in the world is a result of intransgressible laws with causes and effects that make things happen in a mechanical and inevitable way, without leaving any room for the human being to choose his destiny.

*The third group* (Ibid., vol. 8, 38–39) comprises al-Muʿtazila, al-Qadariyya (adeterminists) and Ibn ʿAqīl (d. 513/1119). They believe that God has created human beings and commanded them to follow His guidance for their own benefit and as an act of Divine charity towards them. Wisdom created for the servants of God is limited to them and is not an attribute of God, otherwise, He would be in need of His creation to reach perfection. However, they contradicted themselves as "they affirmed the existence of wisdom, which is to benefit the servants, but they then said that God has created people He knows will be harmed by being created rather than benefitted by it." Ibid., vol. 8, 39. Al-Muʿtazila and al-Qadariyya formulated this idea in line with their pattern of denial of destiny and on the basis of the law of "reasonableness and permissibility" (*taʿlīl* and *tajwīz*). The latter alludes to the idea that God has the obligation to act with goodness, which is a pillar of Muʿtazilite epistemology, and that it is impossible for evil to emanate from Him. Man, in their eyes, is the creator of his own actions, and God did not create them and did not foreordain them. Ibn ʿAqīl, on the other hand, has argued that man's actions are part of God's destiny, but he has approved the Muʿtazilite position that affirms that wisdom is only related to the creatures. Ibid.

*The fourth group* consists of al-Karrāmiyya, who view that man was created for a wise reason that "belongs to the Lord and according to His knowledge. They said that He created them to worship, praise, exalt and glorify Him." He who does so is created for that purpose, "and whoever does not do so is not created for it. […] They said that the Qurʾanic verse: 'And in no way did I create the jinn and humankind except to worship Me' is specific to those required to perform the worship, which is the opinion of a group of salaf scholars and their successors. They said that what is meant here is that whoever is required to perform worship is therefore created for it, and whoever is not required to perform it is not created for it […], however, their statement on the interpretation of the verse is, despite agreeing with some of the salaf, a weak one." Ibid., vol. 8, 39–40.

*The fifth group* comprises those who adopted the same approach as the preceding one but from a different intellectual standpoint. Being a group of salaf scholars, "they have argued so because God Almighty does what He desires, and that if he wanted them to obey Him, he would make them obey Him as He has made the believers do. Al-Qadariyya say that God does not need anything from these or those except obedience, but He did not make either obedient. Will is an act of order that

God uses to command both parties. Hence, one party worshipped Him by creating their will and obedience, while the other disobeyed Him by creating their will and their disobedience. Those [salaf scholars] knew the corrupt view of al-Qadariyya because God created everything, and He is their Lord who rules over them. Whatever He wills, so shall it be, and whatever He does not will, it shall not be, and nothing shall exist in His kingdom except what He wills, creates and ordains, as proved through Revelation and reason. This is the doctrine of all the companions, all of the imams and the majority, and it is the doctrine of the Sunnites. For this reason, they [this fifth group] have altered the interpretation of the verse to make it specific because they could not combine belief in destiny and the fact that God created them for the sake of His worship, while they do not worship him. They thus said that He had not created those made for Hell to worship Him; so, whoever says that God has created mankind so that the believers worship Him is among those who have followed this track." Ibid., vol. 8, 43–44.

*The sixth group* consists of some Sufis who hold the opinion that worship includes believers as well as others, but worship is not an end or purpose for men; rather, it is a cosmic destiny that God has decreed for humans and made them submit to. This group sees that "mankind and jinn worship God, because God's destiny applies to them." Ibid., vol. 8, 47. God "makes them worship Him and He makes them execute His will, and the worship of others, Satan and idols, is a foreordained act. This resembles the position of some latter-day scholars who say: I disbelieve in a Lord who is disobeyed, and they make of anything that consists of obedience, just as the others have made it, an act of worship to God Almighty, because they are under God's will. Some of their scholars used to say about Satan: While he disobeyed the command, he obeyed the will. Those, however, are permissive and they suspend the command." Ibid.

*The seventh group* includes some of the salaf who adopted the same position as the above but from a different intellectual standpoint and in reaction to al-Qadariyya. In interpreting the Qur'anic verse, they said: "It is stated in the general sense, but what is meant by worship is to make humans submit, bring them under His authority and exert His power and will over them, thus making them see the happiness and wretchedness they have been created for. This is the position of Zayd ibn Aslam (d. 136/753) and like-minded scholars. [...] Zayd ibn Aslam is reported to have said: 'And in no way did I create the jinn and humankind except to worship Me' points towards the wretchedness and happiness which God has bestowed upon them by nature. Wahb ibn Munabbih (d. 114/732) said: God has made them prepared for obedience and disobedience by nature." Ibid., vol. 8, 45. While this group's position is in harmony with the preceding one, in the sense that worship is what God has foreordained for man, it disagrees with it in that a person is obedient to God by submitting to the creational command (cosmic will) whatever its shape might be. Ibn Taymiyya said: "As for Zayd ibn Aslam, Wahb ibn Munabbih and like-minded scholars, they were far from being accused of holding such an opinion because they were among the greatest men to glorify commands, prohibitions, promises and warnings. They only intended to respond to those who denied destiny by claiming that God wills that which does not exist, and He does not will that which exists. The latter group pretended that God could not force people to worship Him or make them submit to His will; so, these scholars only wanted to invalidate these arguments. Verily, it is right what they wanted to do, but the argument revolves around what is intended by the verse. [...] The author of this statement only wanted to show what they were created for." Ibid., vol. 8, 48.

*The eighth group* includes "those who interpreted worship in terms of a dictated general command but not as the ordered worship revealed through God's messengers. The interpretation of ibn Abī Talḥa, which is attributed to ibn 'Abbās, reads: "except to acknowledge their submission to Me, willingly or unwillingly." This kind of submission is like the one cited in the Qur'anic verses: "To Him submits whoever there is in the heavens and the earth, willingly or unwillingly" and "To Allah prostrates whoever there is in the heavens and the earth, willingly or unwillingly." Some of them explained "unwillingness" as the inevitability of the law of destiny, which makes the explanation similar to the previous one, but the correct meaning is that human beings are directed towards God's foreordained rule without their choice, such as when they submit to calamities and when they are made to accept legal rulings towards which they have an aversion; so, everyone should be directed towards the rule that God has destined for him, and this is a correct meaning explained in another context, but it is not what is meant by worship. Another party said: "It is only to submit to Me and show humility," adding that the linguistic meaning of worship conveys humility and submission and that every creature of jinn and mankind is subject to the will and destiny of God Almighty and they are submissive to His will. No one can escape the destiny for which God has created him." Ibid., vol. 8, 48–49.

*The ninth group* comprises some salaf scholars whose reaction to al-Qadariyya was different. They commented on the meaning of the same verse, saying: "He created them for worship, and there is worship that is beneficial and worship that is not. God said: 'If you ask them, "Who created the heavens and the earth, and disposed of the sun and the moon?" They will surely say, "Allah"' (Q 29:61), this is an act of worship performed by them, but it will not be of any benefit for them because of their polytheism. This meaning is valid, but the polytheist worships Satan, and the fact that he made the right statements about God is not worship, since a mere acknowledgment of the Creator, is not called worship when other deities are associated with Him. [...] This is similar to others who said that it [the previous verse] means 'except to affirm my Unicity.' The believer affirms the Unicity of God in times of adversity as in prosperity, while the unbeliever does so when encountering adversity and in testing times rather than those of prosperity." Ibid., vol. 8, 50.

*The tenth group* includes some salaf whose reaction was to say that "to worship Me" signifies "to know Me." "Qatāda is cited as the author of this interpretation, which is also mentioned by al-Baghawī in his citation of Mujāhid (d. 104/722)." The latter said: "This is an acceptable view because if He had not created them, His existence and Unity would not have been known, and the evidence for this is: 'If you ask them, "Who created the heavens and the earth, and disposed of the sun and the moon?" They will surely say, "Allah"' (Q 29:61). This meaning is valid, but the fact that God is only known through their creation requires that their creation is a condition of their knowledge of God. This does not mean, however, that what they obtained in terms of knowledge is the purpose for which they were created. This is similar to al-Sadī's opinion. They all share this general affirmation in interpreting the verse: 'When your Lord took from the children of Adam' (Q 7:172), but this is not what 'worship' means." Ibid., vol. 8, 50–51.

Ibn Taymiyya commented on the position of the above four groups, clarifying that they came as reactions to the al-Qadariyya school: "These four perspectives represent the views of those who know that the verse is general, so they sought to explain worship as an act that includes mankind and jinn, but they assumed that if it was interpreted in terms of the familiar worship, which is obedience to God and to His messengers, it would have been a worship that should have been performed but it is not. Hence, they wanted to explain it in terms of a perforce worship, assuming that if they had explained it as a form of worship that was not performed, they would be required to adopt the position of al-Qadariyya, namely, that God created people to worship Him, but they disobeyed Him against His will and His power; so, they shunned the viewpoint of al-Qadariyya. Their attitude is understandable; however, they explained it in a way that is not intended by the verse." Ibid., vol. 8, 51.

*The eleventh group* is made up of deniers of destiny (al-Qadariyya) who argue that the purpose of the creation of mankind is to achieve worship. However, they say that because some people fall short of performing worship, although God has destined all people for worship, there are certain things in the universe that are not subject to God's will and that God wills things that cannot be fulfilled. Moreover, "they argue that what He has created them for, did not happen because He wills what does not happen, and what He does not will, happens." So, "Al-Qadariyya adeterminists do not say that He wills only in the sense of commanding, for in their view whatever does not constitute obedience in the actions of the servants is what He does not will, because from their perspective He does not create it." Furthermore, "in their viewpoint, the actions of the servants do not fall within His creation, power, will or will to do; but God's will in relation to those actions is only in the sense that they fall within His command. Hence, they say that He creates them to worship Him and He commands them to do so; therefore if they do not do it, it amounts to disobeying His command." Ibid., vol. 8, 54–55.

*The twelfth group* consists of Ahl al-Sunna (Sunnites) who agree with the above statement that worship is a universal goal intended for all people and that it alludes to the realisation of God's command. They, however, disagree with the above group by attributing the establishment of destiny to God. Ibn Taymiyya said: "The Sunnites whose belief in destiny is firm say that the Qur'anic verse: 'And in no way did I create the jinn and humankind except to worship Me' does not stipulate the occurrence of worship, as the authors of the previous statements said, and it does not stipulate denial of destiny to have in God's Kingdom what He does not will or what He wills not to be, as al-Qadariyya claim. These [al-Qadariyya] say: What He creates them for does not happen because He wills what does not happen, and what He does not will happens. Those [Sunnites who have espoused the four aforementioned positions], however, say: If what He wills happens and what He does not will does not happen, then what does not happen is what He does not will, and what does not happen at the level of worship is what He does not will, which is a correct view. They then say: He must have willed what He has created them for, and what He does not will to create, He has not created them for." Ibid., vol. 8, 54. However, the correct view, ibn Taymiyya argues, is the one adopted by this twelfth group in its interpretation of the meaning of the Qur'anic verse as "He has created them but to worship Him, but they may worship Him or they may not." Ibid., vol. 8, 58.

137 Ibid., vol. 19, 160.

138 The Atharī (Salafī) creedal school remained the main tendency within Sunni Islam until it was overruled by the Ash'arī school which started to become the dominant trend during the eleventh century through the Ash'arī scholar Niẓām al-Mulk (d. 1092), who took power of the Seljuq Empire (between 1064 and 1092) and imposed Ash'arism in the schools he founded in Iraq and Persia. It then expanded to Egypt and the rest of North Africa until it became the official majority Sunni doctrine in the twelfth century. See for instance: 'Izz al-Dīn ibn al-Athīr, *al-Kāmil fī l-Tārīkh* [The Integral Book of History] (Beirut: Dār al-Kitāb al-'Arabī, 1997), vol. 6.

139 Al-Shāṭibī, *al-Muwāfaqāt*, 99–100.

140 Ibid., vol. 2, 328–29.

141 Ibid., vol. 2, 303–4.

142 Al-Iṣfahānī, *al-Dharī'a ilā Makārim al-Sharī'a*, 84.

143 Ibid., 85.

144 Ibid.

145 The Māturīdī theological school denied the Divine action-attributes and reduced all the Divine attributes to self-attributes, entailing that wisdom and rationale follow Divine action and that Divine action is not motivated by the wisdom, rationale or purpose that are stemming from it. That is because if God would have created things and established rulings for a wisdom or a purpose behind it, He would not have been characterised with that wisdom before having created or revealed or before the realisation of that purpose, which goes against His perfection. Hence wisdom and purpose that are consequences or outcomes of His creation and Revelation cannot be attributed

to God (are not Divine attributes). Accordingly, God does not act based on wisdom or purpose, but those are but consequences of His actions related to his creation and not to Him. Consequently, wisdom and purpose are but a Divine grace and relative (secondary) matters that are not intended as such. See:

- Abū Manṣūr al-Māturīdī, *al-Tawḥīd*, ed. Fatḥ Allāh Khalīf (Alexandria: Dār al-Jāmiʿāt al-Miṣriyya, n.d.), 47
- Ibn Taymiyya, *Darʾ Taʿāruḍ al-ʿAql wa-l-Naql* [Averting the Conflict between Reason and Revelation], ed. Muḥammad Rashād Sālim (Riyadh: Imām Muḥammad ibn Saʿūd Islamic University, 2nd ed., 1991), vol. 4, 3–18
- Muḥammad Amīr Badshāh al- Ḥanafī, *al-Taysīr wa-l-Taḥrīr* [The Facilitation and Verification] (Beirut: Dār al-Fikr, n.d.), vol. 3, 303–5

146 Al-Iṣfahānī, *al-Dharīʿa ilā Makārim al-Sharīʿa*, 88.

147 Al-Shāṭibī, *al-Muwāfaqāt*, 358–72.

148 Yūsuf al-Qaraḍāwī, *Ethics of Islam* (Doha: Research Center for Islamic Legislation and Ethics, 2017), 260–62.

## Bibliography

ʿAbd al-Razzāq, al-Ṣanʿānī. *Tafsīr ʿAbd al-Razzāq*. Edited by Maḥmūd ʿAbduh. Beirut: Dār al-Kutub al-ʿIlmiyya, 1419AH.

Ibn ʿAbd al-Salām, ʿIzz al-Dīn. *Fawāʾid fī Mushkil al-Qurʾān [Lessons about Problematic Qurʾanic Verses]*. Edited by Sayyid Riḍwān ʿAlī al-Nadwī. Jeddah: Dār al-Shurūq, 1982.

Ibn ʿAbd al-Salām, ʿIzz al-Dīn. *Tafsīr al-Qurʾān*. Edited by ʿAbd Allāh al-Wahbī. Beirut: Dār ibn Ḥazm, 1996.

Abū Dāwūd, Sulaymān. *Sunan Abī Dāwūd*. Edited by Shuʿayb al-Arnaʾūṭ and Muḥammad Kāmil. Beirut: Dār al-Risāla al-ʿIlmiyya, 2009.

Abū Ḥayyān, Athīr al-Dīn. *Al-Baḥr al-Muḥīṭ fī l-Tafsīr [The Vast Expanse of Exegesis]*. Edited by Sidqī Muḥammad Jamīl. Beirut: Dār al-Fikr, 1999.

Ibn ʿĀdil al-Ḥanbalī, Sirāj al-Dīn. *Al-Lubāb fī ʿUlūm al-Kitāb [The Core Sciences of the Book]*. Edited by ʿĀdil Aḥmad and ʿAlī Muḥammad. Beirut: Dār al-Kutub al-ʿIlmiyya, 1998.

Al-Ālūsī, Shihāb al-Dīn. *Rūḥ al-Maʿānī fī Tafsīr al-Qurʾān al-ʿAẓīm wa-l-Sabʿ al-Mathānī [The Spirit of Meanings in the Interpretation of the Great Qurʾan and the Seven Verses]*. Edited by ʿAlī ʿAbd al-Bārī. Beirut: Dār al-Kutub al-ʿIlmiyya, 1994.

Amīr Badshāh, Muḥammad. *Al-Taysīr wa-l-Taḥrīr [The Facilitation and Verification]*. Beirut: Dār al-Fikr, n.d.

Anjum, Ovamir. *Who Wants the Caliphate?* Texas: Yaqeen Institute for Islamic Research, 2019.

Ibn ʿArabī, Muḥyī al-Dīn. *Fuṣūṣ al-Ḥikam. [The Ringstones of Wisdom]*. Beirut: Dār al-Kitāb al-ʿArabī, n.d.

Al-Ashʿarī, Abū al-Ḥasan. *Al-Ibāna ʿan Uṣūl al-Diyāna [The Elucidation Concerning the Principles of Religion]*. Edited by Fawqiyya Ḥusayn Maḥmūd. Cairo: Dār al-Anṣār, 1977.

Ibn al-Athīr, ʿIzz al-Dīn. *Al-Kāmil fī l-Tārīkh [The Integral Book of History]*. Beirut: Dār al-Kitāb al-ʿArabī, 1997.

Al-Baghawī, Abū Muḥammad al-Ḥusayn. *Sharḥ al-Sunna [Explanation of the Sunna]*. Edited by Shuʿayb al-Arnaʾūṭ. Damascus: al-Maktab al-Islāmī, 1983.

Al-Baghawī, Abū Muḥammad al-Ḥusayn. *Maʿālim al-Tanzīl fī Tafsīr al-Qurʾān [Qurʾanic Exegesis]*. Edited by ʿAbd al-Razzāq al-Mahdī. Beirut: Dār Iḥyāʾ al-Turāth al-ʿArabī, 1999.

Ibn Baṭṭāl, al-Qurṭubī. *Sharḥ Ṣaḥīḥ al-Bukhārī*. Edited by Abū Tamīm Yāsir. Riyadh: Maktabat al-Rushd, 2nd ed. 2003.

Al-Bayḍāwī, Nāṣir al-Dīn al-Shirāzī. *Anwār al-Tanzīl wa-Asrār al-Taʾwīl [The Lights of the Revelation and the Mysteries of Interpretation]*. Edited by Muḥammad al-Marʿashilī. Beirut: Dār Iḥyāʾ al-Turāth al-ʿArabī, 1997.

Chittick, William C. *Science of the Cosmos, Science of the Soul the Pertinence of Islamic Cosmology in the Modern World*. Oxford: Oneworld Publications, 2007.

Al-Dasūqī, Fārūq Aḥmad. *Al-Khilāfa al-Islāmiyya Uṣūluhā wa-Ḥaqīqatuhā wa-Ḥatmiyyat ʿAwdatihā [The Islamic Caliphate: Its Origins, Truth and the Imperative of its Return]*. Cairo, 1998.

Al-Dulābī, Muḥammad. *Al-Kunā wa-l-Asmāʾ [Nicknames and Names]*. Edited by Muḥammad al-Fārayābī. Beirut: Dār ibn Ḥazm, 2000.

Faraḥāt, Aḥmad Ḥasan. *Al-Khilāfa fī l-Arḍ, [Vicegerency on Earth]*. Kuwait: Dār al-Arqam, 2003.

Al-Ghazzālī, Muḥammad Abū Ḥāmid. *Mīzān al-ʿAmal [The Balance of Work]*. Edited by Sulaymān Dunyā. Egypt: Dār al-Maʿārif, 1964.

Ibn Ḥamīd, al-Kassī ʿAbd. *Al-Muntaghab min Musnad ʿAbd ibn Ḥamīd [Selections from Musnad ʿAbd ibn Ḥamīd]*. Edited by Ṣubḥi al-Badrī and Mahmūd Khalīl. Cairo: Maktabat al-Sunna, 1988.

Ibn Ḥanbal, Aḥmad. *Al-Zuhd [Asceticism]*. Beirut: Dār al-Kutub al-ʿIlmiyya, 1999.

Ibn Ḥanbal, Aḥmad. *Musnad al-Imām Aḥmad ibn Ḥanbal*. Edited by Shuʿayb al-Arnaʾūṭ and ʿĀdil Murshid, et al. Beirut: Muʾassasat al-Risāla, 2001.

Al-Ḥarālī, Abū al-Ḥasan. *Turāth Abī al-Ḥasan al-Ḥarālī al-Marākishī fī l-Tafsīr [The Tafsīr Legacy of Abū al-Ḥasan al-Ḥarālī]*. Edited by Muḥammādī al-Khayyāṭī. Rabat: al-Markaz al-Jāmiʿī, 1997.

Al-Hindī, al-Muttaqī. *Kanz al-ʿUmmāl [Treasures of the Doers of Good Deeds]*. Edited by Bakrī Ḥayyānī and Ṣafwat al-Saqā. Beirut: Muʾassasat al-Risāla, 5th ed., 1981.

Idris, Jaafar Sheikh. "Is Man the Vicegerent of God?" *Journal of Islamic Studies* 1 no. 1 (1990): 99–110.

Al-Iṣfahānī, al-Rāghib. *Tafsīr al-Rāghib al-Iṣfahānī, [The Exegesis of al-Rāghib al-Iṣfahānī]*. Edited by ʿĀdil ibn ʿAlī al-Shādī. Riyadh: Dār al-Waṭan, 2003.

Al-Iṣfahānī, al-Rāghib. *Al-Dharīʿa ilā Makārim al-Sharīʿa [The Book of Means to the Noble Qualities of Sharīʿa]*. Edited by Abū Zayd al-ʿAjamī. Cairo: Dār al-Salām, 2007.

Al-Iṣfahānī, Abū Nuʿaym. *Ḥilyat al-Awliyāʾ [The Adornment of the Saints]*. Cairo: Dār al-Saʿāda, 1974.

Ibn al-Jawzī, Jamāl al-Dīn. *Zād al-Masīr fī ʿIlm al-Tafsīr [The Victuals of the Journey in the Exploration of the Science of Exegesis]*. Edited by ʿAbd al-Razzāq al-Mahdī. Beirut: Dār al-Kitāb al-ʿArabī, 2001.

Ibn Khaldūn, ʿAbd al-Raḥmān. *Dīwān al-Mubtadaʾ wa-l-Khabar fī Tārīkh al-ʿArab wa-l-Barbar wa-Man ʿĀṣarahum min Dhawī al-Shaʾn al-Akbar [Book of Lessons, Recordings of the Beginnings and Events in the History of the Arabs, the Berbers and their Powerful Contemporaries]*. Beirut: Dār al-Fikr, 1988.

Ibn Māja, Muḥammad. *Sunan ibn Māja*. Edited by Muḥammad Fuʾād ʿAbd al-Bāqī. Cairo: Dār Iḥyāʾ al-Kutub al-ʿArabiyya, n.d.

Al-Makkī, Abū Ṭālib. *Qūt al-Qulūb fī Muʿāmalat al-Maḥbūb wa-Waṣf Tarīq al-Murīd ilā Maqām al-Tawḥīd [The Sustenance of Hearts]*. Edited by ʿAṣim Ibrāhīm al-Kayyālī. Beirut: Dār al-Kutub al-ʿIlmiyya, 2005.

March, Andrew F. *The Caliphate of Man: Popular Sovereignty in Modern Islamic Thought*. Cambridge, MA; London, England: Harvard University Press, 2019.

March, Andrew F. "Modern Islamic Conceptions of Sovereignty in Comparative Perspective." In *The Oxford Handbook of Comparative Political Theory*, edited by Leigh K. Jenco, Murad Idris, and Megan C. Thomas. New York: Oxford University Press, 2020.

Al-Marwazī, Naʿīm. *Kitāb al-Fitan [The Book of Tribulations and War]*. Edited by Samīr al-Zuhayrī. Cairo: Maktabat al-Tawḥīd, 1992.

Al-Māturīdī, Abū Manṣūr. *Al-Tawḥīd*. Edited by Fatḥ Allāh Khalīf. Alexandria: Dār al-Jāmiʿāt al-Miṣriyya, n.d.

Al-Māwardī, ʿAlī Abū al-Ḥasan. *Al-Aḥkām al-Sulṭāniyya [The Ordinances of Governance]*. Cairo: Dār al-Ḥadīth, n.d.

Al-Maydānī, ʿAbd al-Raḥmān Ḥabanka. "Hal al-Insān Khalīfa ʿan Allāh fī Arḍihi? [Is Man the Vicegerent of God on earth?]." *Majallat Kuliyyat al-Daʿwa wa-Uṣūl al-Dīn bi-Makka al-Mukarrama*, 1, no. 1 (1983): 3–47.

Al-Maydānī, ʿAbd al-Raḥmān Ḥabanka. *Lā Yaṣiḥ an Yuqāl al-Insān Khalīfa ʿan Allāh fī Arḍihi fa Hiyya Maqūla Bāṭila [The Impropriety and Invalidity of the Belief that Man is the Vicegerent of God on Earth]*. Mecca: Maktabat Iḥyāʾ al-Turāth al-Islāmī, 1991.

Ibn Miskawayh, Abū ʿAlī. *Tahdhīb al-Akhlāq wa Taṭhīr al-Aʿrāq [Refinement of Morals and Purification of Provisions]*. Edited by ibn Khaṭīb. Cairo: Maktabat al-Thaqāfa al-Dīniyya, n.d.

Ibn al-Mubārak, ʿAbd Allāh. *Al-Zuhd wa-l-Raqāʾiq [Asceticism and Spirituality]*. Edited by Ḥabīb al-Raḥmān al-Aʿẓamī. Beirut: Dār al-Kutub al-ʿIlmiyya, n.d.

Al-Najjār, ʿAbd al-Majīd. *Fiqh al-Tadayyun Fahman wa-Tanzīlan [The Jurisprudence of Religiosity: Understanding and Implementation]*. Mohammedia, Algeria: Dār Qurṭuba, 3rd ed. 2006.

Al-Nāṣir, ʿAbd Allāh ibn Ibrāhīm. "The Principle of Vicegerency in the Islamic Economy: A Study in the Light of the Qurʾan." *Journal of Qurʾanic Studies* 7, no. 1, (2005).

Al-Naysabūrī, al-Ḥākim. *Al-Mustadrak ʿalā al-Ṣaḥīḥayn*. Edited by Muṣṭafā ʿAbd al-Qādir. *Beirut: Dār al-Kutub al-ʿIlmiyya*, 1990.

Al-Qaraḍāwī, Yūsuf. *Fatāwā Muʿāṣira [Contemporary Fatwas]*. Vol. 2. Kuwait: Dār al-Qalam, 2005.

Al-Qaraḍāwī, Yūsuf. *Ethics of Islam*. Doha: Research Center for Islamic Legislation and Ethics, 2017.

Al-Qaṣṣāb, Aḥmad. *Al-Nukat al-Dālla ʿalā al-Bayān fī Anwāʿ al-ʿUlūm wa-l-Aḥkām [Issues in Clarifying Different Types of Sciences and Rulings]*. Edited by Ibrāhīm al-Junayd. Cairo: Dār al-Qiyam, 2003.

Ibn Qayyim al-Jawziyya, Shams al-Dīn. *Badāʾiʿ al-Fawāʾid [The Amazing Insights]*. Edited by Hishām ʿAṭā, ʿĀdil al-ʿAdawī and Ashraf Aḥmad. Mecca: Maktabat Nizār Muṣṭafā al-Bāz, 1996a.

Ibn Qayyim al-Jawziyya, Shams al-Dīn. *Madārij al-Sālikīn bayna Manāzil Iyyāka Naʿbud wa-Iyyāka Nastaʿīn [The Wayfarers' Stages]*. Edited by Muḥammad al-Muʿtaṣim Billāh. Beirut: Dār al-Kitāb al-ʿArabī, 1996b.

Ibn Qayyim al-Jawziyya, Shams al-Dīn. *Miftāḥ Dār al-Saʿāda wa-Manshūr Wilāyat al-ʿIlm wa-l-Irāda [Key to the Blissful Abode]*. Beirut: Dār al-Kutub al-ʿIlmiyya, n.d.

Al-Qurṭubī, Muḥammad Shams al-Dīn. *Al-Jāmiʿ li-Aḥkām al-Qurʾān [The Compiler of the Rulings of the Qurʾan]*. Edited by Aḥmad al-Bardūnī and Ibrāhīm al-Aṭafīsh. Cairo: Dār al-Kutub al-Miṣriyya, 1964.

Al-Rāzī, Muḥammad Fakhr al-Dīn. *Al-Tafsīr al-Kabīr [The Great Exegesis]*. Beirut: Dār Iḥyāʾ al-Turāth al-ʿArabī, 1999.

Al-Samʿānī, Abū al-Muẓaffar Manṣūr. *Tafsīr al-Qurʾān [The Interpretation of the Qurʾan]*. Edited by Yāsir ibn Ibrāhīm and Ghunaym ibn ʿAbbās. Riyadh: Dār al-Waṭan, 1997.

Al-Samarqandī, Naṣr ibn Muḥammad. *Baḥr al-ʿUlūm [The Vast Expanse of the Sciences of Sharīʿa]*. Edited by ʿAlī Muḥammad Muʿawwaḍ. Beirut: Dār al-Kutub al-ʿIlmiyya, 1993.

Al-Shajarī, Yaḥyā. *Tartīb al-Amālī*. Edited by Muḥammad Ḥasan. Beirut: Dār al-Kutub al-ʿIlmiyya, 2001.

Al-Shāṭibī, Abū Isḥāq. *Al-Muwāfaqāt [The Reconciliation]*. Annotated by Mashūr ibn Ḥasan. Cairo: Dār ibn ʿAffān, 1997.

Steppat, Fritz. "God's Deputy: Materials on Islam's Image of Man." *Arabica* 36, no. 2 (1989): 163–72.

Al-Ṭabarī, Muḥammad ibn Jarīr. *Jāmiʿ al-Bayān ʿan Taʾwīl Āyī al-Qurʾān [The Comprehensive Exposition of the Interpretation of the Verses of the Qurʾan]*. Edited by Aḥmad Muḥammad Shākir. Beirut: Muʾassasat al-Risāla, 2000.

Takeshita, Masataka. "The Theory of the Perfect Man in ibn ʿArabī's Fuṣūṣ al-Ḥikam." *Tokyo: Orient* 19 (1983): 87–102.

Ibn Taymiyya, Taqī al-Dīn. *Minhāj al-Sunna al-Nabawiyya fī Naqḍ Kalām al-Shīʿa al-Qadariyya [The Way of the Prophet's Sunna: a Critique of the Theological Discourse of al-Qadariyya Shiites]*. Edited by Muḥammad Rashād Sālim. Riyadh: Imām Muḥammad ibn Saʿūd Islamic University, 1986.

Ibn Taymiyya, Taqī al-Dīn. *Al-Fatāwā al-kubrā [Major Fatwas]*. Beirut: Dār al-Kutub al-ʿIlmiyya, 1987.

Ibn Taymiyya, Taqī al-Dīn. *Darʾ Taʿāruḍ al-ʿAql wa-l-Naql [Averting the Conflict between Reason and Revelation]*. Edited by Muḥammad Rashād Sālim. Riyadh: Imām Muḥammad ibn Saʿūd Islamic University, 2nd ed., 1991.

Ibn Taymiyya, Taqī al-Dīn. *Majmūʿ al-Fatāwā [The Compilation of Fatwas]*. Medina: King Fahd Complex for the Printing of the Holy Quran, 1995.

Ibn Taymiyya, Taqī al-Dīn. *Bayān Talbīs al-Jahmiyya fī Taʾsīs Bidaʿihim al-Kalāmiyya. [Exposition of the Falsehoods of al-Jahmiyya in the Establishment of their Theological Innovations]*. Medina: King Fahd Complex for the Printing of the Holy Qurʾan, 2005.

Al-Ṭībī, Sharaf al-Dīn. *Sharḥ al-Ṭībī ʿalā Mishkāt al-Maṣābīḥ [The Explanation of al-Ṭībī on Mishkāt al-Maṣābīḥ]*. Edited by ʿAbd al-Ḥamīd Hindāwī. Mecca: Maktabat Nizār Muṣṭafā al-Bāz, 1997.

Ibn Tūhāmī, al-Jīlānī. *Falsafat al-Insān ʿinda ibn Khaldūn [The Philosophy of the Human Being in the Work of Ibn Khaldūn]*. Beirut: Dār al-Kutub al-ʿIlmiyya, 2011.

Umlīl, ʿAlī. *Al-Khiṭāb al-Tārīkhī: Dirāsa li-Minhajiyyat ibn Khaldūn [Historical Discourse: A Study of ibn Khaldūn's Methodology]*. Beirut: Dār al-Tanwīr, 1985.

Al-Zamakhsharī, Maḥmūd. *Al-Kashāf ʿan Ḥaqāʾiq Ghawāmiḍ al-Tanzīl [The Discoverer of Revealed Truths]*. Beirut: Dār al-Kitāb al-ʿArabī, 1987.

Al-Zaylaʿī, Fakhr al-Dīn. *Ṭibyān al-Ḥaqāʾiq Sharḥ Kanz al-Daqāʾiq [The Explanation of Kanz al-Daqāʾiq]*. Cairo: al-Maṭbaʿa al-Kubrā al-Amīriyya, 1313 AH.

Al-Zayūt, Yūsuf. "Madā Ṣiḥḥat al-Qawl bi-ʾanna al-Insān Khalīfat Allāh fī l-Arḍ [The Extent of the Validity of the Statement that Man is the Vicegerent of God on Earth]." *Majalat Jāmiʿat Dimashq* XVII, no. 2 (2001): 265–288.

# 4 Vicegerency as Existential Function in Contemporary Reformism

As the human existential function that makes the human being a vicegerent of God, the concept of *istikhlāf* or *khilāfa* (vicegerency) gained prominence within the modern Islamic reformist movement, to the extent of virtually becoming a common denominator among the pioneers of intellectual reform in the previous century. This was in line with the increasing trend in the exploration of the major principles and values governing Islamic thought and civilisation in the face of the problematic of fragmentation of knowledge as one of the greatest challenges confronting the endeavour to integrate Islamic thought in the era of modernity and counter modern materialistic worldviews. Most contemporary reformists hailing from various backgrounds have referred in their works to this broad sense of the concept of vicegerency, as exemplified by the writings of leading reformist figures amongst the Qurʾan exegetes such as Muḥammad ʿAbduh (d. 1905), Muḥammad Rashīd Riḍā (d. 1935), Sayyid Quṭb (d. 1966), Muḥammad al-Ṭāhir ibn ʿĀshūr (d. 1973) and Abū al-Aʿlā al-Mawdūdī (d. 1979). This concept also featured in the writings of influential Sunni reformists in general, including Muḥammad Iqbāl (d. 1938), Badīʿ al-Zamān Saʿīd al-Nūrsī (d. 1960), ʿĀʾisha Bint al-Shāṭiʾ (d. 1998) and ʿAbd al-Wahhāb al-Masīrī (d. 2008), as well as in the works of leading Shia scholars, such as ʿAlī Sharīʿatī (d. 1977), Muḥammad Bāqir al-Ṣadr (d. 1980) and Murtaḍā Muṭahharī (d. 1979). Moreover, in the context of the *Islamisation of Knowledge project*, the prominent figures of the International Institute of Islamic Thought, such as Ismāʿīl al-Fārūqī (d. 1986), ʿAbd al-Ḥamīd Abū Sulaymān (d. 2021), Munā Abū al-Faḍl (d. 2008) and Ṭāhā Jābir al-ʿUlwānī (d. 2016) have also highlighted the importance of the concept of vicegerency. Furthermore, a number of academic studies, doctoral theses, preaching literature and some applied studies[1] have been devoted to the study of this concept as will be developed in this chapter. However, it becomes clear after extensive reflections on this literature that the concept of vicegerency has not, to date, received due consideration, nor has it been subject to an appropriate rooting process in the relevant literature. In addition, there is no trace of any study that shows interest in the examination of the Islamic intellectual heritage around the concept of *istikhlāf* as an existential function, a topic addressed in the preceding chapter. Nor is there any comparative study dealing analytically with contemporary views of the concept of vicegerency as an existential function, a gap that we will try to fill here.

DOI: 10.4324/9781003335948-4

Hence, this chapter seeks to examine the concept of vicegerency as existential function from the perspective of contemporary Muslim scholars. The primary concern of this study is not the political, social or intellectual contexts within which contemporaries have dealt with the concept; rather, the focus will be on the comparison between the views of contemporary and classical scholars and whether the former's views have actually broken any new ground in the field. The focus will also be on attempts at rooting the concept of vicegerency as an existential function in the Qur'an and in Islamic theology, and the extent to which they can be relied upon to formulate a theory of vicegerency as such. There will also be an attempt at diagnosing the shortcomings or distortions that have marked the study of the concept of vicegerency among contemporaries and prevented the development of a coherent theory. The questions raised in this chapter consist mainly of the following: How have contemporary scholars defined the concept of *istikhlāf* as existential function? What is the object of vicegerency (*al-mustakhlaf fīhi*) in the perception of contemporary scholars? What is the contribution of contemporary scholars to this field? In what way has the concept of *istikhlāf* been rooted in the Islamic worldview, and how have contemporary scholars related it to the major principles of Islam? What are the shortcomings or flaws in contemporary perspectives on the concept of vicegerency?

In the following sections, the answers to the above questions will be framed within a single main approach that consists of analysing the views of contemporaries about the object of *istikhlāf*; or, in other words, the nature of the responsibility conferred upon the human being in the act of delegation on behalf of God. If, as commonly agreed upon by contemporary scholars, *istikhlāf* is defined as God's deputisation of the human being, then the diagnosis of the locus of the deputisation should be viewed as the main pillar in the identification of the meaning of *istikhlāf* as a human existential function and the elaboration of a theory that hinges upon it. Thus, consideration of this pillar is deemed the highest priority, because the accuracy of all other issues and underlying principles related to the concept of vicegerency and their potential to establish a theory will depend on the accurate diagnosis of this pillar.

Many of the contemporary writers who have consistently acclaimed the concept of *istikhlāf* as an existential human function did not attempt to define its meaning. This study will examine the assertions of these scholars only insofar as they relate to the topical issues under study. Some, on the other hand, have loosely taken the concept as an overall title for their writings, dealing under that title with several theological issues without referring to the concept of *istikhlāf* at all,[2] or while referring to it ambiguously and unsystematically.[3] Such studies, and others we did not find worth mentioning here, will not be covered in this chapter. This will not be a loss since whatever was said in these writings on vicegerency has already been tackled above or will be tackled below. Those that have either defined or explained the concept of *istikhlāf* as a human existential function can be divided into five categories based on their identification of the nature of the object of vicegerency. The first category, which represents the predominant trend, reduces the object of vicegerency to the earth and its resources.

The second category defines the object of vicegerency in terms of adherence to God's commands and their implementation on Earth. The third category identifies the object of vicegerency in terms of the responsibilities of free choice and disposition that have been conferred upon the human being. The fourth category ascribes the object of vicegerency to the endeavour of manifesting Divine attributes and ethics on Earth. Finally, the fifth category puts forward definitions in which the object of vicegerency is made to assume several material and moral meanings.

In what follows, the opinions articulated within the five categories will be outlined and analysed, using this type of commentary as a starting point to get acquainted with the conditions of contemporary perceptions of *istikhlāf* and to answer the questions raised in this chapter. Most of the comments will focus on studies devoted to the concept of vicegerency as an existential function, or, occasionally, those that have devoted a chapter, a research section or a self-contained title to this concept. The data about these studies have been, to the best of the author's ability, adequately identified and collected. However, some of these studies, though concerned with the concept of *istikhlāf* as an existential function, will be excluded because their attempts to define the concept of *istikhlāf* and identify its object barely provide an exposition of some of the thoughts of classical scholars and attempts at weighting one over the other.[4] This study will also disregard the preaching literature revolving around the topic of *istikhlāf*, as they merely consist of loose thoughts offering moral guidance to the reader. These are impressionistic in nature and do not fulfil the minimum criteria of academic research.[5]

## 4.1 Building and Populating the Earth (*ʿimārat al-arḍ*) and Utilising its Resources

Most contemporary advocates of vicegerency subscribe to the definition of *istikhlāf* as a human existential task consisting in the exploitation of the universe and the utilisation of its resources. This trend emerged at the rise of the modern reformist movements. The definitions that fit into this first category have reduced vicegerency into building the earth and utilising its resources.[6] However, some of them have included concepts like lordship, domination or control over the earth, or to rule over the universe and harness it in their definition of vicegerency, while others have not. The most prominent contemporary reformists who reduced the object of vicegerency to building and populating the earth (*ʿimārat al-arḍ*) and utilising its resources without referring to those concepts include Muḥammad ʿAbduh (d. 1905),[7] ʿAbd al-Ḥamīd ibn Bādīs (d. 1940)[8] and ʿAbd al-Wahhāb al-Masīrī (d. 2008),[9] followed by many researchers.[10]

As for contemporary pioneers of Islamic reformism who defined vicegerency in terms of *ʿimārat al-arḍ* while adding notions like ruling over the earth, dominating, harnessing or controlling it, or to be a master or a lord over it, those include ʿAbd al-Qādir ʿAwda (d. 1954)[11] and Sayyid Quṭb (d. 1966),[12] followed by several researchers.[13]

The above position with its two variants represents the overwhelming majority of the definitions of *istikhlāf* as human function among the contemporaries that we have observed. Consequently, it appears that the majority of contemporary proponents of the concept of vicegerency as an existential human function have reduced it to the exploitation, utilisation and development of the resources of the earth. The problematic posed here is that the Qurʾanic texts regarding the overall purpose of human creation suggest that this function transcends the mere building and population of the earth and use of its resources. The most conspicuous of these texts include the previously cited verse: "And in no way did I create the jinn and humankind except to worship Me" (Q 51:56). Although many of those classified under this category have not specifically addressed this problem, some of them are aware of it and have tried to resolve it in different ways.

### *4.1.1 The Problem of Vicegerency and Worship*

Among those attempts to solve that issue, we find the claim that man is not only created for vicegerency, but that he was "created for two main things, namely the achievement of complete servitude (*ʿubūdiyya*) and total submission to God Almighty besides the accomplishment of the objectives of the vicegerency of God on earth."[14] Hence, a person bears a "dual responsibility: the first consists of his responsibilities and obligations towards his Lord, and the second includes the obligations and responsibilities arising from his relation to the world."[15] However, we find no basis for this differentiation between the two responsibilities, since the human responsibility vis-à-vis the world is, perforce, a responsibility towards God, for it is He who assigned him this responsibility. Nevertheless, this distinction is in line with the Ashʿarī epistemology, which argues for the dualism of worship (*ʿibāda*) and interest (*maṣlaḥa*) and dualism of religion and the world, whereas these binary concepts have no basis in the Qurʾan, as previously stated. Excluding the Ashʿarī epistemology, in Islam there is no responsibility that is merely an obligation towards God and unrelated to a worldly interest or another right (vis-à-vis self, the other or the universe). As for what scholars of jurisprudence have agreed upon in terms of classifications of God's rights and man's rights, they did not, within the context of this classification, account for God's rights as abstract ones that are separate from man's, but rather they considered them as public rights that are not exclusive to a single individual.

The approach to this problematic of the human existential function beyond mere worldly interests and benefits has been debated by some authors classified in this category in different ways by arguing that vicegerency is part of worship and that the latter is more comprehensive. Therefore, "it is evident that the meaning of worship, as the objective of human existence or as the primary human function, is broader and more comprehensive than mere rituals, and that the function of vicegerency is definitely included in the meaning of worship."[16] The counterargument here, however, is that if vicegerency were only part of the human existential function, why is it that when God commended Adam before the angels, He only informed them about one part of his function on earth and

He has given him a name (*khalīfa*) that does not indicate everything that he has been created for? Rather, it was thought that God would inform them about the entirety of man's function. This implies that *khilāfa* includes all aspects of the human function.

Perhaps this is why some of these authors have overturned the argument claiming that vicegerency is broader than worship; worship is thus a part of vicegerency. This argument is espoused by al-Dasūqī (d. 2017), the author of the most extensive treatise devoted solely to the topic of vicegerency, and it is for this reason that in the course of this study, he will be given, to some extent, more space and critical consideration. In al-Dasūqī's view, vicegerency is broader than worship, and it constitutes both "servitude and lordship."[17] In other words, it is both worship and sovereignty:[18]

> In the realm of servitude, the human being interacts with both his Lord and with people. That is an interaction in which a person is subject to God and is humble before Him, while being equal with people. The human being's behaviour in relation to sovereignty, however, concerns his relationship with objects and living beings on earth other than humans, and the nature of this behaviour is marked by control, domination and sovereignty. The latter reflects the human being's effort to assert his vicegerency and establish his sovereignty over the earth. The acts of servitude, on the other hand, consist of steering this vicegerency in a way that makes the human being appear a servant of God alone and who devotes this servitude exclusively to Him.[19]

Hence, sovereignty over the earth is vicegerency in the sense that it is the function for which the human being is created, and worship is vicegerency in the sense that it makes this sovereignty dedicated to God. Consequently, vicegerency may be performed on behalf of an entity other than God if it is a form of sovereignty but without worship.[20] If the human being neglects worship and "no longer holds firm and absolute Divine values, his life is transformed from being a vicegerency of God to a vicegerency of other than God."[21] Al-Dasūqī continued:

> Therefore, the community of polytheism and disbelief is a community of vicegerency as well, but it is a vicegerency to others than God. The evidence for this position is that God Almighty has designated man as His vicegerent on earth without making a distinction between the Muslim and the disbeliever in this regard. Furthermore, the human being was only made a vicegerent in a deterministic way, he is, however, vicegerent of God Almighty or of others by choice, for God has made him a vicegerent by virtue of innate disposition and creation, then sent him on earth and left him to determine, of his own volition, the party whose vicegerent he wants to become.[22]

Al-Dasūqī considers that the modern Western world fulfils vicegerency in its sovereign dimension, as it has

> enhanced it with the advances in science and technology, but it has forgotten, become oblivious to or denied servitude towards God. In doing so, the Western man thought that he has acquired everything on earth, while in reality his sovereignty over matter, as a result of refusing servitude towards God, has relapsed into servitude to matter.[23]

In the main, it should be understood from al-Dasūqī's thesis that the objective of the human being's existence is sovereignty and lordship over the earth, and that worship is a means that steers this objective towards the right direction. Hence, he defines *khilāfa* as an existential human function in terms of utilising and extending sovereignty over nature without including worship.[24] This position poses a large number of problems, but it will suffice here to raise the following.

One of these problems is his view that *khilāfa* means sovereignty, lordship, domination and control of the universe as widely as possible. Al-Dasūqī tries to justify this idea using a strange form of logic, which is that if man is incapable of exhibiting superiority over the universe and subjugating it, he cannot be said to subject to God but rather to the universe. Thus, the worship of God can only be achieved through sovereignty. He goes on: "This means that the sovereignty of man on earth is one of the pillars of monotheism (*tawḥīd*)."[25] This is a strange form of logic that raises the question: What is the basis of the assumption that worship can only be achieved through domineering and exerting control over Earth?[26] The fact that man may not control the universe does not necessarily mean that he becomes subject to it. Accordingly, should a human being be, for instance, a master over Buddha or Shiva or Satan so that he can avoid becoming their servant? There are many elements, phenomena and laws in the universe that are beyond the control of human beings. Does this mean that the human being is subject to them rather than to God? Is it possible for humans to control the earth and all its phenomena in the first place? Moreover, if the human being is responsible for the management and utilisation of the earth's resources, does this imply the obligation of good management or the obligation of domineering? Does the fact that, for example, a person is responsible for resources or employees entail domination and tyranny towards them so that they do not react to him in the same way? There seems to be no logical support for al-Dasūqī's position, nor is there evidence for this in the texts of Revelation indicating that it is the human being's duty or purpose in life to dominate the universe and subjugate it to himself. Rather, it appears that the Qur'anic text backs a different position, as will be shown later. Hence, just as the human being appears in his dealings with God, self and others "a humble subject to God," he is equally so in his dealings with the universe without the slightest difference. As for the fact that the human being occupies the highest position among the creatures of the universe, this is a *fait accompli* that relates to God's cosmic will and destiny, and not what man was entrusted to achieve or seek.

Another problematic that emerges in this thesis is that of the dichotomy of religion and world, which al-Dasūqī calls worship and sovereignty. It is true that he has drawn attention to the fact that "work in the field of sovereignty, or what some call worldly matters, is a form of worship in Islam, but the distinction between servitude and sovereignty is for the purpose of clarification only." However, he goes on to claim that "differentiation should be made between them in terms of the type of attitude in each of them and in terms of the other party in relation to the attitude."[27] He then mentions that this differentiation resides in the fact that worship is submission and that sovereignty is control, which is an invalid argument, as I pointed out. Moreover, although he asserts that sovereignty is a form of worship, he differentiates between them in several contexts. For example, he asks: "Is it possible to restrict the meaning of vicegerency to servitude? No [...] because vicegerency does not only mean servitude, for it must stand for something else as well."[28] The author could not distance himself from the dichotomy of worship versus world and religion versus world, and although he asserts that this is a non-Islamic division,[29] he falls into the same trap by virtue of the differentiation he has made himself and his neglect of the fact that the worship of God is never dissociated from man's connection with other than God (self, other and universe), and that there is no such thing in relation to man's existential function that involves more than worship. There is no form of worship, in the sense of religious responsibility, in which there is no benefit related to self, the other or the universe, unlike the claim made by the Ashʿarī school, as previously stated. Moreover, the conjunction "except" in the Qur'anic verse "And in no way did I create the jinn and humankind except to worship Me" (Q 51:56) refutes the assumption that the human being is created for something other than worship.

Furthermore, the argument that vicegerency may be for God, for Satan[30] or others entails a problem resulting from the lack of ontological control of the meaning of vicegerency and a deficiency in the rooting of the concept at the theological level. Submission to an entity other than God or to material and civilisational progress is not a form of vicegerency in any Qur'anic sense, as will be explained later through the ontological and theological analysis of the concept. Al-Dasūqī tried to argue for this position by stating that God made man a vicegerent on Earth with no differentiation between the believer and the non-believer, hence they are all deputising somebody or something.[31] However, this argument does not hold, for God, in the same way, has described the human being as being created for the purpose of worshipping Him irrespective of his status as Muslim or non-Muslim. Notably, the fact that God has proclaimed the existential function for which He created human beings does not mean that all of them will fulfil it. Presenting a person or a group of people as deputies does not necessarily entail that all of them are good deputies and that all of them are faithful to their task, though it does mean that it is their function initially.

Al-Dasūqī's argument that the human being is "vicegerent by virtue of destiny and determinism" requires all creatures on Earth to be considered vicegerents, since they are predestined to submit to God and perform their existential function on Earth. If the human being has been created a vicegerent in a predetermined manner, i.e., he is prepared to act as the vicegerent of anything, then vicegerency is no longer deemed an existential function but merely a question of inevitable fate. God, in this case, will be informing the angels in the verse about *khilāfa* that

He has created a being capable of good and evil. *Khilāfa*, accordingly, does not determine man's existential function, but it rather determines an inevitable existential fact, which is that man is prepared to pursue both good and evil. The verse of *khilāfa* refutes this claim, because if it were a proclamation of a *fait accompli*, then the angels would have surrendered to it without being surprised. However, when they realised that it was a task that had been assigned to man, while they thought they were in a better position to accomplish God's intent behind it, they reacted with surprise. This proves that it is not merely a matter of predetermined fate. This is why God did not reproach them for questioning His decision, He rather showed them that the human being is capable of performing the vicegerency task thanks to the innate characteristics of humans that the angels did not experience and that were not part of their nature. In other words, the fact that God revealed to the angels the virtuous characteristics that qualified humans, and not angels, to accomplish God's intent behind vicegerency indicates that vicegerency is an ethical task and not merely a predisposition to pursue good and evil, as al-Dasūqī claimed. So, his point of view, once again, reflects the distortion in the ontological control of the meaning of vicegerency.

Among the consequences of al-Dasūqī's identification of the object of vicegerency in terms of domination over the earth and the utilisation of its resources is that he does not limit this task to worldly life, arguing that "whoever fulfils the vicegerency of God Almighty on earth [and] achieves a level of sovereignty that is commensurate with his era [...] gets the reward of eternal vicegerency in Heaven where he will become the *wālī* (governor) of God, the Exalted, and master over creatures in an absolute manner."[32] He continues:

> There is no doubt that this conclusion, i.e. the belief that vicegerency on earth is not confined to worldly life, but is rather an existential, otherworldly reality as well, makes of the reality of vicegerency a major fact of the Islamic faith, even raising the human being to the level of the supreme objective of humanity and the noble objective of not just human life in a worldly existence, but also for eternal existence in the Hereafter.[33]

However, it is questionable if there is any evidence in support of this opinion. Rather, the Qur'an and the *Sunna* indicate that the responsibility of humans concerns only worldly life and does not extend to the Hereafter. Yet, it seems that al-Dasūqī argues that vicegerency in the Hereafter is not an act of trial but rather an "existential fact." However, the verse of *khilāfa* (Q 2:30) is clear in determining worldly life as the locus of vicegerency. Notwithstanding the author's attempt to react to this, his far-fetched interpretations make his position unconvincing.[34] Nothing in the Qur'an or *Sunna* validates the argument that man in Heaven becomes "the *wālī* (governor) of God and master over creatures in an absolute manner," as the author claimed. This interpretation is a projection of an abstract opinion onto a metaphysical world that the mind cannot recognise or comprehend without relying on Revelation. So, what if Revelation contradicts it explicitly? Indeed, the only master over creation, as per the Qur'an, is its Creator.

Furthermore, how can a human being be a master "in an absolute manner" over God's creation?

### *4.1.2 The Lordship-Wordship Dichotomy*

To conclude the remarks on al-Dasūqī's thesis, another point can be raised from the above commentary on the problematic of the transcendence of the human function beyond the sole responsibility for the earth and its resources. Al-Dasūqī, among others, has reduced the concept of *istikhlāf* within the confines of the utilisation of the resources of Earth and its control, and has made worship the means that orients this objective in the right direction so that it would be for God. This reduces the objective of human existence by confining it to material aspects and by making the spiritual and ethical aspects no more than means for those material objectives.

Several scholars seem to emulate the idea of dividing the concept of vicegerency into worship and sovereignty. Abdelaziz Berghout, for instance, writes:

> Civilizational vicegerency means the expression of servitude towards God Almighty and sovereignty over the earth through harmony with God's universal rules and laws, benefitting from the land and its bounties and offering, in return, obedience and thanksgiving, being prepared to meet God is the existential function of man in the realm of this world.[35]

Another researcher says: "Vicegerency is sovereignty over the earth and servitude towards God."[36] However, al-Dasūqī was not the originator of the lordship-worship division but was only following in the footsteps of others before him. The first contemporary Muslim reformist we found referring to that idea is Muḥammad ʿAbduh (d. 1905) who writes that the human being is a "servant to God alone and a master of everything else."[37] We also find this idea clearly articulated by Sayyid Quṭb (d. 1966) in his arguments against the materialistic worldview,[38] which leads us to believe that al-Dasūqī borrowed it directly from Quṭb.

ʿAbd al-Qādir ʿAwda uses the word "control" or "domination," in his definition of vicegerency, in the sense that it is "the right to dominate and control the universe in order to benefit from its bounties."[39] He, however, does not use it in the sense of sovereignty and lordship. Muḥammad Abū al-Qāsim Ḥājj Ḥamad (d. 2004), in turn, used the terms "dominance" and "control over nature" when defining the concept of *istikhlāf*. He alluded to the issue of Lordship as well. However, he reduced *istikhlāf* into a "cosmic vicegerency" that had taken place at an extinct historical period in which God chose one person as His vicegerent. Ḥaj Ḥamad says that vicegerency expresses "the shift from the logic of Divine domination by extraordinary miracles to the logic of 'harnessing,' which reflects 'Divine delegation' to man in the control of nature and beings."[40] "The human being's vicegerency of God is not an expression of mere 'political authority,' but it is a 'cosmic vicegerency' and the domination over nature and beings 'with Divine delegation.'"[41] In the same vein, Seyyed Hossein Nasr writes: "Islam sees men and women as God's vicegerents on earth. Therefore, in the same way that God has power over His creation but is also sustainer and protector, human beings must also combine power over nature with responsibility for its protection and sustenance."[42]

The duality of servanthood and lordship is not a novel idea as it has its roots in Akbarian (in reference to ibn ʿArabī) tradition. Ṣadr al-Dīn al-Qūnawī (d. 672/1274), one of ibn ʿArabī's most influential students wrote: "The perfect man is a bridge between the unseen and the seen worlds and a mirror in which appears the truth of servanthood and lordship."[43] Having said that, one cannot affirm that this division relates to the division adopted by some contemporary scholars, in the sense that lordship in the Akbarian tradition is not about man's obligation to subject and dominate other creatures. Rather, it is God that manifests His lordship over creation through the vicegerent (perfect man), as he is the intermediary between God and creation, and is therefore simultaneously a manifestation of worship and lordship. In the words of another Akbarian scholar describing servanthood and lordship: "The word servant is but an expression that designates the manifestation of the Lord in the form of a servant. The essence is thus a Lord and the appearance is that of a worshipper. The servant is thus a Lord who adores Himself through the form of a worshipper."[44] This marks a clear difference with lordship in the sense of the material domination of man over the creatures. Therefore, we do not see an emphasis in (at least classical) Akbarian writings on material exploitation of the earth as a human existential function, in contrast to what we find in those contemporary advocates of lordship and domination.

The idea of the human being simultaneously being a servant and a lord and bearing the responsibility of worshipping God and dominating creation is, however, first and foremost a biblical one, known under the name "cultural mandate" or "*dominium terrae*."[45] Indeed the Bible reads:

> Then God said, Let us make man in our image after our likeness. And let them have domination over the fish of the sea and over the birds of the heavens and over the livestock and over all the earth and over every creeping thing that creeps on the earth. (Genesis 1:26)

It is in this sense that the biblical interpretation of the naming of all creatures by Adam was directed. Hence, "in the Semitic context of the Bible, the act of naming is rightly interpreted as exercising absolute power."[46]

Charles Peter Wagner (d. 2016) writes:

> Adam and Eve were ready to receive their first recorded Divine commandment: "Have many children, so that your descendants will live all over the earth and bring it under their control. I am putting you in charge of the fish, the birds, and all the wild animals..." (Gen. 1:28, GNB). These first human beings were given what Robert Webber calls "delegated sovereignty" over God's earthly creation. They were to treat creation as God himself would treat it. That was the cultural mandate.[47]

The reformist Christian priest and theologian John Wycliffe (d. 1328) divided *dominium* into "civil *dominium*," which is lordship according to "human law" and "Evangelical" or "Christian" *dominium*. This division is comparable to that of many contemporary Muslims when dividing vicegerency into what is based on Islam and what is not, as we saw with al-Dasūqī and will discuss again below. Wycliffe considered Christian *dominium* superior and more pure than civil *dominium*, as it prevents servitude of man to other than God. He wrote in terms remarkably similar to those of al-Dasūqī saying: "[T]he servant or minister insofar as he is such, looks upon his lord relatively, but every Christian should reciprocally minister to another; therefore he is reciprocally lord and servant… it is clear that evangelical lordship and servitude are not opposites but mutually follow upon one another."[48]

Therefore, it seems that some contemporary scholars tried to project the biblical conception of kingship and domination or Lordship and servanthood on the Qurʾanic notion of *khilāfa*. After affirming that the metaphor of "God as king primarily evokes praise for his magnificence and boundless power and control," in both the Bible and the Qurʾan, Ruben Schenzle writes on the possible similarities between the Bible and the Qurʾan in this context:

> The anthropological bias of ruling and controlling what is on earth (*dominium terrae*) is located in this context. It can be found in the exegetical traditions on Genesis 1:26-30, where the point was already made by early rabbinic exegetes that man's creation in His image (*be-tsememū*) should be regarded as an appeal for acting on God's behalf and in His way (*ki-demūtenū*), thus shifting the anthropomorphic notion of *Imago Dei* in favour of an understanding of *Imitatio Dei*. This concept was supported by Stefan Schreiner, professor of Religious and Jewish Studies, who pointed out the potentially synonymous meaning of the term *khalīfa* in Q 2:30. Moreover, the Anglican scholar Kenneth Cragg in his monograph "The Privilege of Man" noted on this matter: "It is nearly, if not precisely, this notion of the 'dominion' of man which is denoted in the Qurʾanic term *khalīfa*."[49]

This supposed convergence between the Bible and the Qurʾan on man's dominance and kingship on Earth was admitted by several researchers.[50] Hence, it seems that many Muslim reformists went in this direction.[51] However, as we saw in the previous chapter, none of the classical Muslim scholars have interpreted *khilāfa* in this sense. The closest we could find in Islamic tradition, besides the Akbarian opinions that did not go in that direction either, is the opinion of some Sufi scholars who argued that man "is a vicegerent whom God has deputised to act on His behalf in managing the kingdom for he is in His image in this respect."[52] However, they, and the other classical scholars, were not of the opinion that man deputises for God in his attribute as a King or in dominating, controlling, subjugating or ruling over His kingship,[53] unlike the statement by Ruben Schenzle: "as concluded by the 12th century exegete al-Zamakhsharī who commented Q 2:30 as follows: 'we made thee a deputy (*istakhlafnā-ka*) over the kingdom (*mulk*) in the earth.'"[54] However, al-Zamakhsharī was not commenting Q 2:30 but Q 38:26, i.e., a verse where God is attributing *khilāfa* to Dāwūd (David), whom God made a king.[55]

One of the reasons for the abstinence of classical scholars from qualifying man as a lord or a king or dominator or sovereign over the earth may be the fact that the Qur'an explicitly denies any share for man in God's kingship: "Do they have some share in the kingship? - if it were, they would not give to mankind even a single sesame." (Q 4:53, Ahmad Khan). Furthermore, the Qur'an is explicit in attributing lordship to God exclusively, to the extent that one of the major forms of monotheism in Islamic creed is the "monotheism of lordship" (*tawḥīd al-rubūbiyya*), which consists in rejecting any form of true lordship over creation to other than God. Moreover, the majority of classical scholars prohibited the use of the title "vicegerent of Allah" for a political leader because he does not act on behalf of God in his reign, as previously stated. As for those who did allow it, they were not of the opinion that the political leader is vicegerent of God in the sense of domination, control or lordship over his creatures, but only in the sense of executing His will in the management of their affairs, as we saw.

Muḥammad Zarmān, in his approach to the problematic of utilisation of the resources of nature and the question of worship, adopts a thesis similar to al-Dasūqī's. He suggests that worship is a means for the achievement of vicegerency, which lies in the utilisation of the resources of the earth and the exercise of sovereignty over it.[56] Although he argued that worship is broader than vicegerency, and that vicegerency is included in the concept of worship, he also says, after defining vicegerency in the sense of utilisation of the resources of the earth, that its "achievement is the very realisation of the purpose of human existence."[57] He states that it is higher than other religious obligations, such as faith, spirituality and rituals. He says, for example:

> On this basis, we can divide worship – as the supreme objective of creation – into two forms, metaphorically speaking: a minor worship which consists of performing religious obligations and rituals, such as prayer, fasting, *zakāt*, pilgrimage, seeking repentance, and remembering God, among other things which tame human instincts, keep people away from the maze of anxiety, loss and turmoil, make them feel reassured and tranquil, as well as linking them in a strong and lasting manner with God Almighty. The other worship is the major one which is represented in vicegerency on earth by building it, population it, exploiting its bounties, and harnessing its interests for the sake of the human beings. The relationship between the two forms of worship is close-knit and they are rather two sides of the same coin, given that the system of worship in its totality is the ethical framework of vicegerency on earth and its construction.[58]

He continues: "Spiritual elevation makes hearts vivid and consciences clear so that they are ready to undertake the burden of vicegerency."[59] In other words, the purpose of spiritual elevation, which ranks among "minor worship," is vicegerency, that is, the utilisation of the resources of nature, which makes up "major worship." Hence,

> because of the overriding importance of the process of spiritual and moral elevation in implementing the provisions of the project of vicegerency in the

> manner that pleases God Almighty, it is something that Islam has given special attention to and considered an essential and original goal of vicegerency, and one of its strongest dimensions.[60]

Zarmān continues:

> Based on the foregoing, the process of vicegerency [which he previously defined as the utilisation of the resources of the earth and its building and population] – in Qurʾanic discourse – cannot be properly manifested unless it integrates faith (*ʾīmān*) and the building and population of the earth (*ʿumrān*), and wherein an equilibrium exists between the pursuit of spiritual elevation and the endeavours of material and civilizational advancement. If the human being's attention heads towards one side at the expense of the other, his movement becomes slanted and his sense of equilibrium is lost.[61]

Zarmān then engages in expressing viewpoints that adopt the dichotomies of religion and worldly life and worship and interest.[62]

What was previously noted applies equally to this thesis in the sense that if vicegerency is only a part of worship, then why does God present Adam as a "*khalīfa*" (vicegerent) and not in a way that includes his entire function? The answer may lie in Zarmān's view that vicegerency, in the sense of utilising the resources of the earth, is the major worship, while faith and spirituality make up minor worship, and the latter has been established in order to be able to achieve the former. This type of argument poses a serious problem. In addition to the fact that the author did not put forward any argument that could justify this hierarchical division, the final purpose of worship, religion and spirituality is reduced to material meanings. Although Zarmān stated that spiritual elevation is one of the means of vicegerency in some contexts, the role of this elevation is ambiguous in others. It is not clear if he meant that it was merely a means to vicegerency or that it was simultaneously one of its goals or dimensions. Be that as it may, the problem remains in the meaning of the human being's deputisation for God in terms of spiritual aspiration, or the meaning of deputisation for God as the goal of spiritual elevation. How can a human being act on behalf of God in worshipping God or in getting closer to Him? It is a problematic that exists, once again, due to the lack of rooting of the meaning of vicegerency theologically and ontologically.

Overall, it appears that the majority of contemporary Muslim intellectuals have reduced the concept of vicegerency, as a human existential function, to building and populating the earth (*ʿimārat al-arḍ*) and the utilisation of its resources. This reductionist approach dismisses some aspects of the Qurʾanic text regarding man's existential duties. As I have explained, the attempts to reconcile those aspects with the material aspect of the function of man could not resolve the problem. There is yet another major problem in these definitions that exacerbates the problem of reductionism. This problem relates to the distortion at the level of theological and ontological rooting of the concept of vicegerency, in the sense of man's deputisation on behalf of God. These studies argue that man is a vicegerent of God in utilising the resources of the earth, caring for it, and benefitting from it or dominating it. However, the earth and its laws exist with the command of God and are not in need of the work of man; so, a human being cannot act as a vicegerent of God in that. On the other hand, building, populating and utilising the earth cannot be called an act of vicegerency. Did God utilise the resources of the earth and benefit from its wealth so that man could be his vicegerent in that? This is one of the many aspects of distortion and confusion in the rooting of the concept of vicegerency, as will be explained further in this study. If the meaning of *istikhlāf* on behalf of God had been controlled ontologically and theologically, it would have been impossible to argue that man is the vicegerent of God in this sense.

We could not find any of the contemporary scholars paying attention to the above problem, except the illustrious Tunisian exegete Muḥammad al-Ṭāhir ibn ʿĀshūr (d. 1973).[63] The solution proposed by ibn ʿĀshūr is to divert the meaning of vicegerency to a metaphorical meaning, since building and populating the earth is not a Divine action. However, I do not see any reliable consideration justifying this interpretation, because I consider that God did entrust man with one of his actions according to the proper sense of vicegerency, which will be developed in the following chapters. Moreover, I did not find evidence supporting the idea that the object of vicegerency resides in building and populating the earth or any of the concepts (such as "to rule over the things on earth"[64]) that forced ibn ʿĀshūr to interpret the concept of vicegerency and to divert its meaning to a metaphorical one.

The definition of the concept of *istikhlāf* adopted under this first category is not a novel one. It transpires from the previous chapter that a number of classical scholars defined the concept of *istikhlāf* in the same sense, as an act of building and populating the earth, ploughing, planning, manufacturing and extracting the benefits of nature, or organising and harnessing the means of the universe, possessing the earth and managing it, etc. However, some of the problematics identified in these definitions do not apply to all the definitions given by classical scholars because, unlike contemporaries, some of them did not provide this definition in the context of man's vicegerency of God on Earth or in the context of man's religious duties. Indeed, some of them expressed this view in the context of man's *khilāfa* of man, or in the context of vicegerency or *ʿimārat al-arḍ* as an inevitable existential fact and not a religious responsibility, which is the case for ibn Khaldūn as we saw and also for al-Iṣfahānī as we will see in the last chapter. The idea that the meaning of vicegerency refers to sovereignty, lordship, control and domination over the earth, as a human function, also seems to be part of these novel contemporary definitions, as argued before. We were unable to find any classical scholar who espoused this point of view.[65] This also holds true for the argument of some authors that, as a human existential function, vicegerency may be carried out on behalf of God or others[66] and that it applies to worldly life as to the Hereafter. Furthermore, one novelty among contemporaries is their extensive debate on vicegerency as a human function and their attempt to root it and apply it to certain areas, such as economic and environmental issues.

## 4.2 Adherence to God's Will and Commands and their Implementation on Earth

The most notable reformists who defined vicegerency in terms of adherence and implementation of God's commands on Earth are Badīʿ al-Zamān Saʿīd al-Nūrsī (d. 1960),[67] Abū al-Aʿlā al-Mawdūdī,[68] Muḥammad al-Ṭāhir ibn ʿĀshūr[69] (d. 1973), and other contemporary scholars.[70] Some of these scholars, however, hold that "the meaning of *khilāfa* is the building and population of the earth (*ʿimārat al-arḍ*) in accordance with God's orders."[71]

It appears from the definitions of the tenets of this category that the object of vicegerency is God's will and His orders. It is true that some of the authors of these definitions have introduced many meanings to the concept of vicegerency, such as "the elevation of man in his individual self, social entity, and his method in dealing with the environment to seek God's favour in nature,"[72] among other meanings of vicegerency, its goals, results or means. However, our focus in this context remains on the object of vicegerency. Assuming that vicegerency means deputisation for God, then the starting point for the determination of the meaning of vicegerency should be to identify the locus of that deputisation before talking about its means, goals and results.

It seems that most of the definitions under this category have adopted a comprehensive meaning of the concept of vicegerency and that they have not reduced it to one thing or another. This is due to the identification of the object of vicegerency in the role of commitment and fulfilment of Divine will, which, of course, encompasses all aspects of religion. Nevertheless, this definition of *istikhlāf* and identification of the object of vicegerency are not immune to numerous problems that have not been resolved by the authors of these definitions.

The problems raised in this respect include the fact that the identification of the object of vicegerency in the Divine will and command strips the human being of his uniqueness within the function of vicegerency. All creatures are implementers of Divine will and commands, as is clear from the texts of Revelation, which would imply that they are all vicegerents. Moreover, it should be noted here that God's will is already achieved in the universe and in human natural disposition (*fiṭra*), as will be explained later in detail; therefore, the human being cannot be assigned to achieve what is already achieved. Hence, it cannot be said that the human being deputises for God in achieving the Divine cosmic will (*irāda kawniyya*), and the most that can be said in this regard is that man is entrusted to preserve the existing will of God. However, the outstanding question here is: Can a person act on behalf of God in order to achieve the revealed will (*irāda sharʿiyya*)? The revealed will, that is, Revelation, does not bring about anything additional to the universe or to the *fiṭra* that has not yet been achieved. It is only a means to preserve the Divine will that exists in the universe, as will be explained later. If we assume that the object of vicegerency is Divine will, then the human being is not a vicegerent of God in achieving it, because it is already achieved. Rather, he may be a vicegerent of God in preserving some of its aspects, but the outstanding question still lies in identifying those aspects. As for the revealed orders, they serve only as means for that preservation and are not an object in themselves, as they do not achieve anything additional. Moreover, the opinion that the human being is God's vicegerent in the sense of deputising for Him in achieving His revealed orders or abiding by them, is vague, as the fulfilment of these orders or commitment to them is not intended in itself, but is a means to achieve the object of vicegerency. Hence, the concept of vicegerency must be defined by identifying the object of vicegerency before its means.

The problem of lack of clarity in distinguishing between the ontological meaning of vicegerency by determining the object of vicegerency, on one hand, and its objectives, results, means and foundations, on the other, is recurrent in the writings of most of those who have dealt with this topic. A case in point here is ʿAbd al-Majīd al-Najjār, the author of one of the most sophisticated theses in this field.

Al-Najjār incorporates many meanings and theories to the concept of vicegerency, such as individual, group, material and methodological elevation, *jihād* and the use and preservation of the environment.[73] Nonetheless, he does not clearly indicate how all of these meanings are integrated into the concept of vicegerency. Are they part of its dimensions, foundations, means, outcomes or purposes? How does this relate to deputisation, and how can it be done on behalf of God? Al-Najjār argues that Islamic civilisation can only be based on what he calls the "jurisprudence of *khilāfa*"[74] or the "jurisprudence of *istikhlāf*."[75] He believes that the jurisprudence of vicegerency is an element that "characterises Islamic civilization with permanent elevation of the human being, be it within his individual self, his social self or in his method of life. All of these three manifestations of elevation are thus governed by the jurisprudence of vicegerency."[76] While he considers these three dimensions (elevation of the individual, group and methodology in dealing with the environment) manifestations of elevation in this context, in another study he considers them "the pillars that constitute the principle of vicegerency as a basic principle in the jurisprudence of Islamic civilization."[77] He then proceeds in both studies to elaborate upon these three "manifestations" or "pillars." However, the position of these three elements in the function of vicegerency is not clear in his arguments. Sometimes, he considers them to be manifestations of civilisational elevation governed by vicegerency, while at other times, he considers them to be the pillars that constitute the principle of vicegerency. Furthermore, he gives the impression that they are "among the requirements of vicegerency on earth."[78] However, it is very likely that he does not see them either as constituting vicegerency or a part of it, but rather as the means for its achievement. So,

> the three of them are a major jurisprudential principle of Islamic civilization in the elevation of the human being so that man's vicegerency of God may be fulfilled. [...] Since it is a jurisprudence that derives its strength from the doctrine of vicegerency, we entitled it "the jurisprudence of vicegerency of God in Islamic civilization."[79]

It transpires that much of what al-Najjār has said about the concept of vicegerency, whether in his book *Khilāfat al-Insān bayna al-Waḥy wa-l-ʿAql* (The

Vicegerency of Man, Between Revelation and Reason), in the research study on "al-Istikhlāf fī Fiqh al-Taḥaḍḍur al-Islāmī" (Vicegerency in the Jurisprudence of Islamic Civilization), in his book *Fiqh al-Taḥaḍḍur al-Islāmī* (The Jurisprudence of Islamic Civilization) or in his other works in which the term is extensively used, revolves around the means and approaches leading to the achievement of vicegerency or its applications in theory and practice. However, there is no substantial explanation or discussion of the essence of vicegerency, or what he calls the "the doctrine of vicegerency." This lack of consideration of the very concept of vicegerency can be observed through the absence of the establishment of any ontological link between these "principles of vicegerency" (elevation in its three meanings) and the very concept of vicegerency as man's deputisation of God. For example, on the "pillar" or "principle" of "the vicegerency of/in individual elevation," he writes: "Individual elevation becomes 'vicegerencial' (*khilāfī*) through the individual's continuous development of his own capabilities." He further argues: "It is a 'vicegerencial' type of elevation when it is intended for servitude towards God; otherwise, it is not a 'vicegerencial' elevation."[80] He then proceeds to differentiate between what is "vicegerencial" and what is not by including those elements that are compatible with the principles of Islam within the "vicegerencial" category and excluding those that are contrary to them. Nonetheless, he does not draw any link between the meaning of vicegerency and these principles or explain the relationship of vicegerency as a human task in the deputisation on behalf of God and spiritual elevation and other points he has copiously discussed. It appears as though the terms *khilāfa* or *istikhlāf* for al-Najjār are nothing but synonyms for the word "Islam." This also applies to all other concepts that al-Najjār has considered part of the pillars of elevation, such as monotheism (*tawḥīd*), etc. He does not explain the meaning of what he calls "the doctrine of vicegerency," nor does he develop a vicegerency theory as such. On account of the absence of an ontological link and theological rooting of the meaning of vicegerency, it seems that what al-Najjār has developed is closer to being a theory of the doctrinal principles of Islamic civilisation bearing the title of "vicegerency" than to a philosophy or theory of vicegerency. This applies, first and foremost, to most of the contemporary writings on vicegerency as an existential function, as will be discussed below.

Furthermore, al-Najjār falls prey to the dichotomies of soul/body, worship/interest and religion/world or interest/Hereafter. He argues that in order to achieve vicegerency, a balance must be created between the spirit that connects man to God and the body that connects man to the earth. He cites the Qur'anic verse: "By the means of what Allah has given you, seek the abode of the Hereafter, while not forgetting your share of this world" (Q 28:77, Ali Qarai). As has already been clarified, this verse indicates that the quest for the Hereafter is attained through what the human being has achieved in this world, but it does not say that the quest for the share of worldly life is detached from the quest for the Hereafter. Nothing in the verse justifies the dichotomy of interest/religion or world/worship, nor does the verse imply the view that "the quest for the Hereafter is attained through purification of the soul and taming it to adjust to worship and the share of worldly life lies in the nourishment of the body and its material needs."[81] Rather, the purification of the soul and worship are worldly interests before being quests for rewards in the Hereafter, and the gratification of the body and the satiation of its material needs reinforce the quest for the Hereafter. What is required is not just the establishment of a balance between the soul and the body, but rather a balance between all aspirations and human impulses, since conflict may occur between two spiritual demands and not only between material and spiritual ones. The conflict, therefore, is not between the soul and the body, as will be discussed later.

The problematic of harmonising worship and the utilisation of the natural resources of the world, which occurred in the definitions under the first category, does, at first glance, not seem to apply to this second category. That is because of the fact that the obligation to comply with God's orders covers the meaning of worship, which would mean that vicegerency is synonymous to worship. Nevertheless, the relationship between vicegerency and worship remains shrouded in ambiguity in the theses of this second category. In ʿAbd al-Majīd al-Najjār's thesis, for instance, the relationship between vicegerency and worship lacks clarity. If vicegerency, as he has defined it, is the deputisation of God in the execution of His orders, does this mean that vicegerency is worship itself, or something separate or a part of it or more than that? We could not find the answer in the theses of this category.

Al-Najjār sometimes conveys that vicegerency is worship and that the latter "equals its meaning," and that vicegerency includes all human actions in the way of obedience to God, be they individual, collective, material or moral, thus constituting "a movement of worship devoted to God." Other times, however, the impression the reader gets is that vicegerency and worship are two different things, as in al-Najjār's statement: "Both of them are objectives for human existence." Again, at other times, he implies that vicegerency is only a part of worship, as in his argument that the concept is "imbued with the meaning of servitude." Likewise, it may be inferred from what he has written that worship is one of the foundations of vicegerency, as in his statement that vicegerency is "based on worship" and his statement: "servitude upon which vicegerency is based."[82]

This again highlights the deficiency in the rooting of the concept of vicegerency among contemporary scholars. It should be reckoned that theorisation about or the rooting of the concept of vicegerency as an existential human function may not transpire or develop except after resolving this problematic in a way that fulfils the purpose. What is the precise relation between vicegerency and worship? If vicegerency is yet another name for worship, then the reason for dubbing it so should be clarified, as should be the manner in which the human being should be distinguished through the task of vicegerency, since all creatures are worshippers. Or, if vicegerency is only a part of worship, then why is Adam, i.e., the human being, described only in terms of a part of his existential function? Or if vicegerency and worship are two distinct objectives, then why did the Qurʾan limit the objective of the creation of the human being to worship alone in *sūrat al-Dhāriyāt* (Q 51:56)?

Besides defining the object of vicegerency in terms of the obligation to abide by God's guidance and laws, Aḥmad Faraḥāt says that vicegerency in this sense is the "voluntary worship of God."[83] This may justify why the privilege of vicegerency is conferred upon man rather than any other creature, since the obedience of other creatures is but an involuntary act. Faraḥāt, however, does not clarify if vicegerency is but another name for worship or a part of it or broader than that, etc. By stating that vicegerency is the obligation to "comply with God's guidance and laws,"[84] and not their implementation or realisation, Faraḥāt is spared the problematic of having to address the fact that Divine command and will are already achieved before man's intervention, as pointed out before. In other respects, however, all the comments made in connection with the category under discussion apply equally to Faraḥāt's definition.

As he approaches it within the definition given above, Faraḥāt makes vicegerency a duty for all human beings, saying that "disbelief that may be associated with some people does not, in essence, stand in contradiction with the principle of vicegerency of the human being on earth."[85] Later, however, he restricts the function of vicegerency, as defined above, to believers only. He says: "We can distinguish two types of vicegerency: a cosmic one common to all people, and an Islamic vicegerency specific to believers only."[86] This appears to be clearly contradictory, for he had defined vicegerency as "the voluntary worship of God by complying with His guidance and laws," and asserted that it is a duty "that includes the entire human race – believers and nonbelievers."[87] This also implies the existence of some form of determinism, since non-believers were not created for the existential function that the believers were created for.

Perhaps what Faraḥāt meant was that the fruits of Islamic vicegerency will only be reaped by the believers in accordance with the Qur'anic verse: "Allah has promised those of you who have faith and do righteous deeds that He will surely make them successors/vicegerents in the earth" (Q 24:55, b.o. Ali Qarai). However, this does not mean that vicegerency is specific to believers only, but rather all human beings have been created for this purpose and have been entrusted with it. If some people do not adhere to their existential function and do not, consequently, reap its fruits, it does not mean that they are not concerned with vicegerency and that it is specific only to believers.

In the conclusion of his study, Faraḥāt states briefly that what he meant by cosmic vicegerency is the succession of a generation that did not achieve the mission of Islamic vicegerency by another generation. It is, therefore, "a cosmic vicegerency that takes place when the defunct nation is superseded by another one without the latter having any will or choice in that."[88] The following Qur'anic verses may contextualise this process: "Remember when He made you successors after the people of Noah." (Q 7:69, Sahih Int); "He said, 'Maybe your Lord will destroy your enemy and make you successors in the land, and then He will see how you act.'" (Q 7:129, Ali Qarai); and "Your Lord is the All-sufficient dispenser of mercy. If He wishes, He will take you away, and make whomever He wishes succeed you, just as He produced you from the descendants of another people." (Q 6:133, Ali Qarai).

However, the failure of the generation that had been entrusted before the one that took over to realise the mission of vicegerency does not mean that their vicegerency was cosmic in the sense that it was inevitably hereditary. It just means that they were vicegerents who did not abide by their mission; so, they were vicegerents in the sense of being entrusted with *khilāfa* just like the rest of mankind. They, however, were not true vicegerents given that they did not fulfil their mission. The emergence of the inheriting nation in lieu of the succeeded one, without the former's volitional choice, does not mean that its vicegerency is cosmic, that is, inevitable, as it has the choice to perform the function of vicegerency in any case. It is true that the fact of succeeding the disbelieving nation is inevitable or cosmic, a process in which the successor does not have any choice, but does this justify its exclusion from "Islamic vicegerency" and the restriction of the latter to only those believers who have succeeded a believing nation? Is the mere succession of one nation over another called vicegerency, or is it the succession related to an existential function? Animal nations succeed one another without their choice, but does this make the animal a vicegerent in the cosmic sense? In any case, there does not seem to be any justification for the use of the concept of "cosmic vicegerency," especially if we take into consideration that vicegerency and worship are inextricably linked. Faraḥāt himself defines vicegerency as something "common to all people" by virtue of being an act of "voluntary worship of God." So, can voluntary worship be divided into material and Islamic worship? Or does he mean that this voluntary worship is what he calls "Islamic vicegerency" that excludes "the cosmic one"? Accordingly, Islamic vicegerency becomes "common to all people." Hence, there is no justification for the term "cosmic vicegerency" at any rate. Or does he perhaps mean that this voluntary worship is the vicegerency in the sense of being the existential function of man, and that the cosmic vicegerency is that in the sense of a cosmic and inevitable truth for the human being? However, this again does not justify the exclusion of non-believers from Islamic vicegerency. All of this compromises the very basis for this kind of division. However, it seems that this confusion goes back to a disruption at the terminological level.

Indeed, one of the problems of Faraḥāt's thesis is that it does not establish the meaning of vicegerency. For example, on the issue of the object of vicegerency, he cited some scholars, some of whom we mentioned in the previous chapter, who argue that vicegerency could be on behalf of other human beings, God or in relation to God, but only as an honorific title. However, he does not clearly settle on a certain opinion, but seems to embrace the idea that *khilāfa* is the succession of generations and that the human being is called the vicegerent of God as an honorific title only, not because he is really a vicegerent or deputy of God. If this is the case, it becomes necessary to justify the labelling of the human existential function as *istikhlāf* in the sense of deputisation of one generation over another, and not with a label that conveys a more honourable or superior state reflected by human reality. Generational succession is self-evident and does not foreshadow any existential function, in addition to the fact that it is not specific to human beings. Besides this, it is also necessary to explain the relationship between the definition of *khilāfa* as an obligation on the part of man to comply with God's commands and the question of intergenerational succession. Be that as it may, the problem of ontological control and doctrinal rooting of the meaning of *istikhlāf* resurfaces here. Consequently, Faraḥāt's ideas fell into contradiction and got entangled as he tried to reconcile the idea of vicegerency as an existential function for all human beings and the idea of vicegerency as the inheritance of the former generation. How can the human existential task consist in the deputisation on behalf of or succession of a disbelieving nation? Indeed, here comes into play the loophole of "cosmic vicegerency."

Overall, it appears that the identification of the object of vicegerency in terms of the obligation to execute or abide by God's will and orders is not of much help in determining man's existential function, on account of the vagueness of this definition, in addition to the fact that it is not impervious to numerous objections and is not supported by an ontological rooting of the concept of vicegerency. It emerges from the previous chapter that the description of the object of vicegerency in terms of execution of the Divine will and orders is an opinion adopted by some classical scholars. However, what is new in contemporary literature, in addition to the attempt at providing a detailed explanation of the means and the outcomes of vicegerency, is the division of vicegerency into an Islamic and a cosmic one, a division that does not appear to have a justifiable ground, as it were, since all generations can be said to have succeeded their predecessors (an inevitable succession) in order to achieve the mission of vicegerency with no distinction that could justify this division. This division is thus the consequence of another innovation in contemporary thought, i.e., the argument that vicegerency as an existential function means the succession of generations. Indeed, classical scholars that defined vicegerency as generational succession did not regard this existential fact as a function or religious responsibility.[89]

## 4.3 The Responsibility of Choice and Disposition

If one of the problematics in determining the object of vicegerency in terms of worship or compliance to the Divine commands or utilisation of the goods of the earth is the fact that all creatures are worshippers, abiding by God's will and utilising the goods of the earth, it remains that what distinguishes the human being in those aspects is his freedom of choice and will. It is perhaps this perception that has prompted the third category to identify the object of vicegerency in terms of these concepts.

Some of the earliest contemporary writers to espouse this point of view are the Shiite sociologist ʿAlī Sharīʿatī (d. 1977)[90] and the Egyptian author ʿĀʾisha Bint al-Shāṭiʾ[91] (d. 1998), among others.[92]

While resolving some of the problematic issues related to the definitions provided under the previous two categories, as highlighted above, the identification of the object of vicegerency under this category is not free of counterarguments that bring about even more problems than the preceding ones. One of them is that freedom of will, disposition and choice is a general matter that does not in itself determine the existential function of the human being. Freedom in itself is not a task, notwithstanding being a responsibility required by man's existential function. Having been created to worship God like all other creatures, the human being is distinguished by virtue of the choice he has been given to perform this task or not perform it. It is this freedom of choice, among other qualities, that gives man the specificity and elevation of status, but it is not worship as such, that is to say, it is not man's function as such. Hence, the problem of determining the object of vicegerency still persists.

Moreover, if the meaning of vicegerency is to deputise God, then there is no basis for the argument that man is a vicegerent of God in the matter of freedom. There are several considerations for this, including the fact that human freedom is different from God's. The scope of human freedom of choice within the framework of his/her existential role is within the limits of what is possible in terms of good or evil and from within his/her position as an entrusted being. God, however, is not entrusted with anything and is not asked about anything, His freedom is limitless and He is not obliged to choose between good or evil. If the freedom of the human being lies within the framework of his mission to choose between good and evil, then he is not a vicegerent of God in that, because God's freedom is not likewise. The human being's freedom is not a real or, at least, an absolute one, in the sense that he is only free to choose from the choices God has made available; the Qurʾan reads: "And your Lord does create and choose as He pleases: no choice have they." (Q 28:68, Hilali & Khan).

There is no aspect of the relationship between human freedom and God's freedom in which the human being could be a deputy of God in terms of freedom. Sharīʿatī tried to justify this definition on the basis of a similarity between God's freedom and human freedom, in that the human being is able to "act even against his nature and instinct" and that God is able to act "even contrary to the universal system and laws."[93] Nevertheless, this is an analogy that entails a variation that invalidates the comparison. The human being, whom Sharīʿatī describes as capable of "acting in the same way as God Almighty, doing whatever he wants even if it is contrary to the physical laws and to nature,"[94] is, in Qurʾanic terms, engaging in an evil act when he does what is "contrary to the physical laws and to nature" since he is in violation of Divine will. As for God, He is the establisher of these laws, through which He acts as He wishes, upholding them, transcending or violating them. He is not bound by them, unlike the human being who has been entrusted to uphold them. Therefore, how can it be said that the human being deputises for God in a mission (i.e., in choosing between good and evil and taking responsibility for doing so) that is not God's at all?

Moreover, one of the considerations that challenges the argument that the human being is God's vicegerent in the matter of freedom is the fact that freedom is not a Divine act, task or goal. It is true that one of God's attributes is that He is "*faʿʿālun li-mā yurīd*" ("Indeed, your Lord does whatever He desires." Q 11:107, Ali Qarai), and also that He is the Omnipotent, All-Powerful and Supreme Determiner. However, these attributes are in the nature of God and are inherent to His Divine Entity, but they are not Divine acts or functions such that the human being can act as God's vicegerent in this regard. This section of God's attributes is what some Muslim theologians called "self-attributes" (*ṣifāt dhātiyya*), which are the eternal attributes inherent to God's Entity and are not related to a Divine act in His creation. For example, one of the Divine self-attributes is Life. Accordingly, is the human being God's vicegerent in Life? God is also the All-Knowing; so, can man be a vicegerent of God in Knowledge? Rather, vicegerency lies in performance, not in mere attributes, i.e., it lies in a characteristic from those that theologians have called "action-attributes" (*ṣifāt fiʿliyya*), which are attributes related to the creation and are not eternal or inherent to His Entity; rather, they are attributes that occur after the Divine act in His creation.[95] God has extended to many creatures some imperfect aspects of His own attributes so that they can fulfil their existential function, such as life, hearing, sight, mercy, power, etc. This, however, does not mean that they are vicegerents in that, because vicegerency, as per its Qurʾanic meaning, is entrustment with the responsibility of acting on behalf of God in a mission that belongs to Him initially,[96] as will be developed in the next chapter. The similarity in some attributes does not imply that the one who looks alike represents the One who is resembled in that similitude. Just as hearing, for example, is a characteristic that enables the human being to perform his existential task, and for the use of which he is held accountable, so is freedom. The fact that the human being is uniquely free does not mean that freedom is the task with which he has been entrusted, but rather it means that the nature of the human existential function necessitates freedom as a means to achieve it, contrary to the case of other creatures. Vicegerency in the sense of entrusting the human being to act on behalf of God in executing a Divine mission requires freedom, because without it the human being cannot be a deputy of God, but rather an inevitable executor like all other creatures. However, freedom does not determine the nature of that same Divine mission. Hence, freedom to choose between good and evil is not a Divine task, which means that the human being cannot be a vicegerent of God in that.

Inspired by the idea of freedom, ʿAbd al-Salām al-Aḥmar divided vicegerency into a "faith-based" (*istikhlāf ʾīmānī*) type in which the choice of the human being is directed towards faith and the other teachings of Revelation, and a "positive vicegerency" (*istikhlāf waḍʿī*) whereby the human being builds and populates the earth and uses its bounties on the basis of "reason alone" without choosing faith and religion.[97] This division is comparable to Faraḥāt's division of vicegerency into "Islamic" and "cosmic" vicegerency as we have seen.

As discussed before, vicegerency is only determined by the human being's execution of the task for which he is created; else, it cannot be called vicegerency. Therefore, there is no justification for ascribing the term "vicegerency" to the work of anybody who shuns Revelation and depends on "reason alone." In what sense should this be called vicegerency? Is it so by virtue of being just a "choice"? Rather, vicegerency is a function, whereas freedom of choice is a means. Furthermore, vicegerency (as admitted by the author himself)[98] is on behalf of God, and the choice of evil cannot be done on behalf of God in any sense, as stated above. Also, how can, for instance, the objective of the "materialists" be deemed a form of vicegerency as claimed by al-Aḥmar? This position is due to the identification of vicegerency in terms of mere choice and the absence of a comprehensive view of the human existential function upon which the concept should be based.

Accordingly, al-Aḥmar argues that all human actions, regardless of their intentions and executors, are considered acts of vicegerency:

> It is worth noting that all the actions of human beings on earth achieve the objective of vicegerency, in that they are an exercise – in some ways – of the responsibility of freedom of action, and they bear the outcomes of the human being's choice and the toil and affliction of his performance, as well as the consequences in the form of either a blessed or wretched life in this world and in the Hereafter.[99]

Thus, according to this view, vicegerency is not an existential function, but rather an existential fact. On this basis, al-Aḥmar also divided vicegerency into two other categories: The first is general vicegerency, which is represented in "the human freedom that is restricted by the human being's responsibility for his various actions on earth."[100] The general objective of this type of vicegerency is "the building and population of the earth in any direction that it takes place – temporally and spatially."[101] The second type is particular vicegerency, which is the "entrustment and choice of the believing category, should the conditions be conducive for it, to carry out leadership tasks over other nations."[102] I do not know the source of the author's argument that vicegerency may be specific to the believers alone and that one of the tasks of vicegerency of the believing group is "leadership over other nations." Rather, vicegerency is the mission of all human beings and nowhere in the texts of Revelation is there evidence that it is exclusive to the believers. As for the fact that its rewards and outcomes concern the believers who have performed their mission, it is an obvious matter, as previously stated, and it does not mean that non-believers are not required to undertake it. Regarding the idea that it is a mission of leadership over other nations, we could not find any instance from the text of Revelation that defines vicegerency in this sense or that supports this idea in one way or in another. So, there is no justification for this division which, like the previous one, is distorted as a result of defining the object of vicegerency in terms of the freedom of action and choice.

Another consequence of al-Aḥmar's identification of the object of vicegerency in terms of freedom is his opinion that jinn, in addition to humans, are vicegerents who deputise for God.[103] The fact that jinn are free to choose either the path of good or evil does not, however, mean that they are vicegerents, as there is no evidence that the function of vicegerency in the sense of deputisation for God concerns jinn, in addition to human beings. Rather, the Qur'an named Adam a vicegerent and did not ascribe the vicegerency title to another creature besides the human being, while angels, as well as Satan, who is of the jinn, were asked to prostrate to Adam by virtue of that title. As for the fact that jinn were created to worship God, this task is common to all creatures and does not imply that they are vicegerents.

Whereas vicegerency, as per this category, lies in the freedom to choose between good and evil, all the good that a human being produces and the teachings of religion that he adheres to are forms of vicegerency, and anything that is evil or contradictory to the teachings of religion is an act of vicegerency as well. The choice between belief and disbelief, for example, is the task of the human being in vicegerency, and the human being is deputised to take care of his soul, in the sense that he is entrusted to either embrace belief or disbelief.[104]

Since the faith-based type of vicegerency is only a matter of choosing acts of goodness and the teachings of religion, the concept of vicegerency as an existential human task becomes a loose term gathering all the teachings of religion without offering a philosophical frame that rules those teachings and connects them to that function. So, the difference between the concept of vicegerency as a function and the concept of Islam as a religion disappears. Al-Aḥmar incorporates all of the teachings of religion into the concept of vicegerency without showing how the concept controls these teachings within a coherent system; rather, he considers everything that is Islamic to fall under the faith-based form of vicegerency. Thus, the term "vicegerency" becomes no more than a synonym or a substitute for the term "Islam." After drawing a list of religious teachings which consist of professing monotheism, fearing God, appealing to God and remembering Him, repenting, supplicating, being pious, spending wealth in the way of God, praying, fasting, performing pilgrimage, enjoining good and forbidding evil, doing justice, being righteous and obedient towards parents, etc., al-Aḥmar says that

> all of these objectives and the like are considered an extension of the objective of vicegerency and its behavioural application. By complying with them and manifesting them in one's thought and behaviour, the basic objective of the responsibility of vicegerency, which assumes many forms, whether as beliefs in one's heart, behavioural obligations, or a combination of the two, is established.[105]

If we were to amend al-Aḥmar's terms slightly by saying, "All of these objectives and the likes are considered an extension of the Islamic religion and its behavioural application. By complying with them and manifesting them in one's thought and behaviour, the basic objective of the responsibility of Islamic religiosity is established," it would have made no difference at all. The issue here again is that of replacing Islam with the title "vicegerency," without any addition in developing a theory or philosophical vision of man's existential function, in a way that controls the teachings of religion, thought and other human activities. This applies to all that al-Aḥmar has said in describing vicegerency as a way to achieve the welfare of the human being in the worldly life and the Hereafter, and as "a strong incentive for people to build the land and populate it, promote virtue and guidance among human beings, reduce evil and the causes of corruption,"[106] among other thoughts expressed in connection with the merits of vicegerency. He did not, however, link faith and the other teachings of religion to vicegerency, except by saying that the human being is a vicegerent in choosing or refusing to accept these teachings, that these teachings are objectives or extensions and applications of vicegerency, and that they reinforce this responsibility. But he does this without establishing any ontological connection or theological rooting of the relationship of these concepts to deputisation. Neither does he demonstrate how vicegerency applies in the teachings of religion, or how the latter contribute to the realisation of the mission for which the human being is created. This in addition to the fact that that very function or mission remains unclear, as it remains connected to the mere choice between good and evil. This applies equally to the rest of al-Aḥmar's ideas. For instance, he further argues that the implementation of *Sharīʿa* is part of vicegerency because humans have been entrusted with that, and this would help them achieve faith-based vicegerency. However, once again, the author does not draw any ontological connection between this and the function of vicegerency.

Al-Aḥmar calls for the consideration of vicegerency as a general objective framing "all Qurʾanic objectives" because it is "capable of revealing the systemicity of the Qurʾanic discourse" as "the primary objective of God Almighty behind the creation of the human being." Therefore, vicegerency is appropriate for the "framing of the overall Divine objectives, especially those of the Qurʾan, *Sharīʿa* and civilization" and is capable of "absorbing the various intellectual and human trends and stimulating Islamic civilizational achievement."[107] However, none of these appear in al-Aḥmar's thesis, given that what he has put forward in view of the meaning of vicegerency is not an existential function but merely an existential fact, which is not the purpose for which God created the human being, but rather a means to achieve that purpose. In what way then could the fact of the human being's freedom of choice of good and evil frame all the objectives of Revelation, demonstrate the systemicity of its discourse, absorb various intellectual and human trends and stimulate civilisational achievement? This is, as per his definition of vicegerency, only possible when (faith-based) vicegerency is made to appear as merely another name for Islam. In that case, there is no point talking about vicegerency as the word "Islam" dispenses with its use.

All of the above perceptions that serve to determine the identity of the object of vicegerency in terms of the responsibility for choice are not suitable for the formulation of a vicegerency theory, in the sense that choice is not a function and that the human being's existential function is not determined by it. It seems that the identification of the object of vicegerency in terms of the responsibility of choice is a modern idea that was not debated in classical scholarship. This is equally true for the division of vicegerency into a faith-based form and a positivistic one, and also into general for all people and specific to the believers only. Even though some classical Muslim scholars have argued that *istikhlāf* concerns only the prophets and those who are in "obedience to God and ruling justly among His creation,"[108] they did not proceed to a similar division. They excluded from *istikhlāf* those who do not belong to the righteous group, but they did not merge the latter into another section of *istikhlāf*, as some contemporaries have done. It is also a modern innovation to claim that jinn are, in addition to human beings, concerned with the mission of vicegerency, as well as the argument that all human actions – good and bad – are considered acts of vicegerency.

## 4.4 The Manifestation of Divine Attributes and Ethics on Earth

The Egyptian scholar al-Bahī al-Khūlī (d. 1977) ranks together with the founder of the International Institute of Islamic Thought Ismāʿīl al-Fārūqī (d. 1986) among the most prominent advocates of this definition of the object of vicegerency. Their position is closely related to the opinion of some Sufi scholars in the classical heritage that defines vicegerency as an act of deputisation of God in manifesting His attributes, as we saw before. Al-Khūlī rejected the views and definitions of contemporary scholars in their claim that the object of vicegerency lies in harnessing nature, exploring its laws, exerting sovereignty over it and managing and benefitting from its resources.[109] In the eyes of al-Khūlī, the nature of vicegerency, that is, its object, or the role entrusted to the human being, is to introduce into this material world uncharacteristic traits and values derived from his spirit, which is of heavenly nature.[110] Ismāʿīl al-Fārūqī's conception of vicegerency is not far away from al-Khūlī's.[111]

Al-Khūlī and al-Fārūqī agree on two main ideas that constitute the basis of their understanding of the function of vicegerency. The first idea is that ethical values can only be achieved by God or by the human being, who deputises on behalf of Him. This is because the human being is free in his actions and he is a combination of terrestrial matter and heavenly spirit, whereas the laws of nature and other creatures cannot realise ethics. This is evident from al-Khūlī's statement:

> The Angels are unable to do so, neither are the laws of nature that make up everything we need. Only God is capable of doing so, but the Most High has willed that you deputise for Him in that and act as His vicegerent in it, and He has equipped you accordingly.[112]

Likewise, al-Fārūqī says that the mission of man in terms of

> fulfilment of the Divine will can take place only in freedom; that is, under the real possibility of man's capacity to do otherwise than he ought. It is in this sense that he is God's vicegerent on earth; for only he can realise the ethical-and hence higher values, and only he can have for an objective the realisation of the whole realm in its totality.[113]

It is also articulated in the rest of al-Fārūqī's argument: "What the Qur'an meant to say is that only man may realise ethical value because only he has the freedom necessary therefore; that only he may pursue the totality of values because only he has the mind and vision requisite for such pursuit."[114]

The second idea around which the two scholars concur is the corollary of the first one and it relates to the identification of the object of vicegerency as the task of manifesting Divine attributes and ethics on Earth. As the only being consisting of spirit and body, the human being serves as a bridge between the upper and lower worlds; so, his existential mission is to bring "beings," "values" or "morals" from the upper world to the lower one. Al-Khūlī refers to the human being as "the carrier of a 'spirit' from one horizon to another, a 'truth' from one universe to another and a 'nectar' from a sacred world to a world intended to become so." He further says: "The core of the actions of vicegerency is for the human being to create the kind of living beings who are unlike the beings of nature."[115] In the same vein, al-Fārūqī said that the human being is: "a sort of cosmic bridge through which the Divine will, in its totality and especially the higher ethical part of it, can enter space-time and become actual."[116]

It is worth noting that these arguments seem similar to those of the German philosopher Immanuel Kant (d. 1804) who, like al-Khūlī and al-Fārūqī, states that the human being is the only ethical being in existence and that what the laws of nature and other creatures achieve in terms of purposes does not fall within the area of ethics.[117] Kant also considered that the purpose for which creation is made must be sought outside of nature, as it does not indicate the ultimate purpose of creation. He argues that the only being who is in a position to manifest that higher purpose is the human being as a rational, free and ethically motivated being.[118] It seems that Kant considers that, in his ethical dimensions, the human being lies outside the purview of the universe, which is also what is suggested by al-Khūlī and al-Fārūqī. The former said, for instance, that it is within the possible "for man to create the kind of living beings who are unlike the beings of nature" and that "the laws of nature that make up everything we need" are unable to do so.[119] This can also be understood from al-Fārūqī's statement regarding man being a cosmic bridge between the upper and lower worlds. Kant, furthermore, considers that man, as the only moral being, concentrates all the intermediary purposes for which all beings were created (which in themselves do not say anything about the nature of God, His attributes and intents from creation) in one ultimate purpose, i.e., the ethical purpose.[120] This is close to al-Fārūqī's statement:

> The ethical functions realise the moral values and these are the higher occupants of that realm, the higher imperatives of Divine will. The Divine will includes imperatives of a lesser order such as food, growth, shelter, comfort, sex, etc; for everything in creation partakes of the Divine purposiveness; and in fulfilling them, in the hierarchical order proper to them, man realizes the Divine will.[121]

There are other similarities between the position of this group and Kant's views, yet we will halt the comparison here.

I am currently unable to affirm with full certainty whether al-Khūlī and al-Fārūqī were in fact influenced by Kant's teleology and moral philosophy or whether this congruence in opinion was merely coincidental. Likewise, I am not in a position to assess a possible influence of Akbarian thought on Kant's thesis. Nonetheless, these ideas are not impervious to criticism in their application to Islamic theology as crystallised through the Qur'an. The first objection to such a thesis relates to the first idea agreed upon by both scholars, which Kant adopted in his teleology. The human being, according to Kant, is a unique moral entity, for he alone has a moral mission that other beings are incapable of performing or because their functions are devoid of any moral value in themselves as they only realise intermediary objectives that do not say anything about God's intent and nature. The Qur'an, however, says the complete opposite by affirming that all creatures are "Muslims": "to Him surrenders (accepted Islam) whoever[122] there is in the heavens and the earth" (Q 3:83, b.o. Ali Qarai), and that they all follow Divine guidance: "He who gave everything its creation and then guided it." (Q 20:50, Ali Qarai). If Revelation came down with the Truth, that is, ethics, as stated in the Qur'anic verse: "With the truth did We send it down, and with the truth did it descend" (Q 17:105, Ali Qarai), that Truth/ethics pre-existed Revelation and human existence: "He created the heavens and the earth with the truth" (Q 39:5, Ghali). Moreover, while Revelation came down with the Balance that enables man to preserve that truth/ethics in the universe and not to violate it, as stated in the Qur'anic verse: "It is God who has sent down the Scripture with the Truth and the Balance" (Q 42:17, b.o. Ahmad Ali),[123] that Balance had existed in the universe before man was entrusted to preserve it: "He raised the sky and set up the Balance" (Q 55:7, b.o. Ali Qarai). The goal of man is not to achieve something that is unfulfilled, but rather his goal is to embrace cosmic Islam, i.e., cosmic ethics: "O believers, enter into the integral peace (*silm*)" (Q 2:208, b.o. Maududi), and not to violate the cosmic balance: "so that you may not transgress in the balance." (Q 55:8, b.o. Ali Qarai). The purpose, thus, is not to achieve something unfulfilled or to create something unprecedented in the universe; rather, the Qur'an states that the religion of man, i.e., his morals, is ultimately the religion of the universe: "Do they, then, seek a religion other than Allah's, while to Him surrenders (accepted Islam) whoever there is in the heavens and the earth?" (Q 3:83).

The following Qur'anic verses show that what is meant by the "Truth" with which Revelation came down is justice, good and guidance: "These are the signs of Allah which We recite to you in truth, and Allah does not desire any injustice for the creatures." (Q 3:108, b.o. Ali Qarai); "O mankind! The Messenger has certainly brought you the truth from your Lord. So have faith! That is good (*khayr*) for you." (Q 4:170, b.o. Ali Qarai); and "Say, 'O mankind! The truth has already come to you from your Lord. Whoever is guided, is guided only for [the good of] his own soul." (Q 10:108, Ali Qarai). Thus, Truth is juxtaposed with injustice in the first verse, belief in Truth is described as good in the second, and guidance as an outcome of Truth in the third verse, which conveys that truth in the Qur'anic sense carries the meanings of justice, good and guidance, that is, ethics. Evidence that what is meant by the Truth as the foundation of the universe and its creatures is good and ethics is contained in the following Qur'anic verse: "Had the Truth followed their desires, the heavens, the earth, and all who live in them would have surely been corrupted." (Q 23:71, b.o. Khattab). The juxtaposition of Truth and cosmic corruption indicates that what is meant by Truth is ethics, that is, the universe is based on Truth in the sense of goodness and virtue. This is also evidenced by the Qur'anic verse: "And do not cause corruption on earth after it has been set good." (Q 7:56, b.o. Maududi). The earth, accordingly, was good and established on goodness before the advent of humans, which refutes the need for human intervention to introduce ethics in the world.[124] There are more Qur'anic verses that support the idea that the Truth entrusted to man and that he is required to observe, to advise others to do so, and to preserve, is the same Truth that Revelation came down with and by which the universe was created, and not something that the human being introduced to the universe.

As for the reason why ethics is called Truth (*Ḥaqq*) by the Qur'an, that is because of the fact that ethics has an established ontological existence in its own.

Ethics has a true existence in reality beyond ethical creatures, acts and values. That reality is the ontological source of ethical creatures, values and acts without which they would never have existed. Ethical creatures, behaviours and values are but a manifestation or concretization of something that ontologically exists outside of them and from which they are derived, i.e., the Divine attributes of perfection. Hence, justice, mercy, love, peace, generosity, beauty, forgiveness, etc., are nothing but a minor manifestation/extension of an ontological established Truth, i.e., God being the Just, Merciful, Loving, Generous, Beautiful, Forgiving, etc. Whereas unethical values or behaviours are called falsehood (*bāṭil*) because they do not draw their existence from an ontological fact, i.e., there exists no ontological evil. Even though created by God, they are not true but false, because their reality is not derived from what is ontological true. They are not a manifestation of what truly exists outside of them, but rather the result of a deviation from that.

Hence, on account of the above Qur'anic arguments and of the fact that every creature, and the entire universe, is noting but an outcome of God's perfect attributes, the idea that the human being is the only moral creation is alien to the Qur'an. The argument adopted by al-Fārūqī in support of this thesis is the exact same one adopted by Kant, that is, freedom. However, if freedom is to raise the status of the human being in relation to other creatures, in that the human being achieves the ethical values by his free will, this does not mean that the achievement of ethics in an inevitable way requires the deprivation of the other creatures and what they achieve from ethical values. The inevitable realisation of God's will in His creation is, rather, a Divine realisation of ethics (Truth, Justice, Guidance, etc.) through these beings.

Al-Khūlī, for his part, based that idea on the spiritual nature of the human being. If the human being is made up of a heavenly spirit and a material body, then he is the only being who carries the values of heavenly attributes and is able to manifest them in the material world. It is true that the other creatures, from an Islamic point of view, do not carry the Divine "breath" of which the human being is made up, but this does not mean that they are unable to achieve Divine ethics. If God has guided man through the two paths of *fiṭra* and Revelation as stated in the Qur'anic verse: "Light upon light" (Q 24:35),[125] He has also guided the universe through His Light, as clarified in the same verse: "Allah is the Light of the heavens and the earth." (Q 24:35, Ali Qarai). If the human being is thus innately guided by the Divine Light, so is the universe. Moreover, although the human spirit (*rūḥ*) grants him a special status among creatures on account of being of a different nature from the terrestrial nature, and although this nature encompasses values and qualifications that are not shared by other creatures, this does not mean that the universe is devoid of ethical values or cannot fulfil any. Rather, the universe, just like man, is illuminated by God's Light, as the above Qur'anic verse indicates, albeit this is done in a different way.

Hence, God is not in need of a "cosmic bridge through which the Divine will" can be implemented in the universe, nor the existence of a carrier of "Truth from one universe to another," or "nectar from a sacred world to a world intended to become so," as argued by al-Fārūqī and al-Khūlī. God acts alone in His universe and guides His creation without the need for a medium, as stated in the previous verses, and as will be developed in detail later. In describing the universe, the Qurʾan shows that all creatures in the universe are but a manifestation of what the Japanese Qurʾan scholar Toshihiko Izutsu (d. 1993) has called "Divine ethics."[126] They manifest mercy, justice, wisdom, beauty, generosity, knowledge and all the other Divine attributes, while the human being has no role in transmitting these values from one world to another; rather, it is God who: "rules (all) affairs from the heavens to the earth" (Q 32:5, Yusuf Ali). In his own world, the ethical human being does not transfer these values from the heavenly world to the earthly one, but he rather activates and preserves the ethics that God has instilled in his *fiṭra*.

The views of al-Fārūqī and al-Khūlī are in affinity with the Ashʿarī epistemology, which considers that the universe (i.e., the Divine cosmic will) is devoid of any ethical value and that creatures and universal laws are neither good nor evil in themselves or in what they achieve, nor do they convey any value. Al-Khūlī's arguments imply differentiation between God's will and the will of nature. For example, he says: "The laws of nature [...] are unable to do so [...] and only God Almighty is capable of doing so." This is as if to say that nature has a capability in its own right or that its laws are not God's. Likewise, al-Fārūqī differentiates between cosmic Divine will, which he excludes from the field of ethics, and revealed Divine will, which he includes exclusively in the field of ethics. He says that the fulfilment of the Divine will

> takes place involuntarily as in the physiological and psychic function; and freely, as in the ethical. The ethical functions realise the moral values and these are the higher occupants of that realm, the higher imperatives of Divine will. [...] man realises the Divine will. But his vocation lies in the moral realm where fulfilment of the Divine will can take place only in freedom; that is, under the real possibility of man's capacity to do otherwise than he ought.[127]

That is, the human being's vocation in realising the Divine will lies under the revealed Divine will that al-Fārūqī has made the only one related to ethical values, an argument that lies at the heart of the Ashʿarī epistemology. It is true that the Ashʿarites went further than that by denying that the revealed will could ever be related to the achievement of objective ethical values, for they are rather subjective ethical values since God has said that they are so, not in terms of their nature, as previously explained. Therefore, I say that this position is in affinity with the Ashʿarī epistemology instead of arguing that it is in full congruence with it.

Concerning the relationship between vicegerency and worship, al-Khūlī recognises that worship is a human task, but it is a common task among all creatures; so, it is not reasonable to argue that it is vicegerency.[128] However, he does not show the relationship between worship and vicegerency as two existential human tasks. The problematic of whether man is created for more than one teleological end or if vicegerency includes worship, and vice versa, thus persists. What is more problematic in this scholar's argument is that the verse of worship restricts the purpose of man's creation in worship alone "except to worship Me"; so, how can it be said that man is created for an additional purpose? Moreover, is there any religious responsibility that is not considered a form of worship at all?

Al-Fārūqī, on the other hand, discusses vicegerency vaguely in the course of his talk about the major principles that make up the Islamic worldview, but he does not link vicegerency to worship or any other principles of the Islamic worldview, nor does he build upon it. He devotes a title to the relationship between *khilāfa* and monotheism (*tawḥīd*), but ends up discussing *khilāfa* in the sense of the political responsibility of the Islamic nation, instead of in the sense of the human being's existential function.[129]

One of the implications of al-Khūlī's identification of the object of vicegerency in terms of the embodiment of heavenly spiritual ethical values in worldly life is his consideration of a conflict within the human being between what he calls his "humanity" and "spirituality." Accordingly, one of the purposes of the human being is to purify his humanity with the values of his heavenly spirituality. As for the forces of his humanity, they "work in the field of man's animality," while the instincts related to his spirituality appertain to

> an upper field because they represent the characteristics of the spirit that God Almighty has breathed into man; and while the former tends to pull towards the earth, the latter take man upward in the heavenly sphere. If the characteristics which bear materialistic and animalistic tendencies can be called "instincts," the disposition towards religiosity should, first and foremost, be called "instinct" because the power of the soul in man comes from God's order, and it is stronger, more durable and more original that the former.[130]
>
> It is known that man is governed by two forms of instinct: one that inspires strife and disobedience and the other which paves the way for repentance and forgiveness. These constitute the consequences of man's constitution from the specificities of "dust" and "soul," his life takes thus the form of a struggle between these two instinctive tendencies: darkness and light, impurity and purity and disobedience and repentance.[131]

This clash, which resembles the one between body and soul, and matter and ideals in Greek philosophy, especially in Platonism, has no basis in the teachings of the Qur'an. All human instincts, including corporeal and "sensual" ones, eventually lead to their (ethical) objective, which is to enable man to fulfil his existential mission. As previously mentioned, the role of man does not lie in giving precedence to his spiritual inclinations over material ones, for both are designed by Divine will to have an instinctive inclination towards good, i.e., ethics. Rather, what is required is a sense of balance between all of these so that one does not overpower the other. It is possible, for instance, that the natural inclination (*fiṭra*) for worship overpowers a material *fiṭra*, which may create disruption and lead man towards disobedience and immorality. The Prophet (ﷺ) said of those who make their spiritual instincts prevail over their physical ones: "Whoever turns away from my *Sunna* (path) does not belong to me!"[132] It therefore makes no sense to claim that spiritual instincts are godly and material ones are animalistic; rather, they all emanate from God and each contributes to the same ultimate purpose. Moreover, it is meaningless to classify material instincts under such labels as darkness, impurity and disobedience, while classifying the spiritual ones under light, purity and repentance, especially given that al-Khūlī himself admits that they are both from the *fiṭra*. In fact, the *fiṭra* that God has instilled in human beings, in all their dimensions, is a fundamentally ethical nature, as God Almighty says: "(Adhere to) the *fiṭra* of Allah upon which He has created [all] people. No change should there be in the creation of Allah. That is the correct religion" (Q 30:30, Sahih Intl). This "*fiṭra*" (instinct/natural disposition/nature) permeates the universe: "All praise be to Allah, the Fashioner (*Fāṭir*) of the heavens and earth (according to a natural disposition)" (Q 35:1, b.o. Maududi). The issue, again, is not that of conflict between body and soul, but rather it is a matter of balance between all the capabilities and inclinations of humans.

Overall, it appears that the identification of the object of vicegerency in this task is no less problematic than the previous ones, in addition to the fact that it does not precisely define the human existential function, except in vague ideas about the embodiment of spiritual ethical values. Consequently, this category, as the previous ones, does not appear to have developed a theory of vicegerency or a fully fledged view of man's existential function that governs the teachings of Revelation and human thought and activity.

As previously mentioned, the identification of the object of vicegerency in the sense demonstrated above is not alien to Islamic heritage. Some aspects of this can be found in the works of ibn ʿArabī in particular, and Sufi scholars in general, as highlighted in the third chapter. The comparison makes all the more clear the interplay of this definition and some of the views discussed previously. Al-Bayḍāwī (d. 685/1286), an adherent of the Ashʿarī school, referred to this meaning when he said that the *khalīfa* is someone that God has made vicegerent

> to build and populate the earth, manage the political affairs of people, fulfil their needs and implement God's command among them, not because God Almighty needs anyone to act on His behalf, but rather on account of the limitations of the world (*al-mustakhlaf ʿalayhi*) in receiving the bounties of God and His orders without an intermediary.[133]

That is, the world (*al-mustakhlaf ʿalayhi*) cannot receive the bounties and commands of God (i.e., ethical values) except through the human being. Ismāʿīl Ḥaqqī al-Brūsawī (d. 1127/1725), a Sufi exegete influenced by ibn ʿArabī, writes:

> The wisdom of vicegerency lies in the limitations of *al-Mustakhlaf ʿalayhi* in receiving the bounties of God and His orders without an intermediary because the Conferrer, Most Exalted, is in an absolute state of transcendence and sacredness, while the recipient is mostly immersed in such debased activities as eating, drinking, etc., and is also crippled by natural obstacles such as depravities. Hence, the profuse bounties of God are channelled through

someone who is characterised by both "abstraction" and "attachment," which is the vicegerent – whoever he might be.[134]

However, it should be emphasised here that vicegerency in the sense of the emulation of God in articulating some of His attributes and assuming some of His functions, is not an exclusive Akbarian idea. As noted before, this is clearly expressed by different scholars, as we saw in al-Iṣfahānī's words, "It is the emulation of God Almighty, to the extent of the capacity of human beings."[135] Al-Shāṭibī also wrote, "What is required from him [the vicegerent] is to assume the position of the One Who deputized him."[136] Moreover, the very notion of deputisation on behalf of God that many classical scholars (the majority of them according to ibn Khaldūn, as quoted in the previous chapter) adopted (since the early history of Islam)[137] in their understanding of *istikhlāf*, reflects, per se, the idea of assuming some Divine functions and attributes, as will be further covered later.

Consequently, it is clearly erroneous to assert that the "conception in which man is more than just God's object: a creature charged with certain Divine functions and therefore resembling God in certain ways – God's deputy on earth," is particularly a modern reinterpretation of the Qur'an "against its original meaning. Muslims must have felt a strong urge indeed to attain this high rank."[138] This, again, is one of the countless hasty conclusions about vicegerency that we encountered in contemporary literature.

## 4.5 Nature and Beyond

Some scholars have deviated from the definitions of vicegerency provided by the first category, i.e., mainstream contemporaries, by adding a number of issues to the object of vicegerency in addition to building, populating and harnessing the earth.

One of these scholars is the Indian poet and philosopher Muḥammad Iqbāl (d. 1938) who classified vicegerency or "Divine deputization" under the third and final stage of the pursuit of human perfection, or the stages of self-education, after obedience to Divine law and self-control. So, "Divine deputization in this world is the highest level of human grace. The deputy of the Truth – God – is the vicegerent of God on Earth. It is the most complete state that humanity aspires to, which is the spiritual path of life."[139] The stage of vicegerency, or "Divine deputization is a stage in which man controls the world, harnesses the forces of the universe, breathes life into everything and rejuvenates the old, endowing life with the miracle of work, renewing the standards of work and returning the world to brotherhood and peace."[140] Iqbāl's discussion of vicegerency is encapsulated in a vague poetic style. Although it is clear that he had reinforced the definition of the term by adding several elements to the acts of building and populating the earth, they remain rhetorical statements whose meaning is esoteric, in addition to the fact that he did not elaborate on the subject beyond these brief statements. Iqbāl argues that one of the meanings of vicegerency is control, a definition that I have contested earlier.

The Shiite scholar Muḥammad Bāqir al-Ṣadr (d. 1980) considered vicegerency as a collective rather than an individual human responsibility and the vicegerent (*mustakhlaf*) as the entire human race, not the individual as such. He also defined vicegerency as more than an act of deputisation on behalf of God in building and populating the earth and using its resources. In addition to that, the object of vicegerency is the good care and management of the human society. He writes: "*Al-Mustakhlif* is God Almighty, *al-Mustakhlaf* is the human being collectively and the object of vicegerency is the earth and whoever and whatever dwells on it."[141] He continued:

> God's designation of a vicegerent on earth does not concern only the land, but it includes all the matters belonging to the Almighty *Mustakhlif*. God Almighty is the Lord of the earth and its goods and He is the Lord of humans, animals, and every creature that lives in this vast universe, which means that the vicegerent of God on earth is deputized over all these things. [...] Since the human community – as represented in the person of Adam – is the one upon whom this vicegerency has been bestowed, it is then this community that has been entrusted to care for the universe, manage the affairs of the human being and steer humanity towards the designated path for Divine vicegerency. This conveys the fundamental Islamic concept of vicegerency, which is that God Almighty has delegated the human community to govern, lead the universe and build it and populate it socially and naturally, and it is on this basis that the theory of people's governance over themselves is founded, as well as the legitimacy of the exercise of the human community of self-governance as vicegerents of God.[142]

According to Bāqir al-Ṣadr, the vicegerency of the human community is realised through the human quest for Divine ethics as a model.[143]

Bāqir al-Ṣadr's definition of vicegerency and its object are broader than the definitions provided under the first category, for he did not confine it only to the material side but defined it in terms of building and populating the world, in addition to the assumption of leadership over it in society and nature. He also made vicegerency general for all human beings, considering that the Trust that the human being has accepted to undertake, unlike the rest of creation, is that of vicegerency. Nevertheless, from his perspective, even if vicegerency carries a broader meaning than *khilāfa* (caliphate) as a political position or institution, it does not really lie outside the purview of the political meaning related to the management of natural resources and human society and the implementation of God's rule in that. However, as understood from his statements above, he reserved this position for the Islamic nation and not for a single person. He considered this form of *khilāfa* the line of demarcation between a Muslim society and a non-Muslim one. This position represents the bulk of Bāqir al-Ṣadr's thesis on vicegerency. He says, for example, that

> the human community that bears the responsibility of *khilāfa* on earth only exercises this role as a vicegerent of God, which is why it is not authorized to

> govern on the basis of whim or a reasoning independent from the guidance of God Almighty, because this is incompatible with the nature of vicegerency; rather, it governs with truth and it bears the trust that God Almighty has giving it by applying His provisions over His servants and lands. In this way, collective vicegerency as a Qur'anic and Islamic concept is distinguished from collective governance in Western democratic systems, because the sovereignty in these systems belongs to the group which does not act on behalf of God in its exercise. This entails that it is not responsible towards anybody or bound by any objective standard in governance [...] whereas collective governance based on vicegerency is a responsible one and the group in it is obliged to apply the principles of right and justice and reject injustice and tyranny.[144]

While vicegerency is the political responsibility of the human community that is unfulfilled to date, as the Islamic nation has not borne it on account of the oppression and tyranny prevailing in the world, this responsibility moved from the sphere of collective responsibility to that of scholars (*marājiʿ* or religious references) alone. This, in turn, reaffirms the political dimension of the concept of vicegerency as elaborated by Bāqir al-Ṣadr, which owes to the theory of Twelver Shias in the *Wilāyat al-Faqīh* (Guardianship of the Islamic Jurist) on behalf of the "Hidden Imam" in leading the Muslim nation. Bāqir al-Ṣadr says in this regard:

> As long as the nation is governed by tyranny and is excluded from its right to general vicegerency, this line will be practiced by the *marjiʿ* [Shiite religious reference] and the two lines then merge – vicegerency and testimony – in the person of the *marjiʿ*. This merger is not dependent on infallibility, because the line of vicegerency in this case is practically represented only in a narrow range and within the limits of people's actions, and as long as the owner of the right to a general vicegerency fails to exercise his right on account of a tyrannical regime, the *marjiʿ* should take care of this right within the possible limits, and he should be responsible for overseeing the matters of the one who has failed to undertake the mission, thus leading the nation to overcome this deficiency and restore its right to general vicegerency. If, however, the nation has liberated itself, then the line of vicegerency is transferred to it in order to exercise by itself political and social leadership within the nation by applying God's provisions.[145]

Ultimately, vicegerency in the eyes of Bāqir al-Ṣadr is not the human existential function, and it does not transcend the political sphere and the application of *Sharīʿa* provisions in society. Although he made it a mission for all human beings, in the end it does not go beyond the circle of the Twelver Shiites, and today it does not even transcend the realm of individual Shiite scholars. As a result of that, one cannot find in Bāqir al-Ṣadr's thesis what could constitute a comprehensive theory or vision of vicegerency as an existential function.

The views of al-Ṣadr are closely related to those of al-Mawdūdī[146] and many other modern theorists of Islamic popular sovereignty in the twentieth century. If contemporaries did not go far beyond classical definitions of *istikhlāf* as human existential function (regardless of the abundant unfounded classifications and pointless elaborations), as asserted before, they did develop a new interpretation of the concept when basing their theory of the political sovereignty of the *umma*, as an alternative to Western democracy, on *istikhlāf*.[147] However, in both cases they did not develop a vicegerency theory. As for the second group (theorists of popular sovereignty), we can, at best, say that they based their political theories on (a wonky conception of) *istikhlāf*, but it cannot be said that they built a theory of *istikhlāf*, on account of the same critique that we addressed to the above authors.[148] Even though we did not pay much attention to the theses that addressed *khilāfa* as a collective political responsibility or as a central concept in modern Islamic political theories, we did not come across any study devoted to the development of the concept of vicegerency within that framework besides that of Bāqir al-Ṣadr,[149] which itself does not establish a proper vicegerency theory as noted.

## 4.6 Concluding Remarks

It should be reaffirmed at the end of this chapter that contemporary Islamic thought has not offered any clear or comprehensive vision or theory of the existential function of man. Worse, the concept of vicegerency as an existential function remains loose and often incorporates everything considered Islamic. It is an ambiguous concept that has not been rooted ontologically and is fraught with various shortcomings noted throughout this study. In addition, there is no interplay between these studies that have dealt with the concept of vicegerency as an existential human function. Furthermore, they did not provide an in-depth study of the concept as elaborated in the Islamic intellectual heritage. The concept of vicegerency is often dealt with on the basis of some isolated Qur'anic verses[150] by presenting the author's point of view and perceptions but without adopting a clear methodology in its study or applying the hermeneutical and theological methods developed in classical Islamic scholarship. There exists no single study that has dealt with the history of the concept or examined its development.[151] The existing studies did not place the concept of vicegerency in the Islamic worldview by situating its role within that vision or explaining how it controls all the other teachings of Islam and relates to the major principles of Islam. For example, one of the researchers who attempted to build the theory of governance in Islam on the concept of vicegerency wrote:

> The aim of governance in Islam, unlike any other version of governance, is to achieve human wellbeing through the distribution of trust and the organization of resources on the basis of *tawḥīd, amāna, ʿadl wa iḥsān* [justice and benevolence], *ukhuwwa* [universal solidarity], *iṣlāḥ* [reform], *ikhtiyār* [free-will], *tazkiya* [purification], *rubūbiyya* [Divine arrangement for nourishment],[152] and *maqāṣid al-Shariʿah'* [objectives of *Sharīʿa*] through the articulation of *khilāfa* (vicegerency).[153]

This researcher has listed here, and in a chapter devoted to these principles, a set of Islamic principles and major values but without linking them ontologically to vicegerency, i.e., without explaining how these principles contribute to the achievement of the deputisation of God in the task assigned to man, or the relationship between monotheism, and the rest of those principles, and vicegerency.

In the same vein, another researcher said that the goal of vicegerency is

> to achieve the objectives of worship on earth according to God's will alone in His commands and injunctions and in all matters in their minuteness as in their grandeur. It is also to achieve God Almighty's attributes of justice, knowledge, power, mercy for the weak, revenge on the tyrants, His command in understanding the objectives of life, the jurisprudence of its movement and drives, establishing truth and justice, strengthening the weak on earth, spreading monotheism and subjecting every quest in life to what He requires. All of these are values that control the society of vicegerency and the goals of man as a vicegerent.[154]

The researcher, however, has listed all of these values without rooting them in the concept of vicegerency or drawing any ontological connection between them, in order to articulate the concept into a theory. Therefore, with no added value in perspective, the term "vicegerency" remains, once again, a synonym for the term "Islam."

In another context, Munā Abū al-Faḍl (d. 2008) attempted to establish the Islamic "frame of reference" on the basis of four pillars that represent a

> systematic pattern consisting of pivotal concepts as representatives of a number of other interrelated concepts within the framework of the parent concept, and which form at the same time the basis of an integrated structure whose layers make up an airtight and consistent fabric. This will lead to the formation of circles whose centers cohere and dimensions come to completion within the framework of this integration and through this cohesion around a descending arrangement and a proportional relationship that entails a specific vision of priorities. Consistency is a characteristic of this systematic pattern, whether it concerns its formational and structural basis or its vital origins. This framework rests on four pillars that can be likened to the four foundations of the Kaʿba in Mecca, the orbit of Islamic rites and the site of building and construction. The first pillar, the creed of monotheism, is the basis on which the other pillars are established and their features take shape. The second is vicegerency – the reason and purpose of creation and the standard of the Trust and its operative term. The third pillar is the receptacle of this vicegerency and its instrument, and it is the ground of that creed and its seed, i.e., the *umma* (nation). Then comes, as its basis that secures the means to accomplish the mission, the *Sharīʿa*, which requires the nation to guarantee fulfilment of vicegerency. That is the fourth pillar that brings the systematic pattern full circle, around which the reference framework for dealing with the

> Noble Qur'an (and sources of theorization in general) is pinned in the attempt to establish our methodological foundations in the field of social sciences. There is no doubt that this frame of reference that derives from the Islamic worldview is considered a frame of reference for civilizational action insofar that it comprehends the pillars of this action.[155]

Abū al-Faḍl continues:

> We adopt vicegerency as one of the framework concepts in the civilizational act; so, we will follow it through the sub-concepts in the context of the creed-value system, and verify the existence of interdependence, sequencing and consistency within the frame of reference at its various levels, whether across the framework concepts themselves, or at the level of the offshoots stemming from them.[156]

As a result of these bright promises, we expected to see the way this system maintains its coherence, its foundations and method of comprehension of all the concepts and teachings of Islam "that gather and interconnect within the framework of the parent concept," among the other promises discussed above. However, none of that was realised. It seems that what Abū al-Faḍl offers is closer to a map or a general plan for the major principles or values composing the Islamic frame of reference rather than a rooted theory. Moreover, she does not even define vicegerency or explain the foundations or criteria of the choice of the four pillars in support of the Islamic frame of reference, nor the ontological relationship between them, among other requirements of theorisation that guarantee the genuineness, coherence and inclusiveness of the frame of reference. As for the promise to consider the ramifications of the concept of vicegerency to ensure coherence and consistency within the frame of reference, Abū al-Faḍl comes up with a list of values, principles, creedal and spiritual concepts, and practical obligations, which she includes under the concept of vicegerency, but without explaining their relation to vicegerency, nor does she show how they contribute to its achievement, nor how and why they were selected to the exclusion of others.

These observations apply equally to all scholars who have categorised vicegerency as one of the founding principles of the Islamic worldview, or as its highest principle. For example, ʿAbd al-Ḥamīd Abū Sulaymān, one of the leading proponents of the integration of knowledge project, ranks vicegerency as the second of the principles of the Qur'anic worldview, bringing the total numbers of principles to 14. Nonetheless, he does not link it to the other principles, explain its meaning – except for the very short and vague arguments – or use it in the building of the Qur'anic worldview he advocates for.[157] Vicegerency thus remains a mere title on the list of principles without having any impact on the formulation of an Islamic worldview, as is the case with many similar examples related to the loose use of the concept of vicegerency we provided in this chapter.

It also becomes evident from the above discussion that failure to control the concept of vicegerency and the absence of solid theological rooting resulted in many problems and disruptions. This is clearly exemplified by the topologies of vicegerency made by these scholars in terms of faith-based versus satanic, faith-based versus positivistic, *Sharīʿa*-based versus worldly, general for all human beings versus specific to the believers, and worldly vicegerency versus vicegerency in the Hereafter, as well as the participation of jinn in the function of vicegerency and their perception of the concept as conveying domination, control and Lordship. In addition to the aforementioned limitations, the deficiency in conceptual rooting among contemporary scholars also caused confusion and disruption at the terminological level. It also appears that some of the epistemological problems besetting aspects of classical Islamic scholarship are still omnipresent in contemporary thought, even though the majority of the scholars discussed in this study are from reformist backgrounds. These problems still persist in a way or in another through, for instance, the dichotomies in the works of some scholars, such as soul versus body, worship versus worldly life, ethics versus universe and worldly interest versus interest of the Hereafter.

Furthermore, it is evident that these studies came mostly in the context of the search for an Islamic alternative to the Western materialistic view of human civilisation. This is highlighted in the titles of many of the above studies, such as "vicegerency in the jurisprudence of Islamic civilisation," "the civilisational values of Islam," "the cosmic civilisational vision of the Qurʾan," "the function of vicegerency in the Noble Qurʾan, its implications and civilisational dimensions," "vicegerency and civilisation," etc. This is also reflected in the fact that, in their discussion of the concept of vicegerency, most of these studies have debated and criticised what they considered to be the materialistic worldview of civilisation. Comparing what they considered an Islamic worldview of civilisation and its Western counterpart, they attempted to justify the superiority of the former over the latter. This, in my opinion, explains why the majority of contemporary scholars, including many who have not been mentioned in this study, focused on the material aspect and reduced vicegerency to the concept of building and populating the land and utilising its resources, adding, in the process, some spiritual and faith-based elements. One of the most important differences between the Islamic and Western civilisational worldview, according to these studies, is that the former is based on vicegerency in the sense of responsibility over the earth on behalf of the real Owner, while the latter is based on the belief in true ownership. Moreover, the former is based on spiritual values and metaphysical beliefs, while the latter is devoid of that. This differentiation came in the context of demonstrating the advantage of the Islamic view on civilisation, building and populating the earth and utilising its resources on its Western counterpart. Therefore, vicegerency for these scholars was an appropriate concept in the process of searching for an Islamic alternative to modern civilisation and material progress. However, in the process, many of them ended up adopting a capitalistic worldview (with an Islamic flavour) with regard to the relation between man and the earth. Accordingly, permanent growth, development, full employment, technological progress, maximum exploitation of natural resources, etc. became an integral part of the very Qurʾanic existential function for which man was created, according to some of them.[158] Hence, "Man in Islam Is the Alpha and Omega of Global Development."[159] This is not to mention the fact that most of them have reduced the main function of man on Earth to a material function in the first place, as we have seen. This, again, reflects the fact that the idea of vicegerency, among contemporary Muslim reformists, came as a reaction to Western (material) progress, and not as an original endeavour to deduce the Qurʾanic conception of the human existential function, as we will discuss later.

The views we presented and analysed in this chapter refute Raḍwān al-Sayyid's assertion that the idea of vicegerency emerged when revivalists in the 1960s tried to offer an ideological alternative to counter the idea of natural law on which human rights are based. Al-Sayyid stated that ʿAbd al-Qādir ʿAwda (d. 1954) was

> the first to use the idea of *istikhlāf* in an ideological context in his book *Islam and our Political Situation* (1951). Sheikh Muḥammad ʿAbd Allāh Drāz (d. 1958) was also one of the scholars who showed interest in the question of rooting of the concept of *istikhlāf* in his well-known book, *The Moral World of the Qurʾan* (1959). Scholarly interest in the issue grew significantly in the 1960s and 1970s in Islamic writings and the trend has continued since.[160]

However, it seems clear from what has been discussed above that ʿAwda was not the first contemporary scholar to bring up the question of vicegerency the way he did. He was preceded in this by Muḥammad ʿAbduh (d. 1905), Muḥammad Rashīd Riḍā (d. 1935) and Muḥammad Iqbāl (d. 1938), among others. There were also others born before him, such as Nūrsī (d. 1960), Sayyid Quṭb (d. 1966), Abū al-Aʿlā al-Mawdūdī (d. 1979) and other scholars who came up with similar opinions but who preceded ʿAwda. In fact, he did not break new ground in the field or discuss the topic in a way that is uncommon in classical Islamic scholarship. Rather, in emulation of some classical scholars, ʿAwda used the concept of *istikhlāf* in the sense of building and populating the earth and utilising its resources.[161] He, likewise, made it appear as though it were just another term for Islam. He said that it includes "many obligations, all of which fall under the general heading of obedience to God, i.e. following His command and abstaining from what He forbids."[162] In fact, none of the theses on vicegerency discussed in this chapter (and many others that I have been exposed to) critiqued the Universal Declaration of Human Rights, or even alluded to it, including ʿAbd al-Qādir ʿAwda's thesis.[163] As a result, the hypothesis of Raḍwān al-Sayyid in this regard seems groundless.

Therefore, we rank Raḍwān al-Sayyid's statement with those critiqued in the previous chapter on account of their hasty judgements on contemporary reformists' use of the concept of vicegerency. They have judged those definitions of vicegerency as new totally unprecedented ideas introduced by contemporaries. Submitting unquestioningly to Raḍwān al-Sayyid's hypothesis, one of these researchers said:

> Islamic scholars began early on, that is, in the early 1950s, to use some Qurʾanic concepts, such as Divine vicegerency, with which they wanted to

> replace the concept of "natural law" that was considered one of the references in the contemporary discourse of human rights. So, ʿAbd al-Qādir ʿAwda was the first to use the concept of vicegerency, then ʿAbd Allāh Drāz developed the idea of the Divine honouring of man.[164]

Another researcher argued that the interpretation of vicegerency "based on such notions as civilization, science, and material progress, is clearly modernist and has its roots in nineteenth century European thought."[165] These claims were refuted in the previous chapter through the definition of *istikhlāf* given by some classical scholars in terms of "building and populating the earth, planting, harvesting, and planning," "manufacturing and extrapolating the resources of beings and moving them from power to action," "using thought to organise and harness the resources of the universe" or "learning and education," among other previously discussed definitions.

It is true that the popularity of these definitions of vicegerency in the sense given above has increased among contemporary reformers in their bid to confront the intellectual and civilisational challenges posed by modernity and the decline vis-à-vis the West. As noted before, the stake was, more often than not, to react to Western civilisational progress and to defend Islamic identity, or to attempt to catch up with Western material progress by conferring religious legitimacy on it through the concept of vicegerency. However, this does not mean that these uses are new or alien to classical scholarship, as claimed by many of these writers. From what we saw, it seems evident that contemporary intellectuals have not added anything significant in this regard, regardless of the fact that many of them used those classical views to project an "Islamic" variant of Western progress on the Qurʾan.

As discussed in the second chapter, one of the most important critiques levelled at Islamic scholarship, and Islamic thought in general, by contemporary scholars concerns the problem of fragmentation, and the best-appropriated remedy proposed was that of epistemological integration and the elaboration of a worldview as one of the most important premises of this integration. Many researchers regarded the concept of vicegerency as the most important component of that worldview, considering it the "supreme human goal,"[166] a general objective framing "all the Qurʾanic objectives" and "the primary objective of God Almighty behind the creation of man," and it is thus appropriate "to frame the overall Divine objectives, especially those of the Qurʾan, *Sharīʿa* and civilization."[167] Or, as one of these scholars has said, "The main purpose of the Islamic worldview can be summarised in one word i.e., *istikhlāf* or vicegerency. [...] Given all these explanations the article prefers to name the Islamic worldview as the 'vicegeral worldview.'"[168]

If it is correct to argue that vicegerency stands on top of all the priorities in addressing the problems faced by Islamic scholarship, as it constitutes the overarching goal of Islamic thought that governs the Islamic worldview and frames Islamic scholarship, it is then equally correct to say that, to date, the treatment of these problems remains in suspense due to the absence of a clear and integrated vision of the human existential function that is capable of framing thought and *ijtihād*.

## Notes

1 Among the applied studies that we will not mention below because their focus is mainly on the applied side and they do not elaborate much on the meaning of vicegerency is: Nimat H. Barazangi, "Vicegerency and Gender Justice in Islam," in *Islamic Identity and the Struggle for Justice* (Gainesville: University Press of Florida, 1996).

2 See for instance: Muḥammad Amīn Jabr, *al-Insān wa-l-Khilāfa fī l-Arḍ* [Man and Vicegerency] (Cairo: Dār al-Shurūq, 1999); and Mahdī Ḥashmtī, *Khalīfatu Allāh al-Insān al-Kāmil: Maʾāthir al-Shaykh Murtaḍā Muṭahharī* [Vicegerent of God or the Perfect Man: The Legacies of Sheikh Murtaḍā Muṭahharī] (Beirut: Dār al-Safwa, 2009).

3 See for instance: Muḥammad ʿArab, *al-Ishrāq Khilāfat al-Insān fī l-Arḍ* [Illumination of the Vicegerency of Man on Earth] (Damascus: Union of Arab Writers, 2001).

4 These include, but are not limited to:
- ʿAbd al-Raḥmān al-Maṭrūdī, *Al-Insān, Wujūduh wa-Khilāfatuh fī l-Arḍ fī Ḍawʾi al-Qurʾān al-Karīm* [Man, His Existence and Vicegerency on Earth in the Light of the Noble Qurʾan] (Cairo: Maktabat Wahba, 1990)
- ʿAbd Allāh ibn ʿAlī al-Bārr, "Mafhūm al-Istikhlāf wa-ʿimārat al-Arḍ fī l-Islām" [The Concept of Vicegerency and Building and Populating the Earth in Islam], *Journal of Ṣāliḥ ʿAbd Allāh Kāmil Center for Islamic Economics*, no. 20 (2003), 57–108
- Jayyād, "Mafhūm al-Khilāfa al-Ilāhiyya li-l-Insān," 133–155
- Zaynab Aḥmad Dāwūd, "Mafhūm al-Istikhlāf fī l-Qurʾan al-Karīm Shurūṭuh wa-Maqāṣiduh" [The concept of vicegerency in the noble Qurʾan: conditions and objectives] (MA diss., The International Islamic University Malaysia, 2006)
- Gurbet Sayilgan, "The Ur-Migrants: The Qurʾanic Narratives of Adam and Eve and Their Contribution to a Constructive Islamic Theology of Migration" (PhD diss., Georgetown University, 2015)

5 These include, for example:
- ʿAmru Khālid, *Innī Jāʿil fī l-Arḍ Khalīfa* [I Will Set a Vicegerent on Earth] (Beirut: Dār al-Maʿrifa, 3rd ed., 2012)
- Aḥmad Khayrī al-ʿUmarī, *Sīrat Khalīfa Qādim, Qirāʾa ʿAqāʾdiyya fī Bayān al-Wilāda* [Biography of the Incoming *Khalīfa*: A Doctrinal Reading in the Profile of Birth] (Egypt: Dār Ajyāl, 2013)
- Aḥmad al-Mubārak, *Wa-Ṭafiqā Yakhsifān, Khalq al-Insān wa-Khilāfatuh* [And They Began to Stitch Over Themselves: Human Creation and Vicegerency] (Beirut: al-Dār al-ʿArabiyya li-l-ʿUlūm Nashirūn, 2015)

6 Some of these researchers have even reduced the object of vicegerency into only some aspects of worldly life, i.e., the exclusive aspect of "the adornments of life on earth." See: Muḥammad al-Ḥasan Barīma, "Al-Ẓāhira al-Ijtimāʿiyya wa-Niẓāmuhā al-Maʿrifī fī l- Qurʾān al-Karīm" [Social Phenomenon and Its Epistemological System in the Noble Qurʾan], in *Naḥwa Niẓām Maʿrifī Islāmī* [Towards an Islamic Epistemological System] (Amman: The International Institute of Islamic Thought, 2000), 236.

7 Riḍā, *Tafsīr al-Manār*, vol. 1, 217.

8 ʿAbd al-Ḥamīd ibn Bādīs, *Tafsīr ibn Bādīs* [The Exegesis of ibn Bādīs] (Beirut: Dār al-Kutub al-ʿIlmiyya, 1995), 89.

9 ʿAbd al-Wahhāb al-Masīrī, *Mawsūʿat al-Yahūd wa-l-Yahūdiyya wa-l-Ṣuhyūniyya* [Encyclopedia of Jews, Judaism and Zionism] (Egypt: Dār al-Shurūq, 2002), vol. 1, 157.

10 Including:
- Aref T. M. Atari, "Christian 'Service-Stewardship' and Islamic 'Khilafah': Emerging Models in Educational Administration," *The American Journal of Islamic Social Sciences* 17, no. 2 (Summer 2000), 40
- Muḥammad ʿAbd al-Fattāḥ al-Khatīb, *Qiyam al-Islām al-Ḥaḍāriyya, Naḥwa Insāniyya Jadīda* [The Civilizational Values of Islam: Towards a New Humanity] (Doha: Kutub al-Umma, 1431 AH), 35–36, 44

- Farīda Zūzū, "Maqṣad Ḥifẓ al-Bī'a wa-Atharuhu fī 'Amaliyyat al-Istikhlāf" [The Objective of Preserving the Environment and Its Impact on the Vicegerency Process], *Majallat Islāmiyyat al-Ma'rifa* 48 (Summer 2007), 85
- Muḥammad Banī 'Īsā, "Naẓariyyat al-Istikhlāf wa-Atharuhā fī l-Iqtiṣād al-Islāmī" [The Theory of *Istikhlāf* and Its Effect on Islamic Economics], *Journal of Ṣāliḥ 'Abd Allāh Kāmil Center for Islamic Economics*, 14, no. 40 (2010), 11
- Maszlee Malik, "Constructing the Architectonics and Formulating the Articulation of Islamic Governance: A Discursive Attempt in Islamic Epistemology" (PhD diss., Durham University, 2011), 198, 260–61. Durham E-Theses Online: http://etheses.dur.ac.uk/832/
- Aḥmad al-Mubārak, *Wa-Ṭafiqā Yakhsifān*, 245
- Muḥammad 'Ayyād Qaraybi', *al-Istikhlāf wa-l-Ḥaḍāra, Dirāsa fī l-Istikhlāf al-Ilāhī li-l-Insān fī Ḍaw'i al-Qaṣaṣ al-Qur'ānī* [Vicegerency and Civilization: A Study on Divine Vicegerency in the Light of Qur'anic Narratives] (Amman: Dār Zahrān, 2013), 44

11 'Abd al-Qādir 'Awda, *al-Islām wa-Awḍā'unā al-Siyāsiyya* [Islam and Our Political Conditions] (Beirut: Mu'assasat al-Risāla, 1981), 28.

12 Sayyid Quṭb, *Fī Ẓilāl al-Qur'ān* [In the Shadows of the Qur'an] (Beirut: Dār al-Shurūq, 17th ed., 1991), vol. 1, 56, and vol. 6, 3387.

13 Including:

- Al-Dasūqī, *al-Khilāfa al-Islāmiyya*, 423, 471
- 'Abd al-Ḥamīd Abū Sulaymān, *Azmat al-'Aql al-Muslim* [The Crisis of the Muslim Mind] (Beirut: Dār al-Hādī, 2003), 143
- Muḥammad Zarmān, "Waẓīfat al-Istikhlāf fī l-Qur'ān al-Karīm wa-Dalālātuhā wa-Ab'āduhā al-Ḥaḍāriyya" [The Function of *Istikhlāf* in the Noble Qur'an: Its Civilizational Meanings and Dimensions], Qatar University, *Journal of the College of Sharī'a, Law and Islamic Studies* 16 (1998), 195

14 Qaraybi', *al-Istikhlāf wa-l-Ḥaḍāra*, 44.

15 Ibid., 52 and see for a similar division also: Nu'mān 'Abd al-Razzāq al-Sāmurrā'ī, *Naḥnu wa-l-Ḥaḍāra wa-l-Shuhūd* [We, Civilization and Witnessing] (Doha: Kutub al-Umma, 1421 AH), 101–12.

16 Quṭb, *Fī Ẓilāl al-Qur'ān*, vol. 6, 3387.

17 Al-Dasūqī, *al-Khilāfa al-Islāmiyya*, 436. See also: Fārūq Aḥmad al-Dasūqī, *Istikhlāf al-Insān fī l-Arḍ* [Vicegerency on Earth], (Alexandria: Dār al-Da'wa, n.d.), 24.

18 Al-Dasūqī, *al-Khilāfa al-Islāmiyya*, 471. See also: al-Dasūqī, *Istikhlāf al-Insān fī l-Arḍ*, 11–13. This position is also adopted by other scholars. See for instance: Banī 'Īsā, "Naẓariyyat al-Istikhlāf," 30.

19 Al-Dasūqī, *al-Khilāfa al-Islāmiyya*, 471.

20 See: al-Dasūqī, *Istikhlāf al-Insān fī l-Arḍ*, 47.

21 Ibid.

22 Ibid., 58.

23 Ibid., 109.

24 Al-Dasūqī, *al-Khilāfa al-Islāmiyya*, 423, 471.

25 Ibid., 34.

26 It is worth noting here that some classical scholars have used this kind of logic but in a totally different context. Indeed, in the spiritual context (far away from al-Dasūqī's thesis), as established in Islamic teachings in general, if one is not master over his desires, aspirations and tendencies, the latter will become master over him. Hence, there is no way to be only God's servant (monotheism) if one does not control all influences that may submit him to their dictates. In this context, al-Munāwī (d. 1031/1621) writes, "Fasting was only prescribed to break the desires of souls and to cut off the causes of enslavement and devotion to things. For if people persisted on [satisfying] their needs, [these] things would enslave them and cut them off from God. Fasting, cuts off the means of devotion to other that God and confers freedom from enslavement to suspicious things. That is so because the meaning of freedom

is to possess things and not to be possessed by them, because he [the human being] is God's vicegerent in his property. Hence, if these [things] would possess him, the wisdom would be reversed; the favoured would become disfavored and the highest the lowest." Al-Munāwī, *Fayḍ al-Qadīr*, vol. 4, 211.

27 Al-Dasūqī, *al-Khilāfa al-Islāmiyya*, 471.

28 Ibid., 232.

29 Ibid., 471.

30 Ibid., 477 ff.

31 We found some classical scholars describing disobedient people as vicegerents of Satan. For example, the renowned Andalusian Mālikī Judge, Abū Bakr ibn al-ʿArabī (d. 543/1148) writes commenting on Q 24:55, "Whoever acts as such is the vicegerent of God, and whoever disobeys him is the vicegerent of Satan." Abū Bakr ibn al-ʿArabī, *ʿĀriḍat al-Aḥwadhī* [Commentary on al-Tirmidhi's Ḥadīth Collection] (Beirut: Dār al-Kutub al-ʿIlmiyya, n.d.), vol. 9, 70. Nevertheless, unlike al-Dasūqī, these scholars are not arguing that the vicegerency of Satan is part of the vicegerency for which the human being was created and placed on earth as described in Q 2:30 and other verses. On the contrary, these scholars' argument is that if people do not assume their task to be God's vicegerents, they will be following the footsteps of the devil. Indeed, the human being was created to worship God, but he may worship Satan; in the same way, he was created to act as God's vicegerent, but he may follow the footsteps of Satan.

32 Al-Dasūqī, *Istikhlāf al-Insān fī l-Arḍ*, 44.

33 Al-Dasūqī, *al-Khilāfa al-Islāmiyya*, 119.

34 Ibid., 119 ff.

35 Abdelaziz Berghout, "Mawqiʿ Naẓariyyat al-ʿIlm fī ʿAmaliyat al-Istikhlāf wa-l-Taḥaḍḍur ʿind al-Ustādh Badīʿ al-Zamān Saʿīd al-Nūrsī" [The Position of the Theory of Knowledge in the Process of Vicegerency and Civilised Life in the Works of Badīʿ al-Zamān Saʿīd al-Nūrsī], *al-Nūr for Studies in Civilization and Thought*, no. 2 (Summer 2010), 126.

36 Banī ʿĪsā, "Naẓariyyat al-Istikhlāf," 30.

37 Riḍā, *Tafsīr al-Manār*, vol. 1, 277.

38 Quṭb, *Fī Ẓilāl al-Qurʾān*, 56.

39 ʿAwda, *al-Islām wa-Awḍāʿunā al-Siyāsiyya*, 28.

40 Muḥammad Abū al-Qāsim Ḥājj Ḥamad, *Al-Ḥākimiyya* [Sovereignty] (Beirut: Dār al-Sāqī, 2010), 63–64.

41 Ibid., 67.

42 Seyyed Hossein Nasr, *The Heart of Islam: Enduring Values for Humanity* (New York: Harper San Francisco, 2002), 142–43.

43 Ṣadr al-Dīn al-Qūnawī, *Iʿjāz al-Bayān fī Tafsīr Umm al-Qurʾān* [The Miraculous Allocution in the Explanation of the Mother of the Qurʾan] (Qum, Iran: Maktab al-Iʿlām al-Islāmī, 1381 AH), 113.

44 ʿAbd al-Qādir ibn Muḥyī al-Dīn, *al-Mawāqif al-Rūḥiyya wa-l-Fuyūḍāt al-Subūḥiyya* [Spiritual Attitudes and Sublime Effusions] (Beirut: Dār al-Kutub al-ʿIlmiyya, 2003), vol. 1, 325.

45 W. Harold Mare, "The Cultural Mandate and the New Testament Gospel Imperative," *Journal of the Evangelical Theological Society*, 16 no. 3 (Summer 1973), 139–47.

46 Ruben Schenzle, "If God Is King, Is Man His Vicegerent? Considering *Ḫalīfah* in Regard to Ancient Kingship," in *New Approaches to Human Dignity in the Context of Qurʾanic Anthropology*, ed. Rüdiger Braun and Hüseyin I. Çiçek (Newcastle-upon-Tyne: Cambridge Scholars Publishing, 2017), 137–38.

47 Charles Peter Wagner, *Church Growth and the Whole Gospel: A Biblical Mandate* (Eugene, OR: Wipf and Stock, 1998), 12.

48 Stephen E. Lahey, *Philosophy and Politics in the Thought of John Wyclif* (New York: Cambridge University Press, 2003), 122.

49 Ruben Schenzle, "If God is King, Is Man His Vicegerent?" 134–35.
50 See for instance:
- David L. Johnston, *Earth, Empire and Sacred Text: Muslims and Christians as Trustees of Creation* (London: Equinox, 2010, paperback in 2013), ch. 3
- David L. Johnston, "A Muslim and Christian Orientation to Human Rights: Human Dignity and Solidarity," *Indiana International & Comparative Law Review* 24 (2014), 902
- Stephen Myongsu Kim, "Transcendence of God – A Comparative Study of the Old Testament and the Qur'an" (PhD diss., University of Pretoria, 2009), 85
- Mathew Thekkemuriyil, "Image and Likeness of God – An Understanding and Appraisal of the Christian and Islamic Concept of Human Beings in Light of the Creation Narratives in the Bible and in the Qur'an" (MA diss., University of Leuven 2011), 36

51 It is noteworthy, however, that advocates of Christian *dominium* did not restrict this notion to material exploitation of the earth only.
52 Ibn Taymiyya, *Minhāj al-Sunna al-Nabawiyya*, vol. 6, 589.
53 We found a sixth/twelfth-century Persian Sufi esoteric exegete who wrote about the interpretation of Q 2:30: "The dust-dwelling Adam is granted chieftainship over all the empires. His exalted breast will be bright with the light of recognition. In him the subtleties of My generosity and the artifacts of My bounteousness will become apparent." Also, in the context of the interpretation of Q 15:26 he wrote: "He created Adam from all of these kinds so as to honor him and make him eminent. Thus he would be superior to all the creatures of the world. All are subjected to him, and he is given ruling power over all. This is why the Lord of the Worlds says, 'We indeed honored the children of Adam, and We carried them on land and sea, and We provided them with goodly things, and We made them much more excellent than many of those We created [17:70].'" Online: https://quranx.com/Tafsir/Asrar/2.30; https://quranx.com/Tafsirs/15.26. However, it is obvious that this opinion is not about rulership as a function entrusted to man, but rather as a mere existential fact, a *fait accompli* that raises man in rank. Furthermore, man is not qualified here as a lord or a king nor is he charged to control or dominate. Hence, we are far from those contemporary opinions that state that it is a human function and a religious obligation to dominate, subjugate and rule over the creation and control it.
54 Schenzle, "If God Is King, Is Man His Vicegerent?"140.
55 Al-Zamakhsharī, *al-Kashāf*, vol. 4, 89.
56 Zarmān, "Waẓīfat al-Istikhlāf fī l-Qur'ān al-Karīm," 195.
57 Ibid.
58 Ibid., 204–5.
59 Ibid., 206.
60 Ibid., 208.
61 Ibid., 211–12.
62 He says: "The following are some of the many Qur'anic texts in which this call to strike a balance between spiritual and material values is revealed: 'By the means of what Allah has given you, seek the abode of the Hereafter, and do not forget your share of this world' (Q 28:77, b.o. Ali Qarai), and 'He has produced you from the earth and settled you in it, so ask forgiveness of Him and then repent to Him. Indeed, my Lord is near and responsive.' (Q 11:61, Sahih Intl). These two verses clearly express this idea, for God Almighty's words 'By the means of what Allah has given you, seek the abode of the Hereafter' and 'So ask forgiveness of Him and then repent to Him' represent an invitation to pay attention to spiritual aspirations and faith values. On the other hand, the Almighty's words: 'Do not forget your share of this world' and 'He has produced you from the earth and settled you in it' are a parallel invitation to build and populate the land in its material aspect, by utilizing its wealth and enjoying its bounties." Ibid. Notice how the author establishes a dichotomy between the spiritual and the material "values,"

and the worldly life and the Hereafter, as if the building and populating of the earth is a religious obligation without any spiritual value. Also, it is as if the quest for the worldly life cannot be for the sake of the obtainment of the reward of the afterlife. Moreover, it is as if the quest for the afterlife and repentance are spiritual and faith values that are not related to this world and its benefits, and as if "spiritual aspirations and faith values" are for the Hereafter and "the building and populating of the earth in its material aspect" is "parallel" to that, and it is not part of faith and spiritual values nor part of the quest for the afterlife. If building the earth, populating it and utilising its bounties are "part of religious entrustment," or "the supreme objective of the human being," as he claimed, then how can it not be part of faith and spiritual values, and how can it not be for the sake of the afterlife? How can the existential function (i.e., utilisation of the resources of the earth as per Zarmān's definition) for which the human being was created be devoid of spiritual aspirations, faith values and after-worldly purposes? This is again in line with the Ash'ari epistemology, whereby the values of faith and spirituality set the Hereafter, and not worldly life, as their only purpose, and they are among the interests of religion and not of those of the earthly world. Faith and spirituality cannot be achieved without work and endeavour on earth and are pleasures experienced in this life in the first place. Hence, there is no justification for the argument of "the balance between spiritual and material values" and the "invitation" for "the building and populating of the earth" as "parallel" to the invitation for faith and spirituality, because they overlap. This is inferred from the same verse, which he cited, "By the means of what Allah has given you, seek the abode of the Hereafter." What is meant by "of what Allah has given you" is the wealth that God has given to Korah, i.e., you should invest your money for the purpose that will benefit you in the Hereafter. Hence, the verse actually rejects the establishment of any differentiation or "parallelism," and even "balance" between "material values" and "spiritual" ones, as the obligation is rather to unify them. In other words, the human being is not tasked to work for the worldly life and hold material values on one side, and work for the after-worldly life and hold spiritual values on the other, while trying to balance both. Rather, all his endeavours should be directed to the reward of the afterlife, which will give them spiritual value while making them, at the same time, beneficial for the worldly life, whether they represent material or ritual endeavours. Hence, the afterlife can only be reached through seeking the genuine benefits of this world. The second part of the verse, on the other hand: "Do not forget your share of this world," does not imply that that share is dissociated from the quest for the afterlife and spiritual values, or that the quest for the afterlife in the verse is dissociated from the share (benefits) of the world. Rather, it indicates that the former (dedicating worldly efforts to the afterlife) does not contradict enjoying the bounties of the world and satisfy one's (material and spiritual) desires. In this very enjoyment and gratification lies the means to realise the benefits of this world leading to the retribution of the Hereafter. Furthermore, that gratification is a satisfaction of the *fiṭra* and is considered obedience to God if it is for the purpose of compliance, hence there is no "parallelism" here. Thus, the recommendation here is not to merely enjoy the goods of the world. Indeed, the Qur'an recounts that Korah, to whom the recommendations of the latter verse were addressed, was absorbed by the enjoyment of the goods of the world, so why would he be recommended to enjoy the goods of the world? Based on the above, we could paraphrase the verse as follows: "Invest your wealth for the purpose that will benefit you in the Hereafter and, in doing so, you must realise that this is the genuine way to enjoy the worldly life, so bear in mind (do not forget) the share of bounties of the worldly life that you will obtain by that." This meaning, in substance, is what is referred to in the following verse: "Whoever desires the reward of this world, [should know that] with Allah is the reward of this world and the Hereafter." (Q 4:134, Ali Qarai). For a similar interpretation of the former verse (Q 28:77), see Muḥammad al-Ṭāhir ibn 'Āshūr, *al-Taḥrīr wa-l-Tanwīr* [The Verification and Enlightenment] (Tunis: al-Dār al-Tūnisiyya, 1984), vol. 20, 179. As for God's words, "He has produced you from the earth and settled you in it," these are a reminder of His bounties addressed to the people of Thamūd, and there is no "invitation," recommendation or injunction whatsoever in these words as we will see later.

63 Ibn ʿĀshūr, *al-Taḥrīr wa-l-Tanwīr*, vol. 1, 398–99.

64 Ibid.

65 One may argue that this is understood from the previously quoted definition of ibn Khaldūn: "The actions of humans have appropriated the world's creatures and everything that it encompasses, and all of it has become subordinate to the human being. This reflects the meaning of *istikhlāf* mentioned in the Qurʾanic verse: 'I will create a vicegerent on earth' (Q 2:30)." Ibn Khaldūn, *Dīwān al-mubtadaʾ wa-l-khabar*, 593. However, as discussed earlier, ibn Khaldūn was not speaking about appropriation of the things of the earth as a human mission or function but rather as a mere existential fact. This is in addition to the fact that ibn Khaldūn did not use terms like sovereignty, lordship, control or domination.

66 The classical scholars who supported the idea that man is a *khalīfa* of man did not consider *khilāfa* to be an existential function, but an inevitable Divine decree in the way He created man, nor did any classical scholar categorise *khilāfa* in two categories, one as a function and the other as a fate.

67 Badīʿ al-Zamān Saʿīd al-Nūrsī, *Ishārāt al-Iʿjāz fī Maẓān al-Ījāz* [Signs of Miraculousness: The Inimitability of the Qurʾan's Conciseness] (Cairo: Sözler Publications, 3rd ed., 2002), 240.

68 Abū al-Aʿlā al-Mawdūdī, *Niẓām al-Ḥayāt fī l-Islām* [The Order of Life in Islam] (Pakistan: Dār al-ʿUrūba, 2nd ed., 1958), 27–28.

69 Ibn ʿĀshūr, *al-Taḥrīr wa-l-Tanwīr*, vol. 1, 399.

70 Including the following authors:
- Aḥmad Ḥasan Faraḥāt, *al-Khilāfa fī l-Arḍ*, 20
- Al-Najjār, *Khilāfat al-Insān bayna al-Waḥy wa-l-ʿAql*, 61–62
- ʿAbd al-ʿAzīz ʿAyyādī, "al-Insān al-Khalīfa wa-Muhimmat al-Iʿmār: Ruʾya Qurʾāniyya li-l-Ḥaḍāra al-Insāniyya al-Muthlā" [The Man-Vicegerent and the Mission of Building and Populating: A Qurʾanic View of the Ideal Human Civilization], *Algeria, Social Sciences Journal* 20 (2015), 76

71 ʿAbd al-Majīd al-Najjār, "al-Istikhlāf fī Fiqh al-Taḥaḍḍur al-Islāmī" [Vicegerency in the Jurisprudence of Islamic Civilization], *Malaysia, Attajdid Journal*, no. 1 (Winter 1997), 94, and see: al-Najjār, *Fiqh al-Taḥaḍḍur al-Islāmī*, 51–52.

72 Al-Najjār, "al-Istikhlāf fī Fiqh al-Taḥaḍḍur al-Islāmī," 94.

73 Ibid., 93–94.

74 Ibid., 94.

75 Al-Najjār, *Fiqh al-Taḥaḍḍur al-Islāmī*, 53.

76 Ibid.

77 Al-Najjār, "al-Istikhlāf fī Fiqh al-Taḥaḍḍur al-Islāmī," 94.

78 Ibid., 95.

79 Ibid., 123–24. For virtually the same argument, see also: al-Najjār, *Fiqh al-Taḥaḍḍur al-Islāmī*, 79.

80 Ibid., 53.

81 Al-Najjār, "al-Istikhlāf fī Fiqh al-Taḥaḍḍur al-Islāmī," 97.

82 Ibid., 93–94. See also: al-Najjār, *Fiqh al-Taḥaḍḍur al-Islāmī*, 51–52.

83 Faraḥāt, *al-Khilāfa fī l-Arḍ*, 20.

84 Ibid.

85 Ibid., 22.

86 Ibid., 35.

87 Ibid., 22.

88 Ibid., 51–52.

89 We found in some classical *tafsīr* books a misunderstanding initiated by al-Māwardī, followed by a few *tafsīr* scholars. Like most *tafsīr* scholars, al-Māwardī merely mentions the three opinions reported by al-Ṭabarī around who the *khalīfa* is succeeding/

deputising (the jinn, previous generations or God). However, when mentioning the second opinion, attributed, according to al-Ṭabarī, to al-Ḥasan al-Baṣrī, al-Māwardī introduces an idea that is contrary to that which is attributed to al-Ḥasan al-Baṣrī and which no one before al-Māwardī reported. Al-Māwardī writes, "The second [opinion] is that it means that people from the children of Adam will succeed each other. They succeed their father Adam in establishing the truth and populating the earth. This is the opinion of al-Ḥasan al-Baṣrī." Al-Māwardī, *al-Nukat wa-l-ʿUyūn*, vol. 1, 95. However, this is not at all the opinion of al-Ḥasan al-Baṣrī as reported by al-Ṭabarī. When reporting this second opinion, al-Ṭabarī said that, according to that opinion, it means "Those are the children of Adam who succeed their father Adam, and each generation of them succeeds the previous one. This is an opinion ascribed to al-Ḥasan al-Baṣrī." Al-Ṭabarī, *Jāmiʿ al-Bayān*, vol. 1, 451. Indeed, before al-Māwardī and after him, apart from a very few scholars who just copied al-Māwardī to the letter, this second opinion was never about establishing the truth and populating the earth, but it was merely about generations succeeding each other, period. The fact that that idea is not at all the one ascribed to al-Ḥasan al-Baṣrī is further confirmed by al-Ṭabarī's comments on that opinion. The latter relates a narration, attributed to some companions of the Prophet (ﷺ), that suggests that the one to whom corruption and bloodshed is ascribed is not the *khalīfa* himself but his progeniture. So, remarks al-Ṭabarī, according to this narration, the *khalīfa* (Adam and those who follow his example) is the one who deputises for God, and corruption and bloodshed is not emanating from the *khalīfa*. Then, al-Ṭabarī further comments, "Even though this interpretation contradicts the meaning of *khalīfa* as per ascribed to al-Ḥasan [al-Baṣrī] in one aspect, it agrees to it from another aspect. As for the agreement, that is in the fact that those who interpreted it that way [as per the respective narration] ascribe corruption on earth and bloodshed to other than the *khalīfa* [who is, in their view, Adam and his righteous offspring]. As for the contradiction, that is because both of them [ibn Masʿūd and ibn Abbas], ascribe *khīlāfa* to Adam, in the sense that God has deputized him on it on His behalf, while al-Ḥasan [al-Baṣrī] has ascribed *khīlāfa* to his children, in the sense that they succeed each other, and that each generation replaces the previous one, and [because al-Baṣrī has] ascribed corruption on earth and bloodshed to the *khalīfa* [Adam's children according to him]." Ibid., vol. 1, 452. Hence, al-Ḥasan al-Baṣrī does not see *khīlāfa* as an ethical function or religious responsibility, but rather as a mere existential fact, since, as per al-Ṭabarī's explanation, he sees *khīlāfa* as mere generational succession that is intrinsically related to corruption and bloodshed, and not as the establishment of good or any other responsibility. Therefore, it is not ascribed to Adam and those who follow his example but to his offspring in general. Hence, the opinion that vicegerency as generational succession entails a religious responsibility, or an existential function that the human being should endeavour to fulfil, cannot be accurately attributed to any classical Muslim scholar.

90 ʿAlī Sharīʿatī, *al-Insān wa-l-Islām* [Man and Islam], trans. Abbās al-Turjumān (Beirut: Dār al-Amīr, 2nd ed., 2007), 22–25.

91 ʿĀʾisha Bint al-Shāṭiʾ, *al-Qurʾān wa-Qaḍāyā al-Insān* [The Qurʾan and Human Issues] (Cairo: Dār al-Maʿārif, 1999), 37, 52, 72, 75.

92 Including:

- Abū Sulaymān, *al-Ruʾya al-Kawniyya al-Ḥaḍāriyya al-Qurʾāniyya*, 120
- ʿAbd al-Salām al-Aḥmar, "Istikhlāf al-Insān fī l-Arḍ, Naḥwa Ruʾya Qurʾāniyya Kulliyya" [Vicegerency on Earth: Towards a Comprehensive Qurʾanic Vision], *Proceedings of the International Symposium: The Noble Qurʾan and Worldview: Paths of Reflection and Management* (Rabat: Muḥammadiyya League of Scholars, 2014), 307
- ʿAbd al-Salām al-Aḥmar, "Istikhlāf al-Insān fī l-Arḍ bi-Waṣfih Maqṣad ʿĀmm li-l-Qurʾān wa-l-Sharīʿa wa-l-Ḥaḍāra" [Vicegerency on Earth as a General Objective of the Qurʾan, *Sharīʿa* and Civilization], *Majallat Islāmiyyat al-Maʿrifa* 89 (Summer 2017), 111–12, 126

93 ʿAlī Sharīʿatī, *al-Insān wa-l-Islām*, 23.
94 Ibid.
95 Or it may be one of the self-attributes, on one hand, and action-attributes, on the other; so, it is counted among the self-attributes in that it characterises God regardless of His creation, and among the practical attributes in that it relates to His creation. For example, God is the Creator regardless of creation, and He was characterised by this attribute before He created, but He is also the Creator of the heavens and the earth, and this creation is not inherent to His Entity but is an occurrence. This attribute, that is, the "Creator of the heavens and the earth," in this consideration is one of the action-attributes. For this division, see for instance: Shams al-Dīn al-Dhahabī, *al-ʿArsh* [The Throne], ed. Muḥammad al-Tamīmī (Medina: Deanship of Scientific Research at the Islamic University, 2nd ed., 2003), vol. 1, 142.
96 This is further supported by the linguistic meaning of *khilāfa*, as ibn ʿĀshūr wrote: "The vicegerent initially means the one who succeeds somebody or substitutes him in one of his actions that he performs." Ibn ʿĀshūr, *al-Taḥrīr wa-l-Tanwīr*, vol. 1, 398.
97 Al-Aḥmar, "Istikhlāf al-Insān fī l-Arḍ bi-Waṣfih Maqṣad ʿĀmm," 113.
98 Ibid., 126.
99 Ibid., 123.
100 Ibid., 108.
101 Ibid., 119.
102 Ibid., 126.
103 Al-Aḥmar, "Istikhlāf al-Insān fī l-Arḍ Naḥwa Ruʾya Qurʾāniyya Kulliyya," 307.
104 Ibid., 114.
105 Ibid., 115.
106 Ibid., 122.
107 Ibid., 101.
108 Al-Ṭabarī, *Jāmiʿ al-Bayān*, vol. 1, 452; and al-Māwardī, *al-Nukat wa-l-ʿUyūn*, vol. 1, 95.
109 Al-Bahī al-Khūlī, *Ādam ʿAlayhi al-Salām, Falsafat Taqwīm al-Insān wa-Khilāfatuh* [Adam Peace Be upon Him: The Philosophy of Appraising Man and His Vicegerency] (Cairo: Maktabat Wahba, 3rd ed., 1974), 133–37.
110 Ibid., 154–57.
111 Al-Fārūqī, *Tawḥīd: Its Implication for Thought and Life*, 66–67.
112 Al-Khūlī, *Ādam ʿAlayhi al-Salām*, 157.
113 Al-Fārūqī, *Tawḥīd: Its Implication for Thought and Life*, 66–67.
114 Ibid.
115 Al-Khūlī, *Ādam ʿAlayhi al-Salām*, 154–57.
116 Al-Fārūqī, *Tawḥīd: Its Implication for Thought and Life*, 67.
117 Emmanuel Kant, *Critique du Jugement Suivi des Observations sur le Sentiment du Beau et du Sublime*, trans. J. Barni (Paris: Librairie Philosophique de Ladrange, 1846), vol. 2, 156.
118 Ibid., 145.
119 Al-Khūlī, *Ādam ʿAlayhi al-Salām*, 154–57.
120 Emmanuel Kant, *Critique du Jugement*, 145.
121 Al-Fārūqī, *Tawḥīd: Its Implication for Thought and Life*, 66–67.
122 The pronoun "whoever" (*man*) in this verse includes both conscious/rational (*al-ʿāqil*) beings as well as unconscious/irrational beings and inanimate objects (*ghayr al-ʿāqil*). In different occasions, the Qurʾan uses "whoever" (*man*) and "whatever" (*mā*) interchangeably in reference to both groups, as, for example, in: "To Allah prostrates whoever (*man*) there is in the heavens and the earth, willingly or unwillingly and their shadows at sunrise and sunset." (Q 13:15, Ali Qarai), and: "To Allah prostrates whatever (*mā*) is in the heavens and whatever is on the earth, including animals and angels, and they are not arrogant." (Q 16:49, Ali Qarai). Both verses include the worship of both groups. However, in the first verse, the pronoun "whoever" was used to give precedence (*taghlīb*) to the conscious/rational beings as to their rank vis-à-vis

the other creatures. In the second verse, the use of "whatever" is in reference to the precedence of the numerical superiority of the unconscious/irrational beings that worship God.

123 We may also translate this verse as follows: "It is Allah who has sent down the Book with the truth and He has sent down the Balance with the truth," thus conveying the idea that morals/Truth operating in the universe through the Balance, is the same Truth/good that the Revelation came down with.

124 This issue was addressed by some Akbarian scholars (followers of ibn ʿArabī) in the following way: "Before the actualisation of the human form the world existed and the planets revolved. So how can you call man the Pole (*quṭb*) of the cosmos and the means whereby it is maintained? Jāmī replies that although man did not exist in the sensory world, he did exist in the spiritual world, and the effect of his existence was manifest in the lower world." William C. Chittick, *In Search of the Lost Heart: Explorations in Islamic Thought*, ed. Mohammed Rustom, Atif Khalil and Kazuyo Murata (Albany: State University of New York Press, 2012), 151. However, if the human being is regarded as a cosmic bridge between the upper and the lower worlds, how can he transmit the Divine grace to the lower world before being present in it and before espousing a body of its nature? Moreover, what does it mean that the effects of the human being as a spirit manifest in the lower world? Does he act on the world before his presence in it? Which would imply the existence of another actor in creation besides God. Furthermore, is the human being, whether as a spirit or in his actual form, the maintainer of the cosmos? The above argument of ʿAbd al-Raḥmān al-Jāmī (d. 898/1492) reflects the Akbarian conception of vicegerency, as we have seen before, of the vicegerent as the one through whom the cosmos is maintained and polished and through whom God manifests His attributes. However, this is contradicted by a lot of Qurʾanic evidence as we see here, and in other texts that prove that God is not in need of an intermediary between Him and the "lower" world. Moreover, Q 2:31 clearly shows that the angels understood that the vicegerent would be corrupting the earth and not maintaining it, an argument that was not contradicted by God as we will see in following chapters. In addition to that, Q 2:30 clearly indicates that the vicegerent was assigned after the creation of the earth and the maintenance of the universe, which, once more, indicates that (the "perfect") man has nothing to do with that.

125 For the interpretation of this verse in this sense, see: Ibn Qayyim al-Jawziyya, *al-Wābil al-Ṣayyib min al-Kalām al-Ṭayyib* [The Invocation of God], ed. Sayyid Ibrāhīm (Cairo: Dār al-Ḥadīth, 3rd ed., 1999), 52–53. Another verse that indicates this double human guidance translates as follows: "And did We not guide him to the two elevated things?" (Q 90:10, Ahmad Khan).

126 Izutsu, Toshihiko, *Ethico-Religious Concepts in the Qurʾan* (Montreal: McGill-Queen's University Press, 2002), 17.

127 Al-Fārūqī, *Tawḥīd: Its Implication for Thought and Life*, 66–67.

128 Al-Khūlī, *Ādam ʿAlayhi al-Salām*, 128.

129 Al-Fārūqī, *Tawḥīd: Its Implication for Thought and Life*, 142–43.

130 Al-Khūlī, *Ādam ʿAlayhi al-Salām*, 175.

131 Ibid., 177.

132 Narrated by al-Bukhārī in his *Ṣaḥīḥ* (no. 5063) and Muslim in his *Ṣaḥīḥ* (no. 1401). Muḥammad ibn Ismāʿīl al-Bukhārī, *Ṣaḥīḥ al-Bukhārī*, ed. Muḥammad Zuhayr al-Nāṣir (Beirut: Dār Tawq al-Najā, 1422 AH); Muslim ibn al-Hajjāj al-Naysabūrī, *Ṣaḥīḥ Muslim*, ed., Muḥammad Fuʾād ʿAbd al-Bāqī (Beirut: Dār Iḥyāʾ al-Turāth al-ʿArabī, n.d.).

133 Al-Bayḍāwī, *Anwār al-Tanzīl wa-Asrār al-Taʾwīl*, vol. 1, 68.

134 Ismāʿīl Ḥaqqī al-Brūsawī, *Rūḥ al-Bayān* [The Spirit of Illumination] (Beirut: Dār al-Fikr, n.d.), vol. 1, 93.

135 Al-Iṣfahānī, *al-Dharīʿa ilā Makārim al-Sharīʿa*, 83–84.

136 Al-Shāṭibī, *al-Muwāfaqāt*, vol. 3, 25.

137 As we saw in the previous chapter, several reports from early scholars describe *khilāfa* as a task that should be performed by all religiously responsible/accountable (*mukallaf*) human beings, and by which one becomes a vicegerent of God. As noted before, this means deputisation on behalf of God in some of His acts or/and attributes, as the other meanings of *khilāfa* (like succession or replacement) are not applicable to God.
138 Steppat, "God's Deputy," 172.
139 ʿAbd al-Wahhāb ʿAzzām, *Muḥammad Iqbāl, Sīratuh wa-Falsafatuh wa-Shiʿruh* [Muḥammad Iqbal: His Life, Philosophy and Poetry] (Cairo: Hindāwī Publishing Corporation, 2014), 68.
140 Ibid., 89.
141 Muḥammad Bāqir al-Ṣadr, *al-Madrasa al-Qurʾāniyya* [The Qurʾanic School] (Cairo: Dār al-Kitāb al-Islāmī, 2nd ed., 2013), 96.
142 Muḥammad Bāqir al-Ṣadr, *al-Islām Yaqūd al-Ḥayāt* [Islam at the Forefront of Life] (Tehran: Ministry of Religious Guidance, 2nd ed., 1403 AH), 134, and Muḥammad Bāqir al-Ṣadr, *Khilāfat al-Insān wa-Shahādat al-Anbiyāʾ* [Vicegerency of Man and Testimony of Prophets] (Beirut: Dār al-Maʿārif al-Ḥikmiyya, 2014), 54–55.
143 Bāqir al-Ṣadr, *al-Islām Yaqūd al-Ḥayāt*, 141–42.
144 Ibid., 136–37.
145 Ibid., 170–71.
146 See for instance: Abū al-Aʿlā al-Mawdūdī, *al-Khilāfa wa-l-Mulk* [Caliphate and Kingship] (Kuwait: Dār al-Qalam, 1978), 21.
147 See for instance: Andrew F. March, *The Caliphate of Man: Popular Sovereignty in Modern Islamic Thought.*
148 This includes the fact that these authors often used vicegerency as a loose title or principle without clearly defining it, rooting it in the Qurʾan, linking it consistently with other Islamic concepts, developing the frame in which it operates explaining its theological foundations and hermeneutical arguments, and distinguishing between its means, objectives and outcomes, beside many other issues.
149 Especially the chapter in his book, *Al-Islām Yaqūd al-Ḥayāt*, titled "Khilāfat al-Insān wa-Shahādat al-Anbiyāʾ" [Vicegerency of Man and the Testimony of Prophets], which was later published as a monograph under the same title.
150 This will be discussed at the beginning of the next chapter.
151 In an unpublished MA thesis entitled *Mafhūm al-Istikhlāf fī l-Qurʾān al-Karīm Shurūṭuh wa-Maqāṣiduh* [The Concept of *al-Istikhlāf* in the Noble Qurʾan: Its Conditions and Objectives], that was submitted to the International Islamic University Malaysia (2006), Zaynab Aḥmad Dāwūd examines some of the views of classical and contemporary scholars of the concept, but the study lacks critical analysis and does not add anything significant to the subject matter.
152 These are the terms the author used to translate this concept.
153 Maszlee Malik, "Constructing the Architectonics and Formulating the Articulation of Islamic Governance: A Discursive Attempt in Islamic Epistemology" (PhD thesis, Durham University, 2011), 314. Available at Durham E-Theses Online: http://etheses.dur.ac.uk/832/
154 Muḥammad ʿAbd al-Fattāḥ al-Khatīb, *Qiyam al-Islām al-Ḥaḍāriyya*, 37–38.
155 Munā Abū al-Faḍl, *Naḥwa Minhājiyya li-l-Taʿāmul maʿa Maṣādir al-Tanẓīr al-Islāmī* [Toward a Methodology for Dealing with the Sources of Islamic Theorization] (Herndon, VA: The International Institute of Islamic Thought, 1996), 39–40.
156 Ibid., 45.
157 Abū Sulaymān, *al-Ruʾya al-Kawniyya al-Ḥaḍāriyya al-Qurʾāniyya*, 120, and *Azmat al-ʿAql al-Muslim*, 143.
158 See for instance: Malkāwī, *Manẓūmat al-Qiyam al-ʿUlyā*, 139, and al-Dasūqī, *al-Khilāfa al-Islāmiyya*, 435.
159 Muḥammad al-Ḥabīb Balkhūja, "Man in Islam Is the Alpha and Omega of Global Development," *The Ḥasanian Lectures*, 188, (1995), 199–200, retrieved from:

Jason Morgan-Foster, "Third Generation Rights: What Islamic Law Can Teach the International Human Rights Movement," *Yale Human Rights and Development Law Journal*, 8, no. 1 (2005), 94.

160 Al-Sayyid, *al-Ṣirā' 'alā al-Islām*, 161.

161 This is in 'Awda's view related to "general *istikhlāf*." He further divides vicegerency into "particular *istikhlāf*," which he considers to be vicegerency in ruling (*ḥukm*), whether it is related to a single individual, as ascribed in the Qur'an to the prophet Dāwūd and frequently discussed in classical scholarship, or to an entire nation in the sense of its empowerment on earth, as understood from Q 24:55. However, this latter division does not differ much from the former, as they both relate to ruling over and controlling the resources of the earth, the former being a general reality for the human being and the latter in respect of the predominance of a particular nation or individual in that regard. Overall, 'Awda does not really look at *istikhlāf* (with its categories) as an existential function, mission or religious responsibility, but rather as a Divine favour that is attained by abiding by the principles of Islam. Indeed, he considers that "*istikhlāf* in ruling, with its two categories [individual and collective], is another favour that God bestows on who He wants among his servants, whether nations or individuals, after he has bestowed them all with the favour of *istikhlāf* over the earth." 'Awda, *al-Islām wa-Awḍā'unā al-Siyāsiyya*, 18. "God's rule with regards to the vicegerency of nations and individuals is that He gives *istikhlāf* to the nations and individuals who deserve it. [...] If they abide by God's commands, call to Him, worship him alone without taking any partner besides Him, perform prayer, give alms, do good deeds, avoid bad deeds, recommend the good and forbid the evil [...] in that case, God will empower them on earth and grant them means to access everything." Ibid., 20–21. Hence, even though these divisions made by 'Awda between general and particular vicegerency are not familiar to classical scholarship, there is no substantial novelty in his views on *istikhlāf*. 'Awda concludes his expositions of the two categories by stating that both *istikhlāf* in the sense of *'imārat al-arḍ* and in the sense of the ruling (empowerment) of a particular nation or individual are composed of a set of rulings that are nothing more than the rulings of Islam. Vicegerency is thus nothing more than a result of abiding by Islam or being a good Muslim individual or nation. He says: "We conclude from the entire study above that the vicegerents on earth, whether in the general or particular sense, have many obligations that can be summed up in one title: obedience to God, in other words: following his commands and abstaining from what He forbids." Ibid., 31.

162 Ibid.

163 We do not consider Rāshid al-Ghannūshī's views on human rights to be an exception in this regard. Al-Ghannūshī does not develop a thesis on vicegerency, since he did not properly write on the subject but only superficially referred to it among many other Islamic concepts. Like many contemporary reformists/Islamists, al-Ghannūshī asserts that the vicegerency of man on earth, in the sense of *'imārat al-arḍ*, is the central idea in Islamic civilisation. Rāshid al-Ghannūshī, *al-Ḥurriyāt al-'Āmma fī l-Dawla al-Islāmiyya* [Civil Liberties in the Islamic State] (Beirut: Markaz Dirāsāt al-Wiḥda al-'Arabiyya, 1993), 97. He refers repeatedly to the concept of *istikhlāf* when elaborating his thesis on public sovereignty in Islam and his views on the Islamic conception of human rights. However, besides vicegerency, he uses many other Islamic concepts by including them broadly under the banner of vicegerency without elaborating their relationship and without grounding the concept theologically, in the same fashion of those who used *istikhlāf* as a mere synonym for Islam without developing the concept into a consistent theory. Furthermore, vicegerency, whether in his overall thesis or in the context of Islamic human rights, is only addressed passingly or just mentioned without any substantial development or addition. For instance, in his attempt to point out "the general framework of human rights in Islam," he did not say anything about vicegerency besides the fact that "the human being in Islam is deputized on behalf

of God, and it is within the covenant of vicegerency – Islamic *Sharīʿa* – that the sum of his rights and obligations operate." Ibid., 42. In the same way, he said that one difference between Western and Islamic human rights is that in the Islamic conception "the rights remain sacred obligations without any right for God's servant, the vicegerent, to undermine or neglect them. It is not his property but God almighty is its sole owner, the human being is deputized in this regard with the obligation to handle that function according to the will of the Owner." Ibid., 41. Moreover, when talking about the right to marry and its purpose he says: "Islam has encouraged the propagation of the humankind on earth to realize the object of vicegerency, which is *ʿimārat al-arḍ*." Ibid., 62. When talking about the right for social security he said, "These rights are related to the dignification of man with vicegerency." Ibid., 66. Besides the plain fact that al-Ghannūshī only passingly used vicegerency in his overall thesis and in his view on human rights by alluding to it superficially, as illustrated in the above examples, he uses many Islamic principles to portray the "Islamic" variant of human rights besides the concept of vicegerency without clearly and consistently linking them together and elaborating the overall framework in which they operate. This confirms the fact that his view of human rights is only based on vicegerency as a loose title or another name for Islam, not as a consistent theory. Furthermore, as noted above, al-Ghannūshī does not actually write about vicegerency.

164 Shams al-Dīn al-Kīlānī, *Mufakkirūn ʿArab Muʿāṣirūn: Qirāʾa fī Tajribat Bināʾ al-Dawla wa-Ḥuqūq al-Insān* [Contemporary Arab Thinkers: A Reading in the Experience of State Building and Human Rights] (Doha: Arab Center for Research and Policy Studies, 2016), 42.

165 Şükran Vahide, "Man as Vicegerent of the Earth: How New is Said Nursi's Interpretation?" in Hasan Hörküç, *God, Man, and Mortality: The Perspective of Bediuzzaman Said Nursi* (Tughra Books, 2015), 55.

166 Al-Dasūqī, *al-Khilāfa al-Islāmiyya*, 473.

167 Al-Aḥmar, "Istikhlāf al-Insān fī l-Arḍ bi-Waṣfih Maqṣad ʿĀmm," 101.

168 Abdelaziz Berghout, "Concept of Worldview between Assumption and Truth (Observation on Selected Western and Muslim Views)," *Jurnal Ushuluddin*, 23–24 (2006), 137.

## Bibliography

Abū al-Faḍl, Munā. *Naḥwa Minhājiyya li-l-Taʿāmul maʿa Maṣādir al-Tanẓīr al-Islāmī [Toward a Methodology for Dealing with the Sources of Islamic Theorization].* Virginia: The International Institute of Islamic Thought, 1st ed., 1996.

Abū Sulaymān, ʿAbd al-Ḥamīd. *Azmat al-ʿAql al-Muslim [The Crisis of the Muslim Mind].* Beirut: Dār al-Hādī, 1st ed., 2003.

Abū Sulaymān, ʿAbd al-Ḥamīd. *Al-Ruʾya al-Kawniyya al-Ḥaḍāriyya al-Qurʾāniyya, al-Munṭalaq al-Asās li-l-Iṣlāḥ al-Insānī [The Qurʾanic Civilizational Worldview: the Main Entry for Human Reform].* Cairo: Dār al-Salām, 2009.

Al-Aḥmar, ʿAbd al-Salām. "Istikhlāf al-Insān fī l-Arḍ, Naḥwa Ruʾya Qurʾāniyya Kulliyya [Vicegerency on Earth: Towards a Comprehensive Qurʾanic Vision]." *Proceedings of the International Symposium: The Noble Qurʾan and Worldview: Paths of Reflection and Management.* Rabat. Muḥammadiyya League of Scholars, 2014.

Al-Aḥmar, ʿAbd al-Salām. "Istikhlāf al-Insān fī l-Arḍ bi-Waṣfih Maqṣad ʿĀmm li-l-Qurʾān wa-l-Sharīʿa wa-l-Ḥaḍāra [Vicegerency on Earth as a General Objective of the Qurʾan, Sharīʿa and Civilization]." *Majallat Islāmiyyat al-Maʿrifa* 89 (Summer 2017).

ʿArab, Muḥammad. *Al-Ishrāq Khilāfat al-Insān fī l-Arḍ [Illumination of the Vicegerency of Man on Earth].* Damascus: Union of Arab Writers, 2001.

Atari, Aref T. M. "Christian "Service-Stewardship" and Islamic "Khilafah": Emerging Models in Educational Administration." *The American Journal of Islamic Social Sciences* 17 no. 2 (Summer 2000).

ʿAwda, ʿAbd al-Qādir. *Al-Islām wa-Awḍāʿunā al-Siyāsiyya [Islam and our Political Conditions]*. Beirut: Muʾassasat al-Risāla, 1981.

ʿAyyādī, ʿAbd al-ʿAzīz. "Al-Insān al-Khalīfa wa-Muhimmat al-Iʿmār: Ruʾya Qurʾāniyya li-l-Ḥaḍāra al-Insāniyya al-Muthlā [The Man-Vicegerent and the Mission of Building and Populating: A Qurʾanic View of the Ideal Human Civilization]." *Algeria, Social Sciences Journal* 20 (2015): 76.

ʿAzzām, ʿAbd al-Wahhāb. *Muḥammad Iqbāl, Sīratuh wa-Falsafatuh wa-Shiʿruh [Muḥammad Iqbal: His Life, Philosophy and Poetry]*. Cairo: Hindāwī Publishing Corporation, 2014.

Ibn Bādīs, ʿAbd al-Ḥamīd. *Tafsīr ibn Bādīs [The Exegesis of ibn Bādīs]*. Beirut: Dār al-Kutub al-ʿIlmiyya, 1st ed., 1995.

Balkhūja, Muḥammad al-Ḥabīb. "Man in Islam is the Alpha and Omega of Global Development." *The Ḥasanian Lectures* (1995). Retrieved from: Morgan-Foster, Jason. "Third Generation Rights: What Islamic Law Can Teach the International Human Rights Movement." *Yale Human Rights and Development Law Journal* 8 no. 1 188 (2005): 199–200.

Banī ʿĪsā, Muḥammad. "Naẓariyyat al-Istikhlāf wa-Atharuhā fī l-Iqtiṣād al-Islāmī [The Theory of Istikhlāf and its Effect on Islamic Economics]." *Journal of Ṣāliḥ ʿAbd Allāh Kāmil Center for Islamic Economics* 14 no. 40 (2010): 11–53.

Al-Bārr, ʿAbd Allāh ibn ʿAlī. "Mafhūm al-Istikhlāf wa-ʿimārat al-Arḍ fī l-Islām [The Concept of Vicegerency and Building and Populating the Earth in Islam]." *Journal of Ṣāliḥ ʿAbd Allāh Kāmil Center for Islamic Economics – Egypt*, 7 no. 20 (2003): 75–108.

Barazangi, Nimat H. "Vicegerency and Gender Justice in Islam." in *Islamic Identity and the Struggle for Justice*. Gainesville: University Press of Florida, 1996.

Barīma, Muḥammad al-Ḥasan. "Al-Ẓāhira al-Ijtimāʿiyya wa-Niẓāmuhā al-Maʿrifī fī l-Qurʾān al-Karīm [Social Phenomenon and its Epistemological System in the Noble Qurʾan]." in *Naḥwa Niẓām Maʿrifī Islāmī [Towards an Islamic Epistemological System]*. Amman: The International Institute of Islamic Thought, 1st ed., 2000.

Al-Bayḍāwī, Nāṣir al-Dīn al-Shirāzī. *Anwār al-Tanzīl wa-Asrār al-Taʾwīl [The Lights of the Revelation and the Mysteries of Interpretation]*. Edited by Muḥammad al-Marʿashilī. Beirut: Dār Iḥyāʾ al-Turāth al-ʿArabī, 1997.

Berghout, Abdelaziz. "Concept of Worldview between Assumption and Truth (Observation on Selected Western and Muslim Views)," *Jurnal Ushuluddin* 23–24 (2006): 117–138.

Berghout, Abdelaziz. "Toward an Islamic Framework for Worldview Studies: Preliminary Theorization." *The American Journal of Islamic Social Sciences* 24, no. 2 (2007): 22–43.

Berghout, Abdelaziz. "Mawqiʿ Naẓariyyat al-ʿIlm fī ʿAmaliyat al-Istikhlāf wa-l-Taḥaḍḍur ʿind al-Ustādh Badīʿ al-Zamān Saʿīd al-Nūrsī [The Position of the Theory of Knowledge in the Process of Vicegerency and Civilized Life in the Works of Badīʿ al-Zamān Saʿīd al-Nūrsī]." *Al-Nūr for Studies in Civilization and Thought*, no. 2 (Summer 2010).

Bint al-Shāṭiʾ, ʿĀʾisha. *Al-Qurʾān wa-Qaḍāyā al-Insān [The Qurʾan and Human Issues]*. Cairo: Dār al-Maʿārif, 1999.

Al-Brūsawī, Ismāʿīl Ḥaqqī. *Rūḥ al-Bayān [The Spirit of Illumination]*. Beirut: Dār al-Fikr, n.d.

. Chittick, William C. *In Search of the Lost Heart: Explorations in Islamic Thought*. Edited by Mohammed Rustom, Atif Khalil, and Kazuyo Murata. Albany: State University of New York Press, 2012.

Al-Dasūqī, Fārūq Aḥmad. *Al-Khilāfa al-Islāmiyya Uṣūluhā wa-Ḥaqīqatuhā wa-Ḥatmiyyat ʿAwdatihā [The Islamic Caliphate: Its Origins, Truth and the Imperative of its Return]*. Cairo: 1998.

Al-Dasūqī, Fārūq Aḥmad. *Istikhlāf al-Insān fī l-Arḍ [Vicegerency on Earth]*. Alexandria: Dār al-Daʿwa, n.d.

Dāwūd, Zaynab Aḥmad. "Mafhūm al-Istikhlāf fī l-Qurʾān al-Karīm Shurūṭuh wa-Maqāṣiduh [The Concept of Vicegerency in the Noble Qurʾan: Conditions and Objectives]." MA diss. The International Islamic University Malaysia, 2006.

Al-Dhahabī, Shams al-Dīn. *Al-ʿArsh [The Throne]*. Edited by Muḥammad al-Tamīmī. Medina: Deanship of Scientific Research at the Islamic University, 2nd ed., 2003.

Al-Fārūqī, Ismāʿīl Rājī. *Tawḥīd: Its Implication for Thought and Life*. Herndon, Virginia: International Institute of Islamic Thought, 1992.

Faraḥāt, Aḥmad Ḥasan. *Al-Khilāfa fī l-Arḍ, [Vicegerency on Earth]*. Kuwait: Dār al-Arqam, 2003.

Al-Ghannūshī, Rāshid. *Al-Ḥurriyāt al-ʿĀmma fī l-Dawla al-Islāmiyya [Civil Liberties in the Islamic State]*. Beirut: Markaz Dirāsāt al-Wiḥda al-ʿArabiyya, 1993.

Ḥājj Ḥamad, Muḥammad Abū al-Qāsim. *Al-Ḥākimiyya [Sovereignty]*. Beirut: Dār al-Sāqī, 2010.

Ḥashmtī, Mahdī. *Khalīfatu Allāh al-Insān al-Kāmil: Maʾāthir al-Shaykh Murtaḍā Muṭahharī [Vicegerent of God or the Perfect Man: The Legacies of Sheikh Murtaḍā Muṭahharī]*. Beirut: Dar al-Safwa, 1st ed., 2009.

Al-Iṣfahānī, al-Rāghib. *Al-Dharīʿa ilā Makārim al-Sharīʿa [The Book of Means to the Noble Qualities of Sharīʿa]*. Edited by Abū Zayd al-ʿAjamī. Cairo: Dār al-Salām, 2007.

Izutsu, Toshihiko. *Ethico-Religious Concepts in the Qurʾan*. Montreal: McGill-Queen's University Press, 2002.

Jabr, Muḥammad Amīn. *Al-Insān wa-l-Khilāfa fī l-Arḍ [Man and Vicegerency]*. Cairo: Dār al-Shurūq, 1st ed., 1999.

Jayyād, ʿAbd al-Riḍā Ḥasan. "Mafhūm al-Khilāfa al-Ilāhiyya li-l-Insān fī l-Qurʾān al-Karīm wa-Kitābāt al-ʿUlamāʾ al-Muslimīn [The Concept of Man's Vicegerency of God in the Noble Qurʾan and in Islamic Scholarship]." *Adab al-Kūfa Journal*, 1 no. 2 (2008): 133–155.

Johnston, David L. *Earth, Empire and Sacred Text: Muslims and Christians as Trustees of Creation*. London: Equinox, 2010.

Johnston, David L. "A Muslim and Christian Orientation to Human Rights: Human Dignity and Solidarity." *Indiana International & Comparative Law Review* 24 (2014): 899–920.

Kant, Emmanuel. *Critique du Jugement Suivi des Observations sur le Sentiment du Beau et du Sublime*. Translated by J. Barni. Paris: Librairie Philosophique de Ladrange, 1846.

Khālid, ʿAmru. *Innī Jāʿil fī l-Arḍ Khalīfa [I Will Set a Vicegerent on Earth]*. Beirut: Dār al-Maʿrifa, 3rd ed., 2012.

Al-Khaṭīb, ʿAbd al-Fattāḥ. *Qiyam al-Islām al-Ḥaḍāriyya, Naḥwa Insāniyya Jadīda [The Civilizational Values of Islam: Towards New Humanism]*. Doha: Kutub al-Umma, 1431 AH.

Al-Khūlī, al-Bahī. *Ādam ʿAlayhi al-Salām, Falsafat Taqwīm al-Insān wa-Khilāfatuh [Adam Peace be upon Him: The Philosophy of Appraising Man and his Vicegerency]*. Cairo: Maktabat Wahba, 3rd ed., 1974.

Al-Kīlānī, Shams al-Dīn. *Mufakkirūn ʿArab Muʿāṣirūn: Qirāʾa fī Tajribat Bināʾ al-Dawla wa-Ḥuqūq al-Insān [Contemporary Arab Thinkers: A Reading in the Experience of*

*State Building and Human Rights].* Doha: Arab Center for Research and Policy Studies, 1st ed., 2016.

Kim, Stephen Myongsu. "Transcendence of God-a Comparative Study of the Old Testament and the Qurʾan." PhD diss. University of Pretoria, 2009.

Lahey, Stephen E. *Philosophy and Politics in the Thought of John Wyclif.* New York: Cambridge University Press, 2003.

Malik, Maszlee. "Constructing the Architectonics and Formulating the Articulation of Islamic Governance: A Discursive Attempt in Islamic Epistemology." PhD diss. Durham University (2011).

Malkāwī, Fatḥī Ḥasan. *Manẓūmat al-Qiyam al-ʿUlyā: al-Tawḥīd wa-l-Tazkiya wa-l-ʿUmrān [The Higher Value System: Monotheism, Purification and Civilization].* Virginia: International Institute of Islamic Thought, 2013.

March, Andrew F. *The Caliphate of Man: Popular Sovereignty in Modern Islamic Thought.* Cambridge, MA; London, England: Harvard University Press, 2019.

Mare, W. Harold. "The Cultural Mandate and the New Testament Gospel Imperative." *Journal of the Evangelical Theological Society* 16, no. 3 (Summer 1973): 139–47.

Al-Masīrī, ʿAbd al-Wahhāb. *Mawsūʿat al-Yahūd wa-l-Yahūdiyya wa-l-Ṣuhyūniyya [Encyclopedia of Jews, Judaism and Zionism].* Egypt: Dār al-Shurūq, 1st ed., 2002.

Al-Maṭrūdī, ʿAbd al-Raḥmān. *Al-Insān, Wujūduh wa-Khilāfatuh fī l-Arḍ fī Ḍawʾi al-Qurʾān al-Karīm [Man, His Existence and Vicegerency on Earth in the Light of the Noble Qurʾan].* Cairo: Maktabat Wahba, 1st ed., 1990.

Al-Māwardī, ʿAlī Abū al-Ḥasan. *Al-Nukat wa-l-ʿUyūn [The Exegesis of al-Māwardī].* Edited by Sayyid ibn ʿAbd al-Maqṣūd. Beirut: Dār al-Kutub al-ʿIlmiyya, n.d.

Al-Mawdūdī, Abū al-Aʿlā. *Niẓām al-Ḥayāt fī l-Islām [The Order of Life in Islam].* Pakistan: Dār al-ʿUrūba, 2nd ed., 1958.

Al-Mawdūdī, Abū al-Aʿlā. *Al-Khilāfa wa-l-Mulk [Caliphate and Kingship].* Kuwait: Dār al-Qalam, 1978.

Ibn Muḥyī al-Dīn, al-Amīr ʿAbd al-Qādir al-Jazāʾirī. *Al-Mawāqif al-Rūḥiyya wa-l-Fuyūḍāt al-Subūḥiyya [Spiritual Attitudes and Sublime Effusions].* Beirut: Dār al-Kutub al-ʿIlmiyya, 2003.

Al-Mubārak, Aḥmad. *Wa-Ṭafiqā Yakhsifān, Khalq al-Insān wa-Khilāfatuh [And They Began to Stitch over Themselves: Human Creation and Vicegerency].* Beirut: Al-Dār al-ʿArabiyya li-l-ʿUlūm Nashirūn, 2015.

Al-Munāwī, Zayn al-Dīn. *Fayḍ al-Qadīr Sharḥ al-Jāmiʿ al-Ṣaghīr [The Blessings of the Mighty in the Explanation of the Small Treatise].* Cairo: al-Maktaba al-Tijāriyya al-Kubrā, 1937.

Al-Najjār, ʿAbd al-Majīd. "Al-Istikhlāf fī Fiqh al-Taḥaḍḍur al-Islāmī [Vicegerency in the Jurisprudence of Islamic Civilization]." *Malaysia, Attajdid Journal* 1 (Winter 1997).

Al-Najjār, ʿAbd al-Majīd. *Fiqh al-Taḥaḍḍur al-Islāmī [The Jurisprudence of Islamic Civilization].* Beirut: Dār al-Gharb al-Islāmī, 1st ed., 1999.

Al-Najjār, ʿAbd al-Majīd. *Khilāfat al-Insān bayna al-Waḥy wa-l-ʿAql [The Vicegerency of Man, Between Revelation and Reason: A Critique of the Dialectic of the Text, Reason, and Reality].* Herndon, Virginia: International Institute of Islamic Thought, 3rd ed., 2005.

Nasr, Seyyed Hossein. *The Heart of Islam: Enduring Values for Humanity.* New York: Harper San Francisco, 2002.

Al-Nūrsī, Badīʿ al-Zamān Saʿīd. *Ishārāt al-Iʿjāz fī Maẓān al-Ījāz [Signs of Miraculousness: the Inimitability of the Qurʾan's Conciseness].* Cairo: Sözler Publications, 3rd ed., 2002.

Qaraybi', Muḥammad 'Ayyād. *Al-Istikhlāf wa-l-Ḥaḍāra, Dirāsa fī l-Istikhlāf al-Ilāhī li-l-Insān fī Ḍaw'i al-Qaṣaṣ al-Qur'ānī [Vicegerency and Civilization: a Study on Divine Vicegerency in the Light of Qur'anic Narratives]*. Amman: Dār Zahrān, 1st ed., 2013.

Ibn Qayyim al-Jawziyya, Shams al-Dīn. *Al-Wābil al-Ṣayyib min al-Kalām al-Ṭayyib [The Invocation of God]*. Edited by Sayyid Ibrāhīm. Cairo: Dār al-Ḥadīth, 3rd ed., 1999.

Al-Qūnawī, Ṣadr al-Dīn. *I'jāz al-Bayān fī Tafsīr Umm al-Qur'ān [The Miraculous Allocution in the Explanation of the Mother of the Qur'an]*. Qum, Iran: Maktab al-I'lām al-Islāmī, 1381 AH.

Riḍā, Muḥammad Rashīd. *Tafsīr al-Manār [Interpretation of the Illuminator]*. Cairo: al-Hay'a al-Miṣriyya, 1990.

Al-Ṣadr, Muḥammad Bāqir. *Al-Islām Yaqūd al-Ḥayāt [Islam at the Forefront of Life]*. Tehran: Ministry of Religious Guidance, 2nd ed., 1403 AH.

Al-Ṣadr, Muḥammad Bāqir. *Khilāfat al-Insān wa-Shahādat al-Anbiyā' [Vicegerency of Man and the Testimony of Prophets]*. Beirut: Dār al-Ma'ārif al-Ḥikmiyya, 1st ed., 2014.

Al-Sāmurrā'ī, Nu'mān 'Abd al-Razzāq. *Naḥnu wa-l-Ḥaḍāra wa-l-Suhūd [We, Civilization and Witnessing]*. Doha: Kutub al-Umma, 1421 AH.

Al-Sayyid, Raḍwān. *Al-Ṣirā' 'alā al-Islām [The Fight for Islam]*. Beirut: Dār al-Kitāb al-'Arabī, 2004.

Sayilgan, Gurbet. "The Ur-Migrants: The Qur'anic Narratives of Adam and Eve and Their Contribution to a Constructive Islamic Theology of Migration." PhD diss. Georgetown University, 2015.

Schenzle, Ruben. "If God is king, is man his Vicegerent? Considering *Ḥalīfah* in regard to Ancient Kingship." In *New Approaches to Human Dignity in the Context of Qur'anic Anthropology*. Edited by Rüdiger Braun and Hüseyin I. Çiçek, 132–147. Cambridge: Cambridge Scholars Publishing, 2017.

Sharī'atī, 'Alī. *Al-Insān wa-l-Islām [Man and Islam]*. Translated by Abbās al-Turjumān. Beirut: Dār al-Amīr, 2nd ed., 2007.

Al-Shāṭibī, Abū Isḥāq. *Al-Muwāfaqāt [The Reconciliation]. Annotated by Mashūr ibn Ḥasan*. Cairo: Dār ibn 'Affān, 1997.

Steppat, Fritz. "God's Deputy: Materials on Islam's Image of Man." *Arabica* 36, no. 2 (1989): 163–72.

Al-Ṭabarī, Muḥammad ibn Jarīr. *Jāmi' al-Bayān 'an Ta'wīl Āyī al-Qur'ān [The Comprehensive Exposition of the Interpretation of the Verses of the Qur'an]*. Edited by Aḥmad Muḥammad Shākir. Beirut: Mu'assasat al-Risāla, 2000.

Ibn Taymiyya, Taqī al-Dīn. *Minhāj al-Sunna al-Nabawiyya fī Naqḍ Kalām al-Shī'a al-Qadariyya [The Way of the Prophet's Sunna: a Critique of the Theological Discourse of al-Qadariyya Shiites]*. Edited by Muḥammad Rashād Sālim. Riyadh: Imām Muḥammad ibn Sa'ūd Islamic University, 1986.

Thekkemuriyil, Mathew. "Image and Likeness of God-an Understanding and Appraisal of the Christian and Islamic Concept of Human Beings in Light of the Creation Narratives in the Bible and in the Qur'an." MA diss. University of Leuven 2011.

Al-'Umarī, Aḥmad Khayrī. *Sīrat Khalīfa Qādim, Qirā'a 'Aqā'diyya fī Bayān al-Wilāda [Biography of the Incoming Khalīfa: A Doctrinal Reading in the Profile of Birth]*. Egypt: Dār Ajyāl, 2013.

Vahide, Şükran. "Man as Vicegerent of the Earth: How New is Said Nursi's Interpretation?" In *God, Man, and Mortality: The Perspective of Bediuzzaman Said Nursi*, edited by Hasan Hörküç. New Jersey: Tughra Books, 2015.

Wagner, Charles Peter. *Church Growth and the Whole Gospel: A Biblical Mandate*. Oregon, Eugene: Wipf and Stock, 1998.

Al-Zamakhsharī, Maḥmūd. *Al-Kashāf ʿan Ḥaqāʾiq Ghawāmiḍ al-Tanzīl [The Discoverer of Revealed Truths]*. Beirut: Dār al-Kitāb al-ʿArabī, 1987.

Zarmān, Muḥammad. "Waẓīfat al-Istikhlāf fī l-Qurʾān al-Karīm wa-Dalālātuhā wa-Abʿāduhā al-Ḥaḍāriyya [The Function of *Istikhlāf* in the Noble Qurʾan: its Civilizational Meanings and Dimensions]." Qatar University, *Journal of the College of Sharia, Law and Islamic Studies* 16 (1998).

Zūzū, Farīda. "Maqṣad Ḥifẓ al-Bīʾa wa-Atharuhu fī ʿAmaliyyat al-Istikhlāf [The Objective of Preserving the Environment and its Impact on the Vicegerency Process]." *Majallat Islāmiyyat al-Maʿrifa* 48 (Summer 2007).

# 5 The Object of Vicegerency

## Identifying Human Existential Function

In the previous chapter it has been demonstrated that vicegerency as an existential function has not been addressed and studied adequately in contemporary Islamic thought. Until the present day, we find no studies that could develop a theory of vicegerency or define its outlines, let alone a comprehensive theory about the existential function of the human being.[1] It was also suggested that a major cause for this deficit is the failure to ground the concept in solid theological and Qur'anic grounds. One of the reasons behind this failure that prevented the development of an integral theory is the deficiency in determining the object of vicegerency (*al-mustakhlaf fīhi*) based on coherent theological hermeneutics. This deficiency in determining the object of vicegerency in addition to the deficiency in grounding the concept has resulted in myriad problems that disrupted the very conditions for the establishment of a vicegerency theory. These problems include the lack of establishment of the ontological correlation between vicegerency and the higher principles of Islam that constitute the Islamic worldview, such as the correlation between vicegerency, monotheism, worship and other concepts and values. Further issues include the lack of establishment of the ontological correlation between vicegerency and its ramifications in the Qur'an as well as the lack of clarity regarding the distinction between vicegerency as a human function, its purpose, objectives, fruits, means, foundations and conditions. Another problem is the absence of theological rooting of the way in which vicegerency, as the function that Revelation came to enable human beings to perform, governs all teachings and rulings of Revelation and how the latter contribute to the realisation of vicegerency and operate within it.

Based on the above and on the analysis and critique provided in the previous chapter as to the current state of affairs in the literature on vicegerency, the present chapter is an attempt to lay the groundwork for developing the features of a vicegerency theory. The goal is to overcome the deficiencies that have prevented the development of this theory to this day. In doing so, we will, in this chapter and in the following one, adopt a methodological approach that is meant to guarantee the coherency and inclusiveness of our arguments as much as possible based on the following criteria:

- Studying vicegerency within the Qur'anic view of existence and universe
- Rooting the object of vicegerency theologically

DOI: 10.4324/9781003335948-5

- Clarifying the ontological correlation between the object of vicegerency and deputisation on behalf of God
- Clarifying the ontological correlation between vicegerency and the higher principles and values of Islam
- Clarifying how the teachings of Islam are coherently organised under the function of vicegerency
- Clarifying the standards upon which we base our choice of the governing Islamic principles and values
- Clearly distinguishing between the human function and its purposes, fruits, means, conditions and consequences
- Clarifying the ontological correlation between vicegerency and the principles and issues that stem from it

The failure of the contemporary attempts to develop a vicegerency theory is a result of the absence of all of the aforementioned elements from the contemporary studies that tackled the subject matter. The development of a vicegerency theory can only be realised after these problems are adequately solved, an enterprise that we will attempt to undertake through this chapter and the following. This is precisely what we mean by the necessary ontologico-theological rooting for the development of the said theory.

In the previous chapter, it became clear that the object of vicegerency determined by contemporary researchers warrants criticism when examined in light of the Qur'an and Islamic creed and is not appropriate for the articulation of a vicegerency theory. Hence, we cannot but bypass those studies and seek the object of vicegerency elsewhere. However, before embarking upon that, it is important to take a brief look at the evidence that was produced by those researchers in support of their views, in order to gauge their validity and decide to what extent they can be relied upon, and in order to justify our rupture with those studies. Indeed, when tracking the evidence used to determine the object of vicegerency, it became apparent to us that contemporary writers did not attach much importance to proving their arguments. We could only find some extremely brief and superficial arguments in this regard. Some of them did not even produce proofs as though they believed that their views were incontestable axioms.[2]

## 5.1 Deducing the Object of Vicegerency

The first group from our previous classification, which identified the object of vicegerency in building and populating the earth (*'imārat al-arḍ*), in addition to the dominance and sovereignty over it, according to many of them, did not spend much effort in proving their view. It appears that they considered the idea that *'imārat al-arḍ* is the very meaning of vicegerency to be a self-evident supposition. Some of them based that view merely on the fact that God has given human beings the faculties of innovation, discovery and development.[3] However, this in itself cannot stand as evidence since the human being was given many more faculties besides these. Furthermore, the faculty to perform something does not necessarily imply that that matter is the very purpose or mission of the human being. Otherwise, reproduction, destruction, conflict and whatever else the human being is capable of becomes an existential function.

Another proponent argued that since the human being was created from clay, he is implicitly associated with the elements of nature "and it is, therefore, only natural that his interaction with nature is one of utilisation, especially when God assigns to him the tasks of worshipping Him alone and building and populating the earth, which is the vicegerency mission assigned to man."[4] If this logical correlation between the creation of the human being from the elements of nature and his utilisation of it holds true, then this should similarly apply to the rest of animals and is in no way indicative that such utilisation is one of the human being's existential tasks. Likewise, this does not mean that it is a duty with which Revelation entrusted man. The Qur'an extensively states the purposes behind the creation of the earth and its existents and the ways the human being interacts with it, and this includes numerous purposes over and above the mere utilisation of the earth. The material dimension does not constitute the sole common denominator between man and nature. Both of them share multiple common grounds that define the nature of man's interactions with the universe and the purposes behind the creation of the earth. These include, but are not limited to, spiritual, creedal, intellectual, psychological, aesthetic and ethical purposes. In the next chapter we have listed 13 human-related purposes that the Qur'an explicitly states among the numerous reasons behind the creation of the existents of the earth. We will further elaborate in this chapter on how both the human being and the universe partake in achieving the same existential and ethical purposes. Moreover, the proponent of the previous argument did not present any proofs that substantiate the supposition that building and populating the earth is one of humans' existential missions and not even that that constitutes an Islamic injunction. It seems that this idea has become so prevalent among contemporary thinkers that some of them believe that it is not in need of argumentation.

Many proponents of this first group[5] merely cited the verse featuring the statement "He has produced you from the earth and settled you in it (*ista'marakum fīhā*)" (Q 11:61, Sahih Intl) without providing further commentary or analysis as if this segment of the verse on its own is explicit in defining vicegerency in terms of *'imārat al-arḍ*. This segment of the verse is repeatedly quoted by most contemporary advocates of vicegerency as human function. It is also quoted by some of those who addressed the issue of the human existential function outside the context of vicegerency.[6] However, nothing in that verse refers to a relation between *'imārat al-arḍ* and vicegerency. Regardless, the argument that vicegerency is synonymous with *'imārat al-arḍ* lacks evidence on its own. Moreover, the verse does not indicate that *'imārat al-arḍ* entails a value as such. To the contrary, the Qur'an recounts stories of ancient nations who built the earth with the highest manifestations of civilisation, and yet this availed them nothing in the sight of God; "Have they not travelled through the earth and observed how was the end of those before them? They were greater than them in power, and they ploughed the earth and built it up (*'amarūha*) more than they have built it up." (Q 30:9, b.o. Sahih Intl).

Moreover, the same verse on the basis of which those scholars argue indicates, in fact, that building and populating the earth is not an obligation that depends on religiosity, let alone being an existential mission dictated by Revelation, but is merely a cosmic fate. The verse in its entirety reads:

> And to Thamūd [We sent] their brother Ṣāliḥ. He said, "O my people, worship Allah; you have no deity other than Him. He has produced you from the earth and settled you in it (*istaʿmarakum fīhā*), so ask forgiveness of Him and then repent to Him. Indeed, my Lord is near and responsive."

Thus, the people of Thamūd had indeed built and populated the earth in a civilised way before any Messenger came to them. Ṣāliḥ came to call them to belief, not to build the earth, and to remind them of the graces of God Who permitted them to achieve *ʿumrān* and civilisation, which implies belief, asking for forgiveness and repentance. The above is what the Qurʾan explicitly mentions and not an interpretation; hence, a great number of Qurʾanic exegetes recorded it.[7] According to Rashīd Riḍā, for example,

> the phrase "*istaʿmarakum fīhā*" means "God made you constructors (*ʿummār*) in the earth," from the infinitive *ʿumrān*. That is because they were farmers, manufacturers and builders; God says, "And they used to carve from the mountains houses, feeling secure." (Q 15:82, Sahih Intl) [...] The meaning [of Q 11:61] is "God created you and provided you with the means of *ʿumrān* and benefits of the earth; and therefore, you ought not worship any deities other than Him as He alone is the provider of all bounties and the only one deserving to be worshipped. Therefore, you must ask Him for forgiveness and repent to Him."[8]

This purport of the above verse is further reiterated by another verse that recounts the story of the people of Thamūd with their Prophet and shows the aspects of their endeavours in constructing the earth. This verse itself was used by some as evidence that vicegerency is synonymous with construction and population.[9] The verse reads: "And remember when He made you [Thamūd] successors after ʿĀad and settled you in the land, [and] you take for yourselves palaces from its plains and carve from the mountains, homes. Then remember the favours of Allah and do not commit abuse on the earth, spreading corruption." (Q 7:74, b.o. Sahih Intl). Since God's settlement of Thamūd in the land and since their activities of taking for themselves palaces from plains and carving homes from the mountains had already happened before any Messenger came to them to instruct them with the same (they were sent to them to ask them to repent to God as is clear from the verse), then this construction is merely a Divine cosmic will and not the existential mission of man. God indeed destroyed them although they realised *ʿimārat al-arḍ*. The purport of the verse is thus quite the opposite of the opinion of this group. It is indicative of the fact that building the earth is not the existential function that man is entrusted with by virtue of Revelation.[10]

Another proponent cites as evidence the verse reading, "And We have certainly established you upon the earth and made for you therein ways of livelihood. Little are you grateful." (Q 7:10, Sahih Intl). He then said, "there are many other Qur'anic evidences," and referred to a set of verses.[11] However, the aforementioned verse, again, only contains a statement of an established fact, by virtue of which man ought to give thanks to God. It makes no mention of a function or a duty whatsoever. Besides, the verse makes no reference to any relation between its content and vicegerency. In the same way, the other verses that he designates as "Qur'anic evidences" make no case as to his conclusion that vicegerency means building the earth and utilising its resources.

Other advocates from the same group[12] relied on the verses that state that God has subjected the universe for man. Again, these verses as such do not prove a relation between this subjugation (*taskhīr*) and vicegerency. As a matter of fact, all of the verses about subjugation talk, without exception, about God's subjection of the universe as a reminder of His favour on humans, so that, upon reflecting over this fact, the human being attains belief in God. In other words, this subjugation is a cosmic fact necessitating thanksgiving and is not a duty of the human being. This conclusion is evident from all the verses relevant to the question of subjugation. For example, God says: "It is Allah who subjected for you the sea so that ships may sail upon it by His command and that you may seek of His bounty; and perhaps you will be grateful" (Q 45:12, b.o. Sahih Intl);

> Do you not see that Allah has made subject for you whatever is in the heavens and whatever is in the earth and amply bestowed upon you His favours, [both] apparent and unapparent? But of the people is he who disputes about Allah without knowledge or guidance or an enlightening Book [from Him].
> (Q 31:20, b.o. Sahih Intl).

And,

> It is Allah who created the heavens and the earth and sent down rain from the sky and produced thereby some fruits as provision for you and subjected for you the ships to sail through the sea by His command and subjected for you the rivers. And He subjected for you the sun and the moon, continuous [in orbit], and subjected for you the night and the day. And He gave you from all you asked of Him. And if you should count the favour of Allah, you could not enumerate them. Indeed, humankind is [generally] most unjust and ungrateful.
> (Q 14:32–34, Sahih Intl).

In addition, other verses make it clear that subjugation is a cosmic norm and not a human function or responsibility. One of the above-mentioned researchers attempted to refute this argument by dividing subjugation into two kinds: Absolute subjugation, which is not dependent on human actions, and subjugation that depends on human use of the objects in the universe.[13] However, this division as such lacks evidence as the verses refer only to the first kind, and there is no explicit or implicit reference to the second kind. The verses rather indicate that the subjugator is God and that the human being is merely a utiliser and not a subjugator. The author linked the second kind with the incident of Adam being taught all names as mentioned in Q 2:31, and views this kind of subjugation to be "attained through learning the names and through the knowledge of the characteristics of the objects and the living beings to be subjugated, which is currently known as industrial and technological progress."[14] This, again, lacks evidence, in addition to the absence of any justification for limiting the names taught to Adam to the names that are to be learnt to enable industrial and technological progress. The use of these verses to deduce the object of vicegerency is problematic from two perspectives. First, they do not link vicegerency with subjugation, and hence the proof of this relation should be sought elsewhere. Second, they do not indicate that subjugation is a human function or task.

Even if we assume that the utilisation of what God has made usable for man is required, or rather desired by God, that utilisation occurs by the motivation of the human being's innate instinct and is not in need of Revelation or belief. This is evidenced by the conditions of humanity throughout history until today. This is in addition to the fact that this is not subjugation, but rather utilisation and exploitation of what has been subjugated by God. Therefore, we do not find any explicit or strict command in Revelation to achieve "industrial and technological progress," let alone this being the function of vicegerency.

Sayyid Quṭb used a similar argument to defend his view on the object of vicegerency, citing the following verse: "It is He who created for you all of that which is on the earth. Then He directed Himself to the heaven and made them seven heavens, and He is Knowing of all things." (Q 2:29, b.o. Sahih Intl). Our remarks above apply to the use of this verse in support of this view in the same way. However, it can be said that Quṭb's deduction is better founded than the former ones since the verse he cited immediately precedes the verse of vicegerency (Q 2:30), hence Quṭb tried to explain how they relate to each other.[15] Quṭb attempts to link the verse of vicegerency with the verse that precedes it on the grounds that the relation between the two verses resides in the fact that God created everything on the earth for the human being, and this makes man a vicegerent over the resources of the earth and entitled to make use of them. However, this conclusion based on the relation between the two verses is not supported by sufficient evidence. If the link between Q 2:30 and the preceding verse resides in the fact that the latter indicates the domain in which the human being is entrusted with achieving vicegerency, it does not refer to the essence of this function. This is evidenced by the fact that the verse talks about the creation of the universe and that the earthly domain was created for the human being. The verse says nothing about the human being becoming the "master of the earth and the master of the machine"[16] nor does it say that the utilisation and harnessing of everything on Earth is a human task as Quṭb argues. God indeed created everything on the earth for the human being in order to enable him to accomplish the mission of vicegerency, which is a *fait accompli* that does not depend on human responsibility and endeavours. It is quite evident from Quṭb's arguments that his view came as a reaction to the materialistic progress of the Western civilisation, which, according to him, gave priority to the materialistic values over the human being, thus making the human being subordinate to material progress. Thus, interpreting vicegerency as dominance, according to this perspective, frees the human being from servanthood to material by making him dominant over it, and not the other way around. It is on the basis of this very logic that al-Dasūqī divided vicegerency into servitude (*ʿubūdiyya*) and lordship (*rubūbiyya*) as we saw in the previous chapter.

As noted above, the human being, from the Qurʾanic perspective, is of a higher value and rank than the other creatures. However, does this necessarily mean that he is the lord and master over them and that he possesses sovereignty over the earth? The Qurʾan does not state this at all. This supposition is, rather, based on a projection of pre-established ideas on the Qurʾan as a reaction to Western progress, as mentioned above. The Qurʾan actually states that the sole Master and Lord of the universe is the One who created it, and not the one who utilises it as mentioned before.

In any case, all these are superficial deductions that attempt to attribute purports to some Qurʾanic verses, which they do not explicitly or implicitly state, in an effort to make them suit preconceived notions. These preconceived notions were, more often than not, motivated by a reactionary attitude than by a deliberate consideration of the Qurʾanic verses and conception of the human being and his existential function. This attitude grew in proportions to the extent that industrial and technological progress became one of the greatest objectives of the Qurʾan, in the same way that they are one of the greatest objectives of the dominant Western civilisation.

As for the second group, which argues that the object of vicegerency is the fulfilment of God's will, its members were not more profound or sophisticated in rooting their opinion in the Qurʾan or providing other evidence. In fact, they did not provide more than some logical or linguistic arguments. Some of them argued, for example, that if you assign someone to act on your behalf, they should behave according to your will, not according to theirs.[17] Although it is true according to this logic that a condition of vicegerency is that the vicegerent undertakes it according to the will of the one who mandated him with that, it does not mean that that condition is the very object of that function. A similar argument states that, linguistically speaking, "one of the meanings of vicegerency is to execute commands."[18] Like many others, some advocates of this group did not even attempt to provide evidence for their view, as though their opinion were self-evident.[19]

As for the third group, which maintains that the object of vicegerency is free will and choice, it was shown in the previous chapter that some of those who formulated this view based their argument on the understanding that freedom of choice and behaviour are what distinguish humans from other creatures.[20] However, humans have other characteristics that differentiate them from other creatures. Thus, why should this characteristic in particular, and not any other, be the object of vicegerency? Furthermore, we have already explained that freedom as such is not a function or action, and thus cannot be the object of vicegerency.

Another researcher from this group quoted the following Qur'anic verses in support of his opinion: "Indeed, We guided him to the path, he may be grateful and he may be ungrateful." (Q 76:3, b.o. Sahih Intl); "And [by] the soul and He who proportioned it harmoniously. And inspired it [with discernment of] its wickedness and its righteousness, he has succeeded who purifies it, and he has failed who instils it [with corruption]." (Q 91:7–10, b.o. Sahih Intl); and "Have We not made for him two eyes and a tongue and two lips and guided him to the two elevated things?" (Q 90:8–10, b.o. Ahmad Khan). The researcher did not demonstrate how these verses denote that freedom is the object of human vicegerency. He only briefly commented, "Thus, vicegerency and the freedom of action and choice it entails are the essence of human life and its purpose in doing good deeds, innovating and constructing."[21] These verses, however, do not indicate whatsoever that the object of vicegerency is freedom of choice. This author has thus contented himself with listing verses that do not relate to the topic under discussion, without even trying to relate them to vicegerency. This is another blatant example of the lack of interest among contemporary scholars in rooting the object of vicegerency in the Qur'an, despite the fact that the author's book carries the title "The Qur'anic Worldview."

Another researcher maintained that this conclusion

> is obvious from all the verses that touch on vicegerency, including the statement addressed by Moses to his people: "Perhaps your Lord will destroy your enemy and grant you succession/vicegerency in the earth and see how you will do." (Q 7:129, b.o. Sahih Intl); and the *Ḥadīth*: "The world is sweet and green (alluring) and verily Allah is going to install you as vicegerents in it in order to see how you act."[22] Vicegerency, by virtue of these two Texts, is founded on the human being's entitlement to absolute freedom on earth, allowing him either to reform or to corrupt as he desires under the watch of God, Who keeps record of what he does, and for which He will hold him accountable in the Last Day and reward him accordingly. With this understanding, vicegerency means that God has given man the entitlement to act and choose in this world, and that He will hold him accountable in the Hereafter accordingly.[23]

However, these texts can, at best, prove that vicegerency is a responsibility, for which man will be brought to account by God, but they neither specify this responsibility nor indicate that the object of vicegerency is freedom of choice.

In the previous chapter, we presented the evidence used by the fourth group (including implicitly the Akbarian view) to support their opinion that the object of vicegerency is the manifestation of the Divine ethics on Earth. We saw that their argumentation was not based on Qur'anic grounds but rather on a set of philosophical (often esoteric) doctrines. They argued, for instance, on the premise that the human being is the sole ethical creature on Earth and that he is an interface between God and the world, suppositions that proved in opposition to the Qur'an, as explained in the previous chapter.

As for Bāqir al-Ṣadr, who argued that the object of vicegerency is managing and attending to "all the matters belonging to the Almighty *Mustakhlif*," he based his view on the fact that "God Almighty is the Lord of the earth and its goods and He is the Lord of humans, animals and every creature that lives in this vast universe, which means that the vicegerent of God on earth is deputised over all these things."[24] However, this argumentation is flawed on the basis of the fact that most of the existents of the world are managed and attended to by God in such a way that they do not fall within the responsibility of humans. Should that responsibility over "all the matters" be assigned to the human being, the earth and its existents would cease to exist, as asserted by the Qur'an: "Indeed Allah sustains the heavens and the earth lest they should fall apart, and if they were to fall apart, there is none who can sustain them except Him. Indeed, He is All-Forbearing, All-Forgiving." (Q 35:41, Ali Qarai). Humans do not even have knowledge of many animate and inanimate creatures and cosmic laws, let alone the ability to manage and attend to the universe. Thus, vicegerency must be in effect for a limited set of matters that belongs to God, and not for all the matters that belong to Him. These matters are to be determined with better founded evidence than merely stating that it is about matters belonging to God.

All the above confirms that none of the contemporary advocates of vicegerency were able to produce well-founded and well-developed evidence in support of their views regarding the determination of the object of vicegerency from a Qur'anic perspective. The Qur'an did not play a central role in determining the meaning of vicegerency and identifying its object as we saw. The arguments presented to justify the views on the object of vicegerency are superficial and often a projection of pre-established opinions or reactions on isolated Qur'anic texts, or even fragments of texts. The above represents another example that illustrates the reason why we cannot speak about a Qur'anic vicegerency theory, or even a vicegerency theory at all, in contemporary scholarship. Moreover, the relation between deputisation on behalf of God and the object of vicegerency and their ontological connection has not been precisely defined, as we have seen before.

## 5.2 Vicegerency is Deputisation on Behalf of God

Based on the above, the primary condition for identifying the object of vicegerency in the process of the ontologico-theological rooting of vicegerency is to found that identification on sound and holistic Qur'anic deductions and on a consistent correlation between the object of vicegerency and the issue of deputisation on behalf of God. We consider this the first step towards overcoming the aspects of deficiency that characterise the contemporary discussion on vicegerency. Yet, we must first prove that the one who the vicegerent deputises for is God and not somebody or something else, so that our thesis about the mission assigned to the human being on behalf of God is established on a firm basis.

Let us begin here by reiterating the linguistic definition of *khilāfa*. According to the Arabic lexicons, *khilāfa* means to deputise someone to do something on his behalf whether in his absence or presence or otherwise to succeed or replace someone.[25] Accordingly, *khilāfa* entails necessarily the deputisation, replacement or succession of somebody or something. Commenting on Q 2:30, Qur'an exegetes offered three different views about who is deputised or succeeded by the vicegerent (*al-mustakhlaf 'anhu*): The former generations; the jinn or other creatures that inhabited the earth before man; or God, as was detailed in the third chapter. When closely examining Q 2:30, however, it becomes evident that vicegerency is the deputisation of God and not somebody else, for different considerations that we will develop below.

*Khilāfa*, as expressed in Q 2:30, is a human specificity by which no other creature was described, by virtue of certain faculties that the human being does not share with any other creature, as mentioned in the sequence of the verse. Furthermore, the ascription of *khilāfa* to the human being was a great occurrence that merited Divine acknowledgement and the Divine command to the angels to prostrate themselves before Adam. The mere succession of generations, however, is not specific to humans, not unprecedented and does not merit such Divine acknowledgement in an assembly of angels. Moreover, the succession of generations is an inevitable cosmic fate that per se does not denote any function. If the meaning of *khilāfa* was to inform of an inevitable predetermined event, i.e., the succession of generations, the angels would not have been astonished because God predetermines what He wills. The Qur'an underlines the fact that the angels do not question the Divine decree, "They do not speak before He has, and they execute what they are ordered to do." (Q 21:27, b.o. Ahmad Khan). The vicegerency verse does not contain an exception to this rule. Since the vicegerency verse is the only Qur'anic passage that recounts the angels' astonishment at the Divine decree in contrast to their basic attitude of absolute submission to the Divine will, this indicates that this decision is not merely a predetermined fact or cosmic command.

Before the human being was created, there had been successive generations of animal species on earth. If *khilāfa* is the mere succession of generations, why were the angels astonished? Before the human being's advent on Earth, there was what could appear as deprivation, since these animals were shedding each other's blood. Throughout the history of the earth, there had been natural disasters that led to mass extinctions of animal species and caused massive wildfires, extinction of flora and fauna, global climate change and other effects that were discovered by modern science.[26] If God was speaking of a predetermined fact, then why would the angels be astonished at the human being's potential corruption, since these disasters had caused much more destruction than can be achieved by the human being? Moreover, it is an established and consensual fact in Islamic creed that it is the angels themselves that are entrusted with the execution of these disasters and any other Divine decree in His creation, whether in terms of operation, destruction or construction.

Rather, the angels were astonished because they knew that *khilāfa* is a mission that the human being had been entrusted with and could not grasp the rationale behind the Divine decree of placing a vicegerent on Earth while they were capable of putting the Divine decrees strictly into effect without deviating an inch. Therefore, "They said, 'Will You place in it one who causes corruption therein and sheds blood, while we declare Your praise and sanctify You?'" (Q 2:30, b.o. Sahih Intl). This indicates that *khilāfa* is not an inevitable predetermined fact, but rather a mission that the one entrusted with can fulfil or abandon; hence, it cannot be the mere succession of generations. God, therefore, did not blame them for questioning His decree, but instead informed them of the rationale behind it and that the human being is capable of carrying out the mission of vicegerency due to characteristics he has, which the angels were not aware of and do not possess. In other words, the fact that the angels knew that *khilāfa* is not an inevitable predetermination and that, therefore, some people would not abide by it, and the fact that God showed the angels the good qualities that qualify the human being for *khilāfa* and make it superior to the function of the angels, indicate that *khilāfa* is an ethical mission and not the mere succession of generations. Furthermore, if *khilāfa* means the succession of generations, the angels would not have thought that their actions could compensate for it, especially considering that Muslim scholars agree that angels do not reproduce nor come forth in successive generations, unlike human beings, animals and jinn.[27]

What proves that *khilāfa* means deputisation on behalf of God is the argument put forward by the angels to claim that *khilāfa* can be compensated for by the angels' function in the universe when they told God, "while we declare Your praise and sanctify You." They considered that their actions do compensate for man's vicegerency as they never deviate from the Divine will when executing their function in the universe, because they are not vicegerents to God in the execution of their actions, but their actions are God's willed (*mashī'a* or Divine cosmic will) and intended (*irāda* or Divine revealed will) actions (contrary to the actions of the human being which may be God's willed, but not intended actions).[28] This applies also to the actions of all other creatures including animals that succeed each other. As for vicegerency, it means the deputisation of a being on behalf of God in the execution of some actions that are initially God's. This will inevitably lead to actions contrary to God's *irāda* such as corruption and killing, as the angels understood. That is because of the fact that this being is not God, and he does not possess the attributes of perfection, while being entrusted to fulfil one of God's actions; hence it is inevitable that he would engage in what God does not like and that some of his actions would be false (*bāṭil*) in that they are not in themselves an articulation of an ontologically established Truth (*Ḥaqq*), i.e., God's attributes of perfection, but a mere consequence of a deviation from that This is in contrast to the case of angels as they have no religious responsibilities (*taklīf shar'ī*) (though they have cosmic duties (*taklīf kawnī*) as all other creatures), and they will not be held accountable on the Day of Judgment for their deeds, as they "never disobey what God commands them, and do what they are commanded." (Q 66:6, Ahmad Ali).

Had *khilāfa* meant the human being's mutual succession, it would not have been a problem for the Angels to (not) understand the wisdom of this succession. God, with His wisdom that may not be grasped by the minds, decrees whatever He wants, even acts of apparent corruption and killing. What is the problem with God creating beings who would kill each other or practise what appears to be corruption on the earth? Animals kill each other, and before humans, there were creatures who caused more destruction to the earth than humans can cause, as we said. This is not a problematic point at all, as long as it is part of God's decree and Wisdom. However, since *khilāfa* meant the human being's deputisation on behalf of God, which means that he will inevitably fall short of fulfilling that mission, the angels could not comprehend the wisdom behind this, and why God could not just achieve what he wants to achieve through His inevitable cosmic will, realised via the actions of angels. Thereupon, God answered them saying, "I know what you do not know" (Q 2:30). Then God showed them the wisdom behind that and the human being's eligibility for carrying this mission, which is another proof that supports the impossibility for *khilāfa*, in this context, to mean intergenerational succession.

Indeed, to prove the human being's entitlement for carrying out this function (undertaking a divine act), God invoked the fact that Adam was endowed with an appropriate faculty, as stated in the subsequent verses,

> And He taught Adam the names – all of them. Then He showed them to the angels and said, "Inform Me of the names of these,[29] if you are truthful." They said, "Exalted are You; we have no knowledge except what You have taught us. Indeed, it is You who is the Knowing, the Wise.'"
>
> (Q 2:31–32, Sahih Intl)

The quality that enables the human being for *khilāfa* is thus the fact that God has taught him all the names. In other words, he is endowed with the potential consciousness of everything thanks to language. That potential gives him the ability to elicit the unknown from the known facts, i.e., to learn things, express them and act accordingly.[30] This is a faculty that the angels do not enjoy, therefore they replied, after they were asked to inform about the names of things, "We have no knowledge except what You have taught us." That is, "Our knowledge is limited to the names you have taught us, and we cannot depart from that to elucidate what is unknown to us." This is indeed a major difference between the human being and other creatures. The knowledge with which the latter are endowed is limited with the limits of their function and their subsequent nature. As the former is performed unwillingly the latter's cognition is limited to a set of fixed impulses with no access to further information. Furthermore, as the former is not performed on behalf of God, but is God's inevitable willed (*mashīʾa*) and intended (*irāda*) action, the latter is not endowed with the same proportion of Divine attributes. As for the human, being a vicegerent of God, he will not be executing God's intention (*irāda*) in a deterministic fashion. Unlike other creatures, he will need to be conscious of the Divine actions in the universe that he needs to undertake on behalf of God, along with the details of their establishment and correct performance. Hence the knowledge he received is a knowledge based on linguistic cognition that procures him a singular consciousness. This consciousness potentially extends to all aspects of the Divine actions that the human being is tasked to handle on behalf of God. It further extends potentially to all aspects of the cosmic balance ("cosmic worship") that God established, so that the human being could strive to fully embrace "cosmic Islam," which is an overall purpose of his function as will be developed below.[31] It also entails a moral responsibility, as it makes him aware of God's intention and its opposite, of Truth (*Ḥaqq*) and falsehood (*bāṭil*), and enables him to act according to either.

Moreover, and again in contrast to the other creatures, this peculiar faculty is a result of the Divine insufflation of the spirit in the human being, since the angels were commanded to prostrate to Adam after he was taught the names in the above verses, and after he got the Divine insufflation of the spirit in other verses.[32] It also relates to the image/shape/form (*ṣūra*) according to which the human being was created, as the angels were commanded to prostrate to Adam after God give him his image in yet another verse.[33] It is known that the image according to which the human being was created is the image of God,[34] in the sense that the human being is endowed with some (imperfect) Divine qualities, as will be elaborated on below.

Hence, God, in the above-quoted verses, is proving the eligibility of Adam for *khilāfa* by the evidence that he carries some Divine attributes that enable him to deputise for God in some of His actions, i.e., to be His vicegerent. This was further alluded to by the angels when God asked them to inform Him about the names that Adam was taught. Indeed, they argued that this faculty, which God gave Adam and which they were asked to demonstrate, is a Divine faculty which they do not possess, "Indeed, it is You who is the Knowing, the Wise." Therefore, if *khilāfa* was the mere succession of generations, why would there be a need for all these substantiations?[35]

The evidence that was put forward by God to prove the eligibility of the human being to be a *khalīfa* further consolidates that *khilāfa* is deputisation on behalf of God from another perspective. Indeed, if every existent in the universe has a function that fits the natural constitution it was given (or vice versa), as will be elaborated below, the function of deputisation on behalf of God corresponds to the fact that the human being carries some (imperfect) Divine attributes in his natural constitution (*fiṭra*), which was the argument put forward by God to prove his eligibility for that function as we saw.[36] As for the wisdom behind vicegerency and the reason why God does not suffice with the execution of His inevitable cosmic will through the angels' actions in the universe, that has to do with a hidden fact in the "heavens and the earth" (the universe) that God knows and that the angels were not aware of. This made them miss the wisdom behind vicegerency, therefore God advised them before formulating His substantiations in support of the fact that their actions do not compensate for vicegerency, "I know what you do not know" and after those substantiations, "Did I not tell you that I know the hidden of the heavens and the earth?" (Q 2:33, b.o. Sahih Intl). This hidden fact about the universe, which the angels ignored and which is the reason why their actions do not compensate for vicegerency, corresponds to what we discovered to be the essential rationale behind vicegerency. Indeed, as we will demonstrate in detail in the following chapter, the ontological wisdom behind vicegerency and why the angels' actions (or the action of any other creature) could not compensate for it lie in the fact that it articulates in the universe ("the heavens and the earth") what the angels' action do not articulate. What vicegerency precisely articulates in the universe in an unprecedented fashion will also be developed in detail below.

The view of some Qur'anic exegetes that this vicegerency means the human being's succession of the jinn or creatures that lived on Earth before humans and caused corruption, and that this is the reason why the angels knew that the human being would cause corruption and killing on Earth, is equally debunked by the above arguments. Moreover, this view lacks any reliable evidence and actually comes from Persian and Greek mythology, in addition to the fact that it goes against the context of Q 2:30, as demonstrated by some exegetes.[37] Neither the human being nor the jinn[38] had inhabited the earth yet, and there were no humans except Adam; thus, how could the angels issue such judgement on humans? The angels must have realised this through their understanding of the nature of vicegerency, and not through analogy with other creatures, as indicated by Rashīd Riḍā.[39] This is a further argument in refutation of the view that vicegerency means succession of generations.

Some contemporary scholars said that *istikhlāf* means the succession of generations for the purpose of the execution of God's will or for other duties, and that God made man "a *khalīfā* who succeeds those before him and undertakes the tasks that God charged him with."[40] *Khilāfa*, in this sense, is a human specificity not shared by animals. However, this view is contested by the fact that succession of generations is a means, among many others, to fulfil that mission, and not the mission itself. There are many other predetermined means necessary to fulfil human function such as life, free will, intellect, etc. So, why was the human being, in the context of God's announcement of his mission on Earth before the angels, given the title of *khalīfa* and not any other like "alive," "free" or "intelligent," etc.? Had *khilāfa* meant succession of generations in order to achieve their mission, it would have been meaningless to mention it as a praise for Adam before the angels, without referring to other necessary means for the human being to fulfil his duty. It would have been more appropriate in this context to mention the main purpose of the creation of the human being, not to mention one means to fulfil it, especially since this means is neither the most important nor the noblest one. The succession of previous generations or the jinn or any other is not a function by itself, in contrast to the deputisation on behalf of God, which is by itself a function. Ascribing the title "*khalīfa*" to the human being indicates that *khilāfa* is greater than a mere inevitable fate or one of the many means for the human being to fulfil his mission.

## 5.3 Some Hermeneutical Considerations

The foregoing arguments demonstrate that vicegerency as an existential function as presented in Q 2:30 can only be on behalf of God, i.e., in the performance of one of His actions that He intends and wills, and that this mission is given only to the human being. Furthermore, if the linguistic meaning of *khilāfa* is to succeed, replace or deputise, the latter is the only option that was retained as per the previous arguments, i.e., that the human being is the deputy of God. This means that he is mandated with a task that is initially God's, because if he was just charged with a task that is not performed by God initially, that would not convey the meaning of deputisation as per the etymology of the word *khilāfa*. This refutes the statements of those who classified vicegerency into faith-based and satanic, Divine and positivist, or Islamic and cosmic as we saw in the previous chapter. It also refutes the statements of those who say that the jinn are also entrusted with vicegerency. It became clear that such topologies are a consequence of the failure to establish an accurate definition of vicegerency and of other aspects of theoretical deficiency highlighted in the previous chapter.

Classical scholars who were of the opinion that *khilāfa* means to succeed previous generations or jinn, were consistent in their view since they did not see *khilāfa* as an existential function of the human being, and they confined themselves to the linguistic meaning of the term. Modern researchers, however, are not consistent when elaborating those topologies. On one hand, they admit that *khilāfa* is an existential function of the human being, while on the other hand, they do not differentiate between the linguistic meaning of *khilāfa* that indicates mere deputisation or succession and *khilāfa* as the deputisation of the human being on behalf of God in performing an ethical mission enabled by a singular natural constitution and articulating an unprecedented cosmic reality, as emerging from Q 2:30. Hence, they made of *khilāfa* a loose container term whereby anybody could be a vicegerent of anybody in the performance of anything, while at the same time stating that it is a human existential function performed on behalf of God.

The root *khalafa* and its derivatives are used in many occasions in the Qur'an and *Sunna* according to its etymological meaning, which indicates succession, substitution and inheritance.[41] For instance, the Qur'an reads: "Then they were succeeded (*khalafa*) by other generations (*khalfun*) who inherited the Scripture," (Q 7:169, b.o. Talal Itani). Examples from the *Sunna* include the Prophet's saying: "O God, You are the companion in the journey and my *khalīfa* in my family,"[42] and his saying, "Allah is my *khalīfa* in looking after every Muslim."[43]

However, in its literal meaning, *khilāfa* carries no value in itself. It just means that someone succeeds another or deputises on behalf of someone else, whether the task entrusted to the deputy is a good or an evil one and whether the successor succeeded his predecessor in a righteous way or not. This contrasts with the meaning of *khilāfa* as crystallised through Q 2:30, which reflects an inherently ethical existential function, as indicated by the understanding of the angels that the purpose of *khilāfa* is to achieve what God likes, that the human being will fail in that, and that their actions are better able to achieve the (ethical) purpose. This is further supported by God's reply that the human being carries the necessary ethical qualities that guarantee his eligibility for that mission.

For this consideration, *khilāfa* as a human function must be studied as a concept with an independent technical Qur'anic meaning without confusing it with the abstract linguistic one. Although considering the linguistic meaning is necessary to understand the Qur'anic meaning of vicegerency, it does not make any sense to classify vicegerency into topologies without differentiating between the mere linguistic meaning and the technical meaning as crystallised through the Qur'an, while talking about vicegerency as an existential function of the human being. This, in turn, is one of the aspects of the deficiency in the contemporary scholarship on vicegerency. This approach violates one of the established rudiments of understanding the scriptural texts of Islam. Indeed, one basic rule of exegesis and jurisprudence is to understand the Qurʾanic concepts as per their Islamic convention (*al-ḥaqīqa al-sharʿiyya*) before resorting to the customary convention (*al-ḥaqīqa al-ʿurfiyya*)[44] or linguistic convention (*al-ḥaqīqa al-lughawiyya*).[45] That is so because the Qurʾanic Revelation, by the impulse of its worldview and principles, gave a new life to the Arabic vocabulary, even though it came in an Arabic language. Consequently, most of the Qurʾanic concepts have Islamic meanings that are independent of the customary and linguistic meanings.[46]

Even though they had first-hand knowledge of Arabic semantics and vocabulary, the companions of the Prophet (ﷺ) used to enquire about the meaning of many Qurʾanic terms, realising that these had independent Islamic significances and that etymology and convention do not suffice to determine them.[47] Muslim scholars generally agree that the terms of Islamic scripture are to be understood according to their Islamic meaning, and that customary and linguistic meanings only play a secondary role in that understanding.[48] The linguist and Shāfiʿī jurist, al-Isnawī (d. 772/1370) noted in this regard,

> If the utterance emanating from the Legislator comprises different possibilities, then it should be first understood as per its Islamic meaning (*al-maʿnā al-sharʿī*). That is because of the fact that he [the prophet], peace and blessing upon him, was sent to expose religious rulings. If that is not possible, it should be understood as per the customary convention (*al-ḥaqīqa al-ʿurfiyya*) prevailing in his aera, peace be upon him, because speaking as per the usual custom is more common than as per what is meant by the people of the language. If that is not possible, it should be understood as per the linguistic convention (*al-ḥaqīqa al-lughawiyya*) which should be determined according to the context.[49]

The well-known Ḥanbalī scholar, Najm al-Dīn al-Ṭūfī (d. 716/1316) says, "The [Islamic] convention in each term overpowers its linguistic convention and has priority over it. It is therefore that the Islamic convention (*al-ḥaqīqa al-sharʿiyya*) takes precedence over the linguistic one."[50] Al-Ṭūfī's master, ibn Taymiyya, also says, "It should be known that the words found in the Qurʾan and the *Ḥadīth*, if their explanation and their significance were clarified by the Prophet (ﷺ), there is no need to infer that from the sayings of philologists or others."[51]

Hence, in the context of the exegetical exercise, the Qurʾanic language is not to be regarded against the backdrop of the customary and etymological contexts of the Arabic language in the period of Revelation. To the contrary, pre-Islamic Arabic etymological and customary semantics are to be regarded in the context of the Islamic worldview and value system that insufflated a new semantic life into the Arabic vocabulary. Accordingly, the word *ṣalāt* (prayer) in the Qurʾanic convention no longer means mere supplication (as per its overall etymological meaning)[52] or a set of whistling and clapping movements (as per its pre-Islamic customary meaning).[53] Rather, evolving in the context of a distinct worldview and value system, the word now denotes a new reality in which etymology and custom only play a secondary role. Instead, that new reality is to be brought out through two main approaches, namely, intertextual exegesis[54] and worldview exegesis or, we can say, "contextual intertextuality" and "conceptional intertextuality." As per the first, *ṣalāt* is defined as a set of ritual movements and formulas (which start with the *takbīr* or proclamation of greatness, and end with the *taslīm*, the salutation) that represent the first pillar of Islam aiming to realise specific objectives in this life and the Hereafter, and that must be performed five times a day by all accountable persons on specific timings and with particular conditions defining its validity, obligation and good performance. As per the second approach (as will be further exposed below), *ṣalāt* denotes a fact that is in force in the universe resulting in "cosmic Islam," the integration of which is the overall human existential function. Therefore, *ṣalāt* is one of the teleological purposes behind the advent of Revelation, since it is an essential means to preserve one aspect of "cosmic Islam" or, in other words, the "cosmic balance," which the human being is entrusted to maintain on behalf of God, that is the spiritual balance. Hence, *ṣalāt* is an essential means for the human being to purify his *fiṭra* and get closer to his sound humanness that enables him to enrol in cosmic Islam.

The same applies for a countless number of Qur'anic terms and concepts that espouse a distinct meaning when being read through these two approaches that load the words with their Islamic referentiality. If the Islamic intellectual heritage has mobilised an impressive methodological device at the service of the first approach, the second did not benefit at all from the same theoretical attention, a situation that, we hope, our theory below and "worldview exegesis" could contribute to overcoming. The focus of classical Islamic scholarship in this regard was mainly on bringing out the Islamic meaning of concepts through contextual intertextuality. This, it seems, was deemed enough to gear human action and belief towards the overall human existential function, i.e., worshipping God, which, as commonly agreed upon, means to submit to Him alone in belief, practice and spirituality. As developed in the third chapter, this is one of the reasons why little theoretical attention was given to the human existential function as the means of that overall human function, and as the overall frame of those specific rulings. Indeed, worshipping God by abiding to what He commands and avoiding what He forbids, is elaborated with enough theoretical detail in Islamic sciences, for which the standard intertextual approach seems more than sufficient. Hence, by faithfulness to the particular rulings that are organically evolving within the Islamic worldview, the overall existential purposes and objectives are spontaneously met.[55] If this was more or less the case in the context of classical Islamic scholarship, the fact remains that that spontaneity in meeting the cosmic through the particular got lost over time, and especially in modern time with its many conceptual and existential upheavals. Consequently, if the theorisation of the particular (rulings of jurisprudence, creed and spiritual purification) was the essential means in classical scholarship to achieve the cosmic (without the urge of theorising the latter), we can affirm with confidence that theorising the cosmic (which will enable the worldview *tafsīr*) in order to reinforce and properly orient the particular[56] (elicited through the intertextual *tafsīr*) is an urgent need today.

Be that as it may, the numerous contemporary studies about *istikhlāf* (and Islamic worldview in general) that we were exposed to did not establish a new approach in dealing with Revelation beyond the standard intertextual approach. Besides that, many of these writers confuse the Arabic linguistic meanings with what they deem to be the Islamic ones (without properly following neither the intertextual nor the worldview approaches) with no coherence whatsoever as we saw. If we study vicegerency as an independent Qur'anic concept without confusing it with its linguistic meaning, it becomes impossible to claim that the one who follows the work of Satan is also a vicegerent. Accordingly, there is also nothing such as cosmic vicegerency nor positivist vicegerency or any other such classification. This is because vicegerency in its Qur'anic sense can only be on behalf of God, and carries, therefore, an inherent ethical value, besides being a human specificity. This confusion between the linguistic and Islamic meanings of *khilāfa* caused much confusion around the concept of vicegerency in contemporary writings, as we saw.

As for describing God as the *khalīfa* for Muslims or family, as in the above two *Ḥadīths*, that denotes the fact that God provides care and protection regardless of difficulties and the absence of loved ones. It does not mean that God becomes a deputy or successor for the traveller or for the Prophet after his demise. God looks after people, whether they miss their loved ones or not. Indeed, it is the intertextual backdrop (trough which the Islamic meaning is disclosed) that highlights which of its linguistic meanings the word *khalīfa* in both *Ḥadīths* is in accordance with, and not the other way around as we saw in some contemporary writings. Hence, God is the *khalīfa* of people in the sense that He stays with one's family and with the believers and never forsakes them in the absence of the guardians. Thus, God is the *khalīfa* in the sense that He stays after the departure of the one who leaves, but not in the sense that He is his deputy. This is based on the context of these texts and on the fact that among the linguistic meanings of *khalafa* or *akhlafa* is to leave or to keep something or someone behind.[57] In any case (according to both intertextual and worldview approaches), God can never be a deputy of anyone in performing their duties; it is, rather, God Who creates their actions as established in Sunni creed. Thus, the meaning of God being a *khalīfa* in these *Ḥadīths* does not go beyond the fact that He stays with people despite the absence of their loved ones. God does not deputise on behalf of people in their actions, nor does He succeed or inherit[58] them as per these linguistic meanings of *khilāfa*. Thus, why randomly submit this concept to one of its linguistic meanings while ignoring the Islamic one emerging from both the intertextual and worldview backdrops of these *Ḥadīths*? Creation, ownership and command belong to Him only and all the actions are His, as established in Islamic creed. There is no relationship between this linguistic meaning of *khilāfa* (to stay behind) that fits under the Islamic meaning here, related to the fact that God stays with people no matter how lonely they are, and its linguistic meaning (to deputise) that fits under its Islamic meaning emerging from Q 2:30. Having understood this, it becomes meaningless to classify the function of vicegerency into one performed by God in which He is the cosmic vicegerent of the human being, and one performed by the human being in which he is the religious vicegerent of God, as claimed by a contemporary researcher.[59] Furthermore, what comes out when implementing the hermeneutical rules of Islamic theology is that *khalīfa* is not a Divine attribute, in contrast to what this author claims.[60]

Having demonstrated that vicegerency is a human function, that is, deputisation on behalf of God, and that its object is a Divine action, any view suggested by contemporary (and early) scholars that does not fit the above standards is thus excluded. Accordingly, the object of vicegerency is not free will and the faculty to follow good and evil because they are not functions. Excluded also is the subjugation of the earth and its resources because this is a *fait accompli*. The same applies to the construction of the earth, because this does not depend on the human being's religious responsibility, as well as benefiting from the earth because that is not a Divine action. Excluded also is the execution or realisation of the Divine will, because His Will is already realised. The object of vicegerency may be faithfulness to the Divine will, as noted in the previous chapter. However, this does not solve the problem of determining the aspect of the Divine will that must be adhered to, that is, the exact Divine action in which man must act on behalf of God. It is thus necessary to proceed to the identification of that function, that is, the Divine act or acts in which man deputises on behalf of God.

## 5.4 Identifying the Object of Vicegerency

It becomes clear from the above discussion that among the deficiencies in contemporary scholarship on *istikhlāf* is the failure to build it on a strong Qur'anic basis. This deficiency not only resulted in basing the object of vicegerency on weak foundations, but it has also prevented these studies from developing a comprehensive theory of the human function that determines the human being's place in existence and links that function to the cosmos, the teachings of Revelation and to human nature. In short, it prevented approaching *istikhlāf* from a worldview *tafsīr*. In addition, this deficiency has resulted in a state of confusion in many of these studies that produced unfounded classifications and topologies as we have seen. Therefore, in the present chapter and the following one, we will develop a set of methodological entries by which we will abide to identify the object of vicegerency in our attempt to overcome these deficiencies. Among those entries are the following:

1. Placing the human function within the framework of the Qur'anic worldview related to the function of the universe and the nature of the human being
2. Tracing the Qur'anic verses indicative of the human being's existential function, one of his functions, the reason or the purpose of his creation and linking them to the concept of deputisation on behalf of God
3. Tracing the Qur'anic verses indicating the reason of the creation of the universe and its order and linking it to the function of the human being

4. Tracing the Qur'anic verses indicating the function of Revelation and linking it to the function of the human being
5. Basing the object of vicegerency on the concept of deputisation on behalf of God

All these points are absent in contemporary attempts at identifying the object of vicegerency. Hence, they did not place vicegerency within the framework of the function of the universe. Neither did they base the object of vicegerency on deputisation on behalf of God, though they adopted this view. Finally, they did not link it to the concepts through which the Qur'an rationalises the functions of Revelation, the universe or the human being. As we have seen, most of those studies were based on (non-Qur'anic) pre-established ideas and superficial or hasty inferences.

### *5.4.1 Cosmic Worship*

The first step that should be the starting point in identifying the function that the human being was entrusted to perform on behalf of God is God's words: "And in no way did I create the jinn and humankind except to worship Me" (Q 51:56, Ghali). This verse is the most explicit Qur'anic text that indicates the duty for which man was created. It confines this duty to worship alone. Therefore, the object of vicegerency must be related to it. In the previous chapter it was found that worship is not a part of vicegerency, unlike suggestions made by some contemporary researchers, because the verse confined the purpose of the creation of man to worship alone, which indicates that his existential function does not go beyond that. The view of some researchers that vicegerency is a part of worship has also been proven invalid, because in that case, it would be more appropriate to give man a title denoting his whole function rather than a title denoting only a part of it. We have also demonstrated the invalidity of the idea that worship is one of various functions that the human was tasked with.[61] The function for which the human being was created is nothing more and nothing less than worship, as is explicitly indicated by the conjunction "except." Nevertheless, the problem remains that vicegerency is a human specificity that is not shared by any other creature. Hence, vicegerency cannot be a mere synonym for worship, because worship is a function shared by all other creatures. Be that as it may, exploring the concept of worship is what will help us identify the object of vicegerency, because it is the overall function for which man is created. If worship is a function shared by all creatures, then the question that needs to be asked concerns the human being's particular share in that function and what distinguishes him in its performance. This may solve the present problem and open the way for the identification of the object of vicegerency.

A large number of Qur'anic verses support the fact that worship is the function for which all creatures in the universe were created, for instance:

- "There is not one of the beings in the heavens and the earth except he comes to the Merciful as a worshipper." (Q 19:93, b.o. Qaribullah)

- "To God prostrate all who are in the heavens and the earth, willingly or unwillingly, as do their shadows in the mornings and the evenings." (Q 13:15, b.o. Arberry)
- "Everything in the heavens and earth glorifies God – He is the Almighty, the Wise." (Q 57:1, Abdel Haleem)[62]

Numerous verses indicate that this cosmic worship as a whole is a common function of the human being and the universe. The worship performed by all creatures in the universe is, in its general meaning and objectives, the same worship entrusted to man. The verses indicating this include:

- "Did you not see that to Allah prostrate all things that are in the heavens and on earth, – the sun, the moon, the stars; the hills, the trees, the animals; and a great number among mankind?" (Q 22:18, Ahmad Khan). Worship, referred to as "prostration" in this verse,[63] is performed by all creatures and by many people, which indicates that it is the same overall mission.
- "Do they, then, seek a religion other than Allah's, while to Him surrenders (*aslama*, i.e., accepted Islam) whoever[64] there is in the heavens and the earth?" (Q 3:83). Hence, the worship for which the human being was created, which is achieved by submission (*islām*) to God through following His religion, is in force in the universe and is the very religion that the human being is invited to accept.
- "To Him belongs whatever is in the heavens and the earth, and to Him belongs the everlasting religion. Will you, then, be wary of other than Allah?" (Q 16:52, b.o. Ali Qarai). This verse came after mentioning the advent of the Messengers, the descent of Revelation, the prostration of what is in the heavens and the earth, and before mentioning a set of functions performed by the creatures on earth. Since all creatures submit to and obey God by performing their functions permanently, religion was described as "everlasting." Hence, the cosmic religion is, overall, the same religion that was revealed to man. This is why the verse condemned those who submit to other than God despite this cosmic fact: "Will you, then, be wary of other than Allah?"
- "Our Lord is He who gave everything its natural form and then guided it." (Q 20:50, b.o. Ahmad Ali). Man is thus not excluded from the Divine guidance given to all creatures of the universe, and worship is a common denominator of all forms of Divine guidance.

As for the meaning of this general cosmic worship, it is not confined to prayer, prostration and glorification in the sense of ritual acts of worship that have no purpose but to exalt God. Rather, its general meaning is that every being surrenders to God and submits to Him by the performance of the function it was created for. Indeed, "the meaning of worship is to obey God through submission to Him."[65] The obedience of each being and its submission to God are nothing but the fulfilment of what it was created for. As for the fact that many verses describe the worship of the creatures as prostration and glorification, the meaning of that is a point of difference among Qur'anic exegetes. Ibn Juzayy (d. 741/1340) said: "The meaning of this prostration is disputed; some said that it means submission and surrender, while others say that prostration is used in the literal sense."[66] Ibn 'Aṭiyya (d. 541/1146) said:

> We have already elaborated on the meaning of the glorification of the non-living beings covered by the general term of "whatever in the heavens and earth," and that scholars differed in explaining this [glorification]. Some said that it is [glorification] in the literal sense, while other said that it is used in the figurative sense, meaning that the traces of the Divine creation and manufacturing in those creatures as [if those creatures are] performing glorification and is a call for glorification by whoever can make glorification. Makkī said: "Glorifying God means to pray and bow down, all of which refers to submission and surrender."[67]

Though we cannot rule out categorically the possibility that the prostration and glorification of these creatures have metaphysical connotations that cannot be grasped by reason, yet these verses carry indications that the primary meaning of glorification, prostration and prayer is not the ritual acts of worship such as those prescribed to man.[68] Had it been so, glorification, prostration and prayer in that case would have been metaphysical acts that cannot be perceived, as man does not see the sun, trees and seas glorifying, praying and prostrating themselves in that ritual sense. However, these Qur'anic verses indicate that such glorification and prostration are seen and perceived by man, or, rather, that man must be aware of that and ponder upon it. This is understood from the rhetorical question (*istifhām 'inkārī*) in some of these verses, such as in the above-quoted verse: "Did you not see that to Allah prostrate all things that are in the heavens and on earth?" (Q 22:18), and: "Have you not seen that all those who are in the heavens and the earth glorify Allah, and the birds with their wings spread (also glorify Him)? Each knows its [own way of] prayer and glorification and God has full knowledge of what they do." (Q 24:41, b.o Ahmad Khan).

Commenting on the latter verse, ibn 'Āshūr said:

> It is an invitation to ponder on and take heed from how God has guided many of the inhabitants of the heaven and the earth to glorify Him, which necessarily requires [from man] to believe in Him Alone, and to ponder upon how He inspired birds to sing expressing their joy in the grace of their existence and living granted by God. Thus, their sounds are an indication of their status of praising God and glorifying Him and negating any partners with Him. Hence, their sound is a glorification stemming from their condition [...] The vision in God's saying "do you not see" is in the visual sense, because the glorification by humans is seen by the eyes and the glorification by birds is seen according to what this word [i.e., bird] means. Hence, the contemplator has only to know that the thing designated by that word is worth being described by the word "glorification." Having understood this, one realizes that the rhetorical question has a strong effect.[69]

Commenting on the former verse, he said,

> The vision here is related to knowledge [acquired from meditation], the command [to ponder on creation] is directed to an unspecified interlocutor and the question is a rhetorical one. The latter is a blame to the addressees for being unaware of the creatures' conditions that prove the Oneness of God.[70]

If glorification, prostration and prayer were metaphysical and imperceptible facts, then how could God blame some people for not being aware of them?

Among the proofs that the glorification of the creatures (i.e., their worship) means their submission to God and their obedience in performing their function is the following verse: "Do they not see the shadows of all things God has created incline to the right and the left, prostrating in obeisance to God? To Allah prostrates whatever is in the heavens and whatever is on the earth, including animals and angels, and they are not arrogant." (Q 16:48–49, b.o. Ahmad Ali). These verses include two proofs of the above. The first is the rhetorical question "Do they not see…?" If prostration of these beings was metaphysical and imperceptible, there would be no point in denouncing those who "*plan evil plots*" for their negligence of this. The second is the fact that one of the manifestations of prostration expressed in this verse is the movement of the shadow of the beings from one place to another. This shows that their prostrations are not merely ritual imperceptible acts, but rather the performance of their function in the perceptible universe. Indeed, providing shade is one of the many functions for which these creatures were created, as stated in the Qur'an: "It is Allah who made for you the shade from what He has created." (Q 16:81, Ali Qarai).

Another proof is God's saying:

> Say: "Had there been other gods with Him, as they assert, they would surely have sought a way (of opposition) against the Lord of the Throne." Too glorious and high is He, too exalted for what they say! The seven heavens and the earth and all those in them glorify Him. There is not a single thing that does not glorify His praise, though you do not understand their glorification: He is verily Clement and Forgiving.
>
> (Q 17:42–44, b.o. Ahmad Ali)

In these verses, God proves His Oneness through the fact that if there were gods beside Him in the universe, as the polytheists claim, they would have competed with Him in creation, and "they would have challenged Him seeking to be the only lord."[71] This would result in turmoil in the laws and norms of the universe as each god enforces his own laws and cosmic order. This argument is repeated in the Qur'an in different forms, as in God's saying, "Nor is there any god beside Him – if there were, each god would have taken his creation aside and tried to overcome the others." (Q 23:91, Abdel Haleem). Then, after this, God has established the invalidity of this by the proof of the glorification of God by all the creatures of the universe without exception. Since the universe is unified in its laws, course and order, and no single being in the universe is subjugated to anyone other than God, this proves that nobody is competing with God in his creation. This supports the view that glorifying God is not a metaphysical matter and that it refers to the functions that these beings perform, which result in this unified system of disciplined laws that proves the Oneness of the Creator. This is what the Qur'an asserts on various occasions, such as: "You will not see any flaw in what the Lord of Mercy creates. Look again! Can you see any flaw?" (Q 67:3, Abdel Haleem).

As for God's saying, "though you do not understand their glorification" (Q 17:44), there is nothing in the verse indicating that the glorification of the elements of the universe is imperceptible. What it does indicate is that the human being was, and still is, unaware of many details or aspects of that glorification, even though he is aware of it in general terms, as indicated by the arguments mentioned above.[72] One of the objections to this (i.e., understanding prostration in its "literal" sense) is that the rationale of the human being's prostration and glorification in the "literal" meaning is clear, as they bring him/her many spiritual and psychological benefits, contributing thereby to the fulfilment of his/her existential function. As for the prostration and praise of the other creatures in the sense of submission to God by performing the functions for which they were created, the rationale behind that is also clear here, because all this contributes to the orderliness and cohesion of the universe. There is, however, no clear wisdom or rationale behind the prostration and glorification of the elements of the universe in the "literal" sense, i.e., their performance of imperceptible ritual acts intended only to manifest subjugation and surrender. Neither is God in need of that, as He is Self-Sufficient, nor is the human being in need of it, because he cannot perceive it at all, nor are the creatures in need of that, because they do not do it voluntarily and it does not change anything in the good performance of their function.

Moreover, the idea that the glorification, prostration, prayer and guidance of the elements of the universe mean their performance of their respective functions is supported by the fact that many of the verses in this regard have been preceded or followed by the mention of a set of these functions.[73] For example, after mentioning the glorification and prayer of the creatures in one of these verses, a set of functions of these creatures are enumerated:

> Do you not see that all those who are in the heavens and the earth glorify Allah, and the birds with their wings spread (also glorify Him)? Each knows its [own way of] prayer and glorification and God has full knowledge of what they do. For Allah only is the kingship of the heavens and the earth; and towards Allah is the return. Do you not see that God drives the clouds, then gathers them together and piles them up until you see rain pour from their midst? He sends hail down from [such] mountains in the sky, pouring it on whoever He wishes and diverting it from whoever He wishes- the flash of its lightning almost snatches sight away. It is God who alternates night and day. There is surely a lesson in this for those who have sight. God created every moving thing from water: One crawls on its belly, one walks on two

legs, another moves on four. God creates whatsoever He wills. Indeed God has power over everything. (Q 24:41–45, b.o. Ahmad Khan and Ahmad Ali).

The relation in the above verses between the second rhetorical question concerning the observation of the functions performed by creatures, and the first one concerning the observation of their glorification and prayer, is that the former is an explanation of the latter.

The idea that the worship, glorification and prayer of the elements of the universe mean mere ritual acts of worship expressing obeisance and submission may be related to the issue of the rejection of any intended purpose behind worship, as we saw in the last section of the third chapter. As discussed, many scholars have reduced worship to mere ritual acts without any purpose or benefit but submission to God. Hence, worship is not a function but an inevitable fate. Thus, the proponents of this view have likely projected this on the worship of the universe, reducing it to the performance of mere rituals acts just like those of the human being thereby neglecting the fact that worship is a function.

So far, we have shown that worship is a function shared by all creatures, and that it means surrender and obeisance to God by the performance of every being of the duty for which it was created. In other words, cosmic worship is the contribution of every element of the universe to the unity and harmony of the cosmic order by performing its existential function. All creatures were thus created for the same ultimate purpose, including humans. Therefore, according to the Qur'an, all creatures are worshippers (Q 19:93), all of them are Muslim (Q 3:82), all of them are religious (Q 16:52) and all of them are guided (Q 20:50). It can thus be asserted that the human being, according to the Qur'an, is entrusted to achieve the same ultimate purpose that all creatures of the universe contribute to achieve. This is why Revelation came to the human being with the same guidance already existing in the universe (as a consequence/manifestation of an established ontological Truth), as indicated in previously quoted verses: "With the Truth did We send it down, and with the Truth did it descend" (Q 17:105), and: "He created the heavens and the earth with the Truth" (Q 64:3, Ghali). This fact appears more clearly in the following verse: "In fact he brought them the Truth, and most of them dislike the Truth. Had the Truth followed their desires the heavens and the earth and all those within them would have been corrupted." (Q 23:70–71, b.o. Ahmad Khan). These verses indicate that Revelation, which the Messenger (ﷺ) came to proclaim, is the same as the Truth on which the goodness of the universe (the heavens and the earth) is established. If Truth contained in Revelation was according to the desires of the polytheists, the universe would have collapsed because it is established on the same Truth. Since the human being is required to abide by the same cosmic Truth, he must strive to realise the same ultimate purpose shared by all creatures. That purpose is to join that harmonious cosmic order and to be an integral part of it. If all creatures are worshippers, religious, Muslims and guided, as indicated by the Qur'an, then this means that Islam is not limited to scriptural[74] revelation. Rather, it is an overall cosmic order, and Islam as a scriptural revelation is only part of that whole. More precisely, Islam as scriptural revelation is only an enabler to joining cosmic Islam. If the meanings of Islam, based on its etymological roots (*sīn-lām-mīm* or *s-l-m*), include surrender (*istislām*), soundness (*salāma*) and peace (*salām*),[75] these same meanings are present in cosmic Islam as much as they are present in the Islamic religion as a human responsibility that came through scriptural revelation. Surrender to God (*istislām*)[76] is intended to preserve the soundness (*salāma*) of the human being in his natural disposition (*fiṭra*),[77] which in turn leads to the preservation of peace (*salām*) between the human being and his soul and between the human being and his surroundings.[78] This also applies to the universe, or it is, rather, the meaning of its worship. The creatures' surrender to the will of God guarantees their soundness, which leads to peace and harmony among all creatures of the universe, i.e., the harmony of the universal order.

From this, we can conclude that the overall existential purpose of the human being is not different from that of the universe. This is a significant consideration given the many ideas proposed by both traditional and modern Islamic thought, and especially those modern writings on vicegerency, with regard to the position of the human being in the universe and the relationship between Revelation and universe. The fact that the purpose of the human being is to be in harmony with the universe refutes all such views that make of the human being, as a vicegerent on Earth, a lord, sovereign, dominator, controller or subjugator over what is on the earth. This also invalidates those epistemologies based on dualism or contradiction between Revelation and universe, emptying the latter of any ethical value. The key point here is that the object of vicegerency is not something exogenous that the human being introduces to the universe. Rather, it is something through which the human being joins the cosmic harmony, as we will see.

To sum up, the overall function of the human being and the universe are the same, which is worship; the purpose of the human being and the purpose of the universe are also the same, which is cosmic Islam (i.e., surrender, soundness and peace) and the overall means by which the human being accomplishes his purpose and those of the universe are the same, namely Divine guidance. Thus, God's saying "And in no way did I create the jinn and humankind except to worship Me" (Q 51:56), does not mean that only the jinn and humans were created to worship God. Rather, it means that they are not an exception to that, and that this general norm (the creation of the universe for the worship of God) is not affected by the fact that they possess free will or other peculiarities that distinguish them from the other elements of universe and which may give the illusion that they have a different function.

If worship is a common denominator for every creature's performance of its existential function so as to join cosmic Islam, then this means that every creature will have its own form of worship, as indicated in God's words: "Each knows its [own way of] prayer and glorification and God has full knowledge of what they do." (Q 24:41). The contribution of every being to cosmic Islam is different, depending on the nature given to it, which results in a distinct function. This is implied in God's saying, "Our Lord is He who gave everything its natural form and then guided it," (Q 20:50) as well as His saying, "who created all things harmoniously; Who gave them proper measures and then guided them." (Q 87:2–3, b.o. Maududi).

This applies to humans as well. In this way, the relationship between vicegerency as human existential function and worship as a cosmic existential function becomes clear. Worship is not a part of vicegerency, nor is vicegerency a part of worship; nor is worship synonymous with vicegerency, nor are they two different human functions, unlike the statements made by contemporary researchers. Rather, vicegerency is the peculiar worship of the human being. That is to say, vicegerency is what humans must adhere to in order to join cosmic Islam.

### *5.4.2 Human Worship*

From the foregoing arguments, we have now achieved a general view of the object of vicegerency. We now know that it is something that enables the human being to join cosmic Islam with its three meanings as mentioned above. We have also determined that it is neither something that is exogenous to the order of the universe, nor a novelty that the human being introduces to the universe, as per certain opinions expressed by some Muslim scholars mentioned earlier. The outstanding issue now is to determine the specific function that distinguishes the human being from other creatures as to the realisation of that cosmic Islam.

One of the verses that deals with the difference between man and the universe in this regard is God's saying, "We presented the Trust to the heavens and the earth and the mountains, but they refused to bear it and were apprehensive of it; but the human being undertook it. Indeed he is most unjust and ignorant." (Q 33:72, b.o. Ali Qarai). Many contemporary researchers (as well as some early scholars) adopted the view that the "Trust" which mankind carried is the trust of vicegerency. However, this does not determine the meaning of vicegerency nor its object. The above-mentioned verse indicates that the human being differs from the universe by a responsibility that only he/she bears, but it does not specify this responsibility nor the meaning of Trust. Consequently, Qur'an exegetes gave many views when commenting on this verse. Ibn ʿĀshūr enumerated 20 of them and added that this verse was considered as one of the problematic (*mushkil*) verses of the Qur'an.[79] Vicegerency is a suitable interpretation of that trust, because other concepts proposed as explanations of the "trust" (such as freedom, obedience to God, religiosity, monotheism, intellect, etc.) are not peculiar to the human being, but are shared by the jinn and other creatures. However, this view also does not solve the problem of identifying the object of vicegerency. If the trust itself is vicegerency, then what is the duty entrusted to the human being to act as a vicegerent in it on behalf of God? The verse does not specify this, but may help in this regard. The use of the term "trust" to express the function that distinguishes the human being from the rest of the universe hints at the fact that this task does not lie in realising something that is inexistent, but it is the preservation of something that exists. Ibn ʿĀshūr said, "A trust is something that is entrusted to somebody so that he preserves it and meet its obligations without wasting or prejudicing it."[80] This is confirmed by the saying of the Prophet (ﷺ)

"Trust descended in the innermost (root) of the hearts of people. Then the Qur'an was revealed, and they learnt from the Qur'an and they learnt from the Sunna."[81] Thus, Revelation does not realise something inexistent, but came later as a means to preserve it.

If this verse does not specify the nature of the "trust," there are other Qur'anic verses worth considering in our attempt to identify the object of vicegerency, because they define the function assigned to the human being in the context of the general cosmic worship. These verses were omitted by those who studied the concept of vicegerency and the existential function of the human being. These verses are the opening ones of *sūrat al-Raḥmān*:

> It is the Lord of Mercy, who taught the Qur'an. He created the human being and taught him speech. The sun and the moon are [disposed] calculatedly, the plants and the trees prostrate themselves [in submission]. He has raised up the sky and established the balance; so that you may not transgress in the balance. Set up the weight with equity and do not diminish the balance. And the earth – He laid it out for mankind with its fruits, its palm trees with sheathed clusters, its husked grain, its fragrant plants. Which, then, of your Lord's blessings do you both deny? (Q 55:1–13, b.o. Ali Qarai)

These verses cover the cosmic worship referred to above, the worship specific to the human being, as well as vicegerency outlined in Q 2:30. They also refer to the fruits of worship, its purpose and means. In addition, they determine the worship specific to the human being, i.e., the object of vicegerency, according to the following sequence:

1- The *Sūra* starts with God's saying "*Al-Raḥmān*" (the Lord of Mercy) indicating that what will follow are some effects of His mercy. This is the only *Sūra* in the Qur'an that begins with a Name of God not preceded by anything else. Another peculiarity of this *Sūra* is its repeated reminder of God's graces "Which, then, of your Lord's blessings do you both deny?" which is repeated 31 times in the *Sūra*.[82] Among the favours that result from God's Name "Lord of Mercy" is the reference to the worship of the universe and the worship of humans as will be elaborated. Mercy is thus the fruit of worship and worship is a consequence of mercy.
2- After opening the *Sūra* with one of God's Most Beautiful Names, the *Sūra* mentions "teaching the Qur'an" as a result of God's Mercy, which is a guidance given solely to the human being or, in other words, one of the means to realise worship that is specific to the human being. Then came the mention of another of those means, namely the creation of the human being.
3- After the grace of the creation of the human being came the mention of the grace of the human being's innate (spiritual) aptitude that enables him to perform his particular worship, namely that God taught him "speech." Speech here refers to the innate human ability to know all things and express them by giving them names.[83] It is the natural disposition that will facilitate

for him the recognition and awareness of the (material and moral) things of the universe and to name them so as to act on them in the performance of his function. This is the same argument that God used to answer the angels in Q 2:31 to prove the human being's eligibility for performing the function of vicegerency, i.e., teaching him all the names, as demonstrated by ibn ʿĀshūr.[84] In this way, these three verses, that are talking about the specific guidance given to the human being and his creation according to a distinct innate structure, explain the part of the human being in God's saying, "Our Lord is He who gave everything its [natural] form, then gave it guidance," (Q 20:50), as well as His saying, "who created all things harmoniously; Who gave them proper measures and then guided them." (Q 87:2–3). These verses also occur in the context of enumerating the blessings of God.[85] These latter verses mention creation before guidance as they talk about the creation of all beings. In *sūrat al-Raḥmān*, on the other hand, the creation of man is mentioned between two kinds of guidance, the guidance of Revelation and the guidance of the natural aptitudes. This is attributable to the singularity of the function of man compared to the other creatures, which we will elaborate upon later.

4- After reminding of God's mercy in giving the human being revealed and natural guidance to perform his specific function, the *Sūra* proceeds with the reminder of God's mercy related to the shared function among all creatures, that is the overall cosmic worship. The relation between God's saying, "The sun and the moon are [disposed] calculatedly," and the previous verses enumerating the blessings given to humans, in terms of Revelation and a singular natural disposition, lies in the fact that the overall order of the universe runs according to the same laws and norms that are revealed to the human being and according to which his innate faculties are structured. Simply put, the human being is guided with the same general cosmic guidance, as it becomes clear from the above-quoted verse (Q 20:50). This notion is abundantly recurrent in the Qurʾan, as we will see.
5- After reminding of the blessings of God in the creation of all existents in the universe according to a precise order, the *Sūra* states, "the plants and the trees prostrate themselves [in submission]," indicating that this order is a consequence of the worship performed by these beings. The sun and the moon are disposed according to precise measurements and calculations set by God, as are plants and trees; however, at the same time they "prostrate themselves," and so do the sun and the moon. This is further evidence that prostration is the commitment to that Divine order.[86]
6- After affirming that all beings in the universe follow a disciplined order and that they worship God,[87] the *Sūra* proceeds: "He has raised up the sky and established the balance" to show that there is a relationship between that cosmic worship and the balance and harmony upon which the universe is founded. Raising up the sky signifies the creation of the universe.[88] This cosmic order, which is guided according to a disciplined system stemming from its submission to God's will, is one of God's actions in His universe. It is He

who created the universe and established the balance in it. The balance refers to the harmony and stability that God has spread in the universe, that is, it is the cosmic Islam that makes everything balanced in itself ("soundness") and in its relationship with its environment ("peace") as a result of its "surrender" to God.

7- After speaking about God's mercy in giving human beings and the whole universe the Divine guidance, and after God has defined one of His actions in the universe, the Divine discourse turns to the human being by determining the function he is entrusted with in this context. Thus, God says: "So that you may not transgress in the balance." The duty attributed to the human being in this verse is to preserve that cosmic balance. This verse also suggests that the purpose behind the revealed and innate guidance given to the human being, along with the general cosmic guidance, is to fulfil this duty ("…so that…").[89] It further indicates that this duty is not to introduce something that does not exist, but rather to maintain ("not transgress in the balance") something that exists. It also indicates that this duty (maintaining the balance of the universe) is at its origin a Divine act ("He has…established…") entrusted to man's responsibility.[90]

8- The previous verse is followed by a seemingly similar one since it states, "Set up the weight with equity and do not diminish the balance." Qur'anic exegetes differed regarding the reason behind the reiteration of the term "balance" three times in a row in these verses.[91] It seems to us that the context of these verses and some of their clear statements suggest that the first balance is the one placed by God in the universe and that is preserved and looked after by Him. The second is the same general cosmic balance, but in the context of entrusting a part of its maintenance to the human being, as supported by God's saying, "in the balance" as will be explained later. The third balance is that which God placed within the human being in particular, as supported by God's command to the human being to "set up the weight with equity" in the previously quoted verse, as we will elaborate. The human being is entrusted to preserve the second (a part of the general cosmic balance) and the third (the balance existing within him in particular) ones. However, in the third one, the command to set up the weight came before the command to preserve the balance. This is attributable to a peculiarity of human nature (*fiṭra*) and to the difference between the command to not transgress (*taṭghaw*) in the balance and not diminish (*tukhsirū*) it, as will be detailed later.

9- After reminding of God's blessings upon the human being by teaching him Revelation, creating him with a singular nature, creating all beings according to disciplined laws, the worship of all beings, the creation of the universe with an established balance and the responsibility of the human being to preserve it, God concludes all of this by speaking about another grace related to the previous ones, namely the blessing of the earth. He said: "And the earth – He laid it out for mankind, with its fruits, its palm trees with sheathed clusters, its husked grain, its fragrant plants." The relation between these verses and the ones before them is that the earth is the arena where the human being is entrusted to fulfil his duty. Thus, earth is another means that enables the human being to perform his duty. Some of the earth's blessings, embellishments and aesthetic components including plants, fruits and fragrant grasses were mentioned here in indication of the convenience of this field, its stability, beauty and its good life, that is to say, its suitability for this duty. Ibn ʿĀshūr said, "The meaning of 'laying out the earth' is that He tamed it for them, i.e., he spread it under their feet and bodies to enable them to utilise it with all what it offers in terms of benefits and usages."[92]

10- After this overall sketch regarding what distinguishes the human being from other creatures of the universe in terms of the function he is entrusted with and the guidance to perform it, along with the natural constitution that enables him to execute it, until the arena of its performance, God concludes this with the first occurrence of the verse that is repeated 31 times in this *Sūra*: "Which, then, of your Lord's blessings do you both deny?" We believe that the most appropriate opinion about the meaning of "you both," is that it is directed to two categories of humans, as it is a rule in Arabic language that the pronoun must refer to an aforementioned noun. Accordingly, ibn ʿĀshūr adopted the opinion that it is directed to "the believers and unbelievers."[93]

These verses cover all the constituents of the human existential function from within their overall comic context. It thus appears that the object of vicegerency is to maintain the balance set by God. This is confirmed by the different aspects of the interrelationship between vicegerency and maintaining the balance. Among these aspects, as noted through the examination of the vicegerency verse, is that the object of vicegerency is one of the Divine actions, and that vicegerency can only be on behalf of God. The same conclusion appears clear here in *sūrat al-Raḥmān* through the correlation between what God does in the universe in terms of establishing and preserving the balance and what the human being is entrusted with in terms of maintaining that balance. Another aspect of interrelation between vicegerency and maintaining the balance is the fact that vicegerency and trust both denote the preservation of something existing, as we have discussed, and not to introduce something new, which is also confirmed here as we saw. Furthermore, human existential function depends on his innate faculty to learn all names as stated in the vicegerency verses, which is also confirmed by these verses as noted. Moreover, vicegerency is a duty assigned to the human being alone, as indicated in the *khilāfa* verses, and as confirmed in the above verse commanding the human being, in particular, to maintain the balance. These and many other aspects of interrelation between vicegerency and preservation of the balance prove that the verses of *sūrat al-Raḥmān* (Q 55:1–13) can be explored to explain and elaborate on the verses on *khilāfa* in *sūrat al-Baqara* (Q 2:29–38).

The verses of *sūrat al-Raḥmān* have detailed facts related to the vicegerency of man, which were not expounded by the verses of *sūrat al-Baqara*. For example, they placed the duty of the human being in the context of the general Islamic existential view of the universe and the Divine action in it. Also, they determined the one who is deputised (*al-mustakhlaf ʿanhu*, i.e., God), the vicegerent (*khalīfa*, i.e., the human being), the object of vicegerency (*al-mustakhlaf fīhi*, i.e., the balance) and the arena of vicegerency (*al-mustakhlaf ʿalayhi*, i.e., the earth) in a way that leaves no room for the ramified differences among scholars on these elements that we have detailed in previous chapters.

The vicegerency verses in *sūrat al-Baqara* speak about the human existential function and the Divine guidance that qualifies him to carry it out (i.e., his innate faculty (*fiṭra*) to name things (language), hence, be conscious of them and act accordingly), before speaking about Revelation and after mentioning the suitability of the earth as a field for that duty. On the contrary, the verses of *sūrat al-Raḥmān* speak about the duty of the human being after referring to the guidance of Revelation and natural disposition (*fiṭra*) and before mentioning the suitability of the earth for that duty. In both *Sūras*, the mention of the human function is closer in rank to the innate guidance than to the revealed one. In *sūrat al-Baqara*, the innate guidance comes immediately after the verse mentioning the human function, while in *sūrat al-Raḥmān*, it comes just before the verse on the cosmic guidance that preceded the human function. This is because Revelation in its essence confirms the guidance naturally rooted in the human being, as already noted,[94] and as indicated by the Prophet's (ﷺ) statement, "Trust descended from the Heavens and settled in the roots of the hearts of people, and then people learnt it from the Qurʾan and *Sunna*."[95] Hence, the mention of *fiṭra* (human nature) came closer in rank to human function than Revelation because it is the first means for fulfilling that function before Revelation. Moreover, the balance placed in the universe is established in the human being's *fiṭra*, since he is part of that universe. Revelation is thus one of the means by which the human being can maintain the cosmic balance.

Significantly, out of thirty-two *Sūras* of the Qurʾan that begin by mentioning Revelation, we found that 18 of them combine the mention of both Revelation and the universe and its order, along with the mention of the human being and his natural disposition (*fiṭra*) in some occasions.[96] As for the other *Sūras* that begin by mentioning Revelation, we found that they combine both Revelation and people's conditions, except for one *Sūra*. We further found that twenty-five *Sūras* begin by speaking about the universe and its order and/or the creation of the human being and his *fiṭra*.[97] This shows the close link between Revelation, the cosmic order and human nature, since all *Sūras* opening with the mention of Revelation refer also to the universe or the human being and his nature or conditions, except for one *Sūra* that talked about Revelation before it came to Earth.[98] Half of the *Sūras* of the Qurʾan open with either the mention of the former (Revelation combined with universe and/or the human being) or the mention of the universe and its order or the human being and his nature. The Qurʾan therefore describes both Revelation and the universe as the "truth" and that the former was descended "by the truth," and the latter was created "by the truth," as noted before. The Qurʾan also describes both as being signs from God,[99] and that they are both the "light" of God, or enlightened by Him.[100] Therefore, the balance is a cosmic purpose, as presented in Q 55, and, at the same time, one of the purposes of the teachings of Revelation, as stated by God's saying, "It is God who has sent down the Scripture with the Truth and the Balance," (Q 42:17), and His saying, "We sent Our Messengers with clear signs, the Scripture and the Balance, so that people could uphold equity." (Q 57:25, b.o. Abdel Haleem).

From all of this, it can be understood that the object of vicegerency is the harmony that God has placed in the universe, that is, cosmic Islam. This is why the commitment to Revelation, i.e., adopting the religion of Islam, contributes to the preservation of the balance, that is, the harmony of the universe. The object of vicegerency is not to create this harmony, but rather to maintain it, as noted before.

Furthermore, what follows from the examination of the verses of *sūrat al-Raḥmān* is that the object of vicegerency is not to preserve all aspects of Divine action in the universe. This confirms our previous arguments about the impossibility for the object of vicegerency to be "all the matters belonging to the Almighty *Mustakhlif*,"[101] as claimed by some researchers. Evidence of the above in the verses of *sūrat al-Raḥmān* lies in God's saying "in the balance," which denotes that the prohibition applies to neglecting the preservation of a part of the balance, not all of it. Ibn ʿĀshūr said,

> [The proposition] "in" (*fī*) in God's saying "in the balance," signifies that what is prohibited is to cause the least transgression in the balance. The prohibition is thus not to neglect the balance in its entirety but is rather relative to any [possible] transgression related to it as the case in God's saying, "but provide for them and clothe them in it (*fīhā*)."
>
> (Q 4:5, b.o. Sahih Intl)

This means, 'provide them from a part of it.'"[102] This is because, full exceedance in the balance, and, in reverse, full preservation of it are impossible, as this is only within the purview of God. The human being does not have the capacity to preserve or transgress the balance in its entirety, but he was mandated to be a vicegerent to act on behalf of God in looking after and maintaining a part of that cosmic balance. If this is confirmed, the outstanding question is then about the specific aspects of the cosmic balance that the human being has been entrusted to preserve on behalf of God. This is what we will attempt to address by investigating the function of vicegerency on behalf of God in maintaining the balance through the reading grid of the Qurʾanic rationale behind the existence of Revelation, universe and the human being. The concepts and principles used by the Qurʾan as rationale to justify these existential phenomena represent, for considerations that we will highlight below, the higher Islamic concepts that make up the Qurʾanic worldview. The holistic approach to vicegerency through the reading grid of the Qurʾanic outlook on the function of the universe and its teleological relation with the function of the human being, which helped us overcome several of the shortcomings identified in contemporary scholarship in this chapter, will further help us in outlining the contours of a Qurʾanic vicegerency theory in the coming chapter.

## Notes

1 The mission or existential function of the human being has hardly been tackled by contemporary (and even early) Islamic thinkers. We could only find a handful of studies dedicated to the subject, which did not go beyond a few comments on some isolated texts from the Qurʾan, *Sunna* and statements of the early scholars. See for instance: Yūsuf al-Qaraḍāwī, "Qīmat al-Insān wa-Ghāyat Wujūdih fī Ḍawʾ al-Qurʾān wa-l-Sunna" [The Value of the Human Being and the Purpose of His Existence in the Light of the Qurʾan and the Sunna], *Journal of Buhūth al-Sunna wa-l-Sīra*, Qatar University no. 5 (1991). As for the studies that tackled the subject of the human being in Islam in general, they only provide brief and superficial discussions on the issue of human existential function. One of these is the recent edited volume published by the International Institute of Islamic Thought on the subject in question. See Rāʾid ʿUkkāsha and ʿĀʾisha al-Ḥaḍīrī, ed., *Sūrat al-Insān bayna al-Marjiʿiyyatayn al-Islāmiyya wa-l-Gharbiyya* [The Image of the Human Being between Islamic and Western References] (Herndon, VA: International Institute of Islamic Thought, 2020). As for Akbarian writings, we do not consider that they propose a Qurʾanic theory on the human existential function for different reasons. One of them is that vicegerency, according to that paradigm, is only reserved for a small elite. Furthermore, it is more an existential fact than an existential function, in addition to the fact that that theory is not rooted in solid Qurʾanic grounds, but, on the contrary, clearly contradicts many Qurʾanic fundamentals.

2 Among them: Abū Sulaymān, *Azmat al-ʿAql al-Muslim*, and Zarmān, "Waẓīfat al-Istikhlāf fī l-Qurʾān al-Karīm," and several others.

3 Those include ʿAbduh and Riḍā, *Tafsīr al-Manār*, vol. 1, 217.

4 Munyā al-Gharbī, "al-Insān wa-l-Qiyam fī al-Nuṣūṣ al-Taʾsīsyya: Sūrat Luqmān Unmūdhjan" [Man and Values in the Foundational Texts: Sūrat Luqmān as Case Study], in Rāʾid ʿUkkāsha and ʿĀʾisha al-Ḥaḍīrī ed., *Sūrat al-Insān bayna al-Marjiʿiyyatayn al-Islāmiyya wa-l-Gharbiyya* [The Image of the Human Being between Islamic and Western References] (Herndon, VA: International Institute of Islamic Thought, 2020), 51.

5 Including:

- ʿAwda, *Al-Islām wa-Awḍāʿuna al-Siyāsiyya*, 28
- Banī ʿĪsā, "Naẓariyyat al-Istikhlāf,"16
- Zūzū, "Maqṣad Ḥifẓ al-Bīʾa wa-Atharuhu fī ʿAmaliyyat al-Istikhlāf," 84
- Atari, "Christian 'Service-Stewardship' and Islamic 'Khilafah,'" 40

6 See for instance: ʿAbd al-Majīd al-Najjār, "Maqāṣid al-Qurʾān fī Tazkiyat al-Insān" [The Objectives of the Qurʾan in the Purification of Man], in *Sūrat al-Insān bayn al-Marjiʿiyyatayn al-Islāmiyya wa-l-Gharbiyya,* 107.

7 See for instance:

- Al-Rāzī, *al-Tafsīr al-Kabīr*, vol. 18, 36
- Ismāʿīl ibn Kathīr, *Tafsīr al-Qurʾān al-ʿAẓīm* [The Exegesis of the Great Qurʾan], ed. Sāmī Salāma (Riyadh: Dār Ṭayba, 2nd ed., 1999), vol. 4, 331
- Muhhammad al-Qāsimī, *Maḥāsin al-Taʾwīl* [The Virtues of Interpretation], ed. Muḥammad Bāsil ʿUyūn al-Sūd (Beirut: Dār al-Kutub al-ʿIlmiyya, 1418 AH), vol. 6, 112
- Ibn Bādīs, *Tafsīr ibn Bādīs*, 39
- Aḥmad al-Marāghī, *Tafsīr al-Marāghī* (Egypt: Dār Muṣtafā al-Bābī al-Ḥalabī wa-Awlāduh, 1946), vol. 12, 53
- ʿAbd al-Karīm al-Khaṭīb, *Al-Tafsīr al-Qurʾān li-l-Qurʾān* [The Explanation of the Qurʾan by the Qurʾan] (Cairo: Dār al-Fikr al-ʿArabī, n.d.), vol. 6, 1162–63
- Ibn ʿĀshūr, *Al-Taḥrīr wa-l-Tanwīr*, vol. 12, 108

8 Riḍā, *Tafsīr al-Manār*, vol. 12, 101.

9 See: Maszlee, "Constructing the Architectonics and Formulating the Articulation of Islamic Governance," 198.

10 Some classical scholars reported the view that this verse (Q 11:61) implies a command to build and populate the earth. See for instance: Abū Bakr al-Jaṣṣāṣ, *Aḥkām al-Qur'ān* [The Rulings of the Qur'an], ed. Muḥammad Ṣādiq, (Beirut: Dār Iḥyā' al-Turāth al-'Arabī, 1405 AH), vol. 4, 378, and al-Māwardī, *Al-Nukat wa-l-'Uyūn*, vol. 2, 479. Yet, this is contradicted by the context of the verse as we saw, since Thamūd were already engaging in *'imārat al-arḍ* in an unprecedented fashion before the prophet Ṣāliḥ came to them with Divine commandments. Furthermore, it is not clear whether these views regard this "command" as a cosmic or a religious one. In his comment on these opinions, al-Qurṭubī seems to argue for the former and clearly disallows the idea that this is a Divine (religious) command to engage in *'imārat al-arḍ*. See: al-Qurṭubī, *Al-Jāmi' li-Aḥkām al-Qur'ān*, vol. 9, 56–57. Moreover, those few who do regard it as a religious command only see it as one of the many (secondary) commands addressed to the human being, and not as the very existential function for which he was created. Al-Jaṣṣāṣ (d. 370/981), for instance, writes that one of the opinions about this verse is that it indicates that God "commanded you to construct the earth according to your needs, which indicates the obligation to construct the earth in terms of farming, planting and [constructing] buildings." al-Jaṣṣāṣ, *Aḥkām al-Qur'ān*, Ibid. Also, they do not say, in the context of the explanation of this verse, that *'imārat al-arḍ* is synonymous to the *khīlāfa* for which the human was created or a part of it, nor do they explain the verse(s) on *khīlāfa* in the light of this verse, in contrast to these contemporary writers.

11 Qaraybi', *Al-Istikhlāf wa-l-Ḥaḍāra*, 44.

12 Including: al-Dasūqī, *Al-Khilāfa al-Islāmiyya*, 433 ff. and al-Khaṭīb, *Qiyam al-Islām al-Ḥaḍāriyya*, 36.

13 See: al-Dasūqī, *Al-Khilāfa al-Islāmiyya*, 435.

14 Ibid.

15 Quṭb, *Fī Ẓilāl al-Qur'ān*, vol. 1, 54.

16 Ibid.

17 See: al-Mawdūdī, *Niẓām al-Ḥayāt fī al-Islām*, 27–28.

18 Al-Najjār, *Fiqh al-Taḥaḍḍur al-Islāmī*, 51.

19 Including, for instance, Faraḥāt, *Al-Khilāfa fī al-Arḍ* and 'Ayyādī, "Al-Insān al-Khalīfa wa-Muhimmat al-I'mār."

20 Including: Sharī'atī, *Al-Insān wa-l-Islām*, 22–23; and Bint al-Shāṭi', *Al-Qur'ān wa-Qaḍāyā al-Insān*, 72–75.

21 Abū Sulaymān, *Al-Ru'ya al-Kawniyya al-Ḥaḍāriyya al-Qur'āniyya*, 120.

22 Recorded by Muslim in his *Ṣaḥīḥ* (no. 2742).

23 Al-Aḥmar, "Istikhlāf al-Insān fī l-Arḍ Naḥwa Ru'ya Qur'āniyya Kulliyya," 307.

24 Bāqir al-Ṣadr, *Al-Islām Yaqūd al-Ḥayāt*, 134.

25 See: al-Rāghib al-Iṣfahānī, *Al-Mufradāt fī Gharīb al-Qur'ān* [The Dictionary of Complex Qur'anic Terminology], ed. Ṣafwan 'Adnān al-Dawūdī (Damascus-Beirut: Dār al-Qalam, al-Dār al-Shāmiyya, 1412 AH), 294; and ibn Manẓūr, *Lisān al-'Arab*, vol. 9, 83.

26 See George R. McGhee, Jr, Peter M. Sheehan, David J. Bottjer, and Mary L. Droser, "Ecological Ranking of Phanerozoic Biodiversity Crises: The Serpukhovian (Early Carboniferous) Crisis Had a Greater Ecological Impact than the End-Ordovician," *Geology* 40, no. 2 (2012), 147–50; and S. Sahney and M. J. Benton, "Recovery from the Most Profound Mass Extinction of All Time," *Proceedings of the Royal Society B: Biological Sciences* 275, no. 1636 (2008), 759–65.

27 For example, al-Māwardī notes: "The angels are the best and most sane creatures. However, they do not eat, drink or reproduce." Al-Māwardī, *Al-Nukat wa-l-'Uyūn*, vol. 1, 94. Al-Rāzī comments: "It has been agreed that the angels do not eat, drink or reproduce. They exalt God day and night and do not slacken." Al-Rāzī, *Al-Tafsīr al-Kabīr*, vol. 1, 85.

28 Some theologians, particularly ibn Taymiyya, differentiated between Divine *mashī'a* (will) and *irāda* (intention). In their view, everything that happens in the universe is the

*mashī'a* of God. Something may occur in the universe and it is the *mashī'a* of God but not His *irāda*. For example, the human being's corruption is God's *mashī'a* but not His *irāda* (intention), in other words this is God's cosmic will but not His revealed will. It is God's will because He predestined it and gave humans the means and enabled them to do it, but it does not in itself represent an intention of God, because it is contrary to what God likes and ordained in Revelation and it is not in itself an articulation of His attributes of perfection. It is contrary to God's revealed will and it is falsehood (*bāṭil*) in the sense that it does not stem from an ontological Truth (God's attributes) but it rather stems from a deviationfrom that. However, behind this action that is not intended by God in itself is always something that is intended, i.e., that is good, that is true, and that is why it was willed by God. For instance, murder is willed by God but not intended because it goes against the revealed will and in itself also against the intentions behind both the revealed and cosmic wills, i.e., in itself it is evil and falsehood. However, behind murder there is something that is intended, i.e., that is good, that is true, like the ability for a being to choose between murder or not, between elevation and debauchery, etc. Consequently, everything that happens in the universe, including human actions, is in itself always willed by God, because nothing happens against His will, but not always intended in itself, but what is always intended is the inextricable good (Truth) behind it. See for instance: Ibn Taymiyya, *Minhāj al-Sunna al-Nabawiyya*, vol. 5, 409–16.

29 The use of the 'conscious/rational subject' pronouns (*ḍamīr al-'āqil*) "them" (*hum*) and "these" (*hā'ulā'*), in reference to the names of the things that Adam was taught, does not mean that he was only taught the names of conscious/rational beings and their attributes. Rather, the previously explained linguistic rule of "precedence" (*taghlīb*) applies here as well. See for instance, ibn 'Āshūr, *Al-Taḥrīr wa-l-Tanwīr*, vol. 1, 412.

30 As we will see, the Qur'anic verses that highlight the natural faculty on which the human existential function depends, or which give rise to that function, express that faculty in different ways, with the common denominator of being something that God taught human beings. In Q 2:31, it is about the human being having been "taught all the names," referring to this potential consciousness of all material and moral things thanks to language. It is this consciousness that allows him to act on behalf of God as we saw. In Q 55:4, it is about the human being having been "taught speech," referring to the natural potential to express that in spoken language. In Q 96:4, it is about the human being having been "taught by the pen," referring to the ability to represent that consciousness/language through symbols.

31 For instance, identifying different species of fauna and flora by learning their names (a specific human faculty as we saw) provides the human being with a singular state of consciousness of his natural environment, with all the spiritual and moral consequences that entails in getting closer to his humanness, fulfilling his existential function, recognising God's favours and Majesty, understanding the worship of each creature by which it integrates cosmic worship, seeking to be harmonious with these creatures, etc. Nonetheless, as indicated, beyond the consciousness of his material surroundings, language procures the human being with the consciousness of a whole set of universes of existence in different realms, starting from the realm of the Divine (names) which gives him access to the realm of his inner universe, as will be developed.

32 Q 15:28–29 and 38:71–72.

33 Q 7:11.

34 Al-Bukhārī (no. 6227), and Muslim (no. 2612).

35 The angels' substantiation that vicegerency will inevitably go against the Divine intention and that their actions compensate for it, God's substantiation that the human being is endowed with the appropriate faculties and that the angels' actions do not compensate for vicegerency, since, as will be developed below, they do not articulate what vicegerency articulates in the universe, and the angels' substantiation that they do not possess the faculty to name all things because that is a Divine attribute with which they were not endowed.

36 The relation between the fact that the human being was taught all the names and the Divine names and attributes will be explored in the following chapter.
37 See: Ibn ʿĀshūr, *Al-Taḥrīr wa-l-Tanwīr*, vol. 1, 399, and Riḍā, *Tafsīr al-Manār*, vol. 1, 215.
38 As noted before, the idea that the jinn inhabited the earth before the human being is alien to the Qurʾan and the *Sunna*. To the contrary, the Qurʾan clearly states that Iblīs (the father of the jinn) was banished from paradise and sent to Earth after his refusal to prostrate to Adam, thus after Adam was appointed as a *khalīfa*. As for the fact that Iblīs is, according to the Qurʾan, the father of the jinn, this is clear from the fact that the Qurʾan warns against Iblīs and his offspring, as in Q 18:50.
39 Riḍā said: "It goes without saying that this question arose from the understanding of the meaning of being a *khalīfa* and its implications." Riḍā, *Tafsīr al-Manār*, vol. 1, 217. In his commentary on the *tafsīr* of al-Bayḍāwī, Ismāʿīl al-Qūnawī (d. 1195/1780) disputed the idea that the angels could have understood that the human being will corrupt and shed blood through the meaning of the word *khalīfa*, because if that was the case then how could the angels "aspire for *khilāfa*" and pretend that they are more eligible for it? Ismāʿīl ibn Muḥammad al-Qūnawī, *Ḥāshiyat al-Qūnawī ʿalā Tafsīr al-Imām al-Bayḍāwī* [The Footnote of al-Qūnawī on the Tafsīr of al-Bayḍāwī], ed. ʿAbd Allāh ʿUmar (Beirut: Dār al-Kutub al-ʿIlmiyya, 2001), vol. 3, 120. However, as elaborated before, there is no indication in these verses that the angels assumed that they would be better vicegerents or that they aspired for *khilāfa*; rather, as demonstrated, they believed that there is no need for *khilāfa* in the first place, since, they supposed, their actions in the universe do compensate for that.
40 Muḥammad ibn Ṣāliḥ al-ʿUthaymīn, *Majmūʿ Fatāwā wa-Rasāʾil al-ʿUthaymīn* [The Collection of Fatwas and Treatises of al-ʿUthaymīn] (Riyadh: Dār al-Waṭan-Dār al-Thurayya, 1416 AH), vol. 3, 102.
41 For example: Q 7:142, 150; Q 43:60; Q 19:59.
42 Muslim (no. 1342).
43 Muslim (no. 2937).
44 That is the meaning of the words according to the semantic conventions of the pre-Islamic Arab community within which the Revelation came.
45 That is the meaning of the words within the semantic field shaped by the convention of Arabs in general.
46 See ʿAbd Allāh Bin Bayyah, *Amālī al-Dalālāt wa Majālī al-Ikhtilāfāt* [The Impact of Semantics and the Areas of Divergence] (Beirut: Dār ibn Ḥazm, n.d.), 73.
47 Ibid., 71–72.
48 The majority of jurists agree that the words of Islamic scripture should always be understood according to their Islamic meaning unless there is an indication that the latter is not intended. The Ḥanafī school, for its part, holds that they should be understood as per their linguistic meaning as long as there is no indication that the Islamic one is meant. However, all agree that the linguistic meaning is to be sidelined if the word came in the context of its Islamic meaning. See for instance: Shams al-Dīn al-Burmāwī, *Al-Fawāʾid al-Saniyya fī Sharḥ al-Alfiyya* [The Bright Benefits from the Explanation of the *Alfiyya*], ed. ʿAbd Allāh Ramaḍān (Egypt: Maktabat al-Tawʿiyya al-Islāmiyya, 2015), vol. 2, 374–76.
49 Jamāl al-Dīn al-Isnawī, *Al-Tamhīd fī Takhrīj al Furūʿ ʿalā al-Uṣūl* [Prolegomena in Deducing Particular Rulings from Overall Principles], ed. Muḥammad Ḥasan Hītū (Beirut: Muʾassasat al-Risāla, 1400 AH), 228.
50 Najm al-Dīn al-Ṭūfī, *Sharḥ Mukhtaṣar al-Rawḍa* [The Explanation of the Abridgement of al-Rawḍa], ed. ʿAbd Allāh al-Turkī (Beirut: Muʾassasat al-Risāla, 1987), vol. 2, 207.
51 Ibn Taymiyya, *Majmūʿ al-Fatāwā*, vol. 7, 286.
52 See for instance: al-Sharīf al-Jurjānī, *Al-Taʿrīfāt* [The Definitions] (Beirut: Dār al-Kutub al-ʿIlmiyya, 1983), 134.

53 Q 8:35.

54 This approach defines the meaning of the term within the context of the specific verse or *Ḥadīth* in which it was evoked and in relation to other verses and *Ḥadīths* dealing with similar issues. *Uṣūl al-fiqh* (Islamic jurisprudence) is mainly concerned with the study of the methodological rules and devices of this approach, which is also well-established in the discipline of *uṣūl al-tafsīr* (methods of Qur'anic exegesis) and *'ulūm al-Qur'ān* (Qur'ān sciences).

55 Explaining why, in the achievement of worship, it is better to merely abide by the rulings of Revelation (obtained through contextual intertextuality) without seeking to realise the intended benefits behind them or to explore the teleological purposes and objectives (worldview) that control them, al-Shāṭibī writes: "If the intended benefit (*maṣlaḥa*) behind religious responsibilities is known, the accountable person that is responsible for abiding by it can have three possible attitudes: [...] The third: to merely seek to abide by the injunction, whether he understands the intended benefit or not. This is the most perfect and most safe attitude. It is the most perfect because he [the accountable person] constitutes himself as a servant under the [Divine] orders, since he takes nothing in consideration but the mere commands. Furthermore, since he abides by the commands, he delegates the knowledge of the benefits [intended behind them] to the One Who knows them in their integrity. [Hence] his action will not be limited to some of its benefits to the exclusion of others, since God knows every benefit that comes forth from this action. [...] Hence, he enters under the command of His will, the abidance of which is not restricted to some benefits to the exclusion of others. As for it [i.e., merely abiding by the commandments without seeking their objectives] being the safest [attitude], that is because of the fact that he who handles based on mere abidance, handles according to servitude." Al-Shāṭibī, *Al-Muwāfaqāt*, vol. 3, 99–100. Al-Shāṭibī then further explains why this is the safest attitude based on his Ash'arī worldview, which stipulates that the primary intent behind abiding by the rulings of Revelation is mere servitude and that Revelation is not initially intended to realise any human interests in this world other than worship for the sake of worship in the sense of abstract servitude. Hence, the safest is to only focus on abstract worship and to ignore any (accidental) benefit behind Revelation in order to avoid placing it on the same level or above abstract worship. Overall, it is clear from al-Shāṭibī's statements that the human existential purpose, in his consideration, is organically achieved by merely abiding by the commandments of Revelation without the need of considering the worldview in which they operate. Furthermore, that existential purpose does not inherently relate to the achievement of any initially intended worldly purposes, or a concrete worldly mission. Hence, the theorisation of the human existential mission does not appear to have any importance as it were. This is an eloquent illustration of the two hypotheses by which we explained why the human existential function did not receive significant theoretical attention in classical Islamic scholarship in the third chapter, namely, its spontaneous realisation through mere abidance and the epistemological frames through which the different schools of theology apprehended the wisdom behind the creation of the human being.

56 And in order to offer a comprehensive Islamic philosophical frame through which contemporary issues could be envisaged holistically, as previously discussed.

57 See: 'Alī ibn Sīdah, *Al-Muḥkam wa-l-Muḥīṭ al-A'ẓam* [The Conclusive and Most Comprehensive], ed. 'Abd al-Ḥamīd Hindāwī (Beirut: Dār al-Kutub al-'Ilmiyya, 2000), vol. 5, 198; and Ibn Manẓūr, *Lisān al-'Arab*, vol. 9, 85.

58 Indeed, God is al-Wārith (the Inheritor) and the Inheritor of the earth and what's in it after the demise of the human being, as described in the Qur'an (for instance, 19:40). However, this does not mean that He will become the possessor of the earth and what's in it after it has been possessed by the human being. Rather, it means that He will remain the only owner after it has been (partially) borrowed by the human being. This is supported by many verses that establish the fact that God is the real possessor,

that He gives the heritage of the earth to whom He wants, and that the human being is not a real owner but somebody to whom the earth was temporary entrusted, as, for instance, in Q 57:7, 10 and Q 7:128.

59 See: al-Dasūqī, *Al-Khilāfa al-Islāmiyya*, 198, 215 ff.

60 Al-Dasūqī said, "It is established in the Qur'an that God Almighty is al-Walī (the Protecting Associate), al-Wakīl (the Guarantor), al-Wārith (the Inheritor), al-Nāṣir (The Supporter), al-Ḥākim (The Ruler), in the cosmic meaning. This necessitates that one of His attributes is that He is a *Khalīfa*, but also in the cosmic sense. [...] The permissibility of describing God as *Khalīfa* is not inferred only from this, though such inference would be sufficient. Indeed, the Prophet (ﷺ) described God as such in the supplication of travelling." Al-Dasūqī, *Al-Khilāfa al-Islāmiyya*, 216. It seems, however, that the writer omitted the fact that God's Attributes are *tawqīfī* (prescribed by Revelation) and cannot be deduced by way of inference. God's Attributes must be clearly stated in Scripture. Furthermore, the naming of God a *khalīfa* over the family in the *Ḥadīth* did not occur in the context of ascribing a name or an attribute to God, but rather in the context of informing us that God looks after His servants even when they are forsaken by their loved ones, as mentioned above. Thus, it cannot be said that God is a *khalīfa* in an absolute (unrestricted) sense, nor is *khilāfa* a Divine attribute or Name. One of the conditions of the permissibility to ascribe a Name or Attribute to God is that they must occur in the Qur'an or *Sunna* in an unrestricted manner. Ibn al-Qayyim said: "To say something about God as an information about Him is broader than to give Him a Name or an Attribute. For instance, saying that He is 'something' or a 'being' or that He 'stands alone' is giving information about God, but it cannot be taken as Beautiful Names or Higher Attributes." Ibn Qayyim al-Jawziyya, Shams al-Dīn, *Badā'i' al-Fawā'id* [The Amazing Insights] (Beirut: Dār al-Kitāb al-'Arabī, n.d.), vol. 1, 161. He also said, "Ascribing a Name or an Attribute to God can only be *tawqīfī* (prescribed by Revelation). Giving information about Him, however, is not necessarily *tawqīfī* such as saying that He is infinite, something, existing or standing alone, for instance." Ibid., vol. 1, 162. Another condition is that the Names and Attributes of God must be praiseworthy in the absolute. This is a difference between the texts of Revelation that use terms in describing God and those that ascribe terms to God as Divine names or attributes. See: Ibn Taymiyya, *Majmū' al-Fatāwā*, vol. 6, 142. Ibn al-Qayyim said, "If the Attribute comprised both aspects of perfection and shortcomings, then it cannot be applied as a Name of God in an absolute manner. Only the aspects of perfection can be ascribed to Him as a Name. This include, for instance, words like *murīd* (the one who wills), *fā'il* (performer) and *ṣāni'* (maker), these are not names for God. It is, therefore, wrong to call Him a maker without adding anything. He is rather a Performer of what He desires, because will, performance and making may be used in a positive sense or in a negative sense. Will, performance and making have aspects of perfection and others of shortcomings. It is therefore that God only named Himself according to the best aspects of those attributes." *Badā'i' al-Fawā'id*, vol. 1, 161. Therefore, "His Beautiful Names do not include the willer, the speaker, the performer, or the maker, because these names may be used to designate praiseworthy or blameworthy meanings. His Names and Attributes are only the praiseworthy ones such as al-Ḥalīm (The All-Forbearing), al-Ḥakīm (the All-Wise), al-'Azīz (The Mighty) and the Performer of whatever He wills." Ibn Qayyim al-Jawziyya, Shams al-Dīn, *Mukhtaṣar al-Ṣawā'iq al-Mursala 'alā al-Jahmmiyya wa al-Mu'aṭṭila* [The Summary of the Thunderbolts Sent on the Jahmiyya and the Suspenders of Divine Attributes] (Cairo: Dār al-Ḥadīth, 2001), 307. Thus, when a verb or an action is ascribed to God (in Revelation), or an information is given about Him, while it can be used pejoratively, it is not permissible to derive a Divine name or attribute from it. This is the case for *khilāfa*, as an action ascribed to God in the *Ḥadīth*. According to the linguistic meaning of the word, the *khalīfa* can be a good or an evil one; hence, it cannot be taken as an attribute of God. Moreover,

the term *khalīfa* in the description of God was not used in an absolute way but in a restricted one. The *Ḥadīth* did not say that God is a *khalīfa* period, but rather that He is a *khalīfa* in taking care of the family or the Muslims. Thus, *khalīfa* is unquestionably not one of God's Beautiful Names or Higher Attributes.

61 Among those who believe that worship is not the only purpose for which man was created is Muḥammad al-Ṭāhir ibn ʿĀshūr. For him, the conjunction in the verse: "except to worship Me" is "not a restriction (*ḥaṣr*) in the literal sense (*qaṣr ḥaqīqī*). Even if we are not to know the measures of God's wisdoms, we are sure that the purpose of the creation of the human being is not only to worship Him, because the purposes of God's acts are numerous and we cannot comprehend them all. Mentioning one of these purposes here does not exclude other ones. God mentions, on other occasions, purposes other than worship. For example, He says, 'If your Lord had pleased, He would have made all people a single community, but they continue to have their differences – except those on whom your Lord has mercy, and for that He has created them.' (Q 11:118–19, b.o. Abdel Haleem). Moreover, God mentions some purposes behind the creation of specific individuals among humans and jinn, as He says about Jesus: 'We shall make him a sign for people and a blessing from Us.' (Q 19:21, Ahmad Ali)." Ibn ʿĀshūr, *Al-Taḥrīr wa-l-Tanwīr*, vol. 27, 28. However, ibn ʿĀshūr does not differentiate here between worship as an existential function and its means and outcomes. It appears that he includes all these within the meaning of "wisdom" and "purpose." Hence, he interprets the restriction (except to worship Me) as a figurative, and not a literal, one by attempting to prove that the human being was created for other purposes (wisdoms). He gave two examples here: 1) the indication of Q 11:118–19 that God created people to have mercy on them; 2) He created Jesus to make him a sign for humankind and a mercy from God. Nevertheless, mercy is a fruit of worship. The verse even clearly indicates that the exclusion "except those on whom your Lord has mercy" is meant for the worshippers. Furthermore, the mercy for which God created the human being is, first and foremost, an outcome of worship that will be granted in the Hereafter for those who fulfilled their mission, as we can understand from following *Ḥadīth*: "Allah has one hundred (parts of) mercy. He has sent down, out of these, one part of mercy upon the jinn and human beings and animals and insects. It is because of this (one part) that they love one another, show kindness to one another and the beast treats its young one with affection because of that. Allah has reserved (the other) ninety nine parts of mercy for the Day of Judgment to have mercy on His servants." Recorded by Muslim in his *Ṣaḥīḥ* (no. 2752). As for the creation of Jesus to be a sign for humankind, this is but one of the many means to achieve worship. Moreover, God's mercy on Earth for all of His creatures is a fruit of their inevitable worship for him, and God's mercy for the human being is a fruit of the human being's wilful worship of God in actions where the human being is not worshipping God in an inevitable way to complete that mercy. Therefore, ibn ʿĀshūr did not give any accurate example to prove that the human being's function is not limited to worship. Moreover, ibn ʿĀshūr himself said: "Man's worship of God is nothing but the very achievement of the purpose of his creation and the reason for its realisation." Ibid., vol. 27, 27. Hence, a careful examination of ibn ʿĀshūr's thoughts reveals that he does not understand the restriction (*ḥaṣr*) as a figurative one concerning the function for which the human being was created, but only concerning the wisdom for which he was created. Accordingly, the only function for which he was created is worship, but there are different wisdoms behind his creation. Thus, ibn ʿĀshūr holds the literal meaning of the restriction for the human being's function but not for the wisdoms of his creation, based on the fact that this function has many fruits and means that constitute the wisdoms behind man's creation. However, there is no need for such an interpretation as the word "worship" is comprehensive of all its purposes and means.

62 See also: Q 62:1; Q 64:1; and Q 59:24.

63 We will prove later that prostration in this verse and in others means worship, not just the "literal" meaning of prostration.
64 For the inclusion of all elements of the universe in the term "whoever," see the fourth section of the fourth chapter.
65 Al-Ṭabarī, *Jāmi' al-Bayān*, vol. 1. 362. See also for example:
- Abū Isḥāq Ibrāhīm al-Zajjāj, *Ma'ānī al-Qur'ān wa-I'rābuh* [The Meanings of the Qur'an and Its Grammatical Analysis] (Beirut: 'Ālam al-Kutub, 1988), vol. 1, 48
- Muḥammad ibn al-Zamanayn, *Tafsīr al-Qur'ān al-'Azīz* [The Exegesis of the Mighty Qur'an], ed. Ḥusayn ibn 'Ukāsha and Muḥammad al-Kanz (Cairo: al-Fārūq al-Ḥadītha, 2002), vol. 1, 119
- Al-Qurṭubī, *Al-Jāmi' li-Aḥkām al-Qur'ān*, vol. 11, 130

66 Muḥammad ibn Aḥmad al-Kalbī ibn Juzayy, *Al-Tashīl li-'Ulūm al-Tanzīl* [The Facilitation of the Sciences of Revelation], ed. 'Abd Allāh al-Khālidī (Beirut: Dār al-Arqam ibn Abī al-Arqam, 1416 AH), vol. 1, 428.
67 'Abd al-Ḥaqq ibn 'Aṭiyya, *Al-Muḥarrar al-Wajīz fī Tafsīr al-Kitāb al-'Azīz* [The Concise and Verified Exegesis of the Mighty Book], ed. 'Abd al-Salām Muḥammad (Beirut: Dār al-Kutub al-'Ilmiyya, 1422 AH), vol. 5, 283.
68 The famous Mauritanian scholar Muḥammad al-Amīn al-Shinqīṭī (d. 1973) claimed that the opinion that holds that prostration (*sujūd*) in these verses is not the known ritual prostration performed by Muslims, goes against the rule (which we highlighted above) that stipulates that Qur'anic concepts must be understood as per their Islamic meanings before resorting to the linguistic meaning. Muḥammad al-Amīn al-Shinqīṭī, *Aḍwā' al-Bayān fī Īḍāḥ al-Qur'an bi-l-Qur'an* [The Clarification of the Qur'an by the Qur'an] (Beirut: Dār al-Fikr, 1995), vol. 2, 238–39. Nevertheless, the Islamic meaning of terms is not only obtained by mere intertextuality in the sense of the more or less apparent clarification through context or other texts of Scripture, which we previously named "contextual intertextuality." *Sujūd* according to the latter is a ritual act where one places seven body parts on the ground (the forehead, both palms with closed fingers – without touching the ground with the arms and elbows and without adjoining the arms to the body – nose, both knees and feet) while facing the *qibla* (the Ka'ba in Mecca), pointing towards it with the feet and hands, and formulating specific supplications with the intention of glorifying God while remaining in that position until reaching a relaxed state. This is indeed *sujūd* according to contextual intertextuality. However, this is not the Islamic meaning of *sujūd* in the specific context of these verses as per the worldview *tafsīr* (which we called "conceptional intertextuality") that we will develop below. The latter is also based on intertextuality. Yet, the intertextuality of the worldview approach through which the Islamic meaning is obtained is not the one envisioned by classical scholars where the concept (*sujūd* here) is verbally or practically explained in detail by the Prophet (ﷺ) or by other texts of Revelation. Rather, it is an intertextuality that explores the concepts within the frame of their teleological purposes, ontological roots and existential realities, in other terms, within the Islamic worldview, as will become clear throughout the remaining part of this study.
69 Ibn 'Āshūr, *Al-Taḥrīr wa-l-Tanwīr,* vol. 18, 259.
70 Ibid., vol. 17, 226.
71 Al-Zajjāj, *Ma'ānī al-Qur'ān wa-I'rābuh*, vol. 3, 241.
72 See: Ibn 'Āshūr, *Al-Taḥrīr wa-l-Tanwīr*, vol. 15, 114–15.
73 Including: Q 13:15; Q 16:48–49; Q 20:50; and Q 57:1.
74 Besides worship, religion, Islam and guidance, we may add that another shared factor between the universe and the human being, which underlines their common objective, is revelation. Indeed, the Qur'an indicates that God's revelation is in force in the universe (Q 41:12), on Earth (Q 99:5) and that He reveals His will to animals (Q 16:68). We might qualify this form of revelation as "cosmic revelation," and its counterpart as "scriptural revelation." However, our reference to this latter type is mostly through

the word "Revelation" with a capital R. Moreover, the human being, the universe and Revelation, referred to below as "the three main existential phenomena," share the common particularity of carrying the signs of God. Qur'anic verses are called signs (*āyāt*), and the universe and the human being are qualified as signs (*āyāt*) or as carriers of signs, as in His saying, "On the earth, and in yourselves, there are signs (*āyāt*) for firm believers. Do you not see then? (Q 51:20–21, Wahihuddin Khan), and "There are signs (*āyāt*) in the heavens and the earth for those who believe, and in your own creation and all the creatures He has spread about, there are signs for people of sure faith." (Q 45:3–4, b.o. Wahihuddin Khan).

75 Rashīd Riḍā said, "Islam means to enter in *silm*, which means peace, soundness and purity and surrender." Riḍā, *Tafsīr al-Manār*, vol. 3, 295. More meanings related to the root *s-l-m* are indicative of this cosmic Islam, such as "freedom," as this surrender to God frees from any influence from dictates that go against sound nature and peace, or "security" and "safety," as a result of peace, etc. See the definitions of the root *s-l-m* in terms of surrender, soundness, healthiness, peace, freedom, security, safety, to be free from fault, defects, imperfections and vices, etc. in: Edward W. Lane, *An Arabic-English Lexicon* (London: William and Norgate, 1863), book I, part 4, 1412–14.

76 "Turn to your Lord and surrender (*aslimū*) to Him before the punishment overtakes you and you can no longer be helped." (Q 39:54, b.o. Maududi).

77 "The day when neither wealth nor children will be of any avail, only those who come before Allah with a sound (*salīm*) heart [will be saved]." (Q 26:88–89, b.o. Ahmad Ali).

78 "O believers, enter into the integral peace (*silm*)" (Q 2:208, b.o. Maududi).

79 Ibn 'Āshūr, *Al-Taḥrīr wa-l-Tanwīr*, vol. 22, 126.

80 Ibid.

81 Al-Bukhārī (no. 6497), and Muslim (no. 143).

82 Ibn 'Āshūr, *Al-Taḥrīr wa-l-Tanwīr*, vol. 22, 126.

83 Ibid., vol. 1, 419.

84 See: Ibid., vol. 1, 410–413, 419 and vol. 27, 233.

85 Commenting on Q 20:50, ibn al-Qayyim said, "God (glory be to Him) gave every being its distinctive form and then guided it to that which it is created for." Ibn Qayyim al-Jawziyya, *Shifā' al-'Alīl fī Masā'il al-Qaḍā' wa-l-Qadar wa-l-Ḥikma wa-l-Ta'līl* [Healing the Sick about the Issues of Predestination, Wisdom and Rationale] (Beirut: Dār al-Ma'rifa, 1978), 79. Ibn 'Āshūr said: "'Then' signifies sequence in terms of time and order, that is God created beings then guided them to the purpose of their creation and guided them to the truth after he created them, and bestowed upon them many blessings." Ibn 'Āshūr, *Al-Taḥrīr wa-l-Tanwīr*, vol. 16, 233.

86 The proof that all creatures are disposed according to precise measurements and calculations, and that this is their prostration and worship is God's saying, "Did you not see that for Allah prostrate all things that are in the heavens and on earth,- the sun, the moon, the stars; the hills, the trees, the animals; and a great number among mankind?" (Q 22:18). If there is no difference between the prostration of the sun, the moon, stars and trees here, then there is also no difference between these things in the fact that they are disposed according to precise measurements and calculations set and controlled by God. The verse in *sūrat al-Raḥmān* may also be understood in the sense that it highlights a function of the sun and the moon, that is that they are created so that people may calculate time, as some Qur'anic exegetes stated. Nevertheless, they prostrate in any case as indicated by the previous verse. Hence, even according to this interpretation, it is about a form of worship that they perform.

87 Ibn 'Āshūr pointed out that the sun and the moon, in these verses, represent the celestial creatures, while plants and trees represent terrestrial creatures. Ibid., vol. 27, 235.

88 This is understood, for example, from the fact that the Qur'an describes the destruction of the universe (i.e., the opposite of creation) in terms of the collapse of the sky (i.e., the opposite of "raising up"). The Qur'an says about the end of the world:

"That is the Day when We will roll up the sky like the folding of a parchment. We will bring back creation as We began it at first. [That is] a promise binding upon Us. Indeed, We will do it." (Q 21:104, b.o. Ali Qarai). Hence, if the collapse of the sky signifies the destruction of the universe, its raising signifies the creation of the universe.

89 The preservation of the balance (the human existential function) is the only rationale that the Qur'an explicitly establishes as teleological purpose behind each of these existential phenomena (Revelation, human creation, human nature, cosmic worship, creation of the universe and cosmic harmony), as will be highlighted below.

90 Many Qur'anic exegetes argued that the meaning of "weight" and "balance" in God's saying, "set up the weight with justice and do not diminish the balance," is related to the prohibition of giving short measures in sales. Thus, weighing with justice means to give the buyer the full measure, and the balance is the scale by which goods are weighed. However, this understanding does not fit the context of the verse. After mentioning God's graces with regard to Revelation, the creation of man with distinct faculties, the conception of the elements according to disciplined laws, their submission to God, the creation of the universe in a harmonious manner and the prohibition to exceeding that balance; would it be reasonable to speak after that comprehensive existential sketch about sales and the prohibition of giving short measures and fraud in weighing vegetables, fruits and goods? This is out of context as indicated by God's saying after that, "and do not diminish the balance." Thus, it is clear that the verses speak about the universal balance mentioned at the beginning, not the scale that weighs fruits and vegetables.

91 Some Qur'anic exegetes said the first balance is the balance of the lower world (*dunyā*), the second is the balance of the Hereafter and the third the balance of the mind. It was also said that the first and second balances mean justice, while the third means the measuring instrument. Others said that the reiteration denotes confirmation and amplification. Another view is that the second balance refers to the scale of fruits and vegetables, while the third balance refers to the scale of goods, besides other views. See for example:

- Al-Rāzī, *Al-Tafsīr al-Kabīr*, vol. 29, 342
- Niẓām al-Dīn al-Naysabūrī, *Gharā'ib al-Qur'ān wa-Raghā'ib al-Furqān* [The Wonders of the Qur'an], ed. Zakariyya 'Umayrāt (Beirut: Dār al-Kutub al-'Ilmiyya, 1416 AH), vol. 6, 228
- Aḥmad Shihāb al-Dīn al-Khafājī, *Ḥāshiyat al-Shihāb 'alā Tafsīr al-Bayḍāwī* [Commentary on the Exegesis of al-Bayḍāwī] (Beirut: Dār Ṣādir, n.d.), vol. 5, 124

92 Ibn 'Āshūr, *Al-Taḥrīr wa-l-Tanwīr*, vol. 27, 241.

93 Ibid., vol. 27, 243.

94 See also: Ibn al-Qayyim, *Shifā' al-'Alīl*, 79.

95 Al-Bukhārī (no. 6497), and Muslim (no. 143).

96 This is apart from many other occasions in the Qur'an that mention both the universe and Revelation together.

97 1) The *Sūras* that begin by mentioning Revelation along with the universe and its order: Q 3:1–6; Q 10:1–6; Q 11:1–6; Q 13:1–4; Q 14:1–2; Q 16:1–17; Q 20:1–6; Q 25:1–2; Q 26:1–8; Q 32:1–9; Q 42:1–2; Q 44:1–8; Q 45:1–6; Q 46:1–3; Q 55:1–12.

2) *Sūras* that begin by speaking about Revelation and people's attitudes towards it, then speaking about the universe: Q 39:1–6; Q 50:1–11.

3) *Sūras* that begin by speaking about one of the manifestations of the universal order then Revelation: Q 53:1–4.

4) *Sūras* that begin by speaking about Revelation, people's attitudes towards it, the destruction of some nations and the stories of previous nations: Q 2, 7, 12, 15, 17, 27, 28, 31, 36, 38, 40, 41, 47.

5) *Sūras* that begin by speaking about Revelation without speaking about the universe or people's condition: Q 97.

6) *Sūras* that begin by speaking about the universe and its order and/or the creation of the human being and his *fiṭra*: Q 4:1; Q 6:1–7; Q 34:1–2; Q 35:1–3; Q 37:1–6; Q 57:1–6; Q 59:1; Q 61:1; Q 62:1–2; Q 63:1–4; Q 67:1–5; Q 76:1–3; Q 85:1; Q 86:1–3; Q 87:1–6; Q 91:1–7; Q 92:1–3; Q 93:1–2; Q 95:1–5; Q 96:1–5; Q 100:1–8; Q 103:1; Q 113:1; Q 114:1–3.

98 Q 97.

99 For example: Q 45:6.

100 For example: Q 24:35; Q 42:52.

101 Bāqir al-Ṣadr, *Al-Islam Yaqūd al-Ḥayāt*, 134.

102 Ibn ʿĀshūr, *Al-Taḥrīr wa-l-Tanwīr*, vol. 27, 239.

## Bibliography

Abū Sulaymān, ʿAbd al-Ḥamīd. *Azmat al-ʿAql al-Muslim [The Crisis of the Muslim Mind]*. Beirut: Dār al-Hādī, 1st ed., 2003.

Abū Sulaymān, ʿAbd al-Ḥamīd. *Al-Ruʾya al-Kawniyya al-Ḥaḍāriyya al-Qurʾāniyya, al-Munṭalaq al-Asās li-l-Iṣlāḥ al-Insānī [The Qurʾanic Civilizational Worldview: the Main Entry for Human Reform]*. Cairo: Dār al-Salām, 2009.

Al-Aḥmar, ʿAbd al-Salām. "Istikhlāf al-Insān fī l-Arḍ, Naḥwa Ruʾya Qurʾāniyya Kulliyya [Vicegerency on Earth: Towards a Comprehensive Qurʾanic Vision]." In *Proceedings of the International Symposium: The Noble Qurʾan and Worldview: Paths of Reflection and Management*. Rabat. Muḥammadiyya League of Scholars, 2014.

Ibn ʿĀshūr, Muḥammad al-Ṭāhir. *Al-Taḥrīr wa-l-Tanwīr [The Verification and Enlightenment]*. Tunis: al-Dār al-Tūnisiyya, 1984.

Atari, Aref T. M. "Christian "Service-Stewardship" and Islamic "Khilafah": Emerging Models in Educational Administration." *The American Journal of Islamic Social Sciences* 17, no. 2 (Summer 2000).

Ibn ʿAṭiyya, ʿAbd al-Ḥaqq. *Al-Muḥarrar al-Wajīz fī Tafsīr al-Kitāb al-ʿAzīz [The Concise and Verified Exegesis of the Mighty Book]*. Edited by ʿAbd al-Salām Muḥammad. Beirut: Dār al-Kutub al-ʿIlmiyya, 1422 AH.

ʿAwda, ʿAbd al-Qādir. *Al-Islām wa-Awḍāʿunā al-Siyāsiyya [Islam and our Political Conditions]*. Beirut: Muʾassasat al-Risāla, 1981.

ʿAyyādī, ʿAbd al-ʿAzīz. "Al-Insān al-Khalīfa wa-Muhimmat al-Iʿmār: Ruʾya Qurʾāniyya li-l-Ḥaḍāra al-Insāniyya al-Muthlā [The Man-Vicegerent and the Mission of Building and Populating: A Qurʾanic View of the Ideal Human Civilization]." *Algeria, Social Sciences Journal* 20 (2015): 76.

Ibn Bādīs, ʿAbd al-Ḥamīd. *Tafsīr ibn Bādīs [The Exegesis of ibn Bādīs]*. Beirut: Dār al-Kutub al-ʿIlmiyya, 1st ed., 1995.

Banī ʿĪsā, Muḥammad. "Naẓariyyat al-Istikhlāf wa-Atharuhā fī l-Iqtiṣād al-Islāmī [The Theory of Istikhlāf and its Effect on Islamic Economics]." *Journal of Ṣāliḥ ʿAbd Allāh Kāmil Center for Islamic Economics* 14, no. 40 (2010).

Bin Bayyah, ʿAbd Allāh. *Amālī al-Dalālāt wa Majālī al-Ikhtilāfāt [The Impact of Semantics and the Areas of Divergence]*. Beirut: Dār ibn Ḥazm, n.d.

Bint al-Shāṭiʾ, ʿĀʾisha. *Al-Qurʾān wa-Qaḍāyā al-Insān [The Qurʾan and Human Issues]*. Cairo: Dār al-Maʿārif, 1999.

Al-Burmāwī, Shams al-Dīn. *Al-Fawāʾid al-Saniyya fī Sharḥ al-Alfiyya [The Bright Benefits from The Explanation of the Alfiyya]*. Edited by ʿAbd Allāh Ramaḍān. Egypt: Maktabat al-Tawʿiyya al-Islāmiyya, 2015.

Al-Bukhārī, Muḥammad ibn Ismāʿīl. *Ṣaḥīḥ al-Bukhārī.* Edited by Muḥammad Zuhayr al-Nāṣir. Beirut: Dār Tawq al-Najā, 1422 A.H.

Al-Dasūqī, Fārūq Aḥmad. *Al-Khilāfa al-Islāmiyya Uṣūluhā wa-Ḥaqīqatuhā wa-Ḥatmiyyat ʿAwdatihā [The Islamic Caliphate: Its Origins, Truth and the Imperative of its Return].* Cairo: 1998.

Faraḥāt, Aḥmad Ḥasan. *Al-Khilāfa fī l-Arḍ, [Vicegerency on Earth].* Kuwait: Dār al-Arqam, 2003.

Al-Gharbī, Munyā. "Al-Insān wa-l-Qiyam fī al-Nuṣūṣ al-Taʾsīsyya: Sūrat Luqmān Unmūdhjan [Man and Values in the Foundational Texts: Sūrat Luqmān as Case Study]." In *Sūrat al-Insān bayna al-Marjiʿiyyatayn al-Islāmiyya wa-l-Gharbiyya [The Image of the Human Being between Islamic and Western References].* Edited by Rāʾid ʿUkkāsha and ʿĀʾisha al-Ḥaḍīrī. Virginia: The International Institute of Islamic Thought, 2020.

Al-Iṣfahānī, al-Rāghib. *Al-Mufradāt fī Gharīb al-Qurʾān [The Dictionary of Complex Qurʾanic Terminology].* Edited by Ṣafwān ʿAdnān al-Dawūdī. Damascus-Beirut: Dār al-Qalam, al-Dār al-Shāmiyya, 1412 AH.

Al-Isnawī, Jamāl al-Dīn. *Al-Tamhīd fī Takhrīj al Furūʿ ʿalā al-Uṣūl [Prolegomena in Deducing Particular Rulings from Overall Principles].* Edited by Muḥammad Ḥasan Hītū. Beirut: Muʾassasat al-Risāla, 1400 AH.

Al-Jaṣṣāṣ, Abū Bakr. *Aḥkām al-Qurʾān [The Rulings of the Qurʾan].* Edited by Muḥammad Ṣādiq. Beirut: Dār Iḥyāʾ al-Turāth al-ʿArabī, 1405 AH.

Al-Jurjānī, al-Sharīf. *Al-Taʿrīfāt [The Definitions].* Beirut: Dār al-Kutub al-ʿIlmiyya, 1983.

Ibn Juzayy, Muḥammad ibn Aḥmad a-Kalbī. *Al-Tashīl li-ʿUlūm al-Tanzīl [The Facilitation of the Sciences of Revelation].* Edited by ʿAbd Allāh al-Khālidī. Beirut: Dār al-Arqam ibn Abī al-Arqam, 1416 AH.

Ibn Kathīr, Ismāʿīl. *Tafsīr al-Qurʾān al-ʿAẓīm [The Exegesis of the Great Qurʾan].* Edited by Sāmī Salāma. Riyadh: Dār Ṭayba, 2nd ed., 1999.

Al-Khafājī, Aḥmad Shihāb al-Dīn. *Ḥāshiyat al-Shihāb ʿalā Tafsīr al-Bayḍāwī [Commentary on the Exegesis of al-Bayḍāwī].* Beirut: Dār Ṣādir, n.d.

Al-Khaṭīb, ʿAbd al-Karīm. *Al-Tafsīr al-Qurʾān li-l-Qurʾān [The Explanation of the Qurʾan by the Qurʾan].* Cairo: Dār al-Fikr al-ʿArabī, n.d.

Al-Khaṭīb, ʿAbd al-Fattāḥ. *Qiyam al-Islām al-Ḥaḍāriyya, Naḥwa Insāniyya Jadīda [The Civilizational Values of Islam: Towards New Humanism].* Doha: Kutub al-Umma, 1431 AH.

Lane, Edward W. *An Arabic-English Lexicon.* Book 1, part 4. London: William and Nortgate, 1863.

Malik, Maszlee. "Constructing the Architectonics and Formulating the Articulation of Islamic Governance: A Discursive Attempt in Islamic Epistemology." PhD diss. Durham University, (2011).

Ibn Manẓūr, Muḥammad ibn Mukram. *Lisān al-ʿArab [The Tongue of the Arabs].* Beirut: Dār Ṣādir, 3rd ed., 1993.

Al-Marāghī, Aḥmad. *Tafsīr al-Marāghī [The Exegesis of al-Marāghī].* Egypt: Dār Muṣṭafā al-Bābī al-Ḥalabī wa-Awlāduh, 1946.

Al-Māwardī, ʿAlī Abū al-Ḥasan. *Al-Nukat wa-l-ʿUyūn [The Exegesis of al-Māwardī].* Edited by Sayyid ibn ʿAbd al-Maqṣūd. Beirut: Dār al-Kutub al-ʿIlmiyya, n.d.

Al-Mawdūdī, Abū al-Aʿlā. *Niẓām al-Ḥayāt fī l-Islām [The Order of Life in Islam].* Pakistan: Dār al-ʿUrūba, 2nd ed., 1958.

McGhee, George R. Jr; Peter M. Sheehan; David J. Bottjer; Mary L. Droser. "Ecological ranking of Phanerozoic biodiversity crises: The Serpukhovian (early Carboniferous) crisis had a greater ecological impact than the end-Ordovician." *Geology* 40, no. 2. (2012): 147–150.

Al-Najjār, ʿAbd al-Majīd. *Fiqh al-Taḥaḍḍur al-Islāmī [The Jurisprudence of Islamic Civilization]*. Beirut: Dār al-Gharb al-Islāmī, 1st ed., 1999.

Al-Naysabūrī, Niẓām al-Dīn. *Gharāʾib al-Qurʾān wa-Raghāʾib al-Furqān [The Wonders of the Qurʾan]*. Edited by Zakariyya ʿUmayrāt. Beirut: Dār al-Kutub al-ʿIlmiyya, 1416 AH.

Al-Qaraḍāwī, Yūsuf. "Qīmat al-Insān wa-Ghāyat Wujūdih fī Ḍawʾ al-Qurʾān wa-l-Sunna [The Value of the Human Being and the Purpose of his Existence in the Light of the Qurʾan and the Sunna]." *Journal of Buhūth al-Sunna wa-l-Sīra*, Qatar University no. 5 (1991).

Qaraybiʿ, Muḥammad ʿAyyād. *Al-Istikhlāf wa-l-Ḥaḍāra, Dirāsa fī l-Istikhlāf al-Ilāhī li-l-Insān fī Ḍawʾi al-Qaṣaṣ al-Qurʾānī [Vicegerency and Civilization: a Study on Divine Vicegerency in the Light of Qurʾanic Narratives]*. Amman: Dār Zahrān, 1st ed., 2013.

Al-Qāsimī, Muḥammad Jamāl al-Dīn. *Maḥāsin al-Taʾwīl [The Virtues of Interpretation]*. Edited by Muḥammad Bāsil ʿUyūn al-Sūd. Beirut: Dār al-Kutub al-ʿIlmiyya, 1418 AH.

Ibn Qayyim al-Jawziyya, Shams al-Dīn. *Badāʾiʿ al-Fawāʾid [The Amazing Insights]*. Edited by ʿĀdil al-ʿAdawī Hishām ʿAṭā and Ashraf Aḥmad. Mecca: Maktabat Nizār Muṣṭafā al-Bāz, 1996.

Ibn Qayyim al-Jawziyya, Shams al-Dīn. *Mukhtaṣar al-Ṣawāʿiq al-Mursala ʿalā al-Jahmmiyya wa al-Muʿaṭṭila [The Summary of The Thunderbolts Sent on the Jahmiyya and the Suspenders of Divine Attributes]*. Summarized by Shams al-Dīn ibn al-Mūṣalī. Edited by Sayyid Ibrāhīm. Cairo: Dār al-Ḥadīth, 2001.

Ibn Qayyim al-Jawziyya, Shams al-Dīn. *Shifāʾ al-ʿAlīl fī Masāʾil al-Qaḍāʾ wa-l-Qadar wa-l-Ḥikma wa-l-Taʿlīl [Healing the Sick about the Issues of Predestination, Wisdom and Rationales]*. Beirut: Dār al-Maʿrifa, 1978.

Al-Qūnawī, Ismāʿīl ibn Muḥammad. *Ḥāshiyat al-Qūnawī ʿalā Tafsīr al-Imām al-Bayḍāwī [The Footnote of al-Qūnawī on the Tafsīr of al-Bayḍāwī]*. Edited by ʿAbd Allāh ʿUmar. Beirut: Dār al-Kutub al-ʿIlmiyya, 2001.

Al-Qurṭubī, Muḥammad Shams al-Dīn. *Al-Jāmiʿ li-Aḥkām al-Qurʾān [The Compiler of the Rulings of the Qurʾan]*. Edited by Aḥmad al-Bardūnī and Ibrāhīm al-Aṭafīsh. Cairo: Dār al-Kutub al-Miṣriyya, 1964.

Quṭb, Sayyid. *Fī Ẓilāl al-Qurʾān [In the Shadows of the Qurʾan]*. Beirut: Dār al-Shurūq, 17th ed., 1991.

Al-Rāzī, Muḥammad Fakhr al-Dīn. *Al-Tafsīr al-Kabīr [The Great Exegesis]*. Beirut: Dār Iḥyāʾ al-Turāth al-ʿArabī, 1999.

Riḍā, Muḥammad Rashīd. *Tafsīr al-Manār [Interpretation of the Illuminator]*. Cairo: al-Hayʾa al-Miṣriyya, 1990.

Al-Ṣadr, Muḥammad Bāqir. *Al-Islām Yaqūd al-Ḥayāt [Islam at the Forefront of Life]*. Tehran: Ministry of Religious Guidance, 2nd ed., 1403 AH.

Sahney, S., M.J Benton "Recovery from the Most Profound Mass Extinction of All Time." *Proceedings of the Royal Society B: Biological Sciences*, 275, no. 1636. (2008): 759–65.

Sharīʿatī, ʿAlī. *Al-Insān wa-l-Islām [Man and Islam]*. Translated by Abbās al-Turjumān. Beirut: Dār al-Amīr, 2nd ed., 2007.

Al-Shāṭibī, Abū Isḥāq. *Al-Muwāfaqāt [The Reconciliation]. Annotated by Mashūr ibn Ḥasan*. Cairo: Dār ibn ʿAffān, 1997.

Al-Shinqīṭī, Muḥammad al-Amīn. *Aḍwāʾ al-Bayān fī Īḍāḥ al-Qurʾān bi-l-Qurʾān [The Clarification of The Qurʾan by the Qurʾan]*. Beirut: Dār al-Fikr, 1995.

Ibn Sīdah, ʿAlī. *Al-Muḥkam wa-l-Muḥīṭ al-Aʿẓam [The Conclusive and Most Comprehensive]*. Edited by ʿAbd al-Ḥamīd Hindāwī. Beirut: Dār al-Kutub al-ʿIlmiyya, 2000.

Al-Ṭabarī, Muḥammad ibn Jarīr. *Jāmiʿ al-Bayān ʿan Taʾwīl Āyī al-Qurʾān [The Comprehensive Exposition of the Interpretation of the Verses of the Qurʾan]*. Edited by Aḥmad Muḥammad Shākir. Beirut: Muʾassasat al-Risāla, 2000.

Ibn Taymiyya, Taqī al-Dīn. *Minhāj al-Sunna al-Nabawiyya fī Naqḍ Kalām al-Shīʿa al-Qadariyya [The Way of the Prophet's Sunna: a Critique of the Theological Discourse of al-Qadariyya Shiites]*. Edited by Muḥammad Rashād Sālim. Riyadh: Imām Muḥammad ibn Saʿūd Islamic University, 1986.

Ibn Taymiyya, Taqī al-Dīn. *Majmūʿ al-Fatāwā [The Compilation of Fatwas]*. Medina: King Fahd Complex for the Printing of the Holy Quran, 1995.

Al-Ṭūfī, Najm al-Dīn. *Sharḥ Mukhtaṣar al-Rawḍa [The Explanation of the Abridgement of al-Rawḍa]*. Edited by ʿAbd Allāh al-Turkī. Beirut: Muʾassasat al-Risāla, 1987.

Al-ʿUthaymīn, Muḥammad ibn Ṣāliḥ. *Majmūʿ Fatāwā wa-Rasāʾil al-ʿUthaymīn [The Collection of Fatwas and Treatises of al-ʿUthaymīn]*. Riyadh: Dār al-Waṭan-Dār al-Thurayya, 1416 AH.

Al-Zajjāj, Abū Isḥāq Ibrāhīm. *Maʿānī al-Qurʾān wa-Iʿrābuh [The Meanings of the Qurʾan and its Grammatical Analysis]*. Beirut: ʿĀlam al-Kutub, 1988.

Ibn al-Zamanayn, Muḥammad. *Tafsīr al-Qurʾān al-ʿAzīz [The Exegesis of the Mighty Qurʾan]. Edited by Ḥusayn ibn ʿUkāsha and Muḥammad al-Kanz.* Cairo: al-Fārūq al-Ḥadītha, 2002.

Zarmān, Muḥammad. "Waẓīfat al-Istikhlāf fī l-Qurʾān al-Karīm wa-Dalālātuhā wa-Abʿāduhā al-Ḥaḍāriyya [The Function of *Istikhlāf* in the Noble Qurʾan: its Civilizational Meanings and Dimensions]." Qatar University, *Journal of the College of Sharia, Law and Islamic Studies* 16 (1998): 195–242.

Zūzū, Farīda. "Maqṣad Ḥifẓ al-Bīʾa wa-Atharuhu fī ʿAmaliyyat al-Istikhlāf [The Objective of Preserving the Environment and its Impact on the Vicegerency Process]." *Majallat Islāmiyyat al-Maʿrifa* 48 (Summer 2007).

# 6 Vicegerency in the Qur'anic Worldview

From the previous discussions, we have determined that the object of vicegerency is the preservation of a part of the cosmic balance, which is the specific worship for which the human being was created. The teleological relation between the maintenance of the balance, as a human worship, and the general cosmic worship resides in the fact that all the beings in the universe are worshipping God by performing the function they were created for in contribution to the accomplishment of the cosmic balance. Therefore, in *sūrat al-Raḥmān* (Q 55), the worship of creatures and the performance of their respective functions are mentioned ahead of the emergence of the cosmic balance and ahead of the function assigned to the human being. Yet, the creatures of the universe other than the human being do not act as deputies of God in the maintenance of this balance. They instead do this in a spontaneous inevitable fashion, unlike the human being who was entrusted to perform it on behalf of God. This is indeed what caused the angels' astonishment, so they exclaimed, "while we declare Your praise and sanctify You." (Q 2:30). That is, the angels were wondering if the in-progress cosmic worship contributing to the maintenance of the balance was not enough since, they believed, it fulfilled its purpose adequately. Due to this particularity, the human being was created with inborn natural characteristics (*fiṭra*) and given means that were not granted to the rest of creatures. Although *sūrat al-Raḥmān* indicates this fact, it does not explicitly define the aspects of the cosmic balance that the human being has been entrusted to maintain. Yet, the amount of description contained in the verses of *sūrat al-Raḥmān* allows for the proper adaptation of the multiple Qur'anic teleological concepts that describe the rationale behind the existence of the human being, Revelation and universe, so that each of those concepts can be put into its adequate place in a way that organises them consistently to form the outlines of a vicegerency theory. Indeed, the Qur'an articulates several reasons behind these existential facts (i.e., the human being, Revelation and universe). Some of these relate to the object of vicegerency or one of its aspects, characteristics, features, objectives, effects, means or fruits. As a result of this apparent bifurcation of the reasons behind the existence of the human being, Revelation and universe, researchers who did not attempt to formulate a coordinated relation between these concepts or put them together within a coherent theory were plunged into confusion. These fragmented approaches to the Qur'anic texts did not distinguish the

DOI: 10.4324/9781003335948-6

function for which the human being was created from its means, objectives, fruits, features or effects, thus reducing the function to its means or confusing it with its goals, etc.

One researcher, for instance, suggested that the function for which the human being was created is twofold: First, to get to know God; second, to be put through trial, arguing:

> Accordingly, it is to be understood from the explicit verses of the Qur'an that it is the human being for whom the creation of the whole world is meant, and that God created this vast universe together with the heavens and earth it encompasses to enable the human being, being assigned by God as *khalīfa*, to undertake his function on earth and his mission in the universe. This mission is made up of two main elements: 1) an epistemic and scientific element, entailing the human being's knowledge of his Lord and 2) a practical behavioural element, entailing the human being's proper conduct.[1]

To substantiate his supposition as to the first function, he quoted God's saying, "It is Allah who has created seven heavens and of the earth, the like of them. [His] command descends among them so that you may know (*li-ta'lamū*) that Allah is over all things competent and that Allah has encompassed all things in knowledge." (Q 65:12, Sahih Intl). He comments, "Thus, the purpose is clear from the verse, as indicated by *lām al-ta'līl*[2] ('so that you may know')."[3] He added, "Some scholars deduced the evidence from *sūrat al-Dhāriyāt* as one of its verses reads 'And in no way did I create the jinn and humankind except to worship Me' (Q 51:56), noting that Mujāhid (d. 104/722) interpreted 'to worship Me' as meaning 'to know me.'"[4]

He deduces the evidence for the second function from God's saying, "And it is He who created the heavens and the earth in six days – and His Throne had been upon water – that He might test you as to which of you is best in deeds." (Q 11:7, Sahih Intl). He comments, "Thus, God created the heavens and earth in their entirety to test the responsible people (*al-mukallafūn*) as to who is the best in deeds. They were created to work. The whole existence from beneath and above them was actually created for them to work."[5]

This view is problematic from two perspectives. First, there are many Qur'anic verses that define the purpose of or reason behind the creation of the human being and the universe and the descent of Revelation to be other than the mere knowledge of God and trial, making us wonder why he selected these two in particular to the exclusion of others. Second, these two elements are not the functions for which the human being was created. Knowledge of God is one of the means that enable the human being to perform his function, and is not a function per se. The human being may have good knowledge of his Lord, and yet fail to perform his function for some reason. Accordingly, knowledge is not the purpose, let alone being the function or mission. Iblīs (Satan), who used to be a close subject of God and even conversed with Him immediately, knew that "God has power and knowledge over all things," and yet failed to do his function. What is more, the verse contains no indication that the knowledge of God is one of the reasons for which the human being was created. The verse rather states that the universe was created based on an order and norms ("[His] command descends among them") so that the human being, upon reflection, would be able to see the magnificence and competence of God. It is in no way indicative of the knowledge of God being the purpose of the creation of the universe. Should this be the case, creating the universe would be mentioned without adding the characteristic that necessitates this knowledge, i.e., the descent of the command in the universe.[6] The verse rather indicates that the awareness of God's competence and knowledge of everything are the purposes behind the creation of the universe in accordance with and in an order corresponding to the human being's rational perception and cognitive abilities. Hence, this verse does not indicate that the purpose of the mere creation of the universe is the human being's knowledge of God, let alone that this is the human being's existential function or mission. Furthermore, ibn Taymiyya demonstrated that Q 51:56 is in no way indicative that the human being was created to worship God in the sense of knowing Him, and that that interpretation was only a reaction to the Qadarites (adeterminists) as noted in the third chapter. As for trial, it is not a function, but rather a function-defining characteristic portraying the human being's mission as a responsibility and test. The same applies to proper conduct; it is a characteristic of the function for which the human being was created, defining it as an ethical one, and not a precise designation of the function as such.

These two problematic points, i.e., the reliance on some verses to the exclusion of others and the lack of the cited verses' indication of the respective function, are common to those who addressed the human being's existential function from an Islamic perspective. These two problems are attributable to the failure to integrate the concepts articulated by these verses within a conceptual framework capable of encompassing them and attributing to them their proper place by distinguishing between the essence of the function and its purposes, fruits, means, characteristics, etc. Put differently, the problem is considering the human being's existential function through isolated, fragmented, out-of-context verses and not through a comprehensive worldview. We believe that linking these concepts with the above detailed discussion on cosmic Islam, vicegerency, deputisation on behalf of God and maintenance of the balance may enable this approach and overcome those fragmented approaches.

Let us now proceed to the examination of the concepts through which the Qur'an articulates the rationale behind the existence of the human being, Revelation and the universe in light of the above discussion and on the basis of their correlation with deputisation on behalf of God in the maintenance of the balance and enrolment in cosmic Islam. This will enable us to identify the aspects of the cosmic balance that the human being has been entrusted to maintain on behalf of God. Furthermore, it will enable us to place the major Islamic concepts and principles in their proper positions in a way that contributes to outlining the contours of a Qur'anic vicegerency theory within the overall Islamic worldview. In the following discussion, we will attempt to enumerate the reasons behind the creation of the human being, the advent of Revelation and the creation of the universe as mentioned in the Qur'an, and place each of these reasons in its proper place according to their link with deputisation on behalf of God in the maintenance of the balance. The very existence of these three elements (Revelation, human being and universe) is rationalised with one of the Divine names and with the purpose of enabling the human being to perform his existential function. Therefore, they can be considered as the three main existential phenomena. Indeed, according to the Qur'an, as a consequence of God's mercy, Revelation was revealed, the human being was created, endowed with a specific nature, and the universe was created and structured according to determined calculations leading to cosmic worship and harmony "so that" the human being "may not transgress in the balance" (Q 55: 1–8). Hence, all the notions enumerated by the Qur'an as teleological purposes behind these three phenomena must be, in one way or another, related to the human existential function. It is that particular status of these three phenomena (they merely exist in order for the human being to perform his existential function) that legitimates classifying the rationales that justify their existence among the great principles of Islam.

## 6.1 The Major Concepts of Islam from the Perspective of Vicegerency

In this section, we will enumerate the verses that establish the rationale, purposes and causes behind the creation of the human being and the universe, and the advent of Revelation and Messengers. Below we will refer to these terms (rationale, purposes, causes, reasons) interchangeably in reference to the concepts through which the Qur'an justifies those existential facts whether as means, purposes, objectives, outcomes, consequences or characteristics of the human being's existential function, as will be discussed. We will proceed to the induction of those concepts by reading through the Qur'an verse by verse from the opening until the end. Then, we will proceed to classify the concepts through which the Qur'an articulates the rationale behind these existential phenomena – i.e., the concepts constituting the Islamic worldview – in line with how they relate to the maintenance of the balance. Finally, these concepts will be structured based on their relation to the identified aspects of the cosmic balance entrusted to the human being, i.e., the human existential function. This will result in the formation of the outlines of a coherent vicegerency theory and organisation of the concepts constituting the Islamic worldview in a way that sketches its contours.

In our classification, we will only retain the concepts that the Qur'an explicitly establishes as rationales or reasons behind the existence of Revelation, the universe or the human being. We will leave out the reasons that may be deduced by inference and omit the verses that do not explicitly state that what is being mentioned is a reason or rationale. The latter verses include, for example, expressions such as, "in these things there are signs," "verily Allah commands…," "I have been commanded…," etc. We will thus only retain the verses that link the rationale behind those existential facts with explicit or implicit *ta'līl* (linguistic justification/causation/motivation). This includes the rationalisation through infinitives denoting justification (*al-ta'līl bi-l-maṣdar*), as in "*raḥmatan min Rabbik* (as a mercy from your Lord)," and the rationalisation through prepositions denoting justification (*al-ta'līl bi-l-ḥurūf*) as with the Arabic prepositions of *lām al-ta'līl* (to, in order to, so that), *la'allā* and *la'allakum* (so that, so that you may), *kay* and *likay* (so that, in order to, to), *an al-maṣdariyya* (infinitive *an*, such as "*an lā taṭghaw*," "so that you may not transgress"), *fā' al-tartīb* (so that then, so that afterwards, hence, thus, etc.), *ḥattā* (so that, in order to, to), etc. *Ta'līl* may also be denoted by basing a predicate on a qualifier or otherwise by reducing all the injunctions of Revelation to particular injunctions as in "I was only commanded to…" or "they were only commanded to," etc.[7]

One recognised way of *ta'līl* here is to give Revelation certain adjectives, thus indicating that such adjectives are a reason behind the existence of Revelation, in the same way that naming the Qur'an as *al-Dhikr* (the Reminder) indicates that it has been revealed for the purpose of reminding people. We shall omit some of those explicit reasons or rationales as being self-evident and already included in the reasons that will be elaborated on, such as those stating that Revelation came to show the truth or for people to follow it, or that the Messengers were sent so that people would obey them or to proclaim the message etc.

Based on the above, and after a thorough survey of the entire Qur'an, we found the following:

**1. Reasons behind the advent of Revelation and Messengers**:

- For monotheism and worship of God Alone[8]
- To worship only God, repent to Him and ask Him for forgiveness[9]
- To worship only God and reject *ṭāghūt* (false gods)[10]
- To worship only God and observe prayer and give in *zakāt* (charity)[11]
- For *'īmān* (belief)[12]
- To distinguish truth from falsehood[13]
- To communicate warnings[14]
- To warn that there is no God but Allah[15]
- To warn regarding the Hereafter[16]
- As an exposition of everything[17]
- For guidance[18]
- To guide to the paths of peace[19]
- As mercy from God[20]
- As spiritual healing[21]
- To give glad tidings to those who surrender to God[22]
- To give glad tidings and warnings[23]
- To keep Muslims firm[24]
- To test those who are truthful[25]
- For instruction[26]
- For the purification of the soul[27]
- For spiritual revival[28]

- To teach people what they did not know[29]
- To judge between people[30]
- To bring people out of darkness into the light[31]
- As a reminder[32]
- To maintain the balance[33]
- For people to stand by justice[34]
- To establish the religion and not be divided over it[35]
- So that people would not have an excuse for not following the truth[36]
- For reflection[37]
- For reasoning[38]
- For piety[39]
- For the Prophets to be witnesses over people[40]
- For believers to be witnesses over people[41]
- To enlighten people[42]
- To become godly people (*rabbāniyyīn*)[43]

**2. Reasons behind the creation of the human being**:

- To worship God[44]
- For God to have mercy on the human being[45]
- For vicegerency[46]
- To bear the *amāna* (trust)[47]
- To maintain the balance[48]
- For trial[49]
- To give thanks to God[50]
- For God to see how people behave[51]

**3. Reasons behind creating the human being with his specific form and structure**:

- To maintain the balance[52]
- As an exposition for people[53]
- So that the human being would understand[54]
- So that people would have no plea against God on the Day of Resurrection[55]
- So that nations come to know one another[56]
- So that people help each other[57]

**4. Reasons behind the creation, organisation, subjugation and worship of the universe (reasons related to the human being)**:

- To maintain the balance[58]
- To know the magnificence of God[59]
- For trial and test[60]
- To recompense the believers[61]
- To reward each soul in accordance with what it has done[62]

- To complete the favour bestowed upon the human being so that he/she may believe[63]
- So that the human being seeks favours from God[64]
- As mercy from God[65]
- To give glad tidings about God's mercy[66]
- As bounty and delight for people from God[67]
- So that people see God's signs[68]
- As a reminder[69]
- So that the human being gives thanks to God[70]
- As provision for people[71]

This is what we could record as to the concepts and principles that the Qur'an used as rationale and purpose behind the advent of Revelation and Messengers and the creation of the human being and the universe. These are thus the major Qur'anic teleological concepts. These concepts are also mentioned elsewhere in the Qur'an, yet we opted to omit them as they are expressed in terms that do not denote explicit *ta'līl* (causation). However, we made an exception of referring to a few of the verses that do not contain explicit *ta'līl* provided that the same concept they convey is explicitly used as rationale in other verses. Now, after having identified the Qur'anic rationales behind the major existential phenomena related to the human existential function, we will use the concept of vicegerency, as we have defined it until now, as a cement to bind these concepts and classify them accordingly. This is not at all a far-fetched way of connecting these concepts. To the contrary, the human existential function being the very purpose behind the three existential phenomena and the only one through which all three were explicitly rationalised, as we saw, implies that the teleological reasons behind these phenomena organically connect with each other by the cement of that central purpose, i.e., vicegerency. By grounding the categorisation of these reasons or rationales on their relation to vicegerency on behalf of God and the maintenance of the cosmic balance, we arrived at the following classification:

**Section I: Means enabling vicegerency on behalf of God**. This section incorporates the reasons that cannot be considered as the very function for which the human being was created since they are not Divine functions assigned to him. These reasons are, instead, necessary means without which the human function cannot be performed. Based on this consideration, they were used as rationale behind the existence of Revelation, the human being and the universe. This section comprises the following reasons: Belief, distinction between truth and falsehood, warning with all its above-mentioned forms, exposition of everything (in relation to what the human being needs to fulfil his/her function), keeping people firm, instruction, knowledge and education with all its above-mentioned forms, reminder, reflection, reasoning, enlightenment, clarification, observation of God's signs, repentance to and asking for forgiveness from God, observance of prayers, giving in *zakāt*, inter-people acquaintance and mutual support. The relation of most of these reasons to vicegerency on behalf of God with regard to the maintenance of the balance is evident and does not need further elaboration as they all revolve around the human being's epistemic, spiritual and social needs that enable him/her to accomplish his/her mission. Yet, under the topics below, we will elaborate on some details as to how some of these reasons of specific significance relate to the following aspects of the balance with which the human being has been entrusted.

**Section II: Attributes or characteristics of the object of vicegerency**, that is, the mission for which the human being was created. These reasons do not specify the very object of vicegerency, but instead serve as descriptions of some of its essential characteristics. The attributes and characteristics of human function that the Qur'an uses as rationales behind Revelation or the creation of the human being and the universe, because they represent the essence of that function, include: Guidance, healing, trial, giving glad tidings, a bounty from God, bearing the trust and rejecting the *ṭāghūt*. We have already elaborated on the meaning of the human being's performance of his/her existential function as being a guidance within the cosmic guidance. It has also become clear how it is a trial and trust in terms of being a responsibility for which the human being will be held accountable. We will further explain in which sense it is a healing, glad tiding and rejection of the *ṭāghūt.*

**Section III: Consequences or outcomes of the human being's performance of his existential function**. These are ultimate reasons for which Revelation came or for which the human being or the universe were created. They depend on the extent to which the human being fulfils or is aware of his task. These include mercy, rewarding each soul in proportion to what it has done, attaining the favour and provision of God, not allowing people to have plea against God on the Day of Resurrection, the Prophets bearing witness over people, guidance to the paths of peace and coming out from darkness into the light. These consequences are of permanent causal relation to the human being's endeavour of performing and being aware of his/her existential function. In other words, the human being is not tasked to achieve them, as it is not he who carries them out, but they are rather inextricable consequences of his acts in this regard.

**Section IV: Purposes or objectives of the human being's performance of his existential function**. The reasons under this section are not the very function for which the human being was created, but, instead, the intended objectives of this function, i.e., its aims that one must strive for. The purposes or objectives that were used as rationales behind Revelation include *al-taqwā* (piety, proper conduct, God-fear), *al-rabbāniyya* (to be a godly servant), thanksgiving to God, spiritual revival and bearing witness over people. The difference between this section and the previous one is that, unlike the latter, the features of the current section are aims of the human function that he is tasked to carry out and fulfil. Below, we shall elaborate on how these purposes relate to the object of vicegerency.

**Section V: Ontological reasons behind Revelation, the universe, the human being and his entrustment with the function for which he was created**. By "ontological reasons" we mean the primary reasons beyond which there are no other reasons, and which are identifiable with God's attributes of perfection.[72]

Our investigation shows that the existence of Revelation, the human being and the universe are rationalised through the following ontological reasons:

- mercy (al-Raḥmān, the Merciful)
- guidance (al-Hādī, the Guide)
- to the truth (al-Ḥaqq, the Truth)
- to the paths of peace (al-Salām, the Peace, the Source of Peace and Safety)
- vivification (al-Muḥyī, the Giver of Life)
- healing (al-Shāfī, the Healer)
- provision (al-Razzāq, the Provider, al-Wahhāb, the Bestower)
- judgement (al-Ḥākim, the Possessor of Authority, al- Ḥakam, the Judge)
- justice (al- ʿAdl, the Just)
- belief (al-Muʾmin, the One Who accepts the belief of His servants and grants them safety and security)
- teaching (al-ʿĀlīm, the All-Knowing)
- repentance (al-Tawwāb, the One Who accepts repentance)
- forgiveness (al-Ghaffār, the Oft-Forgiving)
- spiritual purification (al-Quddūs, the All-Pure)
- observance of people's actions by God (al-Baṣīr, the All-Seer), etc.

As a matter of fact, the advent of Revelation and the creation of the universe and the human being are manifestations of all the Divine names and attributes without exception. However, our selection here is limited to the above-identified teleological reasons related to the human being accompanied by explicit *taʿlīl*, as noted above.

Multiple verses indicate that Divine perfection is the ontological reason underlying the existence of Revelation, the human being and the universe. This is to say that these existential facts are effects of God's Most Beautiful Names and Supreme Attributes. A case in point is a verse that rationalises the creation of the human being according to a defined order and the creation of the earth according to a similar order, reading: "That is because Allah is the Truth and because He gives life to the dead and because He is over all things Competent." (Q 22:6, Sahih Intl). Thus, an ontological reason behind the creation of the human being and universe according to the laws described before this verse is the fact that God is the Truth, the Giver of Life, the Competent (al-Qādir) and the All-Powerful (al-Qadīr). In another verse, following the mention of the creation of the universe, the infiniteness of God's words, the creation and resurrection of the human being, the subjugation of the creatures of the universe and other existential facts, God says, "That is because Allah is the Truth, and that what they call upon other than Him is falsehood, and because Allah is the Most High, Most Great." (Q 31:30, Sahih Intl). All these existential facts result thus from God being the Truth (al-Ḥaqq) Most High (al-ʿAlī) and the Most Great (al-Kabīr). Another verse rationalises God's support of those oppressed on the grounds of Him being the All-Hearer (al-Samīʿ) and All-Seer (al-Baṣīr): "That is because Allah causes the night to enter the day and causes the day to enter the night and because Allah is Hearing and Seeing." (Q 22:61, Sahih Intl). Reference to the fact that cosmic worship is an effect of Divine perfection can be found, for instance, in the following verse: "To Him belong the Best Names; whatever there is in the heavens and the earth glorifies Him." (Q 59:24, Ali Qarai).

The relation between these ontological reasons, through which the Qur'an rationalises the existence of Revelation, the human being and the universe, and the human existential function lies in that entrusting the human being with this function is an effect of Divine perfection. Some of these ontological reasons are expressions of some aspects of the Divine perfection that have manifested themselves only through the creation of the human being. These include the reasons of spiritual healing, repentance and forgiveness. Moreover, the vicegerency of the human being and his entrustment with the maintenance of the balance entail some manifestations of the Divine perfection that did not appear in other than the entrustment of the human being with that function. These include God being the Upgrader (al-Rāfiʿ) and the Most Generous (al-Akram), etc. Hence, assigning this responsibility to the human being – in addition to God's breathing into the human being, thus giving him a particular innate nature enabling him to perform his function – dignifies the human being and elevates him to a higher rank than that of the rest of creatures. These two Attributes, i.e., the Upgrader and the Most Generous, did not manifest in any creation of God the way they manifest in the responsibility of deputisation of the human being on behalf of God and in the innate nature given to him. This is an ontological reason for the creation of the human being in particular, which is suggested by God's saying, "Recite in the name of your Lord who created; Created the human being from a clinging substance.; Recite, and your Lord is the Most Generous –; Who taught by the pen –; Taught the human being that which he knew not.; No! [But] indeed, the human being transgresses." (Q 96:1–6, b.o. Sahih Intl). This is the only Qur'anic passage that features the name of "the Most Generous" (al-Akram). These were the first verses of the Qur'an to be revealed to Prophet Muḥammad (ﷺ) who was illiterate. This name (al-Akram) is the first Divine name that was revealed to Prophet Muḥammad (ﷺ), and it is the Divine name by which he was first commanded to recite ("Recite in the name of your Lord… Recite, and your Lord is the Most Generous"). Moreover, the name the Most Generous was mentioned in the context of creating the human being and endowing him with the innate ability to elicit the unknown from the known facts, i.e., learning, and likewise in the context of his existential mission that makes him capable of transgression and causing deficiency to the balance. These particularities indicate that the effects of this name manifest themselves through the human being more than through any other element of the creation. If the creation manifests the fact that God is The Generous (al-Karīm), the human being, by virtue of what he is distinguished with in terms of natural disposition and existential function, is the most accomplished manifestation of God's generosity. Hence, he is the only articulation of the name al-Akram. This explains why this Divine name was the first one to be revealed to the Prophet Muḥammad (ﷺ) and why it came in the context of the creation of the human being, his dotation with his innate faculties and entrustment with his existential function. Thus, it can be argued that the human being is distinguished by being a subject of the manifestation of the

Divine perfection over and above the rest of the creation. This applies to many of God's Most Beautiful Names or attributes that manifested themselves through the human being exclusively, including,

- the Loving (al-Wadūd)
- the Gentle (al-Laṭīf)
- the Upgrader
- the Bestower of Honour (al-Muʿiz)
- the Oft-Forgiving
- the Grateful (al-Shakūr)
- the Bringer of Judgement (al-Hasīb)
- the Responsive (al-Mujīb)
- the Resurrector (al-Bāʿith)
- the One Who Accepts Repentance (al-Tawwāb)
- the Pardoner (al-ʿAfuww)
- the Kind (al-Raʾūf), etc.

The relation between the human being's existential function and God's Most Beautiful Names and Supreme Attributes is not limited to this aspect; they further relate to the human being's execution of his/her function, as we shall elaborate below.

**Section VI: Reasons that constitute the function for which the human being was created, but are broad and extend to all other creatures, and hence do not specify the object of vicegerency**. The previously listed reasons included in this section are monotheism, worship of God alone, establishment of religion, Islam (surrender to God) and achievement of equity. Our previous discussion has disclosed the relation of these concepts to the overall existential duty of the human being. Monotheism and worshipping God alone are the purpose behind the creation of all elements of the universe. Everything is subjected to God, engaged in His worship, establishing religion, adopting Islam and achieving equity.[73] The human being is required to contribute to this general cosmic function. Later, we will elaborate on the relation between monotheism and the specific aspects of the cosmic balance which constitute the object of vicegerency, alongside the other reasons included in this section.

**Section VII: Reasons that constitute the very human existential function and specify the object of vicegerency, but in broad terms, i.e., without designating the specific aspects of the Divine actions that the human being has been entrusted to perform on behalf of God**. Of the above-mentioned Qur'anic rationales, this section comprises vicegerency and the maintenance of the balance.

**Section VIII: Reasons that fit as an expression of one of the aspects of the cosmic balance that the human being is assigned to maintain on behalf of God**. This section includes the above-mentioned reasons of purification of the soul and judging among people equitably as we will discuss in detail below. The suitability of these concepts to express one of the aspects of the cosmic balance entrusted to the human being will also be elaborated in detail in the coming sections.

It appears that some of these major Islamic concepts that the Qur'an used as rationales behind the existence of Revelation, the human being and the universe can be subsumed under multiple sections when viewed from different perspectives. Yet, we found only two reasons that could directly express the specific tasks over which the human being has been granted vicegerency on behalf of God. These are: The purification of the soul and judgement among people. It must be noted that the determination by the majority of contemporary scholars of the object of vicegerency as *ʿimārat al-arḍ* (building and populating the earth) is nowhere to be found in the Qur'an, whether explicitly or even implicitly, as a reason behind the advent of Revelation or the creation of the human being or the universe. We have already proven the invalidity of the "Qur'anic arguments" of contemporary scholars in this regard.

We shall devote the rest of this chapter to considering the aspects of the cosmic balance that the human being has been entrusted to maintain as the existential function for which he was created through the Qur'anic reading grids elaborated above. These aspects will further be considered through a closer examination of their relation to the above-listed Qur'anic teleological concepts which, once properly organised, constitute the overall Islamic frame of reference or the Islamic worldview. Indeed, such an exercise, we argue, has the potential to reveal the organised structure of these major concepts within the overall Qur'anic existential conception of God, the human being and universe. It is against this holistic backdrop that the contours of a Qur'anic vicegerency theory are expected to develop.

## 6.2 The Aspects of the Cosmic Balance Entrusted to the Human Being

### *6.2.1 Maintaining the Spiritual Balance*

Purification of the soul (*tazkiya*), as one of the Qur'anic teleological concepts identified above, represents an aspect of the maintenance of the cosmic balance that has been assigned to the human being, since *tazkiya* signifies spiritual purification and elevation.[74] It thus relates to the preservation of a specific aspect of the cosmic balance, i.e., the cosmic balance instilled within the human being's self. The human being as a microcosm is a mirror of the macrocosm, i.e., the universe, meaning that the balance and harmony established by God in the universe, leading to soundness ("weight") and peace ("balance"), are equally instilled within the human being. This is understood from the general meaning of "And [He has] established the balance." (Q 55:7). However, the maintenance of this balance does not happen in a spontaneous fashion as is the case with the rest of creation. It is instead entrusted to the human being as indicated by God's saying, "Set up the weight (*al-wazn*) with equity and do not diminish the balance." (Q 55:9). Thus, before the command to maintain the balance "Do not diminish the balance" and after it "So that you may not transgress in the balance," the human being is instructed to set up the weight with equity, which indicates an additional function to that of the maintenance of the balance. This task does not reside in establishing the balance, for God did not say "establish the balance" as it is already established, but instead commanded: "Set up the weight (*wazn*)."

Al-Rāghib al-Iṣfahānī (d. 502/1108) notes in his reference work on Qur'anic terminology:

> *Wazn* (weight) means, linguistically, to know the measure of something, it is derived from the root verb *wazana* (to weigh). The commonly known meaning of *wazn* is that what is measured with a scale. The verses "and weigh with an even balance" (Q 26:182, Sahih Intl) and "Set up the weight with equity" (Q 55:9) denote that the human being must observe justice and equity as to all of his acts and sayings. God also says, "We will not assign to them on the Day of Resurrection any weight (*wazn*)." (Q 18:105, b.o. Corpus). As for the segment of the verse "We caused to grow therein [the earth] of every thing justly weighed" (Q 15:19, Arberry), it is said that it refers to minerals like silver and gold. According to yet another opinion, it refers to everything that God has created, meaning that He created them well-balanced in parallel to God's sayings "We have created everything in a determined measure." (Q 54:49, Maududi). As for "And the weighing [of deeds] that Day will be the Truth" (Q 7:8, Sahih Intl), and "And We place the scales of justice for the Day of Resurrection" (Q 21:47, Sahih Intl), they denote giving people justice when bringing them to account. *Wazn* linguistically means also parting objects to be of equal weight.[75]

As for *iqāma* (set up, raise up), it means "to make something stand up, which is a figure of speech for the fulfilment of something as per its best intended purpose."[76] According to the above etymological explanations, *wazn* signifies to know the measure of something and to achieve balance between things through the scale. *Tazkiya*, being a teleological rationale behind Revelation as noted above, is an expression of the most significant aspect of the cosmic balance the maintenance of which has been entrusted to the human being, i.e., the balance within the human self (*nafs*). The human self is made up of a plurality of sound natural (spiritual, physical and psychological)[77] forces, aspirations and tendencies. The human being is required to maintain balance between these aspirations through the preservation and restoration of their weight, i.e., their sound proportion that brings them in harmony with the other aspirations and avoids the encroachment of one upon another. *Tazkiya* is a spiritual purification enabling the human being to observe what lies within himself or herself, purge his or her soul from what causes imbalance and elevate it in such a way that enables him or her to keep his or her natural abilities healthy and balanced. Accordingly, and based on the linguistic definitions above, setting up the weight is to restore innate natural (*fiṭrī*) human forces and aspirations to their proper proportions (measures/weight), which results in their mutual harmony, in the best possible way.

Let us now give an example to clarify this point: The human being's innate nature (*fiṭra*) entails a tendency to self-love and self-esteem and an innate feeling of dignity and pride. This is a sound tendency and even necessary in the course of the human being's performance of his mission. However, this tendency may exceed its proper measure and consequently translate into haughtiness, selfishness or narcissism. This is due to transgressing the measure of those innate tendencies, i.e., exceeding its sound natural "weight." This excess results in disturbance within the spiritual balance as the violation of the measure of that tendency (self-esteem) leads to its encroachment upon other natural tendencies. Put differently, when the natural level of self-esteem transgresses its limits, i.e., its measure, it inevitably results in trampling upon other natural tendencies such as justice and generosity, thus causing "diminishment" in the measure of these two tendencies, leading to injustice and greed. Haughtiness, selfishness and narcissism constitute a "transgression" in the balance by exceeding the sound "measure" of the human being's natural tendency to have self-esteem. Injustice and greed constitute a "diminishment" of the balance by diminishing the sound "measure" of the human being's natural tendency to justice and generosity. This latter "diminishment" is caused by the former "transgression."[78] Hence, the proportions ("weight") of human forces and tendencies are closely linked to their "balance." Any "transgression" of any proportion ("weight") of one of the human tendencies (soundness) inevitably disturbs the spiritual balance, i.e., the harmony of human tendencies (peace) because of the resulting diminishment in other tendencies (soundness). *Tazkiya* is all about purging the soul (*takhliya*) from its transgressive tendencies and its replenishment (*taḥliya*) in such a way that compensates for the diminishment caused by such transgression as to the weight of its natural tendencies and forces.[79]

Our argument above is based on God's saying "Set up the weight with equity" that follows His command "So that you may not transgress in the balance" (i.e., do not exceed as to the proportions of the established balance), and precedes His command "Do not diminish the balance" (i.e., do not diminish the proportions of that balance).[80] Setting up the weight with equity is a middle ground between transgression and diminishment, i.e., between excess and neglect. This also indicates that the "weight" that the human being is assigned to set up must be in accordance with what is already established and in order to return to what is established. The human being is not only required to maintain the balance, but also to set up the weight as illustrated above. This additional function resides thus in the fact that he is entrusted to restore the balance after its disturbance, in addition to its maintenance. This distinguishes the human being from the rest of creatures as they contribute to the maintenance of the established cosmic balance without being able to disturb it. Thus, their function does not include setting up the weight, i.e., the restoration of the balance.

The human being's exceedance of the "weight" of his innate natural faculties and disturbance of their balance is called *fisq* (perversion) by the Qur'an. Al-Iṣfahānī says,

> *Fasaqa* [the verb of *fisq*] means to exceed the limits of *Sharī'a*. It is said for example; "the date has *fasaqa*" when it gets out of (exceeds) its skin. *Fisq* is

> wider than disbelief. The term applies when one commits few sins or many sins, though it is commonly used to refer to committing many sins. The term is often used to refer to someone who accepts the rule of *Sharīʿa* but violates all or some of its provisions. The term may be used, however, to describe a disbeliever, in the sense that he departs from and exceeds the requirements of reason and natural disposition (*fiṭra*). God says, "Is one who is a believer like one who is a *fāsiq* (transgressor/pervert)?" (Q 32:18, b.o. Ahmad Ali). Thus, *fisq* here is used as the opposite of belief; the word *fāsiq* is broader than the word disbeliever. [...] Ibn al-Aʿrābī [d. 231/846] said, "In the [pre-Islamic] language of Arabs, the word '*fāsiq*' was not used to describe humans. Rather, it was used for a date that leaves its skin."[81]

Thus, the etymological meaning of *fisq* is close to its Qur'anic usage as it signifies a thing coming forth, departing from or exceeding its original state. Hence, according to Riḍā, "everything that comes forth from its integument is *fāsiq* [...] which may be used in the Qur'an to mean exceeding the sound natural disposition (*fiṭra*) to a corrupted character."[82] Furthermore, "*Fisq* may either occur through excess or neglect [...]. Excess and neglect are two causes of disobedience in opposition to the proofs, similar to Divine Covenants, placed in one's natural disposition (*fiṭra*). Likewise, they are two means to the disease of spiritual life,"[83] as argued by Nūrsī.

The Qur'an uses the term *fisq* to signify the disturbance/exceedance of the sound natural inclinations and conducts in many occasions,[84] or even in all occasions where the word *fisq* and its derivatives are mentioned, given that belief in God is a natural disposition in the human being according to the teachings of Islam.

The relationship between *tazkiya* and maintaining the balance becomes more evident when considering the relationship between *tazkiya* and deputisation on behalf of God. The latter appears in the fact that maintaining the measures of existents, i.e., their weight, in a way that ensures their balance and harmony is a Divine action. This is understood from many Qur'anic verses: "[He has] established the balance" (Q 55:7); "[He] created everything and determined its exact measure" (Q 25:2, Ahmad Ali); "With Him all things are in determined measure" (Q 13:8, Ahmad Ali); "[We] made all things grow upon it [the earth] justly weighed" (Q 15:19, b.o. Arberry) and "Are you more difficult to create or the heavens? He built it, raised it high and harmoniously proportioned it" (Q 79:27–28, b.o. Ahmad Ali), etc.

This fact (God's creation of beings in disciplined measures (weight) that guarantee their harmony (balance) and His maintenance thereof) is in effect in all the creatures of the universe including the human being. This is understood from, for example, the following verse: "Glorify the Name of your Lord, Most High, Who created [all things] and harmonised (*sawwā*) [them]; Who determined their measures (*qaddara*) and then guided them." (Q 87:1–3, b.o. Ahmad Ali). *Taswiyya*, which is the infinitive of the verb *sawwā*, signifies perfection, harmony and lack of disparity.[85] Commenting on the latter verse, al-Ṭabarī (d. 310/923) said that it means "He who created things harmoniously and correctly, *taswiyya* means to equalise (*ta'dīl*)."[86] The verb *qaddara* (determined their measures) signifies that "He instilled the due measures and nature of things with regard to their forms and faculties."[87] Thus, *taswiyya* (harmonisation) relates to the above-mentioned concept of "setting up the weight" in terms of achieving balance between things. As for the fact that God "determined their measures (*qaddara*)" as in the continuation of the verse, it relates to the above-mentioned idea that everything is made according to specific natural innate measures. What results from this Divine harmonisation and determination of measures is the guidance of all these creatures to the duty they were created for ("then guided them").[88]

This general cosmic setting is also true with the human soul (*nafs*).[89] It has been shown that God created the human soul according to certain measurements that determine its sound innate aspirations and (physical and spiritual) faculties, making it (the human soul) balanced in itself and harmonious with its surroundings. This is understood from God's saying, "And [by] the soul and He who proportioned it harmoniously" (Q 91:7). Commenting on this verse, ibn Kathīr (d. 774/1373) said: "That is, He made it straight and balanced on an upright nature (*fiṭra*)."[90] The Qur'an also reads: "We created the human being in the finest symmetry" (Q 95:4, b.o. Abdel Haleem). Ibn Abbās (d. 68/687) commented: "It means the most upright form of creation."[91]

It is thus God Who created the human being with measures that guarantee the balance of his inclinations, aspirations and all of his natural constituents, exactly like all the elements of the universe. However, the human being is entrusted to preserve these measures on behalf of God, unlike other creatures whose weight ("*wazn*") and balance ("*mīzān*") is maintained by God. In other words, it is He Who maintains their measures ("*qaddara*") and harmony ("*sawwā*"). Therefore, in the continuation of the above-quoted verse, "And [by] the soul and He who proportioned it harmoniously" (Q 91:7), God said: "And inspired it [with discernment of] its wickedness and its piety; He has succeeded who purifies it; And he has failed who instils it [with corruption]." (Q 91:8–10). The basic state of the soul is thus that it is proportioned harmoniously. The subsequent wickedness and corruption are not innate to the soul. Rather, this is considered as deviation from and concealment of the innate nature (*fiṭra*), that is, it is disturbance of its balance which the human being is entrusted to avoid. As for "piety" and "purification," they are not parallel to *fiṭra* or different from it. Rather, they are means to preserve, develop and elevate it.[92] Or, better said, they are respectively a goal that should be worked to and an endeavour that should be undertaken in order to bring it back to its original state of harmony, i.e., soundness and balance, which the human being is entrusted with on behalf of God.

Hence, the righteousness and harmony of the human soul correspond to the natural disposition according to which humans are created. The fact that God inspired the human soul with the ability to know its own wickedness and piety does not mean wickedness belongs to its natural setup. It rather means that God taught this to the human being and showed him the path of wickedness and the path of piety.[93] The meaning of inspiration here is that knowledge of immorality and piety is a primary and necessary faculty resulting from the creation in due proportions.[94] This knowledge further relates to the names that Adam was taught and according to which he acquired the aptitude to fulfil his function. The verse also indicates that the criterion of the human being's success and loss is whether or not he purifies his soul from whatever corrupts its innate harmony. This notion is recurrent in the Qur'an, for example, "Gardens of Eden with rippling streams, where they will live forever. This is the recompense of he who purifies [his soul]" (Q 20:76, b.o. Ahmad Ali); "Successful is he who purifies himself" (Q 87:14, Talal Itani); "The day when neither wealth nor children will be of any avail, only those who come before Allah with a sound heart [will be saved]" (Q 26:88–89) and "O you tranquil soul, Return to your Lord, well-pleased and well-pleasing Him." (Q 89:27–28, Ahmad Ali).

The previous sections explained in general terms the relationship between vicegerency and the other major identified Qur'anic teleological concepts. Here, we will elaborate the relationship of some of those concepts that are closely related to the first aspect of the balance entrusted to the human being on behalf of God, namely purification of the soul, in the sense of maintaining the spiritual balance. This will further disclose the meaning and implications of the preservation of the spiritual balance within the Qur'anic worldview. Although all of these concepts are related to vicegerency, as it has become clear, some of them have a particular relevance to this first specific object of vicegerency. Among these concepts are:

**Monotheism (*tawḥīd*)**: In our classification of the major concepts of Islam, which the Qur'an presents as purposes behind the existence of Revelation, the universe or the human being, we listed monotheism in the sixth section. That section includes the teleological reasons that constitute the overall existential function common to all creatures. Therefore, they do not determine by themselves what distinguishes the human being as a deputy on behalf of God. The correlation between monotheism and the maintenance of the cosmic balance is that the latter is established on the former. Indeed, the surrender (*istislām*) of all beings to God alone guarantees the balance of their measures (*salāma*/soundness), resulting in the overall cosmic balance (*salām*/peace). This formation as a whole constitutes the religion of the universe or cosmic Islam, as we explained, and constitutes a cosmic expression of God's oneness, in other words, it constitutes cosmic *tawḥīd*. Being a part of that whole, the maintenance of the spiritual balance also represents a manifestation of *tawḥīd*, in its premise, method, purpose and outcome. As for the premise, this process can only be achieved by surrendering to God alone (in belief, spirituality, practice and behaviour) and emancipation from surrender to other than God, i.e., from all influences that distract the human being from his sound natural disposition (*fiṭra*). As for the method, the maintenance of the spiritual balance is achieved by observing the measures determined by God (Alone) for each of the faculties given to the human being in a way that keeps their soundness and balance. As for the purpose, it is to join cosmic monotheism. As for the outcome, this ends up in the harmonisation of the various and disparate powers ofthe human being into a united and balanced unity, similar to the unity of theuniverse. Related to this is the concept of piety (*taqwā*), which also appeared as one of the identified teleological concepts, since it refers to a spiritual state in which the human being is enabled to remain safe from everything that distracts him from his innate inclination to monotheism and balance.[95]

**Spiritual revival**: The Qur'an presents this as a rationale behind Revelation, saying: "So We have revealed a spirit [Qur'an] to you [Prophet] from our order." (Q 42:52, b.o. Sarwar). Calling the Qur'an a "spirit" indicates that it was revealed for spiritual revival. Makkī ibn Abū Ṭālib (d. 437/1045) said: "The Qur'an is called spirit because it gives life to the hearts and souls because of the goodness they attain by the Qur'an."[96] This is understood from God's saying: "Believers, respond to God and His Messenger when he calls you to that which gives you life." (Q 8:24, Abdel Haleem). This is a teleological rationalisation of the descent of Revelation through the fact that abiding by it results in making the human being live a genuine human life, which is exactly what vicegerency is about. The mission of vicegerency on behalf of God, enabled by Revelation, leads to the preservation of human's innate faculties and harmony, i.e., the maintenance of the spiritual balance, which brings the human being back to his original humanness. In sum, it achieves the humanness of the human being as a result of the purification from all that goes against it. Consequently, he enjoys real human life by virtue of the activation of his spiritual potentials that enlighten his path. This is the purport of God's saying, "Is a dead person brought back to life by Us, and given light with which to walk among people, comparable to someone trapped in deep darkness who cannot escape?" (Q 6:122, Abdel Haleem).

**Spiritual healing**: This is a Qur'anic rationale behind the descent of Revelation since God says about the Qur'an: "Say: 'For those who believe, it is guidance and a healing.'" (Q 41:44, Talal Itani). Spiritual healing is thus one of the reasons behind the revelation of the Qur'an, as is also stated in the following verses: "People, a teaching from your Lord has come to you, a healing for what is in [your] hearts, and guidance and mercy for the believers. Say, 'with God's grace and mercy let them rejoice: these are better than all they amass.'" (10:57–58, b.o. Abdel Haleem). These verses indicate that the spiritual healing for which the Qur'an came down is a grace and mercy from God and that it is better than whatever one accumulates from the ephemeral pleasures and goods of the worldly life, because the former is the subject of true joy. This relates to another concept through which the Qur'an rationalises Revelation and the creation of the universe, namely, the grace of God and the completion of His blessings to the human being. Spiritual healing, which is one of the teleological reasons behind the descent of Revelation, is achieved through the above-explained preservation of weight and balance. Healing is the restoration of the weight to achieve balance, because the deviation from the spiritual balance is considered a disease of the heart, in addition to being considered a perversion. God says, "Do they whose hearts are filled with disease, think that God will not expose their hatred?" (Q 47:29, b.o. Sahih Intl). Hatred, which represents a disturbance of the spiritual balance due to the exceedance in one of the innate faculties leading to a diminishment in another, namely the natural inclination (*fiṭra*) to affection, is thus considered a disease by the Qur'an. Any disease caused by exceeding the innate measures leads inevitably to an additional disease as stated by the Qur'an: "In their hearts is a disease, so Allah has increased their disease" (Q 2:10, Ahmad Khan), and: "But as for those with sickness in their hearts, it has increased them only in wickedness upon their wickedness." (Q 9:125, Khattab). The opposite is also true; if someone restores (heals) some of his innate faculties to their correct weight, the balance of others will follow: "God increases the guidance of those who follow the guidance" (Q 19:76, b.o. Wahiddudin Khan), and: "But as for those who follow guidance, He adds to their guidance, and gives them their god-consciousness (*taqwā*)." (Q 47:17, b.o. Wahiddudin Khan).

**Reminding and remembrance**: The Qur'an presents "reminding" as a teleological reason behind the advent of Revelation and the creation of the universe and its organisation in different occasions referred to in the previous section. Reminding is intimately related to vicegerency over the spiritual balance, as it means that the Qur'an only came to remind the human being of the innate nature (measures and balance) he was created upon in order to abide by it, and that the universe was not created except according to the nature instilled in the human being. Therefore, the Qur'an was called "the Reminder" (*al-Dhikr*). Among the Qur'anic verses indicating this meaning include: "We have sent down to you a Book in which is a reminder of you. Do you not understand?" (Q 21:10, Ahmad Ali); "Had the Truth followed their desires, the heavens and the earth and all those within them would have been corrupted. But, in fact We had sent them a reminder of them, but they turned away from their reminder." (Q 23:71, b.o. Arberry). Accordingly, the truth that Revelation brought is the truth existing in the universe ("the heavens and the earth") and in the human being ("those within them"), and Revelation came only to remind the human being of who he is, i.e., of what is naturally in him ("reminder of them"). Ibn al-Qayyim says:

> "Therefore We have made this (Qur'an) easy in your tongue so that they may remember." (Q 44:58, b.o. Hilali & Khan) This meaning is repeated much in the Qur'an where God tells us that His Book and His Messenger are sent to remind people of what is instilled in their *fiṭra* in terms of their innate knowledge, love, glorification, honoring, submission, devotion to Him, and the love of His Revelation that represents pure justice and its preference over something else. All of this is instilled in humans' natural disposition, which knows that and is aware of it in general and, sometimes, detailed terms. Thus, Prophets came to remind people of this, detail and explain it, and show the distractors opposing their *fiṭra* and deterring them from following the path of this *fiṭra*. [...] What is meant is that God has created His creatures with a *fiṭra* comprising recognition, love, devotion and glorification of God. What is also meant [by those verses] is that the outer person does not instil these notions in the *fiṭra*. Rather, he only reminds of it, explains and details the means that either strengthen or weaken the perfection of these notions in one's soul. This is the same case when driving a baby to suck at its mother's breast, or reminding people of eating, drinking or marrying; this is a reminder of something already instilled in one's soul.[97]

**Thinking and reasoning**: Among the concepts set in the Qur'an as teleological reasons behind Revelation and creation is for the human being to think and reason, as listed above. This is mentioned in, inter alia: "We have sent down the Reminder to you (O Muḥammad) so that you may clarify for the people that which has been sent down to them so that they may think." (Q 16:44, b.o. Ali Qarai). After mentioning the stages of the creation of the human being, God said, "He let you grow old – though some of you die sooner – and reach your appointed term so that you may use reason." (Q 40:67, b.o. Abdel Haleem). In the first verse, the naming of the Qur'an as the "Reminder" is accompanied by two reasons related to reminding the human being of his natural disposition. First: The Messenger's explanation of the Qur'an to people by his conduct that proves that the Qur'an is in line with sound *fiṭra*. Second: To make the human being think. Thinking and reasoning are closely related to *fiṭra* and the preservation of the spiritual balance as they are an activation of one of the innate human faculties, which is reason. Reason in the Qur'anic perception is a spiritual, not a biological, faculty. The brain is just a tool through which the spirit exercises a part of its rational powers in earthly life. Therefore, the use of reason to approach the truth is an intrinsic value as it represents an elevation of the human being to his humanness. Moreover, this spiritual faculty enables the human being to recognise his innate faculties, name them (and their opposites) and act on them in terms of preservation and setting up their weight. This is what the vicegerency verses (Q 2:31) referred to when establishing that reason is the first innate qualification for vicegerency. The same is true of the verses on maintaining the balance in Q 55, "And taught him speech," as this was the only innate qualification mentioned before the command to maintain "the balance." It is also the only fact in which the perfection of Divine generosity (*al-Akram*) manifested to the human being and it is the very first fact that the Qur'anic revelation came to draw attention to, as noted before in Q 96.

**'*Īmān* (belief)**, in terms of intellectual conviction in what is needed to be believed in order to fulfil the human existential function, is another one of these teleological reasons. This is an innate conviction the basis of which is belief in God. Revelation came in order to drive the human being to return to this natural conviction in a way that enables him to perform his duty. The relationship between *'īmān* and maintaining the spiritual balance lies in the fact that the correct conception of the Creator, human being, universe and life is what enables the human being to maintain that balance by being faithful to that belief in his conduct and behaviours in a way that prevents exceedance in the spiritual balance and contributes to restoring it.

**Performing prayer**: One of the reasons for the descent of Revelation is the performance of prayer as indicated by the reduction of the commands of Revelation to worship, monotheism, prayer and charity (*zakāt*) in the following verse: "Though all they are ordered to do is worship God alone, sincerely devoting their religion to Him as people of true faith, keep up the prayer, and pay the prescribed alms, for that is the true religion." (Q 98:5, Abdel Haleem). The relevance of justifying the advent of Revelation with the performance of prayer is that, as stated above, reminding and remembrance are the first means of spiritual purification, which frees the human being from any exceedance and diminishment that cause him to deviate from his *fiṭra*. The first thing the human being remembers about his/her nature is his/her innate *tawḥīd*, bond with and aspiration for God. The fact that one's inclination to God is an innate nature is indicated, inter alia, in the following verse: "Do not be like those who forgot God, so God causes them to forget their own souls: they are *al-fāsiqūn* (the deviating/pervert ones)." (Q 59:19, Abdel Haleem). Forgetting God is thus qualified as *fisq*, i.e., deviation from the *fiṭra*, as defined above. The definite article *al* (the) in the word "*al-fāsiqūn*" (the deviators) designates generalisation (*istighrāq*), meaning that forgetting God is full deviation from the *fiṭra*. Thus, maintaining the innate bond with God is the first way to purify oneself and set up the due measures (weight) of its tendencies. This is understood from the following verse: "Believers, respond to God and His Messenger when he calls you to that which gives you life, and know that God stands between man and his heart, and that you will be gathered to Him." (Q 8:24). There is no way for the human being to know what is in his own soul in order to set up its due measures without returning to God, as He "stands between man and his heart." The first means, established by Revelation, of maintaining this bond are the ritual worships, chief among them prayer, as God says, "I am God; there is no god but Me. So worship Me and keep up the prayer so that you remember Me." (Q 20:14, Abdel Haleem). Therefore, God has made prayer the first condition for the success of the believer in this world and in the Hereafter (Q 23:1 and 11). Islam emphasised the significance of acts of worship in general and prayer in particular as they represent the means through which the human being maintains the spiritual relationship that links him to God and purifies his nature from deficiency in weight and balance that might have afflicted it. The Prophet said: "If there were a river at the door of one of you in which he takes a bath five times a day, would any filth remain on him?" They replied, "No soiling would be left on him." He (ﷺ) said, "So are the five (obligatory) prayers. Allah obliterates the transgressions as a result of performing them."[98] In that way, one becomes a godly servant (*rabbānī*), which is another one of the teleological reasons listed above.

**Guidance to the paths of peace**: We have previously clarified the relationship between deputisation on behalf of God in maintaining the spiritual balance and the soundness of the "weight" of the human being's innate faculties that ultimately leads to its peace, which, in turn, enters the human being in the general cosmic peace. The Qur'an justifies the descent of Revelation on the basis of its clarification of the paths to that peace. The latter is recorded in the following verse: "A light has now come to you from God, and a Scripture making things clear, with which God guides to the paths of peace those who follow what pleases Him, bringing them from darkness out into light, by His will, and guiding them to a straight path." (Q 5:15–16, b.o. Abdel Haleem). In the same vein, the Qur'an reads: "God invites to the abode of peace, and He guides whomever He wishes to a straight path." (Q 10:25, b.o. Ali Qarai).

**Rejecting *ṭāghūt* (false gods)**: Another Qur'anic teleological reason behind the advent of Messengers is the rejection of false gods and the worship of God alone: "We sent a messenger to every community, saying, 'Worship God and shun false gods (*ṭāghūt*).'" (Q 16:36, Abdul Haleem). Above, we listed this reason in section II of our classification, namely, teleological reasons representing characteristics or attributes of the human existential mission. We were tempted to also list it in section VII, which includes the concepts that represent the very object of vicegerency, but in broad terms. This is because this mission (rejecting false gods) is specific to the human being. All other creatures are commanded to worship God, and they are not ordered to avoid false gods, as they are unable to transgress the balance. The human being, however, in his capacity as a vicegerent of God in maintaining the balance, was given the ability to transgress it, and was, hence, commanded to avoid this transgression (*ṭughyān*), which is exactly to avoid *ṭāghūt*. *Ṭāghūt*, thus, does not mean false gods in the strictly confessional sense, but rather refers to anything that can divert the human being from surrendering to God by making him surrender to something else (*ṭāghūt*) and, hence, fall into excess (*ṭughyān*). For this reason, the double testimony that is the first pillar of the five pillars of Islam, and by which pronunciation one becomes Muslim, does not begin by attesting that God is one, but rather by rejecting any divinity besides Him. That is because the oneness of God is an already established fact in the *fiṭra*, which, as per the Qur'an, was attested by the entire humanity before their advent on earth (Q 7:172).[99] Hence the first purpose is not to assert that God is one, but to protect this innate assertion from any alienation by rejecting the *ṭāghūt*.

**To give thanks (*shukr*) to God**: This is one of the aforementioned rationales behind the creation of the human being and the subjugation of the universe for his benefit. Manifesting gratefulness towards God is a task that is common to all existing things in the universe as in previously quoted verse, "There is not a single thing that does not glorify His praise" (Q 17:44). Hence, by performing his existential function, which is the meaning of glorification and praise (*ḥamd*) in this context as developed before, the human being follows the example of the existents of the universe and participates in that cosmic thankfulness. There would be nothing to add here if we were to take the opinion of certain scholars,[100] like al-Ṭabarī,[101] that the word *shukr* (gratitude) is a mere synonym to the word *ḥamd* (praise). Nevertheless, we found the Qur'an ascribing *shukr* to God and to the human being exclusively, in contrast to *ḥamd*, which is performed by all creatures, including angels.[102] Furthermore, we found that the Qur'an only ascribes *shukr* (along with *ḥamd*) to the human being in the context of this earthly life, and never in the afterlife, where only *ḥamd* is ascribed to the human being.[103] This seems to suggest that *shukr* is specific to the human being (besides God), and that it is something related to his earthly mission exclusively.

Careful analysis reveals that *ḥamd* refers to cosmic gratitude while *shukr* refers to conscious and deliberate gratitude.[104] This is supported by much Qur'anic evidence and by the opinion of the scholars who do differentiate between *ḥamd* and *shukr* in meaning. According to the latter, among the differences between the two terms is the fact that *ḥamd* is broader than *shukr*, as it is gratefulness for Who God is in His self-attributes along with gratefulness for what results from that, while *shukr* is only gratefulness for His favours.[105] Moreover, in contrast to *ḥamd*, which is performed by conscious and unconscious beings, *shukr* can only be done in consciousness and in a deliberate manner, as highlighted by some scholars.[106] This is further confirmed by the fact that *shukr* is specific to God and to the Human being, in contrast to *ḥamd*, as noted.

Hence, the human being will never cease to manifest gratefulness in the cosmic sense (*ḥamd*), because everything that realises God's cosmic will, consciously or unconsciously, is expressing *ḥamd*,[107] but he may be ungrateful in the religious sense. Ungratefulness in the religious sense, which is the opposite of *shukr*, is called *kufr* by the Qur'an, the same word that qualifies disbelief. Indeed, the Qur'an uses the word *kufr* as an antonym of *shukr* in different occasions.[108] *Shukr* is thus exclusively a religious responsibility, the absence of which is a form of disbelief (*kufr*), unlike *ḥamd*, which can never be absent as it is an established fact in the universe.[109] Hence, just as the things of the universe are not capable of disbelief (*kufr*), they are not capable of *shukr*, because they (and their *ḥamd*) are an inevitable and involuntary consequence of God's greatness. If the human being refuses to express *ḥamd* by choice, he will still be expressing it by necessity. Therefore, we could not find in the Qur'an any instance of blame or lamentation against those who do not perform *ḥamd*, or even just a simple report of cases of lack of *ḥamd*, in contrast to the numerous reproaches towards those who do not show *shukr*.[110] Also, we could not find any verse promising some kind of reward for those who perform *ḥamd*, in contrast to the many verses promising paradise and other rewards in return for *shukr*.[111]

Moreover, besides the creation of the human being and the subjugation of the universe, the Qur'an explicitly establishes *shukr* as a teleological purpose behind many principles and Divine favours such as spiritual purification,[112] piety (*taqwā*),[113] salvation of the soul,[114] fasting the month of Ramadan,[115] God showing His signs to people,[116] providing His rescue,[117] His forgiveness,[118] His bounties.[119] All this while we could not find the Qur'an presenting *ḥamd* as a teleological purpose in any instance at all.

The vicegerency verses further indicate that *ḥamd* refers to the cosmic expression of gratefulness towards God, since praise (*ḥamd*) was the very argument put forward by the angels to assert that their action in the universe compensates for human vicegerency, "while we declare Your praise and sanctify You?" (Q 2:30). As already noted, the angels assumed that the in-progress Divine cosmic will realised through their actions dispenses from assigning a vicegerent, because they align with both Divine cosmic will (*mashīʾa*) and intention (*irāda*), while the vicegerent aligns with God's cosmic will, but he may transgress His intention since he will be assuming a Divine task while not disposing of the Divine attributes of perfection. Thus, he will not be expressing *ḥamd* in its fullest effect, since he may be expressing gratitude in fact but not in what he intends, he may be grateful by necessity but not by choice, in contrast to the angels and the rest of the universe, by virtue of not having a choice. Then, God showed the angels a human faculty (stemming from the Divine insufflation and image) that they do not possess, namely, the potential consciousness and knowledge of everything. This faculty is a Divine guidance that was (given his task) granted to the human being exclusively and that enables him to be grateful (*shākir*) or ungrateful (*kāfir*), as indicated by God's words, "Indeed, We guided him to the path, he may be grateful (*shākiran*) and he may be ungrateful (*kafūran*)." (Q 76:3, b.o. Sahih Intl). In other words, it is the very guidance that the human being received to the exclusion of other creatures (which is his *fiṭra* as noted before), that enables him to perform *shukr* or *kufr*, to be a believer or not, to be a vicegerent or not. That is because of the fact that *shukr*, as noted from its etymological meaning, must be intentional and in return of the favours one has received, and that can only happen by being conscious of those favours, to know them and, hence, to name them, which was not the case of the angels as they were unable to name the things. Hence, *shukr* can only be performed by God and His vicegerents.

This is why God presented *shukr* as an explicit teleological purpose behind the insufflation of His spirit in the human being and the ensuing attributes that enables him to be aware of God's blessings. The Qur'an reads, "God brought you forth from the wombs of your mothers while you knew nothing, and gave you hearing and sight and hearts, so that you might be grateful." (Q 16:78, Wahihuddin Khan); "Then He harmoniously fashioned him; He breathed from His Spirit[120] into him and gave you hearing, sight, and hearts. And yet how little grateful you are!" (Q 32:9, b.o. Ahmad Ali). Hence, according to the latter verse, "hearing, sight, and hearts" are outcomes of the spirit that God insufflated in the human being.[121] These are also the innate features that enable the human being to be aware of things and name them. The first verse establishes the fact that these features' teleological purpose is *shukr*. The second verse indicates that despite having received the appropriate faculties (spirit and consequent hearing, sight and hearts) that enables him to be aware of God's favours and show gratefulness for them, the human being shows little gratefulness for God's favours. The human being was thus created according to that particular fashion in order to perform *shukr*, which is one of the objectives of vicegerency.[122] Indeed, if the human being performs his existential task and maintains his spiritual balance, he will retrieve full awareness of God's favours (by retrieving his *fiṭra*), be able to name them and express gratitude for that. The more he is aware of God's favours (by being a good vicegerent), the closer he will be to his initial humanness that enables him to name all things.[123]

**Distinction between truth and falsehood**: This is a teleological reason through which the Qur'an justifies the advent of Revelation on various occasions, especially when giving Revelation the title of "*al-Furqān*" (the standard of right and wrong). The purpose of distinguishing between truth and falsehood is extremely relevant to the function of maintaining the spiritual balance as it refers, inter alia, to the spiritual ability of the human being to differentiate between balanced and unbalanced faculties within the human soul. This is a subtle knowledge that needs a high degree of spiritual vigilance. The above is indicated in the following verse: "Believers, if you remain mindful of God, He will give you a *furqān* (standard of right and wrong) and wipe out your bad deeds, and forgive you: God's favour is great indeed." (Q 8:29, b.o. Abdel Haleem). The *furqān* (standard), which is a name of the Qur'an, is something that settles in the human soul through piety, which is the spiritual state that follows from the establishment of the spiritual balance as we explained, giving the human being that spiritual insight in distinguishing between truth and falsehood. Another term close to "*al-furqān*" is the concept of "Light" – one of the names of the Qur'an – which is granted to the human being when he revives his soul, as noted before.

**The exposition of everything**: This is another teleological reason behind Revelation. The Qur'an reads: "We have sent the Scripture down to you explaining everything, and as guidance and mercy and good news to those who devote themselves to God." (Q 16:89, Abdel Haleem). Furthermore: "This revelation is no fabrication: it is a confirmation of the truth of what was sent before it; an explanation of everything; a guide and a blessing for those who believe." (Q 12:111, Abdel Haleem). This rationale is related to the preservation of the spiritual balance in light of the fact that the first means given to the human being to achieve his existential function are the innate faculties granted to him, and the basis for these faculties is the ability to know everything, "He taught Adam all the names [of things]," as already shown. Just as the human being is given the innate faculty to know everything he needs so as to achieve the function of vicegerency, Revelation came down in order to clarify everything the human being needs in order to do so. This relates to another teleological reason behind sending Messengers, namely:

**Teaching people:** Among the missions of Messengers is to teach people the Scripture and wisdom, and to instruct those who have not received a revelation before about the teachings of Revelation. God said: "Just as We have sent among you a Messenger of your own to recite Our signs to you, purify you and teach you the Scripture, wisdom, and to teach you that you knew not." (Q 2:151, b.o. Sahih Intl). The relationship between teaching, as one of the Qur'anic teleological concepts, and maintaining the spiritual balance lies in the fact that the latter depends on the innate knowledge that God has taught the human being, as explained before. One of the duties of Revelation is to help the human being to revive that innate knowledge. Therefore, all verses that justify the advent of Messengers through the notion of soul purification mention the latter before mentioning teaching.[124] The reason for mentioning purification before teaching is that acquiring the knowledge that enables the human being to maintain the spiritual balance is only a result of the purification of one's soul, which brings it back to the innate knowledge he has been given ("taught him speech" (Q 55:4), "taught Adam" (Q 2:31) and "taught the human being" (Q 96:5)). There is countless Qur'anic evidence that knowledge is an innate faculty and that learning results from purification of the soul from whatever distracts it away from its sound nature in a way that revives in the human being his innate knowledge. For example: "Be mindful of God (i.e., have *taqwā*, piety), and He will teach you: He has full knowledge of everything." (Q 2:282, b.o. Abdel Haleem). Thus, learning is the result of piety that one acquires through purification of his soul. God also said, "Be mindful of God, and know that you will be gathered before Him." (Q 2:203, b.o. Hilali & Khan). "Be mindful of God and know that you will meet Him.'" (Q 2:223, b.o. Shakir). "Be mindful of God and know that He has full knowledge of everything." (Q 2:231, Abdel Haleem). "Be mindful of God, and know that He sees everything you do." (Q 2:233, Ali Qarai). Knowing all these facts is thus the result of a spiritual state

(Piety; being mindful of God) that revives the human being's innate knowledge. God said, "The believers know it is the truth from their Lord." (Q 2:26, Ahmad Khan). Thus, knowledge is the result of belief in its general sense covering the meanings of piety and soul purification. Therefore, the Qur'an commands people to get knowledge of God and all the teachings of Revelation through returning to that innate knowledge, as God said: "Know that there is no god except Allah." (Q 47:19, Ali Qarai). God also said: "Know that God knows what is in your souls, so be mindful of Him and Know that God is most forgiving and forbearing," (Q 2:235, b.o. Talal Itani) and said: "These are bounds set by God, which He makes clear for those who know." (Q 2:230, b.o. Maududi). Accordingly, the full knowledge of the Oneness of God, His other Attributes of perfection and the wisdom behind the provisions that he has revealed, is obtained only by those who have revived their innate knowledge, which can only be achieved by the purification of the soul.

The opposite is also true; the more the human being revives his innate knowledge, the more he can purify his soul and maintain its balance. The Qur'an reads: "But (to say): 'You should be *rabbāniyyīn* (godly servants) because you have taught the Scripture and studied it closely.'" (Q 3:79). "*Rabbāniyyīn*," which is a spiritual state that results from the balance of the soul (the achievement of which is one of the identified teleological reasons), depends on learning and teaching. God also said: "Those firmly grounded in knowledge say, 'We believe in it: it is all from our Lord' – only the intelligent will remember." (Q 3:7, b.o. Wahiddudin Khan). Hence, grounded knowledge entails faith, and the mindful people (the intelligent) are the ones who remember their natural disposition. God said, "It is only those of His servants who have knowledge who fear God." (Q 35:28, b.o. Ali Qarai). Fear of God, which is a spiritual state arising from the balance of the soul, is a result of knowledge, and so on. This has a very significant connection with:

**Bearing glad tidings and warning**: Many verses provide this as a teleological rationale of Revelation and prophethood. Some verses speak of bringing glad tidings and warning in an absolute sense, while others talk specifically about "the glad tidings" of "Paradise" and the "warning" against "Hellfire" or the "meeting with God." These teleological reasons are used in an absolute or specific sense, and they mostly speak about the Hereafter, as stated by many Qur'anic exegetes. Among these verses is God's saying: "Verily this Qur'an directs you to the path that is straight, and gives happy tidings to those who believe and do right: For them is a great reward. As for those who do not believe in the Hereafter, We have prepared a painful punishment." (Q 17:9–10, Ahmad Ali). The relationship of giving happy tidings and warning with the preservation of the spiritual balance goes back to the human nature (*fiṭra*). The angels' prostration to Adam, as recorded in Q 2:30–34 was due to Adam's peculiar faculty of knowing all the names, a matter that qualified him for vicegerency. In other Qur'anic passages, the angels' prostration before Adam was also a result of his innate nature, although it was expressed in different terms. This occurs in three other *Sūras*: "Verily We created you and gave you form and shape (*ṣawwarnākum*), and then ordered the angels to bow before Adam." (Q 7:11, b.o. Ahmad Ali). Thus, the angels' prostration before Adam was a consequence of the formation (*taṣwīr*) of the human being. "Your Lord said to the angels, 'I will create a human being out of dried clay, formed from dark mud. When I have fashioned him harmoniously (*sawwaytuhu*) and breathed My spirit into him, bow down before him.'" (Q 15:28–29, b.o. Sahih Intl). In *sūrat Ṣād*, God said: "Your Lord said to the angels, 'I will create a human being from clay. When I have fashioned him harmoniously (*sawwaytuhu*) and breathed from My Spirit into him, bow down before him.'" (Q 38:71–72, b.o. Abdel Haleem). Thus, prostration was a consequence of formation (*taṣwīr*) of the human being in the first verse, and of his natural harmony (*taswiyya*) and the Divine breathing into him in the second and third verses. Basing the angels' prostration before Adam on his innate knowledge, his formation (*taṣwīr*), and breathing from God's Spirit into him, indicates that all these meanings are interconnected.[125] It is thus clear that the innate knowledge granted to the human being, along with his other natural faculties, results from the spirit that God breathed into him. This is what distinguishes the human being from all other beings; the spirit breathed into him is created in an upper world that is different from this world and that responds to an existential referential different from the referential of the lower world. Hence, the human spirit does not respond to the standards of logic, time, space, matter and any other of the standards of this physical world. God says, "They ask you about the Spirit. Say, 'The Spirit is part of my Lord's domain and you have only been given a little knowledge.'" (Q 17:85, b.o. Talal Itani).

The relevance of all this to bearing glad tidings and warning of the Hereafter lies in the fact that as the human being is a human being by virtue of his spirit, not his body,[126] then he is not created for this world because it does not meet the true aspirations of his spirit.[127] Hence, Revelation came down to give him the "glad tidings" that there is a world where his real aspirations will be met, and "warns" him against the deception of the worldly life (*dunyā*) when chasing it in the hope of satiating his aspirations. The Qur'an said:

> O assembly of jinn and men! Did there not come to you Messengers from among yourselves, relating to you My signs, and warning you of the encounter of this Day (of Judgement)? They will say: "Yes, we bear witness against ourselves." They have been deluded (*gharrathum*) by the life of this world, and they will bear witness against themselves that they had disbelieved.
>
> (Q 6:130, Maududi)

Warning given by God's Messengers is thus intended to avoid the delusion (*ghurūr*) of this world.

Belief in and longing for the Hereafter is instilled in the human *fiṭra*, because the human being, by virtue of his celestial spiritual nature, aspires to the infinite; to infinite, pure and absolute happiness, pleasure, freedom, justice, beauty, wealth, serenity, etc. Hence, he naturally aspires to an infinite world corresponding to the origin of his spirit. However, there is nothing in this world that meets the absolute aspirations of the human being. Therefore, the Qur'an pointed out that the human being will only live truly in the Hereafter, since all his human aspirations will be truly met over there: "The present life is nothing but sport and amusement. The true life is in the Abode of the Hereafter; if only they knew." (Q 29:64, Maududi). The Qur'an also reads, "Do you prefer this world to the life to come? How small the enjoyment of this world is, compared with the life to come!" (Q 9:38, Abdel Haleem). Furthermore, "Say, 'Who has forbidden the adornment of Allah which He has brought forth for His servants, and the good things of [His] provision?' Say, 'These will be, for the faithful in the life of this world, pure on the Day of Resurrection.'" (Q 7:32, b.o. Ali Qarai). Hence, the soiled (by finitude inter alia)[128] pleasures one enjoys in this world will be pure, i.e., unspoiled by virtue of being absolute and infinite, in the Hereafter. Therefore, it is not reasonable that the human being satisfies himself with the enjoyment of this worldly life because his innate aspirations go far beyond that. The Qur'an, however, does not impose a choice between this life and that one. Rather, it is a matter of being aware of the true happiness that fits human nature. Therefore, the only occurrence of (the derivatives of) the term "happiness" (*sa'īd, su'idū*) in the Qur'an is in the context of the happiness of the Hereafter (Q 11:105, 108).

As to the happiness and pleasures of the worldly life, the Qur'an describes them as misleading or delusions (*ghurūr*): "As for the life of this world, it is nothing but a misleading (*ghurūr*) pleasure." (Q 3:185, b.o. Ahmad Ali), because it misleads the natural human aspirations and *fiṭra* in its entirety by giving it the illusion that it will fulfil its hopes and absolute desires. This is why God says, "So do not let the present life mislead (*taghrur*) you." (Q 31:33, b.o. Qaribullah). About the satiation of the real aspirations in the Hereafter, the Qur'an says: "They will have all that they wish for there, and We have more for them." (Q 50:35, Abdel Haleem). Moreover, "Everything the souls desire and pleases the eye will be there, where you will abide forever." (Q 43:71, b.o. Ali Qarai).

Consequently, the Qur'an considers denying or neglecting the Hereafter as contrary to the nature instilled in the human soul:

> They know an outer aspect of the worldly life, but they are heedless of the Hereafter. Have they not reflected in their own souls? Allah did not create the heavens and the earth and whatever is between them except with the truth and for a specified term. Indeed, many people disbelieve in the encounter with their Lord.
>
> (Q 30:7–8, b.o. Talal Itani and Ali Qarai)

In other words, the reason they denied or neglected the Hereafter is their satisfaction with the palpable aspect of existence. Had they thought about the nature of their own soul with its innate faculties and aspiration to the infinite, they would not have neglected the Hereafter. If they looked at the universe, they would see that it is true, justice and balanced and would have realised that, in spite of that, it is not what is made to satisfy their *fiṭra*, because it is limited and will continue for a "specific term." Furthermore, they would have realised that since the universe is created "with the truth" (i.e., it is an outcome/expression of an ontological fact) while it does not satisfy all their needs despite of that because of being finite ("for a specified term"), there must be another existential truth that corresponds to their *fiṭra,* i.e., that is a fuller expression of that ontological Truth.

From this point, the belief in and aspiration for the Hereafter is inherent in the human being's *fiṭra*. Revelation comes then to revive this *fiṭra* and guide it by reminding the human being that his soul and his aspirations exceed by far his sensory perceptions, and that his soul will not be satisfied with anything in the world, except by recourse to God and connection with Him. Otherwise, Satan would adorn for him that which is limited and deceive him that it is absolute, so that the human being spends his life seeking to satisfy his infinite aspirations through a finite world to no avail, until he dies. This is the purport of God's saying, "The quest for more and more distracted you, until you ended up in [your] graves." (Q 102:1–2, b.o. Talal Itani).[129]

Accordingly, one of the teleological purposes of Revelation is to warn the human being that the finite means of this world are not able to satisfy his real needs. Moreover, to bring him the glad tidings that there is one means that is able to give him tranquillity in this world, which is to attach himself to the Infinite and attach his hopes to an absolute world that responds to his real aspirations. Furthermore, to warn the human being that denial of the imperceptible (*ghayb*) and the Hereafter is denial of a part of his humanness, or that it is lying to oneself by believing in the finite and demanding the satiation of his infinite aspirations through it. All this constitutes a reduction and a contempt of the humanness of the human being.

Hence, "bearing glad tidings" is about the reminder that there exists a world created for who the human being truly is, responding to his metaphysical needs. Warning is given about, inter alia, the reminder that what is in this world will not fulfil the real needs of the human being, because it is not that world that was created for who the human being truly is, but was only created for a temporary mission. The relation of these teleological concepts with the preservation of the spiritual balance is that those glad tidings enable the human being to maintain his inner balance by attaching his hopes and aspirations to that which suits his *fiṭra* and drives him away from what may disturb the balance of his soul. Indeed, transgression of the spiritual balance is mostly caused by the deception of the natural aspiration of the human being as noted. Moreover, this preservation enables him to join cosmic Islam, which is the only way in this world to meet some of the aspirations of the human being towards the infinite.

**God's Beautiful Names and Supreme Attributes**: We demonstrated above the correlation between vicegerency and God's Most Beautiful Names and Supreme Attributes through which the Qur'an expresses, either explicitly or implicitly, the rationale behind the descent of Revelation and the existence of the universe. Vicegerency is a manifestation of God's Names and Attributes that do not manifest in any other creature. However, the correlation between God's Names and Attributes and vicegerency has also something to do with the human being's execution of the function he was created for. The human being has innate attributes that have their supreme ideals in the Divine attributes. For example, among the human being's innate characteristics is his/her inclination towards or aspiration for knowledge, justice, beauty, mercy, love, etc., and we know that God is the All-knowledgeable, All-Just, All-Beautiful, All-Merciful, All-Loving, etc. This is the meaning of the human being having been created in the image of God. This fact is hinted to by the angels' prostration before Adam after his formation (*taṣwīr*), i.e., after he received his *ṣūra* (image/form), as recorded in *sūrat al-Aʿrāf* (Q 7:11). The Prophet (ﷺ) said: "God has created Adam in His Image (*ṣūratihi*)."[130] Thus, Allah's saying, "We gave you form and shape (*ṣawwarnākum*)" (Q 7:11) means that He created you in the image of God, and this is linked to God's breathing from His Soul into Adam and teaching him all the names as already noted. It is based on this (image/form, breath, teaching) that the angels prostrated themselves before Adam. There is no disagreement among the *Salaf* (early Muslim generations) that God's creation of Adam "in His image" means the image of God, taking into consideration the full *tanzīh* (transcendence) of God.[131] Ibn Taymiyya said,

> The word "image" in this *Ḥadīth* follows the same rule of all other Divine names and attributes which may be applied to creatures in a restricted manner but when applied to Allah gives a sense that is particular to Him, such as the Knowledgeable, the Powerful, the Merciful, the Hearing One, the Seeing One.[132]

The degree of the balance of the human being's soul is thus measured according to the degree of its pursuit of the Divine ideal (in Names and Attributes other than those unique to God), even though it cannot reach it by virtue of not being Divine. The Qur'an, on various occasions, calls for following the Divine attributes. For instance: "O believers, among your spouses and children are enemies for you, so beware of them! Yet if you forbear, overlook, and forgive, God is indeed Forgiving and Kind." (Q 64:14, b.o. Arberry);

> Those who spend their wealth in God's cause, and do not follow their spending with reminders of their benevolence or hurtful words, will have their rewards with their Lord: no fear for them, nor will they grieve. A kind word and forgiveness is better than a charitable deed followed by hurtful [words] and God is Rich and Forbearing. You who believe, do not cancel out your charitable deeds with reminders and hurtful words. (Q 2:262–64, b.o. Talal Itani).

The first verse urges believers to follow God's example in forgiveness and mercy (All-Forgiving, All-Merciful). The second set of verses show that God is "Rich," but yet He is "Forbearing." Thus, the verses urge believers to adopt the morals of tolerance and forbearance, even if they spend on others, because God is richer than them and provides for all creatures, yet He is Forbearing with those whom he provides for, however they may behave. Another obvious example includes: "They should forgive and overlook (their failings). Would you not like God to forgive you? And God is Forgiving and Kind." (Q 24:22, Ahmad Ali).

The more the human being elevates his innate moral qualities by following the example of the Divine attributes of perfection, the more he brings his innate measures closer to their proper weight and to the spiritual balance, i.e., to the Divine "image" according to which he was created. The correlation between the Divine names and attributes with vicegerency does not end at this point, as vicegerency itself is an act of following the example of some Divine attributes since it is deputisation on behalf of God. For instance, vicegerency is about following the example of God's Names "the Preserver" (*al-Ḥāfiẓ*) and "the All-Preserver" (*al-Ḥafīẓ*) in the sense that the human being follows the Divine ideal in preserving the aspects of the cosmic balance entrusted to him. Therefore, the Qur'an promises paradise to those who return to their original *fiṭra* and preserve it:

> And Paradise will be brought near to the righteous, not far, [It will be said], "This is what you were promised – for every returner and preserver (*ḥafīẓ*), who feared the Most Merciful unseen and came with a heart that is returned [to its *fiṭra*]. Enter it in peace. This is the Day of Eternity."
>
> (Q 50:31–34, b.o. Sahih Intl)

In addition, in vicegerency, the human being follows God's example in managing the affairs, as "He manages all affairs" (Q 32:5, Talal Itani), because the human being, as a vicegerent, is entrusted to manage the weight and relations of the faculties of his soul (along with other aspects he is entrusted with) in order to achieve the balance.

We should not omit to note that the correlation between vicegerency and the Divine names and attributes goes all the way back to the fact that the human being was taught all the names. Since the human being is supposed to be God's deputy in some of His actions, and that God acts on his creation according to His Knowledge and different other attributes, He endowed him with Knowledge and other Divine attributes in a manner (and proportions) appropriate to acting on His behalf on the part of creation that he was mandated to act on. This is what is meant by the fact that God taught Adam all the names as indicated before. It was indeed the argument presented by God to the confused angels to demonstrate the suitability of the human being to be a vicegerent, after He said, "I know what you do not know" (Q 2:30). Thanks to this knowledge (which stems from his linguistic faculties as we saw), the human being is conscious of things, able to name them and act on them. It is due to this faculty (Divine insufflation/image/knowledge) that the human being is a unique expression of the Divine names and attributes as we saw. This consciousness, and subsequent ability to acquire knowledge, name things and freely act on them, stemming from the Divine insufflation that provided the human with the Divine image (Some Divine attributes), led the Divine names and attributes to articulate in creation in an unprecedented fashion on four different levels:

**The first** is the articulation of the Divine attributes through what the human being is, such as life (God is the Living one, al-Ḥayy, and the human being, thanks to this consciousness, lives in a more complete form than any other existent), generosity (this particular faculty of the human (knowledge of all the names) makes him an unprecedented expression of the Divine Generosity as explained above) and knowledge (God is the All-Knowing, and the human being, thanks to that particular faculty, achieved knowledge in an unprecedented fashion[133]). The same applies for many other Divine names and attributes that especially articulate through what the human being is in his fundamental nature as a consequence of having learned all the names, such as the fact that God is the All-Seeing, the All-Hearing, the Resurrector, etc.

**The second** is the articulation of these attributes through what the human being needs, such as the fact that God is the Responder (al-Mujīb), the Grateful (al-Shakūr), the Loving, etc. Those human needs are a consequence of this faculty that the human being was granted (knowledge of the names), and through which he is able to be a vicegerent of God. Since this function cannot materialise through the Divine cosmic will alone, that is, through natural stimuli alone, and since, as a consequence of this natural constitution that the human being was granted, he will fall short in performing his task, these Divine names and attributes are articulated in creation through the human being exclusively.

**The third** is the articulation of these attributes through the good that the human being does, is capable of achieving or naturally aspires for, such as maintaining, managing, creating, forgiving, being companionate, generous, bringing about beauty and wisdom, etc. Indeed, all of these are Divine attributes that the human being was endowed with (the Divine image), and must aspire to, as a consequence of his/her function and of the fact that he/she was taught all the names. It is indeed that consciousness and that knowledge, thanks to which he is able to identify things and name them, that enables him/her to follow that Divine ideal. In this way, these Divine attributes manifest themselves in creation through human (potential) action in an unprecedented fashion.

**The fourth** is the articulation of these attributes through the evil the human being does or is able to do. Evil is an inevitable consequence of vicegerency as understood by the angels, as highlighted before. It is also a consequence of the fact that the human being was taught all the names, since the consciousness of all things and their opposites engenders the responsibility to be faithful to the ethical and to reject its opposite, a responsibility that brings about the potentiality of evil. Hence, many Divine names and attributes solely express through the human being due to this reality, such as the fact that God is the Oft-Forgiving, the Pardoner (al-ʿAfuww), the Watchful One (al-Raqīb), the Acceptor of Repentance (al-Tawwāb), The Bringer of Judgement (al-Ḥasīb), etc.

All of the above aspects of correlation between the vicegerency of the human being in maintaining the spiritual balance and the main Qur'anic existential concepts disclose the contours of a tight structure governing all teachings of Revelation. The concept of vicegerency is one of the most prominent links of this interrelationship. The first aspect of the cosmic balance with which the human being is entrusted as a vicegerent of God is the balance established in the human soul. Thus, the human being is entrusted to maintain that balance and restore it again, in case of disturbance, on behalf of God, to Whom this matter belongs initially, as elaborated before. This mission does not lie in balancing the relation between spirit and body, as some contemporary researchers stated, as we saw. Rather, it lies in preserving all human faculties from transgressing their sound measure or falling short of it, thereby losing their harmony. If the human being's innate spiritual aspirations are absolute and infinite, then their satisfaction, in the absolute sense, cannot be achieved in this world due to its finiteness. Thus, the maintenance of the sound measures and harmony of these innate faculties becomes the only possible worldly interim alternative for the absolute satisfaction that is only possible in the Hereafter.

### *6.2.2 Maintaining the Collective Balance*

The second Qur'anic teleological reason behind the descent of Revelation that is appropriate to express as an aspect of the cosmic balance that the human being is entrusted to maintain is "to judge among people." We will elaborate below on the necessity of this reason to be a specific aspect of the human function unlike other teleological concepts. The verses that rationalise Revelation with this teleological purpose are: "We have sent down the Scripture to you [Prophet] with the Truth so that you can judge between people in accordance with what God has shown you." (Q 4:105, Abdel Haleem); "Humankind was a single community, then God sent prophets to give them happy tidings and warnings, and with them He sent the Scripture with the Truth to judge between people in their disagreements." (Q 2:213, Hilali & Khan). Thus, one of the reasons for sending Revelation is to judge among people with truth, which is a social purpose ("between people"). Commenting on this last verse, ibn ʿĀshūr wrote:

> The purport of this verse is to stress that monotheism, guidance and goodness are the *fiṭra* that God created people upon as indicated by the verse "Am I not your Lord?" (Q 7:172, Ahmad Ali). This *fiṭra* was only corrupted by misguidance and promotion of falsehood. Therefore, God sent Prophets to repair this *fiṭra* [...] and sent Muḥammad to complete that reformation, and to bring people back to unity in goodness and guidance. This is the meaning of God's saying: "So by His leave God guided the believers."[134]

Accordingly, the second aspect of the cosmic balance that the human being was entrusted to preserve on behalf of God is harmony and balance between people, that is, collective harmony and balance, resulting in the original unity of the human nation. Therefore, the purposes behind Revelation that this verse explicitly stipulated is to bring people back to that social nature by judging among them with truth, since Revelation came down for this purpose in the wake of the disturbance of that social *fiṭra* that forms the basis of the unity of the human nation.

Among the verses denoting that human unity is an innate nature (*fiṭra*) that God created humans upon is God's saying,

> Stand firm and true in your devotion to the religion. This is the *fiṭra* (nature) according to which He originated humankind. There is no altering God's creation, this is the upright religion, though most people do not realise it. Turn to Him alone, all of you. Be mindful of Him; keep up the prayer and do not be as those who ascribe partners to God, those who divide their religion into sects, with each party rejoicing in their own. (Q 30:30–32, b.o. Corpus)

According to the first verse, "God's creation" is naturally upon "the upright religion," in its general sense. This is similar to God's saying regarding the cosmic religion: "to Him belongs the everlasting religion" (Q 16:52), as noted earlier. Then the verses go on to refer to the means to maintain this natural constitution including recourse to God, being mindful of Him, performing prayers and adhering to monotheism. The third verse, then, refers to a matter contrary to this *fiṭra*, namely, disunity in religion and division into rival sects and groups. Thus, this denotes that collective unity and coherence are a natural disposition that God instilled in human nature.

What we have said on the correlation between the purification of the soul, maintaining the cosmic balance and deputisation on behalf of God also applies to the teleological purpose of judging between people. God's preservation of the harmony among the existents of the universe extends also to the harmony of relations between individuals and groups of human society as shown in the above-quoted verses, and as denoted by the general indication of the verses stating that God has established the balance and created creatures upon a natural harmony. However, the responsibility for maintaining that harmony in human society is entrusted to the human being on behalf of God, to whom this action originally belongs. This harmony, which the human being must strive to restore and preserve, has different aspects, ranging from the harmony between the human being and his relatives to the harmony between nations, and from harmony in family relations to harmony in political, economic and international spheres and all other aspects of human relations. Judging among people is thus about restoring the balance in society, as it has become clear from previously quoted verses. Hence, this is a suitable expression of one of the aspects of the cosmic balance entrusted to the human being, as it relates to an act of maintaining a balance and restoring measurements initially belonging to God and as per the weights instilled by Him.

Since human unity and the harmony of human society are the natural bases upon which humanity was created, the Qur'an expresses this by referring to a means that helps in restoring this social nature, namely to "command the *ma'rūf* (known to be good) and forbid the *munkar* (known to be rejected)." God said, "[Believers], you are the best (*khayr*) nation singled out for people: you command what is *ma'rūf* and forbid what is *munkar*" (Q 3:110, b.o. Ali Qarai).

> But they are not all alike. There is a nation among the People of the Book who is upright, they recite God's revelations during the night, bow down in worship, believe in God and the Last Day, command what is *ma'rūf* and

> forbid what is *munkar* and hasten to do good deeds. These people are among the righteous.
>
> (Q 3:113–14, b.o. Hilali & Khan)

God also said,

> Be a nation that calls for what is good, urges what is *ma'rūf*, and forbids what is *munkar*: those who do this are the successful ones. So be not like those who became disunited and differed among themselves after clear proofs had come to them: a terrible punishment awaits such people
>
> (Q 3:104–5, b.o. Hilali & Khan).

In all these verses, "commanding *ma'rūf* and forbidding *munkar*" is associated with the word "nation" (*umma*), which indicates the social dimension of this function. According to the first verse, the goodness ("*khayr*") of the "nation" is dependent on commanding *ma'rūf* and forbidding *munkar*. The reference to the collective dimension is noted in most verses that spoke of commanding *ma'rūf* and forbidding *munkar*.[135] As for the last set of verses (Q 3:104–5), they denote this idea in a more pronounced way as they put "commanding *ma'rūf* and forbidding *munkar*" in opposition to division and disputation. This proves that "commanding *ma'rūf* and forbidding *munkar*" is a means to achieve human unity and social harmony.

The fact that the concept "commanding *ma'rūf* and forbidding *munkar*" is an expression of the idea that harmony between people is the natural origin of human society stems from the meaning of "*ma'rūf*" and "*munkar*." Indeed, the meaning of these concepts denotes that this social action that aims to collective harmony represents but a return to what the human being already knows by nature and a rejection of what he already rejects by his *fiṭra*. Ibn Taymiyya says:

> General customs shared by all nations are the greatest and most upright customs. Humans will not go astray in something they all agree to, as they only agree to the truth. However, they go astray in that around which they divide and diverge. God said, "They will continue to have their differences, except those on whom your Lord has mercy." (Q 11:118–119, b.o. Ali Qarai). This is why they have a natural disposition to acknowledge the Creator and adopt His religion. This is what they consensually agree to, though they differed by ascribing partners to Him [...]. Therefore, God described His Prophet and his nation that they "command *ma'rūf* and forbid *munkar*." *Ma'rūf* is that which the hearts incline to and aspire for through natural disposition whenever they know it, while "*munkar*" is that which they dislike and hate by nature whenever they know it.[136]

In another of his books, he said,

> God created His servants upon the *fiṭra* through which they know the truth, believe in it and know the falsehood and disbelieve in it. Through *fiṭra*, they

> also know and like what is useful, and know and dislike what is harmful. Thus, what is true and beneficial is known and loved by the *fiṭra*, which will feel good about it. This is what is meant by *ma'rūf.* What is wrong and false is denied and hated by the *fiṭra*, thus *munkar*. Therefore, God said, "He [the Messenger] commands them to do *ma'rūf* and forbids them to do *munkar*." (Q 7:157).[137]

Consequently, the Qur'an instructed the Prophet (ﷺ) to command in accordance with social customs saying "Be tolerant and command in accordance with *'urf* (according to people's customs), and pay no attention to ignorant people." (Q 7:199). The word *'urf*, which designates the customs of people, stems from the etymological root *'arafa*, as is the case for the word *ma'rūf*, thus denoting the notion of pre-existing knowledge. Ibn 'Āshūr considered people's customs and traditions as part of the natural disposition that Revelation commands to preserve. He said:

> It is evident that judging according to upright customs goes in line with the *fiṭra*, as the precondition to accept customs as standards of judgement is their agreement with the established rules of the *Sharī'a*, that is, they should relate to the principle of permissibility (*ibāḥa*). These customs stem from the *fiṭra*, either because they are not contrary to it and therefore people aspire to attain it, or because they are in line with the *fiṭra* – and this does not require further argument.[138]

Custom is thus considered as a part of religion that Revelation came to promote because human activities and achievements either stem from their *fiṭra* or religion (as religion agrees with the *fiṭra*) or are in service thereof, or they stem from a disturbance, of varying magnitude, in the *fiṭra* due to the transgression of its balance. The human being's achievements may also stem from the *fiṭra* while contradicting it as to the use made of them or in their outcomes. From an Islamic perspective, there is no human action or achievement that goes beyond this.

Ibn 'Āshūr said:

> It follows from this that the *Sharī'a* calls its followers to restore the *fiṭra*, preserve the acts stemming from it and revive those aspects of it that have been stifled or blended. Marriage and nursing, for instance, stem from the *fiṭra*, this is testified by the human constitution. Interaction and good manners of companionship are also matters of the *fiṭra* for they are required for cooperation to insure human survival. Also, protecting people's lives and safeguarding their lineal identity (*nasab*) constitute an aspect of the *fiṭra*. Moreover, true civilization is a manifestation of the *fiṭra*, for it is the expression of the movement of the human intellect that is itself part of the *fiṭra*. Similarly, the various branches of useful knowledge are also a matter of the *fiṭra*, as they result from the interaction and exchange between human minds. So too are the different kinds of inventions, for they flow from people's thinking – and

> it is an aspect of the *fiṭra* that people love to see what emanates from their natural constitution manifested in the external world.[139]

The function of preserving the collective balance lies primarily in preserving the part of that balance that already exists, and therefore, Islam has come to acknowledge customs and human achievements that do not contradict its teachings as noted in the words of Ibn ʿĀshūr. Furthermore, this function lies in restoring that part that deviated from the due measure to its right proportion.

If restoring the collective *fiṭra* and maintaining the social balance are duties assigned to the human being on behalf of God, does this mean that building civilisation is a human existential function and one of the meanings or the meaning of vicegerency as a group of contemporary researchers assumed, as mentioned before? Ibn ʿĀshūr's words, quoted above, suggest that this is one of the purposes for which the human being was created, as he said "true civilization is a manifestation of the *fiṭra*," while the human being is vicegerent over the collective *fiṭra* as demonstrated. In our view, however, this is not part of the existential function entrusted to the human being by Revelation. Revelation only commanded him to preserve the existing social *fiṭra* and to restore any aspects affected by disturbance. For example, the human being has a natural disposition to eat and reproduce. Thus, he is driven to do so by a cosmic command, not a revealed one. As long as his natural disposition remains intact with regard to the measures ("weight") of these needs, he needs no revealed command to fulfil them. This meaning is denoted by the valuable maxim in the discipline of *uṣūl al-fiqh* stipulating that "Natural stimuli compensate religious injunctions."[140] The human being is not religiously obliged to eat, reproduce, observe the functions of his heart, stomach, liver, lungs or any organ, as long as all of this goes in line with the natural measures instilled in the human being. The same applies to the establishment of human civilisation, as this does not depend on Revelation, but on the cosmic command, i.e., natural stimulus, as is evident from the ancient and modern history of humankind. What the human being is assigned to do is to restore any disturbance occurring in this civilisation back to its natural "weight" and balance. This is proven by the command of many Messengers to people of great civilisations, such as the people of Eram, ʿĀd, Thamūd, Pharaohs, etc. The purpose of the Messengers was to restore the imbalances in the scale of these civilisations. We could not find one single Qur'anic verse commanding the human being to establish civilisation, not to say a verse stating that that constitutes his very existential function. What the Qur'an does order is to preserve the aspects of human civilisational achievement emerging from his *fiṭra*, and to reform the aspects resulting from its imbalance. The establishment of civilisation, however, is a matter of Divine cosmic will that occurs, in a way or another, inevitably. It may be part of the human responsibility to establish aspects of human civilisation that are required in order to achieve collective balance, but this is just a means to maintain the collective balance and is not one of the existential functions for which the human being was created.

Revelation may order the treatment of social circumstances that cause disturbance in the collective balance, such as those resulting from physical, psychological, circumstantial, social, environmental or other factors that should be overcome in themselves or in their resultant imbalance. For example, the Qur'an said about desert Arabs, "Bedouins are the most stubborn of all peoples in disbelief and hypocrisy. They are the least likely to recognize the limits that God has sent down to His Messenger." (Q 9:97, b.o. Hilali & Khan). The disturbance represented in the great susceptibility for disbelief, hypocrisy and ignorance in Bedouin communities is stemming from their lifestyle. Thus the way to handle that imbalance is to turn from the state of nomadism to sedentarisation or, at least, to address the causes of disbelief, hypocrisy and ignorance prevalent in those nomadic communities.[141] Even if we assume the latter verse carries an implicit command in favour of urbanisation or civilisation, it does not mean that this is an existential function of the human being. Rather, at the most, the verse indicates that civilisation is more appropriate for the fulfilment of the human mission. Ibn Khaldūn, for his part, considered that civilisation bears no objective value, and even stated that "Civilization constitutes the ultimate stage of urbanisation (*'umrān*) and the point where it begins to decay. It also constitutes the ultimate stage of evil and of remoteness from goodness. It has thus become clear that bedouins are closer to the good than urbanised people."[142]

Many of the teleological concepts through which the Qur'an rationalises Revelation and the creation of the human being and the universe are closely related to the function of preserving the collective balance. The first condition of this function is to strive towards the realisation of the first aspect of the human existential function, namely the maintenance of the spiritual balance. Society is composed of individuals, and unless those individuals seek to maintain their spiritual balance, the restoration of the social balance cannot be achieved. This is the purport of the following verses, "This is because God would never change a favour He had conferred on a people unless they changed what is within themselves. God is All-Hearing, All-Knowing" (Q 8:53, b.o. Ahmad Khan); "God does not change the condition of a people unless they change what is in themselves" (Q 13:11, b.o. Qaribullah); "those who respond to their Lord; keep up the prayer; conduct their affairs by mutual consultation; give to others out of what We have provided for them" (Q 42:38, Abdel Haleem). Consultation and spending, which are both social matters contributing to maintaining the social balance, are mentioned after the response to God and the performance of prayer, which both contribute to maintaining the spiritual balance. This denotes that the success of the latter depends on the former.

The reverse is also true; maintaining the collective balance enhances the maintenance of the spiritual balance. This dialectic relation is evident in God's saying: "By the declining day, the human being is in loss, except for those who believe, do good deeds, urge one another to the truth, and urge one another to steadfastness." (Q 103:1–3, Abdel Haleem). Thus, the human being's salvation from loss depends on both individual (belief and good deeds) and collective (urging one another to do what is right) endeavours.

Against this background, it can be asserted that the previously detailed correlation between maintaining the spiritual balance and the major Qur'anic teleological concepts is in close affinity with the preservation of the collective balance as well. Therefore, in the following discussion, we will investigate the relationship between the latter and other Qur'anic teleological concepts that relate directly to the deputisation on behalf of God in maintaining the social balance, which will further disclose the meaning of this maintenance and contours of the vicegerency theory. These include:

**To establish religion and not divide over it**: This is a teleological purpose behind Revelation, as the Qur'an says: "He has prescribed for you the part of religion which He had enjoined upon Noah and which We have [also] revealed to you, and which We had enjoined upon Abraham, Moses and Jesus, declaring, 'Establish the religion, and do not be divided in it.'" (Q 42:13, b.o. Ali Qarai). The correlation between this teleological reason and the maintenance of social balance is related to the idea explained above that unity in religion is a natural cosmic disposition. God's saying, "part of religion" refers to the fact that what was revealed to the human being is a part of that cosmic whole. His saying, "and do not be divided in it" refers to the idea presented above that human unity is a natural disposition, and that maintaining this *fiṭra* is a duty entrusted to the human being alone.

**Witnessing over people**: Another Qur'anic teleological purpose behind the advent of the Prophet (ﷺ) is to be a witness over people, "O Prophet, We have sent you as a witness and a bearer of happy tidings and an admonisher." (Q 33:45, Ahmad Ali). The Prophet's witnessing over people leads to his followers' witnessing over all other nations as God said, "in order that the Prophet be witness over you, and you be witness over mankind." (Q 22:78, Ahmad Ali).[143] The Prophet's followers being witnesses over people leads in turn to the Prophet being a witness over his followers on the Day of Resurrection regarding whether or not they followed him and fulfilled the requirements of this witnessing, "that you act as witness over people, and the Prophet as witness over you." (Q 2:143, b.o. Ahmad Ali). The testimony over humankind by the Prophet's followers is related to many Qur'anic concepts, including: The concepts of *wasaṭiyya* (to be balanced), *ijtibā'* (being chosen), Islam (surrender), *jihād* (struggle) and *qisṭ* (equity, justice, fairness) as they appear in the following verses:

- "We have made you a justly **balanced (*wasaṭ*)** nation that you act as **witness** over people, and the Prophet as witness over you." (Q 2:143, b.o. Ahmad Ali)
- "**Struggle** hard (*jāhidū*) in the way of God as is His due: He has **chosen** you and placed no hardship in your religion, the faith of your forefather Abraham. God has called you **Muslims** – both in the past and in this [message] – so that the Messenger can bear witness about you and so that you can bear **witness** about other people. So keep up the **prayer**, give the prescribed **alms**, and seek refuge in God." (Q 22:78, Arberry)
- "O you who believe, be steadfast in your devotion to God and bear **witness** for God with **equity**." (Q 5:8, b.o. Pickthall)
- "You who believe, uphold **equity** and bear **witness** for God, even though against yourselves or your parents or your relatives." (Q 4:135, b.o. Ahmad Ali)

Accordingly, what qualifies the nation to be a witness over all of humankind is being a justly balanced nation, chosen by God and its surrender to Him (Muslim). The means enabling this nation for this witnessing are: *jihād*, performance of prayer and giving charity. One of the objects by which they witness over themselves, their relatives and all people is equity. All these meanings have something to do with preserving the collective balance:

- **Chosen by God**: This choice is related to the status of the Muslim nation as in God's saying, "[Believers], you are the best community singled out for people." (Q 3:110). God has thus chosen this nation for its "goodness." However, this goodness is not an inevitable feature of all of its individuals, but an inherent characteristic of its teachings. Indeed, as noted before, this characteristic stems from the *umma*'s quality of "enjoining *ma'rūf* and forbidding *munkar*," which are the most important means of preserving the collective balance, as shown above.
- **Islam:** Another qualifier for the Muslim nation to be a witness over all people is its Islam as denoted in Q 22:78. This is relevant to the detailed discussion above regarding the meaning of Islam as the order upon which the universe is based. One of the purposes of Revelation is to realise Islam in the soul and in the community, in a way that manifests for all people this natural and universal dimension of its teachings; this is thus one of the meanings of witnessing over people.
- ***Wasaṭiyya* (middle way, justly balance)**: The concept of *wasaṭiyya* is closely relevant to the concept of maintaining the balance. Commenting on the verse about *wasaṭiyya* that lies in the exact middle (*wasaṭ*) of the largest chapter of the Qur'an (verse 143 of *sūra* 2, which contains 286 verses), al-Iṣfahānī said:

> *Wasaṭ* basically signifies a point that lies at equal distance from all edges in a circle, and at equal distance from both sides in a rectangle. Thus, the word may refer to the centre of a circle or the fulcrum of the scale in relation to its plates. The word also signifies justice, balance, and centre. In that sense, the word refers to anything lying between the two extremes of excess and neglect, such as generosity as falling between waste and greed, and courage as falling between recklessness and cowardice. Then the word came to be used to denote the best of everything, as it is said: "So and so" is from a *wasaṭ* linage, i.e., the best linage. As God made the Muslim community a *wasaṭ* (justly balanced) nation, He made them in the same sense the best nation saying, "[Believers], you are the best community singled out for people."[144]

It thus appears that *wasaṭiyya* is achieved when the scale is justly balanced, that is when the two sides lean neither to "excess" nor to "neglect." This is exactly what the Qur'an expressed when it commanded to set up the weight and forbade both transgression and diminishment in the balance. The notion of being "justly balanced" relates to what we have developed in the previous section in terms of keeping the measures of innate human faculties intact by not exceeding their limits in a way that leads to loss in others. Nevertheless, *wasaṭiyya* in this particular context refers specifically to the collective balance, as the Qur'an uses it to qualify the word "nation" ("a justly balanced nation").

- **Equity (*qisṭ*)**: Al-Iṣfahānī said:

  If it is asked: "Will all followers of the Prophet be witnesses, or just some of them?" It would be answered: "All of them are able to be witnesses, provided that they purify themselves with knowledge and righteous deeds." Thus, he who does not purify himself will not be an acceptable witness. This is why God says, "The one who purifies his soul succeeds" and He said, "Believers, uphold equity and bear witness to God, even if it is against yourselves." Upholding equity means to observe justice, and it has, in general terms, three forms: justice between the human being and himself, between him and other people, and between him and God. He who upholds these three forms will be a just witness before God.[145]

  Accordingly, equity (*qisṭ*) is justice (*'adl*) in its broad meaning. This Justice is the object by which the "nation" ought to act as witness to other people in God's saying, "bear witness for God with equity" (Q 5:8). This Justice is a teleological reason set by the Qur'an as rationale behind sending Prophets, the advent of Revelation and the conformity between Revelation and the cosmic balance: "We sent Our messengers with clear signs, the Scripture and the Balance, so that people could uphold equity." (Q 57:25). Equity also denotes the equilibrium that must be upheld in the balance: "Set up the weight with equity and do not diminish the balance." (Q 55:8–9).

- ***Jihād* (striving in the cause of Allah)**: The command to perform *jihād* came in *sūrat al-Ḥajj* in God's saying "Strive (*jāhidū*) for God as is His due," ahead of His saying, "so that you can bear witness over people," (Q 22:78) referring to this relationship between *jihād* and witnessing. *Jihād* means exerting one's utmost effort to confront the apparent enemy or to resist the (disturbances of the) soul.[146] The Qur'an commanded Muslims to practise *jihād* a long time before giving them the permission to practise armed resistance. For example, in the Meccan *sūras* we can read, "He who strives (*jāhada*) does so for his own soul." (Q 29:6, b.o. Yusuf Ali). Furthermore, "But We shall surely guide to Our paths those who strive (*jāhadū*) hard for Our cause: God is with those who do good" (Q 29:69, b.o. Ali Qarai), and "strive (*jāhidhum*) hard against them with this Qur'an." (Q 25:52, b.o. Maududi). All of these verses relate to moral, spiritual and intellectual *jihād* for a higher purpose, namely, to resist all factors preventing entry into peace with the self and with the surroundings. In addition to being one of the means to become a witness over people, *jihād* is one of the most salient means of maintaining the spiritual balance. The Prophet (ﷺ) said, "The true *mujāhid* (the one who performs *jihād*) is one who does *jihād* against his own soul."[147] The correlation between *jihād* and maintaining the collective and spiritual balances is the same for all the means for witnessing mentioned in *sūrat al-Ḥajj* (Q 22:78) and in the other *sūras*, such as prayer, *zakāt* and resorting to God. The permission for armed resistance came only in Medinan *sūras* (revealed after the Prophet's migration to Medina). The Qur'an's command to practise spiritual *jihād* before its permission for armed resistance indicates the difference between *jihād* in its comprehensive sense and warfare in the narrow sense. Everyone may perform warfare, whether liberated from the chains of whims or not. However, *jihād* cannot be achieved without hard striving to purify one's soul from any deterrent that corrupts the humanness of the human being and prevents his entry into peace with himself and his surrounding world. If this condition is broken, it is not a matter of *jihād* but just fighting.

- **Mutual deterrence (*tadāfu'*)**: If *jihād* of the soul is one of the most important means of achieving the spiritual balance and witnessing over people, which are among the teleological reasons behind the advent of the Prophet (ﷺ), mutual deterrence is a Qur'anic rationale behind *jihād* and one of the most important means of achieving the collective (and environmental) balance. This is evident in God's saying, "If God did not make people deter one another, this earth would indeed be depraved. But gracious is God to the people of the world." (Q 2:251, Ahmad Ali), and "If God did not make people deter one another, monasteries, churches, synagogues and mosques, where the name of God is honoured most, would have been razed. God will surely help those who help Him, verily God is All-Powerful and All-Mighty." (Q 22:40, b.o. Ahmad Ali). Ibn 'Āshūr said:

> In case there is no mutual deterrence, the result would be corruption, not goodness, because corruption often attracts the human being's desires because most forms of corruption include hasty pleasures. Many souls, or even most of them, have tendency to many types of corruption. The nature of the corrupt souls is to pay no attention to harming others; unlike good souls, evil souls are more determined to violate the rights of others because corrupt actions have more quick results. So, a little corruption overwhelms a lot of goodness. Thus, it is not a cause of wonder that had not God caused good people to deter evil ones, corruption would have spread faster to prevail in all of their affairs in a short time. The greatest manifestation of this deterrence is wars. Through an unjust war, a warrior attempts to usurp the properties of others, and through a just war, the right owner restores his rights from the usurper. It is for this war that alliances are formed and calls for restoring the right are launched, the wrong doers and the unfaithful are attacked to be defeated. Moreover, the people's deterrence of one another repels the corrupt from corruption. The corrupt's realization that others may repel him would deter him from many actions of corruption. Corruption in the earth may apply to the corruption of the humans living on it as indicated by attributing defence to "the people of the earth," or it may apply to the corruption of all that which can be corrupted.[148]

**Inter-people acquaintance**: This is one of the teleological causes that the Qur'an sets as rationale behind the creation of the human being with a social *fiṭra*, as God says, "People, We created you all from a single man and a single woman, and made you into ethnicities and tribes so that you may [get to] know one another. In God's eyes, the most honoured of you are the ones most mindful of Him: God is All-Knowing, All-Aware." (Q 49:13, b.o. Abdel Haleem). The purpose of creating people with such diversity of being, men and women, related in nations and tribes is to get to know one another. This acquaintance leads to several mutual benefits, which lead, in turn, to cooperation and harmony among people. Human diversity is thus one of the Divine norms in the universe that aim to enhance the natural harmony among humans. This is closely associated to the following two Qur'anic rationales behind the creation of the human being according to a specific structure as mentioned above, namely:

**Mutual aid between humans**: This is one of the teleological purposes behind the diversity according to which human beings were created. The Qur'an reads: "It is We who distribute among them their livelihood in the life of this world, and raise some of them above others in ranks, so that they may take one another into service." (Q 43:32, b.o. Wahihuddin Khan). The reason why God created diversity among people ("raise some of them above others") is for them to cooperate, collaborate, and share what God has bestowed on them ("so that they may take one another into service"). This is further exposed through another Qur'anic rationale behind the creation of the human being and the universe. This purpose is:

**Trial**: We have referred before to a set of verses indicating that trial is one of the teleological reasons for creating the human being and the universe, as: "Who created death and life to test you [people] and reveal which of you does best – He is the Mighty, the Forgiving." (Q 67:2, Abdel Haleem). The relevance of pluralism and human unity to the concept of trial (as well as to the two previous teleological purposes) appears in God's saying, "It is He who made you successors in the earth and raises some of you above others in rank, to test you through what He gave you." (Q 6:165, b.o. Talal Itani). Human pluralism ("raises some of you above others") resulting from differences in aptitudes, talents, cultures, genders, etc. ("through what He gave you"), is a test of cooperation and solidarity ("to test you through what He gave you") in order to return to the collective balance. The weak needs the strength of the strong; the young needs the wisdom of the old; the poor needs the wealth of the rich; the ignorant or the incompetent, in any field, need the knowledge of the scholar or the skill of the skilled, men need women and vice versa, etc. The plurality of peoples makes each of them in need for the other. All of these are essential factors in the balance of societies and the elevation of the human species in general. Had people and nations been identical in the measures they are created upon, the human being would not have found any need to establish a human community and interact with it, and everyone would have felt self-sufficiency, as he would not be in need of anything from others. This would result in the corruption of the human society, as indicated in God's saying, "If God were to abundantly increase the provisions to His servants, they would transgress on earth; but He sends down in precise measure whatever He wills. Surely, regarding His servants, He is All-Aware and All-Seeing." (Q 42:27, b.o. Ahmad Ali). God's provisions in the verse may be material or moral Divine gifts. If God were to grant them to everyone abundantly without a difference between people, they would act insolently on Earth, and the human community would have been corrupted and its balance would have been disturbed by the disappearance of ties among people as each of them would feel no need for others and for the social entity as a whole. Therefore (as the verse indicated), the amounts of Divine grants given to each individual and group respond to precise measures set by God, enabling the human being to strive to restore social balance.[149]

In all, it appears that the most suitable notions in expressing the object of vicegerency, as per our induction of the teleological reasons behind the advent of Revelation and the creation of the human being and universe, is the preservation of the spiritual and social balances, in other words, the preservation of spiritual and social *fiṭra*, and its restoration in case of disturbance. This human existential function is consistent with the statement of the Prophet (ﷺ) when he stated, as the sole reason for his advent, "I was only sent to complete good morals."[150] Thus, the reason for sending Revelation is not to achieve something new, but to polish something (balance/weight/*fiṭra*) that exists.

The question that arises here is: Is the human being's vicegerency on behalf of God limited to these two aspects? What about the earth and its resources that were created for the human being and subjugated for him to benefit from, as stated in the Qur'an? Is the human being entrusted to be a vicegerent in this regard? It has already been noted above that the development of the earth, the investment and utilisation of its resources and the establishment of civilisation, are not existential functions of the human being, as discussed earlier. But is the human being considered a vicegerent over the earth in the sense of being entrusted to preserve the soundness of its components and their equilibrium as he is entrusted to preserve the balance of his soul and society?

### *6.2.3 Maintaining the Environmental Balance*

Although this objective is not one of the explicit Qur'anic teleological purposes that we have induced, however, the Qur'an commands this maintenance on various occasions without stating clearly that it is a reason or purpose behind the descent of Revelation, or the existence of the human being, or the universe. For example, God says, "Do not cause *fasād* (corruption) in the earth after it has been set good (*iṣlāḥihā*)." (Q 7:56, b.o. Maududi). The prohibition of causing corruption in the earth is a command to preserve its balance, as the meaning of corruption (*fasād*) is "to exceed balance, whether this exceedance is little or much."[151] The earth, like all other existents, was created upon a good (*ṣāliḥ*) and harmonious state, and the Qur'an does not explicitly command to introduce that which is not on the earth in terms of civilisation or urbanisation. The Qur'an, at best, commands the human being to preserve the already standing state of goodness (*ṣalāḥ*) of the earth, as it is clearly stated in the above verse. Moreover, the human being has not been tasked with preserving all aspects of goodness and balance of the earth and the universe. Rather, he was entrusted with the preservation of those aspects of that balance that relate to the resources of the earth that he needs to deal with and invest to be able to live and perform his existential duty on it. Overall, he is entrusted to preserve the elements of his natural surroundings that are under his reach. Thus, he is tasked to preserve all parts of the universe and the earth that he physically deals with. Other aspects out of his reach are preserved by God and require no human preservation. Human preservation becomes due only when the human being approaches nature through investment and utilisation as this is likely to disturb the balance of his environment. Although all aspects of the universe are subjugated for the human being according to the Qur'an, their subjugation means that they enable him to live in the universe and perform his mission, not that he is able to utilise them all. In other terms, all elements of the universe are subjugated "for" the human being and not "to" the human being. The fact that the human being is basically entrusted to preserve what he utilises[152] in this universe is indicated by many Qur'anic verses that command the preservation of the earth and its resources within the framework of what the human being invests and utilises, for example:

- "Eat and drink from God's bounties and do not abuse the earth with corruption." (Q 2:60, Sarwar)
- "O Children of Adam, dress yourself properly whenever you are at worship and eat and drink but do not be wasteful: God does not like wasteful people." (Q 7:31, Wahiddudin Khan)
- "Eat of (the) good things which We have provided you and (do) not transgress therein, lest should descend upon you My Anger." (Q 20:81, Corpus)
- "It is He who produces both trellised and untrellised gardens, date palms, crops of diverse flavours, the olive, the pomegranate, alike yet different. So when they bear fruit, eat some of it, paying what is due on the day of harvest, but do not be wasteful: God does not like wasteful people. [He gave you] livestock, as beasts of burden and as food. So eat what God has provided for you and do not follow in Satan's footsteps: he is your sworn enemy." (Q 6:141–42, Abdel Haleem)

The purport of forbidding corruption (*fasād*) in the earth, being wasteful in clothing, eating and drinking, transgressing the limits when using God's provision and following in Satan's footsteps when utilising the resources of the earth, the purport of all these prohibitions is the order to preserve the balance and harmony that the earth was created upon. Linking this command to the resources of the earth that the human being utilises denotes that this task becomes due when man approaches these resources, and not at all times. This is one difference between this aspect of the preservation of the cosmic balance, and the previous two aspects, as we will show.

After our integral review of the Qur'an, we did not find the preservation of the earth among the teleological purposes behind Revelation or the creation of the human being and the universe. This preservation comes only as an obligation among many other Qur'anic obligations given to the human being. However, what justifies the inclusion of this task as part of the human existential function is that it falls directly under the command to preserve the cosmic balance "so that you may not transgress in the balance." In addition, this aspect is a suitable object of vicegerency on behalf of God, as it is a Divine action in the universe with which the human being is tasked. Since the human being has the ability to disturb this aspect of the cosmic balance, it becomes part of his responsibility to preserve it, in the sense of not disrupting it. As God is the One Who preserves the due measures and balance of the earth, the human being is thus entrusted with this duty on behalf of God with regard to the aspects that he has the ability to corrupt.

The difference between this aspect of the cosmic balance and the previous two is that the human being is not only entrusted to maintain the latter two aspects, but also to restore them after their disturbance. This is evident from the verses quoted above that demonstrate the high susceptibility of the human being to deviate from his spiritual and social *fiṭra* because of his weakness and negligence in carrying out his function. This is also evident from the following verses:

- "We created the human being in the finest symmetry, then reduced him to the lowest of the low." (Q 95:4–5)
- "Indeed, the human being transgresses." (Q 96:6)
- "Indeed he [man] is most unjust and ignorant" (Q33:72, b.o. Ali Qarai)
- "Indeed, We created the human being in trouble." (Q 90:4, b.o. Aberry)
- "The human being is in [deep] loss." (Q 103:2, b.o. Abdel Haleem)
- "The human being was created weak." (Q 4:28, b.o. Ahmad Ali)
- "All people were originally but one single community, but they differed." (Q 10:19, b.o. Ahmad Ali)
- "This community of yours is one – and I am your Lord: be mindful of Me – but they have split their community into sects, each rejoicing in their own." (Q 23:52–53, Abdel Haleem)
- "If your Lord had pleased, He would have made all people a single community, but they continue to have their differences – except those on whom your Lord has mercy." (Q 11:118–19, Abdel Haleem)

These verses demonstrate that the spiritual and social balances are easily disturbed, and need, therefore, sustained efforts and constant endeavours in order to be restored. Or, rather, they are two ideals that the human being is entrusted to constantly strive to achieve, though he will never fully reach them. God said, "O human being, you have to strive and go on striving towards your Lord, then will you meet Him."[153] (Q 84:6, Ahmad Ali). The Prophet (ﷺ) said, "By the One in Whose hand my soul is, if you were not to commit sins, God would replace you with people who would commit sins and then seek forgiveness from God, the Almighty, who would then forgive them."[154] Therefore, it can be said that the human existential function is not to fully preserve the spiritual and the collective balances or *fiṭra*, since this is not only impossible, but it would also deprive the human being of his/her existential purpose as understood from the above *Ḥadīth*. His function is rather to strive perpetually towards that ideal. The same does not apply to the part of the cosmic balance established on Earth. We have quoted above a set of verses proving that this balance is already established without referring to any imbalance that would affect it, contrary to the many verses about the balance set in the human being.[155]

From this general rule we may exclude God's saying, "Corruption (*fasād*) has appeared in land and sea because of the doings of the people's hands, that He may make them taste something of what they have done, so that they may come back." (Q 30:41, Ali Qarai). There are many verses that forbid the human being from causing corruption on Earth or mention his corruption in it, as we have already referred to some above. However, this is the only verse that refers to the disturbance of the balance of the earth, since it speaks about the appearance of corruption in it, and not just of humans causing corruption. However, there is a difference between this verse and the verses speaking of the human being's deviation from his spiritual and social balances. The latter portray that deviation as a common and inevitable fact: "He is ," "then reduce him to," "We created the human being," "The human being was created," "Indeed, the human being is," "they continue to have their differences," "they differed," "they have split their community." Thus, it is an inevitable imbalance and the predominant state of the human being. The above verse, in contrast, does not attribute this disturbance to the environment (land and sea), and does not portray it as inevitable or dominant. Rather, it uses the expression "has appeared" to denote that it is an accidental matter in the universe. Accordingly, maintaining the existing balance in the earth does not require continuous efforts. It is not a duty entrusted to the human being to "set up the weight" in the sense of restoring the *fiṭra* of the earth to its original measures and harmony. It is sufficient here to avoid transgression in the existing cosmic balance.

Therefore, when God expresses the function of the human being in the universe, He said, "So that you may not transgress in the balance: set up the weight with equity and do not diminish the balance." (Q 55:8–9). Verse no. 8 "so that you may not transgress in the balance" denotes the function of the human being in general terms, including all aspects of the cosmic balance whose preservation is entrusted to him. As for verse no. 9 "set up the weight with equity and do not diminish the balance," it specifically refers to the spiritual and social balances, as is evident from the command to set it up before the second command to maintain it.[156] This is because disturbance in that balance corresponds to the usual human condition, as most human beings fall short in fulfilling their duty and in delivering constant endeavours to maintain that balance. This is contrary to the case of the balance established on Earth, since the basic condition of that balance is its non-disturbance. This is why one of the teleological purposes behind Revelation is to bring "healing for what is in [the] hearts" (Q 10:57), i.e., to restore the integrity of one's *fiṭra*, as noted. Nowhere in the Qur'an, however, could we find that restoring the integrity of the *fiṭra* of the earth and the universe is a purpose behind Revelation.[157] Hence, this difference seems to be the reason why the Qur'an did not rationalise the main existential phenomena through the preservation of the environmental balance, despite it being an aspect of the cosmic balance entrusted to man.

In the previous chapters, we have demonstrated that the vast majority of contemporary researchers who tackled the question of vicegerency argue that its meaning, or most prominent meaning, is the construction of the earth, its investment, development, urbanisation and utilisation of its resources. This is referred to as *ʿimārat al-arḍ*, or *ʿumrān*, which some translate as civilisation[158] or as "the Qur'anic concept of civilization."[159] Some have made of *ʿimārat al-arḍ* one of the highest principles of Islam. For example, Ṭāhā Jābir al-ʿUlwānī (d. 2016) attempted to prove that the establishment of *ʿumrān* is one of the higher values of Islam, besides monotheism and purification, based on the angels' arguments in the vicegerency verse. Al-ʿUlwānī said,

> God has established trial and mandate (*taklīf*) for humans on one basis and two pillars: The basis is pure monotheism, and the two pillars are: First; purification through which one can fulfil his duty, trust, carry out the functions of vicegerency and pass the Divine testing. Second; the establishment of *ʿumrān*: as *ʿumrān* is the right of the earth that the angels were afraid that the one entrusted with vicegerency would corrupt and shed blood and propagate destruction on it instead of *ʿumrān*. Therefore, the higher Qur'anic governing objectives are: monotheism, purification and civilization.[160]

Al-ʿUlwānī further made of *ʿumrān* a condition for achieving monotheism.[161] Nevertheless, we found no single evidence in the Qur'an that proves that "*ʿumrān* is the right of the earth," nor that it is a religious requirement or not even that it has any intrinsic value. Furthermore, the cited Qur'anic verse (Q 2:30) does not state that the human being's mission is achieving *ʿumrān* on Earth in any sense. It rather implies that the angels were fearful that the human being may destabilise the established goodness of the earth, with no reference whatsoever to the notion that the human being is commissioned to establish civilisation on Earth or make it thrive, as we have already explained. It is noteworthy here to pinpoint this thoughtlessness in elevating concepts to which the Qur'an did not ascribe any inherent value whatsoever to the status of "higher Qur'anic governing objectives" and greatest pillars of Islam.[162] This practice, we argue, is a result of the influence of the Western material progress over the contemporary Islamic reformist discourse, as noted before. This appears through the engagement of al-ʿUlwānī, and those who adopt the same approach, in debates with and critiques of "Western civilisation" when discussing these concepts.

In his arguments to deny the inherent value that many Muslim thinkers tried to attribute to civilisation, ʿAbd al-Majīd al-Najjār notes,

> It is not unlikely that this perception that overwhelmed the minds [of contemporary Muslim scholars] is a result of the domination of the current civilization, which advocates promote as the model of goodness and welfare, in addition to arousing fascination among the underdeveloped peoples with its achievements and progress. As such, the word civilization, as it refers to today's dominant civilization, has acquired an inherent value by means of

> propaganda, on the one hand, and fascination, on the other hand [...] Hence, civilization is assessed through a materialistic lens, even when evaluating previous civilizations retrospectively. Consequently, materialistic achievement is rendered the ultimate manifestation of human civilization.[163]

Following in the footsteps of al-ʿUlwānī and based on his idea that restricts the higher governing values of Islam to *tawḥīd* (monotheism), *tazkiya* (purification of the soul) and *ʿumrān* (establishing civilisation), Faṭḥī Malkāwī attempted to justify the inclusion of *ʿumrān* among the higher Qur'anic values by following up its occurrences in the Qur'an. He tries to assign it an inherent ethical value, stating,

> In the event that *ʿumrān* collapses and gets corrupted, the human being's life would turn out to be total misguidance and misery. It is stated in the Qur'an, "And whoever turns away from My remembrance – indeed, he will have a depressed life, and We will gather him on the Day of Resurrection blind." (Q 20:124, Sahih Intl). Hence, *ʿumrān* is to lead your life according to Allah's Guidance, and it is goodness and blessing in this life and the Hereafter, whereas corruption is a life of misery and misfortune in the world and in the Hereafter. [...] Hence, achieving *ʿumrān* in the worldly life at the expense of the Hereafter is, at the end of the day, not counted as *ʿumrān*.[164]

One of the objectives of *ʿumrān*, according to Malkāwī, is to "build the earth through its enhancement by agriculture and plantation, and the development of the means of livelihoods so that no piece of land on Earth nor human workforce is left unproductive."[165] This notion is close to the capitalist worldview of development, production, labour and success. Accordingly, production, economic growth, development and full exploitation of natural resources, which are objectives of the capitalist economy, become fundamental objectives of Islam as well. Nevertheless, all of Malkāwī's arguments are based on Qur'anic verses on which preconceived ideas, which he tries to legitimise through the Qur'an, are projected. The methodology followed in his research does not aim at extracting the higher values of Islam through a clear, systematic approach that sets the criteria on which those values, and not others, were chosen. Rather, these concepts were already adopted and Malkāwī's research only attempted to prove or substantiate them. The same applies to al-ʿUlwānī's thesis.

We could not find one single verse in the Qur'anic that proves, either explicitly or implicitly, that *ʿumrān* has an inherent value, nor is there a single verse bearing a command or exhortation to aspire for such an objective. Rather, the Qur'an explicitly considers the achievements of nations that have realised "*ʿumrān* in the worldly life at the expense of the Hereafter" as a great *ʿumrān*, just as mentioned in the Qur'anic verse, "They were greater than them in power, and they ploughed the earth and built it up (*ʿamarūhā*) more than they have built it up." (Q 30:9, b.o. Sahih Intl). Thus, no inherent value is given to the concept of *ʿimārat al-arḍ* by the Qur'an nor is it regarded as a moral act in itself, but rather as a Divine blessing calling for praise and faith in Allah, as previously indicated by some quoted Qur'anic verses. However, Malkāwī and many others used these verses to support ideas that are exactly the opposite of what these verses convey. For instance, Malkāwī states,

> *Khilāfa* on earth means worship and is about thriving and investing the earth (*'imārat al-arḍ*): "And to Thamūd [We sent] their brother Ṣāliḥ. He said, 'O my people, worship Allah; you have no deity other than Him. He has produced you from the earth and settled you (*ista'marakum*) in it, so ask forgiveness of Him and then repent to Him. Indeed, my Lord is near and responsive.'" (Q 11:61, b.o. Sahih Intl). Accordingly, man is brought to this World to establish *'umrān* on earth and to bear the trust.[166]

Besides the fact that he did not bring any proof to the effect that vicegerency means establishing *'umrān* on Earth, he argues on the basis of a verse that proves the opposite of his opinion. Revelation in the respective verse came to command people to worship God alone, not to establish *'umrān*. Furthermore, *'imāra* (constructing the earth, making it thrive, or building civilisation…) had already been achieved by virtue of the cosmic Divine order before the advent of their Prophet. The people of Thamūd who caused the earth to thrive in an unprecedented fashion were destroyed owing to their corruption and immorality, and this prosperity did not avail them anything. Hence, if *khilāfa* "means worship and is about constructing and investing the earth" then the people of Thamūd should have been among the most pious of all nations. Instead, besides the fact that the Qur'an does not ascribe any objective value to *'umrān*, it indicates that *'umrān* may be associated with corruption, or synonyms to it, contrary to his claim that it is intrinsic goodness and blessing. Speaking of the people of Thamūd, the Qur'an states, "And remember when He made you successors after the 'Ād and settled you in the land, [and] you take for yourselves palaces from its plains and carve from the mountains, homes. Thus remember the favours of God and do not commit abuse on the earth, spreading corruption." (Q 7:74, b.o. Sahih Intl). Like no one before, the people of Thamūd made the earth thrive, as mentioned in the Qur'an, and were, nevertheless, corrupt. On what basis, then, can anyone suggest that "the antonym of the Qur'anic term *'umrān* is corruption (*fasād*)"?[167] In addition, the Prophet Hūd chastised his people for going to excess in *'umrān*, as stated in the Qur'an, "Do you construct on every elevation an edifice, amusing yourselves? And take for yourselves palaces and fortresses that you might abide eternally? And when you strike, you strike as tyrants. So fear God and obey me." (Q 26:128–31, b.o. Sahih Intl). Prophet Hūd's directives for the *'umrān* of his people focused on two essential dimensions: First, the disapproval of excess in *'umrān* ("amusing yourselves"), and second, the disapproval of setting that *'umrān* as an ultimate objective ("that you might abide eternally"). Hence, in addition to the fact that achieving *'umrān* is not included in the commandments of Revelation since the human being is already naturally inclined towards it, the Prophets came to forbid any excess in it, in order to maintain the environmental balance. They also came to forbid regarding it as an ultimate life goal, in order to maintain the spiritual balance, since that finite Divine blessing will not satiate human infinite aspirations to possession and pleasure and may, thus, end up misleading his soul and diverting it from its sound measures and balance.

Apart from the many theses of contemporary Muslim reformist thought influenced by Western material progress, and irrespective of the Qur'anic denotation of the concept of *'umrān*, the question that arises here is whether utilising the earth by means of construction, invention, development and discoveries is regarded as one of the duties for which the human being is created. Is this included in the concept of vicegerency and maintaining the balance? If the human being is entrusted to maintain the balance of the earth, as one of his existential functions, by preserving its "goodness," would it (*'umrān*) be deemed one of the aspects or meanings of such preservation?

Based on the previous discussion and investigation of the Qur'anic teleological reasons behind Revelation and creation, it appears that the endeavours in question do not fall under the duties for which the human being was created. This is because these achievements, as such, do not represent the very maintenance of the cosmic balance. In fact, they may contribute to disturbing the (spiritual, social and environmental) balance, which the human being was entrusted to maintain just as they may help in preserving it. Therefore, they do not carry an intrinsic value, in contrast to the objects that represent a very aspect of the maintenance of the balance. Moreover, they do not represent Divine actions, thus how could the human being perform them on behalf of God? This is not to say that the human being is not required to achieve *'umrān*, but what is meant here is that he is only required to achieve in terms of *'umrān* whatever helps him in performing his existential function, just like any other means to this effect.

To enable the human being to perform his existential duties, God created everything on Earth for the benefit of the human being, as stated in the Qur'an, "It is He who created for you all of that which is on the earth." (Q 2:29, Sahih Intl). God, for this purpose, subjugated for him (and not to him) the entire universe, as stated in the Qur'an, "God has made what is in the heavens and what is in the earth subservient for you." (Q 31:20, b.o. Shakir). Therefore, the human being is required to make an epistemic and practical use of the resources God provided that contributes to maintaining the spiritual, collective and environmental balances. In the acquisition of knowledge, for instance, through the discovery of cosmic laws (in addition to the laws of the soul and human society) resides spiritual elevation, as the human being has an absolute natural aspiration to knowledge ("He taught Adam all the names"). By virtue of discovery and knowledge, one can elevate and restore that innate nature. The use of that knowledge to develop the resources of the earth and make inventions can contribute to maintaining the balance. Indeed, myriad benefits are gained from investment and inventions in terms of alimentation, transportation, physical, and psychological health, communication, etc. Nevertheless, these are means that are likely to contribute to setting up the weight and maintain the balance, and not the balance itself. They may even contribute to disturbing it. Accordingly, any such investment, discovery, invention and knowledge used in such a way that disturbs the spiritual, collective or environmental balances is rejected from an Islamic perspective, and any of it contributing in its maintenance is required. However, as already highlighted, cultivation of the earth and the utilisation of its resources do not appear in Revelation as religious requirements since they are mainly stimulated spontaneously by the *fiṭra* and, hence, are not in need of religious injunctions, unless that natural spontaneous stimulation gets itself (exceptionally) disturbed.

Thus, *ʿimārat al-arḍ* in the material sense of construction, discovery, invention, thrive and investment is not the essential purpose of the human being's existence. Rather, it is only a (natural/instinctive) means for accomplishing the human being's mission on Earth. As for *ʿimārat al-arḍ* in the moral sense of administration, policy and organising the affairs of life at the social, economic, financial, legal, educational, cultural and other levels, this may directly fall under the maintenance of the collective balance if it results in its restoration. This is because it represents the very establishment of the equilibrium of the society, in contrast to the material sense of *ʿumrān*, which is not about restoring the balance of the earth, as we have seen. Nevertheless, *ʿumrān* in the moral sense does not appear to be a Qur'anic meaning of the concepts *ʿimārat al-arḍ* or *ʿumrān*. Consequently, once again, we find no justification to consider *ʿimārat al-arḍ* or *ʿumrān* as a Qur'anic value, let alone as one of the "higher Qur'anic governing objectives."

As for maintaining the environmental balance, it also cannot be defined in terms of *ʿimārat al-arḍ* in the sense of nurturing and utilising it. Rather, it is about the entrustment of the human being to preserve the existing environmental balance when he makes use of the earth, as noted. This function has two purposes: First, to maintain the balance of the earth in order that it remains suitable for the performance of the other human existential duties, which are maintaining the spiritual and collective balances; second, to maintain the balance of the earth in order to achieve harmony between the human being (and his society) and the earth, that is, for the sake of joining the environmental and cosmic Islam in general. We have quoted before many Qur'anic proofs in support of this purpose. Let us consider one of them, namely, God's saying,

> No person to whom God had given the Scripture, wisdom, and prophethood would ever say to people, "Be my servants, not God's." But (will say): "You should be *rabbāniyyīn* (godly servants) because you have taught the Scripture and studied it"; He would never command you to take angels and prophets as lords. How could he command you to be disbelievers after you had surrendered yourselves to God?; God took a pledge from the prophets, saying, "If, after I have bestowed Scripture and wisdom upon you, a messenger comes confirming what you have been given, you must believe in him and support him. Do you affirm this and accept My pledge as binding on you?" They said, "We do." He said, "Then bear witness and I too will bear witness."; Those who turn away after this are the *fāsiqūn* (perverts/trespassers).; Do they, then, seek a religion other than Allah's, while to Him surrenders (*aslama*, i.e. accepted Islam), willingly or unwillingly, whoever there is in the

> heavens and the earth and to Him are they brought back?; Say [Muḥammad], "We [Muslims] believe in God and in what has been sent down to us and to Abraham, Ishmael, Isaac, Jacob, and the Tribes. We believe in what has been given to Moses, Jesus, and the prophets from their Lord. We do not make a distinction between any of the [prophets]. It is to Him that we surrender ourselves."; If anyone seeks a religion other than complete surrender to God [*Islām*], it will not be accepted from him: he will be one of the losers in the Hereafter. (Q 3:79–85, b.o. Talal Itani).

The first three verses (79–81) speak about Revelation and the function of the Messengers in calling to *rabbāniyya* (to be godly servants). Then, the next verse (82) came to state that turning away from that is an act of exceeding the *fiṭra* (*fisq*). The next verse (83) came to show that those who are exceeding the *fiṭra* ("*fāsiqūn*") by rejecting the Prophets' messages are also exceeding the order of the universe, and that what Revelation contains is the religion of God adopted by the whole universe ("Do they, then, seek a religion other than Allah's…?") and that it is the universal Islam ("to Him surrenders (*aslama*, i.e. accepted Islam) whoever there is"). Then the following verse (84) came to show that the religion adopted by the universe is the same religion revealed to all Prophets without exception. Thus, there is no way to seek anything other than the standing order of the universe, as the last verse (85) concludes.

Other verses indicate that the disturbance of the spiritual balance entails a disturbance to the environmental balance,

> In their hearts is a disease, so Allah has increased their disease: agonising torment awaits them for their persistent lying. When it is said to them, "Do not cause corruption in the earth," they say, "We are only good-doers," but really they are causing corruption, though they do not realise it.
>
> (Q 2:10–12, b.o. Ahmad Khan)

Therefore, there is no way to enter into peace (*salām*) with the environment and the universe unless the human being seeks to achieve peace within himself.

This is the purpose of creating the earth and subjugating it for the human being. His function is to utilise it to achieve the spiritual and collective balances in a way that does not violate the environmental balance and helps the human being join cosmic peace and Islam. This contradicts many contemporary researchers' opinion that the human being's duty is to dominate the earth, subjugate and control it and have lordship over it or such other views that we have shown to be unfounded. Since joining cosmic Islam is achieved through the human being's performance of his peculiar worship (vicegerency) and since vicegerency enables the human being to achieve harmony and peace within himself and in his society, the Qur'an stated that one of the teleological purposes behind Revelation is guiding those who adhere to their existential duty to the "paths of peace" (Q 10:16), or to "the abode of peace" (Q 10:25) or to "The integral peace" (Q 2:208), i.e., peace in all its manifestations and with all those in it.

This chapter concludes that the object of vicegerency comprises three aspects in maintaining the cosmic balance: The spiritual balance, the social balance and the environmental balance, as shown in Figure 6.1. We may thus define vicegerency as God's entrustment of the human being to act on His behalf in striving to preserve the balance that God has established in the human soul, society and in this natural environment, and to strive to restore any deficiency affecting it. According to our thorough and holistic examination of the Qur'an, this is the existential function for which man was created and established on Earth and for which Revelation was sent to him. This function goes in line with the natural disposition (*fiṭra*) instilled in the human being, and by its performance, the human being can join cosmic Islam. On the basis of our proposed classifications and topologies of the governing Islamic concepts and principles, we have demonstrated the correlation of this human function with all other Qur'anic teleological rationales behind Revelation and the creation of the human being and the universe, as well as with other major principles of Islam. The systematic cohesion of a whole corpus has emerged through the junction of vicegerency, the cosmic order, worship, monotheism, *fiṭra*, *tazkiya*, trust (*amāna*), peace (*salām*), commanding *ma'rūf* and forbidding *munkar*, God's Beautiful Names and Supreme Attributes, and many other central Islamic concepts converging to this end. This has clarified the position of vicegerency in the Qur'anic worldview of existence, universe and human being, in a way that discloses the contours of a vicegerency theory and a coherent and systematic Islamic worldview.

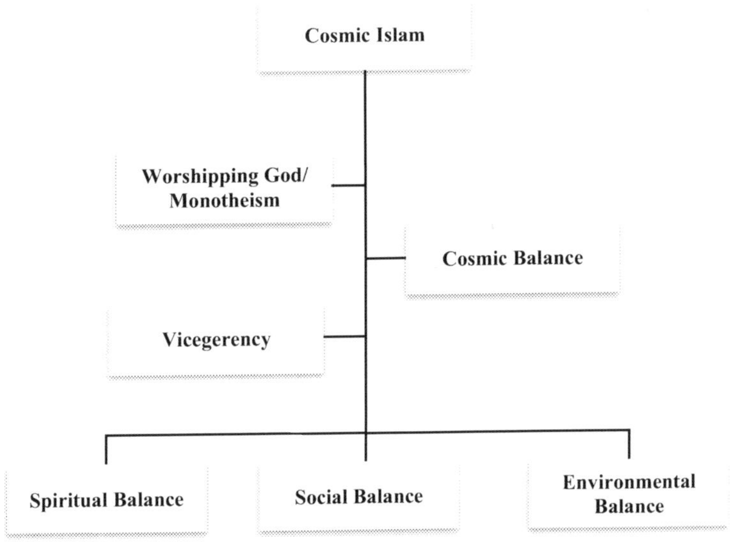


*Figure 6.1* The human existential function consists of maintaining three aspects of the overall cosmic balance on behalf of God. These three objects of vicegerency constitute human worship. By performing his peculiar worship, the human being partakes in the overall cosmic worship and enrols in cosmic Islam.

## Notes

1 Al-Qaraḍāwī, *Qīmat al-Insān*, 27.
2 An Arabic preposition indicating justification, rationale or motivation, e.g., "in order to," "for the purpose of," "so that," etc.
3 Ibid., 21.
4 Ibid., 25.
5 Ibid., 26.
6 The exegetes differed over *lām al-ta'līl* (so that/in order that) in this verse as to whether it relates to the creation of the universe or the descent of His command in it, as mentioned in the verse. We believe that it relates to the latter as the human being's knowledge of the Divine competence and the encompassment of His knowledge has to do with what the human being perceives and learns from the universal order. If the universe was not in correspondence to the human being's cognitive and perceptual abilities in such a way that enables him/her to realise the magnificence of this order's complexity and fine-tuning, he/she would fail to acquire the knowledge referred to in His saying *li-ta'lamū* (so you may know). Such knowledge cannot be attained in a universe where things occur unbound by perceived laws and causes. This view is further substantiated by God's saying, "Allah is He Who raised the heavens without any pillars that you can see. Then, He *istawā* (rose above) the Throne [in a manner that suits His Majesty]. He has subjected the sun and the moon (to continue going round)! Each running (its course) for a term appointed. He regulates all affairs, explaining the signs in detail, that you may believe with certainty in the meeting with your Lord. And it is He Who spread out the earth, and placed therein firm mountains and rivers and of every kind of fruits He made two in pairs. He brings the night as a cover over the day. Verily, in these things, there are signs for people who reflect. And in the earth are neighbouring tracts, and gardens of vines, and green crops (fields etc.), and date-palms, growing out two or three from a single stem root, or otherwise (one stem root for every palm), watered with the same water, yet some of them We make more excellent than others to eat. Verily, in these things, there are signs for people who understand." (Q 13:2–4, Hilali & Khan). Thus, certainty ("that you may believe with certainty"), reflection ("signs for people who reflect") and understanding ("for people who understand") are some of the reasons behind creating the creation with that regulated perceptible order (i.e., subjugation, running through course for an appointed term, regulating the affairs, explaining the signs, etc.). Hence, the main reason for which God has established the universe on determined laws and causal relations between its elements, is for the human being to grasp the greatness of its Author and to be able to utilise it for the sake of his (spiritual, intellectual, social, material, etc.) endeavours. However, these laws are but relative to the human being. Beyond this fact, God does not need the laws of the universe and acts in it without any means or intermediary. Nor is there a causality between its elements for God, Who transcends space, time, causality and any other thinkable laws. This can be understood from several verses in the Qur'an, for instance: "When He wills a thing He has only to say: 'Be,' and it is." (Q 36:82, Ahmad Ali). A case in point here are God's words: "Have you not considered your Lord – how He extends the shadow? If He willed, He could have made it stationary. Then (later, "*thumma*") We made the sun for it a justification." (Q 25:45, b.o. Sahih Intl). Consequently, for God, the shadow and the sun are two different creatures without relation between them. If He had willed, the shadows of things could have been stationary despite the position of the sun. In other words, for God, shadow is not a consequence of the sun (light). It is, however, later ("*thumma*"), after He has created both (independently), that God installed a relation between them by making the sun (light) the cause ("a justification") of shadow. This fact will remain difficult to conceive for the human being due to the impossibility (at least in this world) of conceiving the essence of a Being that transcends time and

space, the way (how) He creates *ex nihilo*, and many other aspects of the imperceptible world (*ghayb*) that do not respond to the laws of our world. Another verse that indicates that God creates things independently before relating them with their cause is His saying: "You did not kill them; rather, it was Allah who killed them; and you did not throw when you threw, rather, it was Allah who threw." (Q 8:17, Ali Qarai). There is no doubt about the fact that the Muslim army killed some of the soldiers of the army of Quraysh with their swords during the battle of Badr, and that it was the Prophet (ﷺ) who threw sand at them. Nevertheless, the Qur'an here is denying these facts because it is talking about the first Divine creation before those creations were linked with their cause. Indeed, it is God who creates phenomena and actions (killing, throwing the sand) without any cause, just like he moves the shadow without any cause. However, he linked those creations to a perceptible cause. This becomes clearer in the last part of the verse as both acts of creation are explicitly referred to, the creation related to its cause: "you threw (the sand)," the Prophet (ﷺ) being the cause (and the chooser) of this act; and the independent creation "Allah threw." The latter may have effects that the former could never achieve, in other words; God achieves with His independent creation that which could not be achieved by his causal creation, like the case of miracles, as was the case of the effect of the sand-throw of the Prophet. This is the reason why the Qur'an did not say, "You did not kill them when you killed them," while adding in the second part, "when you threw." Because that throwing had a miraculous effect (the sand reached the eyes of all the enemies), so the independent creation of God here had an effect that is usually not a consequence of the cause of that creation, therefore a clear distinction was made between "you threw" and "Allah threw." In contrast, His independent creation of killing is usually linked to the cause of that act (the swords here), therefore the Qur'an did not add, "when you killed them," because that's an obvious consequence of their action. This is also understood from the following verse: "And Allah has made for you from your homes a place of rest and made for you from the hides of the animals tents which you find light on your day of travel and your day of encampment; and from their wool, fur and hair He has made furniture and enjoyment for a time." (Q 16:80, b.o. Sahih Intl). The fact that tents and furniture are a consequence of the actions of the human being is obvious; hence, there was no need to mention it here besides God's independent creation of those items. Another example includes "Did they not see the birds above them, stretching out, and flapping their wings? Nothing keeps them up in the sky except the Beneficent God. He certainly watches over all things." (Q 67:19, b.o. Sarwar). This verse mentions the obvious cause of why birds hold in the sky ("stretching out and flapping their wings"), however, this cause was discarded since it is only relative to our perception, and the only cause that was retained is God's direct independent action in this regard. The same applies to the aspects of the cosmic balance that the human being is entrusted to maintain on behalf of God (the spiritual and social balances) as will be elaborated below. These are initially maintained by God through His independent action. The endeavours of the human being to maintain these aspects of the cosmic balance and the means implemented to that effect are only relative to the human perception (they are God's indirect action). For the maintenance of the spiritual balance, this appears, inter alia, in His saying, "Were it not for the favour and mercy of God, none of you would ever have been spiritually purified, but God purifies whomever He wants." (Q 24:21, b.o. Sarwar). As for the maintenance of the social balance, we can mention God's saying, "And He has united their (i.e., believers') hearts. If you had spent all that is in the earth, you could not have united their hearts, but Allah has united them." (Q 8:63, Hilali & Khan).

Remark: After refuting the tenants of *waḥdat al-wujūd*'s interpretation of the above verse (Q 8:17), in the sense that the human being is the incarnation of God, that he is deprived of choice and that his actions are but the actions of God, ibn Taymiyya says: "If we assume that what is meant by this verse is that God created the actions of the humans, then this meaning is true [...] but that does not mean that God is the human and that the existence of the Creator is the existence of the created, nor that God is incarnated in the human being." Ibn Taymiyya, *Majmū' al-Fatāwā*, vol. 2, 323. Indeed, any refutation by ibn Taymiyya (and even ibn al-Qayyim) of the interpretation of the verse in the way we did, i.e., that God creates the actions of the human being (both independent from a cause and with a cause), is to be considered in the context of his refutation of incarnation and anthropomorphism, not in an absolute manner.

7 See for instance: Muḥammad Abū Ḥāmid al-Ghazzālī, *Shifā' al-Ghalīl fī Bayān al-Shabah wa-l-Mukhayyal wa-Masālik al-Ta'līl* [The Satisfaction of the Thirst in Explaining Resemblance, Ambiguity and the Methods of Rationalization] (Bagdad: Maktabat al-Irshād, 1971), 23–106; and Aṣīl Muḥammad Kāẓim and Maḥmūd 'Abd Ḥamad, "Asālīb al-Ta'līl wa-Dalālatuhā fī l-Qur'ān al-Karīm" [The Methods of Rationalization and Their Meanings in the Noble Qur'an], *Journal of al-Qādisiyya fī l-'Ādāb wa-l-'Ulūm al-Tarbawiyya* no. 2 (Sept. 2005).

8 Q 11:26, 50, 61, 84; Q 17:2; Q 18:110; Q 21:25, 108; Q 27:45; and Q 41:14.

9 Q 11:2–3.

10 Q 16:36.

11 Q 98:5.

12 Q 48:9.

13 Q 2:185; Q 21:48; and Q 25:1.

14 Q 6:19, 92; Q 7:2; Q 10:2; Q 25:1; Q 26:194; Q 32:2; Q 35:23; Q 36:6, 7; Q 38:70; Q 46:9; and Q 53:56.

15 Q 16:2.

16 Q 6:130; Q 17:10; Q 18:2; and Q 26:7.

17 Q 16:89 and Q 12:111.

18 Q 2:2, 185; Q 3:4; Q 5:44, 46; Q 6:91; Q 10:57; Q 12:111; Q 16:64, 89, 106; Q 17:2, 9; Q 23:49; Q 27:2, 77; Q 31:2; Q 35:54; Q 41:44; Q 45:20; and Q 46:30.

19 Q 5:16.

20 Q 10:57; Q 12:111; Q 16:64, 89; Q 17:82; Q 21:107; Q 27:77; Q 29:51; Q 31:3; Q 44:6; and Q 45:20.

21 Q 10:57; Q 17:82; and Q 41:44.

22 Q 10:2; Q 16:89, 106; Q 18:2; and Q 27:2.

23 Q 2:119, 213; Q 4:165; Q 6:48; Q 10:2; Q 18:56; Q 25:56; Q 33:45; Q 34:28; Q 35:24; and Q 46:12.

24 Q 16:106.

25 Q 33:8.

26 Q 2:231; Q 5:46; and Q 10:57.

27 Q 2:151; Q 3:164; and Q 62:2.

28 Q 8:24 and Q 26:52.

29 Q 2:151.

30 Q 2:213 and Q 4:105.

31 Q 14:1, 5; Q 57:9; Q 65:11; and Q 5:16.

32 Q 2:221; Q 6:90; Q 7:2; Q 17:41; Q 20:3, 99, 113; Q 21:10, 48; Q 23:71; Q 29:51; Q 38:29, 87; Q 40:54; Q 41:41; Q 43:44; Q 44:58; Q 65:10; Q 68:52; Q 69:48; Q 80:11; Q 81:28; and Q 88:21.

33 Q 55:2–9. This is the only explicit teleological reason behind all three main existential phenomena and their subcategories (Revelation, human creation, human nature, cosmic worship, creation of the universe and cosmic harmony), as already noted.

34 Q 57:25.

35 Q 42:13.

36 Q 4:165; Q 6:156–57; and Q 36:70.

37 Q 2:219 and Q 16:44.

38 Q 2:242.

39 Q 20:113.

40 Q 16:89 and Q 33:45.
41 Q 2:143 and Q 22:78.
42 Q 45:20.
43 Q 3:79.
44 Q 51:56.
45 Q 11:119.
46 Q 2:30.
47 Q 33:72.
48 Q 55:3–9.
49 Q 67:2 and Q 76:2.
50 Q 16:78 and Q 31:14.
51 Q 7:129 and Q 10:14.
52 Q 55:4–9.
53 Q 22:5.
54 Q 40:67.
55 Q 7:172–73.
56 Q 49:13.
57 Q 43:32.
58 Q 55:5–9.
59 Q 65:12.
60 Q 11:7; Q 18:7; and Q 57:25.
61 Q 10:4 and Q 34:4.
62 Q 45:22 and Q 53:31.
63 Q 16:81.
64 Q 16:14; Q 17:66; Q 28:73; Q 35:12; and Q 45:16.
65 Q 28:73.
66 Q 25:48 and Q 30:46.
67 Q 31:31; Q 28:73; Q 78:33; and Q 80:32.
68 Q 31:31 and Q 50:8.
69 Q 25:50, 62; Q 43:13; Q 50:8; Q 51:49; Q 56:73.
70 Q 16:14; Q 25:62; Q 28:73; Q 30:46; Q 35:12; and Q 45:12.
71 Q 2:22 and Q 50:11.
72 Such reasons turn up when the sequence of teleological questions comes to a halt, leaving no room for further why-questions. For example, one may ask, "Why did God create the human being?" to which it could be answered, "To be a vicegerent," which could be followed by the question, "Why did God appoint the human being as a vicegerent?" to which it could be answered, "Because this dignifies the human being over and above any other creature," then comes the question "Why would God want to dignify the human being over and above any other creature?" to which it could be answered, "Because one of God's attributes is *al-Rāfi'* (the One who elevates or promotes) and this entails the elevation of a creature above others as an effect of the Divine perfection." At this point, we arrive at an ontological reason that leaves no room for more why-questions. That is, there is no room for asking, "Why is God *al-Rāfi'*?" because this is similar to asking, "Why is God God?" As noted before, this is why the Qur'an describes both the decent of Revelation and the creation of the universe (including humans), i.e., the three main existential phenomena, as occurring with the Truth (al-Ḥaqq). Indeed they draw their very existence from an ontologically established Truth which closes the teleological chain of truths and beyond which there is no truth, God's names and attributes. Ibn al-Qayyim notes, "Since these Attributes signify perfection, they must have resultant effects, and if all of the creation were like the angels, these Attributes would not be manifested. Such effects include the manifestation of His Names signifying His forbearance, lenience, forgiveness, and covering up of sins, clemency in exacting His rights and emancipating whoever He wishes of His slaves." Ibn al-Qayyim, *Madārij al-Sālikīn*, vol. 2, 191.

73 The evidence that God has created the universe based on harmony and equity is found in the contrast between equity and causing deficiency to the cosmic balance in God's saying, "And set up the weight with equity and do not diminish the balance." (Q 55:9). Thus, the creatures in the universe achieve equity by executing their respective functions in contribution to the cosmic balance.

74 In its linguistic sense, *tazkiya* signifies purification and growth. See ibn Manẓūr, *Lisān al-'Arab*, vol. 14, 358. The relevance of such purification and elevation to spirituality is seen through the association of *tazkiya* with the soul in the Qur'an (for instance, Q 91:9, Q 35:18). The Qur'an attributes *tazkiya* as a religious assignment to the human soul only. This does not conflict with *tazkiya*'s relevance to society and other aspects of human life and interactions, in the sense of purifying them from what contradicts the innate human nature and the human being's ethical (individual and collective) elevation. Yet, the spiritual aspect remains the basis and pivot of *tazkiya* as indicated by several verses (including Q 26:88–89). For instance, charity/alms, which is one of the identified teleological purposes, is called *zakāt* in the Qur'an. Being from the same root as *tazkiya*, it also refers to purification and growth/increase/elevation. However, this *tazkiya* is not directly attributed to money. The Qur'an did not clearly state that *zakāt* is the purification and increase of money or that that is an objective behind *zakāt*, even though it did say that multiplication (of wealth and reward) is a consequence of *zakāt* (and not *zakāt* itself) that is given with a sincere intention as in Q 30:39. On the other hand, the Qur'an did clearly use *zakāt* in relation to the purity and elevation of the human soul as in Q 18:81 and 19:13. Indeed, the first object and objective of purification and elevation (*zakāt/tazkiya*) through charity is the human soul, not the money. This is clearly established in the following verses, "Take charity from their possessions to cleanse them and purify them (*tuzakkīhim*) thereby" (Q 9:103, Ali Qarai), and "Far removed from it [hellfire] will be the righteous, he who gives his wealth to purify himself (*yatazakkā*)." (Q 92:17–18, b.o. Ali Qarai and Pickthall).

75 Al-Iṣfahānī, *al-Mufradāt fī Gharīb al-Qur'ān*, 868–69.

76 Ibn 'Āshūr, *al-Taḥrīr wa-l-Tanwīr*, vol. 27, 240.

77 We do not mention "intellectual" or "rational" here, as reason, according to the Qur'an, is a part of the human spirit (*rūḥ*) as it shall be explained below.

78 And may itself cause diminishment of other tendencies and aspirations in a vicious circle, as will be explained below.

79 The pioneers of the Sufī and ethical thought summarised *tazkiya* in *takhliya* (purgation) and *taḥliya* (replenishment). *Takhliya* means to liberate the heart from whatever thwarts its soundness as all the diseases that afflict the heart result from the lack of such liberation. If such *takhliya* takes place, *taḥliya* occurs spontaneously since the heart that is free from transgression restores the *fiṭra* of monotheism and balance instilled in it.

80 See for example: 'Abd Allāh ibn Qutayba, *Gharīb al-Qur'ān* [Lexical Complexities in the Qur'an], ed. Aḥmad Ṣaqr (Beirut: Dār al-Kutub al-'Ilmiyya, 1978), 436.

81 Al-Iṣfahānī, *Mufradāt Gharīb al-Quran*, 636.

82 Riḍā, *Tafsīr al-Manār*, vol. 10, 211.

83 Nūrsī, *Ishārāt al-I'jāz fī Maẓān al-'Ījāz*, 208.

84 For example: Q 2:26–27, 282.

85 See: Ibn 'Āshūr, *al-Taḥrīr wa-l-Tanwīr*, vol. 27, 85.

86 Al-Ṭabarī, *Jāmi' al-Bayān*, vol. 24, 368.

87 Ibn 'Āshūr, *al-Taḥrīr wa-l-Tanwīr*, vol. 30, 276.

88 Ibn 'Āshūr said, "This means that God guides every being to that which it was created for. [...] The verse means that God created the due proportions of everything and guided all beings to perform their duties as He determined." Ibid., vol. 30, 277.

89 By "soul" (*nafs*) we mean the human being's spirit (*rūḥ*) when present in this life and in connection to the material body, the Qur'an refers to this either as *nafs* or *qalb* (heart).

90 Ibn Kathīr, *Tafsīr al-Qur'ān al-'Aẓīm*, vol. 8, 399.

91 Mujāhid al-Makhzūmī, *Tafsīr Mujāhid*, ed. Muḥammad ʿAbd al-Salām (Egypt: Dār al-Fikr al-Islāmī al-Ḥadīth, 1989), 737.
92 See: Jaafar Sheikh Idris, "al-Taṣawwur al-Islāmī li-l-Insān Asāsun li-Falsafat al-Islām al-Tarbawiyya" [The Islamic Perception of the Human Being as Basis for an Islamic Educational Philosophy], *al-Muslim al-Muʿāṣir*, Issue 12 (September 1977), 73.
93 See: Ibn ʿĀshūr, *al-Taḥrīr wa-l-Tanwīr*, vol. 30, 370.
94 Ibid.
95 Al-Iṣfahānī wrote: "Piety in the Islamic terminology means the preservation of the soul against vice." Al-Iṣfahānī, *al-Mufradāt fī Gharīb al-Qurʾān*, 881. Hence, to have *taqwā* is to be in a state where one has developed a spiritual protection that repels what may affect the weight and balance of his natural tendencies.
96 Makkī ibn Abī Ṭālib, *al-Hidāya ilā Bulūgh al-Nihāya fī ʿIlm Maʿānī al-Qurʾān wa-Tafsīrih wa-Aḥkāmih, wa-Jumal min Funūn ʿUlūmih* [Qurʾanic Lexicography, Exegesis, Jurisprudence and Disciplines] (Sharjah: Faculty of *Sharīʿa* and Islamic Studies, University of Sharjah, 2008), vol. 6, 4281.
97 Ibn al-Qayyim, *Shifāʾ al-ʿAlīl*, 301–2.
98 Muslim (no. 1077).
99 As for the narration attributed to the prophet (ﷺ) suggesting that this testimony happened on earth, it was rejected by several scholars such as Ibn Taymiyya, and his student ibn Kathīr.
100 See some of those in ibn Manẓūr, *Lisān al-ʿArab*, vol. 3, 155.
101 Al-Ṭabarī, *Jāmiʿ al-Bayān*, vol. 138.
102 This is established, for instance, by Q 2:30; Q 42:5; Q 39:75; and Q 40:7.
103 Q 7:43; Q 10:10; Q 17:52; Q 35:34; and Q 39:74; furthermore, the Qurʾan indicates that *ḥamd* is, overall, something especially prevailing in the hereafter, "and to Him belongs [all] praise in the Hereafter" (Q 34:1, Sahih Intl). In another verse it is attributed to both worlds, "And He is Allah; there is no deity except Him. To Him is [due all] praise in the first [life] and the Hereafter." (Q 28:70, Sahih Intl). This contrasts with *shukr*, which is never ascribed to humans in the context of the hereafter.
104 That is why there will be only *ḥamd* and no *shukr* in the hereafter for the human being, since his earthly mission is finished while *shukr* is a voluntary task, contrary to *ḥamd*, which he will perform instinctively in the hereafter, as in the saying of the prophet that the people of paradise "will instinctively perform glorification and praise (*ḥamd*) the same way you instinctively breathe." Narrated by Muslim in his *Ṣaḥīḥ* (no. 2835).
105 See for instance: ibn Manẓūr, *Lisān al-ʿArab*, vol. 3, 155–56.
106 See for instance: ibn al-Qayyim, *Madārij al-Sālikīn*, vol. 2, 238.
107 Even evil and sin belong to His cosmic will as noted before. However, *ḥamd* that includes *shukr* is a more complete expression of gratitude, which is why the Qurʾan calls people to that kind of gratefulness.
108 For instance: Q 2:152; Q 14:7; Q 24:40; Q 31:12; Q 34:15–17; Q 39:7; Q 76:3.
109 This is confirmed, for instance, by God's words, "And to Him belongs praise (*ḥamd*) in the heavens and the earth, and at nightfall and when you are at midday." (Q 30:18, Muhammad Shakir); and, "All that is in the heavens and the earth glorify God. To Him belongs the Kingdom and the praise (*ḥamd*). He has power over all things." (Q 64:1, b.o. Muhammad Shakir). The first verse confirms that praise is always in effect in the universe and that human praise (of which prayers "at nightfall and when you are at midday" are an expression) does not change anything to that cosmic fact, but it is only for his own sake, as explained by ibn ʿĀshūr. Ibn ʿĀshūr, *al-Taḥrīr wa-l-Tanwīr*, vol. 21, 66. As for the second verse, it suggests that the established cosmic praise is a consequence of the cosmic worship. Indeed, as we have explained, the elements of the universe manifest praise by performing their existential function.
110 For instance: Q 2:243; Q 7:10, 17; Q 10:60; Q 12:38; Q 23:78; Q 27:73; Q 32:9; Q 40:61; Q 67:23.
111 For instance: Q 3:144–45; Q 4:147; Q 14:7; Q 34:13; Q 54:35.
112 Q 5:6.

113 Q 3:123.
114 Q 27:40 and Q 31:12.
115 Q 2:185.
116 Q 5:89.
117 Q 8:26.
118 Q 2:52.
119 Q 8:26 and Q 14:37.
120 The ascription of the spirit to God that was blown into the human being does not mean that a part of God's essence resides in the human being or that the human spirit is Divine in its essence, i.e., that the human being is a small God or that he is God's incarnation. Rather, God ascribed that spirit to Himself because, compared to other creatures, it is made of a particular nature only known by Him, as indicated by the Qur'an, "They ask you about the Spirit. Say, 'The Spirit is part of my Lord's domain and you have only been given a little knowledge.'" (Q 17:85). Ibn 'Āshūr writes, "The addition of the spirit to the pronoun of majesty ['His Spirit'] is to point out that amazing secret whose composition is known only to God Almighty. The addition indicates that he is one of God's most particular creatures, otherwise, all creatures are God's." Ibn 'Āshūr *al-Taḥrīr wa-l-Tanwīr*, vol. 21, 217.
121 Indeed, according to the Qur'an, hearing, sight and hearts (i.e., emotion, intellect, etc.) are spiritual faculties that the human being exercises in this worldly life through the interface of his earthly body (auditory, visual and nervous systems) in a bridled manner. Therefore, after he leaves his body, the veil (i.e., that bridle) will be lifted and he will be able to hear, see and understand that which he could not during his earthly life (such as God Himself), as indicated by many Qur'an verses.
122 This was well understood by Iblīs (Satan) since, before being banished to Earth, he promised God that his ultimate purpose will be to prevent the human being from being grateful (*shākir*), as in Q 7:17.
123 That is why the supplication of the righteous people to whom the Qur'an promises paradise (Q 46:16) contains the fact that they ask God, "My Lord, enable me to be grateful for Your favour which You have bestowed upon me" (Q 46:15, Sahih Intl), which was also a supplication of the prophet Sulaymān (Solomon) (Q 27:19). Hence, gratefulness (*shukr*) is not something that is taken for granted, but rather an ideal the enablement of which is coveted by the pious and the prophets. Also, it is reported that the prophet (ﷺ) used to offer night prayer until his feet became swollen. His wife 'Ā'isha asked him "O messenger of God, why are you doing this while God has forgiven your faults of the past and those to follow?" He replied, "Shouldn't I be an all-grateful (*shakūr*) servant?" Narrated by Muslim in his *Ṣaḥīḥ* (no. 2820). He replied with the same to some of his companions when being asked that question (al-Bukhārī, no. 1130). Hence the prophet was teaching his companions that (ritual) worship is not only about clearing oneself from sin and for the only sake of paradise, but it is also to reach a stage of awareness of God's favours in order to become an all-grateful (*shakūr*) servant.
124 Q 2:151; Q 3:164; Q 62:2.
125 The relation between knowledge and the breathing of the spirit also appears in God's saying, "[It is God] who gave everything its perfect form. He first created the human being from clay, then made his offspring from the extract of base fluid, then He harmoniously fashioned him; He breathed from His Spirit into him and gave you hearing, sight, and hearts. And yet how little are the thanks you offer!" (Q 32:7–9). Thus, "hearing, sight, and hearts" are resultants of the Divine breathing. These verses followed a speech on the management of the affairs of the universe and that God entrusted the human being to carry out part of this management given this "Breath" as we shall elaborate below.
126 This appears through a countless number of Qur'anic arguments, some of which we discussed before, like, for instance, the fact that the angels were commanded to prostrate to Adam (the human being) in virtue of the Divine insufflation of the spirit in the

human being and that God justified the vicegerency of man by the spiritual faculties he was granted. Also, as discussed, the humanness of the human being and him being truly alive or death, as per the Qur'an, does not depend on his body but on his spiritual status, etc.

127 The fact that the features of this earthly life do not correspond to the deep aspirations of the human being and, hence, are not able to satisfy them, appears through many Qur'anic angles. For instance, the Qur'an qualifies the pleasures and beauties of this life as ornaments (*zīna*), or that it has been ornamented (*zuyyina*) for the human being, denoting the idea that its features are only apparent and finite pleasures that will not truly satisfy the human aspirations. For instance, the Qur'an reads, "Whatever you have been given is a provision for the life of this world and an adornment of it (*zīnatuhā*). But that which is with Allah is better and more enduring. Do you not use your intellect?" (Q 28:60, b.o. Maududi and Ahmad Khan); "Adorned (*zuyyina*) for the people is the love of desires, such as women, and children, and piles upon piles of gold and silver, and branded horses, and livestock, and fields. These are the conveniences of the worldly life, but with God lies the finest resort." (Q 3:14, Talal Itani). Furthermore, the Qur'an highlights the fact that the purpose of this adornment of which the earthly life disposes is to test the human being and that it is only temporary (finite). For instance: "Indeed We have made whatever is on the earth an adornment (*zīnatan*) for it that We may test them [to see] which of them is best in conduct. And indeed We will turn whatever is on it into a barren plain." (Q 18:7–8, Ali Qarai). Moreover, this worldly adornment, according to the Qur'an, is not pure (absolute): "Say, 'Who has forbidden the adornment (*zīna*) of Allah which He has brought forth for His servants, and the good things of [His] provision?' Say, 'These will be, for the faithful in the life of this world, pure on the Day of Resurrection.' Thus do We elaborate the signs for a people who have knowledge." (Q 7:32, b.o. Ali Qarai). Hence the finite, restricted and smeared pleasures one enjoys in this world will be "pure" (absolute) in the Hereafter, thus corresponding to the initial aspirations of the human being. This knowledge referred to in the above verses (i.e., about the fact that this world was not created to meet the real aspirations of the human being), is an innate knowledge that the human being is commanded to restore by purifying his soul. Therefore, the Qur'an says, after talking about the reverence of the heart to the remembrance of God and to the truth, "Know that the present life is just a game, a diversion, an ornament (*zīna*), a cause of boasting among you, of rivalry for more and more in wealth and children. It is like plants that spring up after the rain: Their growth at first delights the sowers, but then you see them wither away, turn yellow, and become stubble. There is terrible punishment in the next life as well as forgiveness and approval from God; the life of this world is only a misleading pleasure. So race for your Lord's forgiveness and a Garden as wide as the heavens and earth." (Q 57:20–21, b.o. Arberry). These verses point out that what is in this world will not meet the innate aspiration of the soul ("misleading pleasure"), that the expanse of paradise is as absolute as the aspirations of the human soul, and that this is an innate knowledge ("know") that may be restored by purification of the soul and maintaining the spiritual balance.

128 Different classical Muslim scholars considered that there is no such thing as absolute/pure pleasures or benefits/interest (*maṣāliḥ*) in this earthly life, not even in worshipping God. This is not only on account that those pleasures/benefits are finite, but also because one cannot reach them without a portion of inextricable difficulties and some degree of hardship. Al-Shāṭibī, for instance, wrote: "Worldly interests – to the extent that they exist up here – cannot be pure interests. I mean by interests: that which relates to the establishment of human life, to its perfection and to the satisfaction of human desires and intellectual needs in an absolute manner, so that he is in absolute state of enjoyment. This is normally speaking impossible; indeed, those interests entail more or less significant burdens and difficulties associated with, preceding or

followed them." Al-Shāṭibī, *Al-Muwāfaqāt*, vol. 2, 44. The reason for this, according to al-Shāṭibī, is that this temporary life was only intended to test the human being and to distinguish between the good and wrong-doers (and thus not intended to fully satisfy human aspirations). Ibid. This opinion, which we adopt in our elaboration above, is in agreement with Hellenistic Hedonism, since it defines human (worldly and otherworldly) wellbeing and interests (*maṣāliḥ*) in terms of (physical) pleasure (*ladhdha*) and (moral/spiritual) joy (*faraḥ*). Among the most notable scholars who elaborated on this, in addition to al-Shāṭibī, we can name ʿIzz al-Dīn ibn ʿAbd al-Salām (660/1262) and Fakhr al-Dīn al-Rāzī (d. 606/1209). Nevertheless, the portrayal of the ultimate reward for the human being in terms of pleasure and joy is abundant in the Qurʾan. This (pleasure and joy, i.e., human wellbeing) is, according to the Qurʾan, the outcome of the faithfulness to both *fiṭra* and Revelation in this world and in the Hereafter. It is even the outcome of the biggest reward in the Hereafter that is reserved for the righteous people only, which is seeing God. Commenting on some Prophetic reports denoting the pleasure of looking at God in the Hereafter, ibn Taymiyya wrote, "Pleasure is thus linked to looking at Him; they don't love anything more than looking at Him because of the pleasure that procures." Ibn Taymiyya, *Majmūʿ al-Fatāwā*, vol. 7, 537.

129 Moreover, the risk to transgress the balance will always exist due to the infinite aspirations of the human being. When arriving at fulfilled proportions in some of his aspirations, he will tend to transgress them, as indicated by the verses that directly followed the first revealed verses of the Qurʾan, which establish the fact that the human being was endowed with the innate knowledge (resulting from the Divine insufflation and formation according to His image), "Indeed, the human being transgresses when he considers himself fulfilled." (Q 96:6–7). So, the human being tends to transgression when he does not strive to maintain the balance, which opens the way to his fulfilled proportions, propelled by his infinite aspirations, to go beyond their measures. Therefore, even if he achieves balance in some of his aspirations after he had set up their weight, he must be constantly striving for its maintenance.

130 Al-Bukhārī (no. 6227), and Muslim (no. 2612).

131 Ibn Taymiyya, *Bayān Talbīs al-Jahmiyya*, vol. 7, 373–77.

132 Ibid., vol. 7, 131. Ibn Taymiyya further said: "I have demonstrated, when discussing the interpretation of those who said that it [the fact that Adam was created in the image of God] means the attributes and intangible image, that I do not dispute the validity of accurate meanings, such as the fact that a human being has names, attributes and actions as per their interpretation of the *Ḥadīth* [i.e., the *Ḥadīth* that 'God has created Adam in His image'] in attributing human likeness of names, attributes and actions to God. I have no interest in disputing their interpretation of the meaning of this *Ḥadīth* on that basis." Ibid., vol. 6, 579.

133 As noted before, when the angels were asked to inform God about the names Adam was taught, they replied that (in contrast to Adam) they don't have the required faculty for that, and that that is initially an exclusive divine attribute ("Indeed, it is You who is the Knowing, the wise"). Hence, the human carries this divine attribute in an unequalled manner.

134 Ibn ʿĀshūr, *al-Taḥrīr wa-l-Tanwīr*, vol. 2, 301.

135 These include also: Q 9:112, 71; Q 22:41.

136 Ibn Taymiyya, *Bayān Talbīs al-Jahmiyya*, vol. 4, 602.

137 Ibn Taymiyya, *Majmūʿ al-Fatāwā*, vol. 4, 32.

138 Ibn ʿĀshūr, *Maqāṣid al-Sharīʿa al-Islāmiyya*, 266–67.

139 Ibid., 265–66.

140 Tājj al-Dīn al-Subkī, *al-Ashbāh wa-l-Naẓāʾir* [Similar Legal Maxims and Norms] (Beirut: Dār al-Kutub al-ʿIlmiyya, 1991), vol. 1, 368. For a more detailed elaboration on this maxim see: Chauki Lazhar and Khadija Tamaazousti, *Maternité et Islam* (Doha: Research Center for Islamic Legislation and Ethics, College of Islamic

Studies, 2018), 86–87, and 104–5. We also elaborated on this maxim in detail in our book manuscript, *Mafhūm al-Ijtihād bayna al-Iṣṭilāḥ al-Fiqhī wa Takāmul al-Maʿrifa* [The Concept of *Ijtihād* between the Terminology of *Fiqh* and the Complementarity of Knowledge].

141 See: Chauki Lazhar and Khadija Tamaazousti, *al-Umūma wa-l-Unūtha fī al-Islām wa-l-Tamyīz bayna al-Marʾa wa-l-Rajul fī al-Aḥkām al-Sharʿiyya* [Motherhood, Femininity and Gender Differentiation in Islamic Provisions] (Doha: Hamad Bin Khalifa University Press, 2019), 50.

142 Ibn Khaldūn, *Dīwān al-Mubtadaʾ wa-l-Khabar*, 154.

143 The witnessing of the Messenger's followers will be in this worldly life and on the day of resurrection, but our focus here will be on the worldly witnessing.

144 Al-Iṣfahānī, *Tafsīr al-Rāghib al-Iṣfahānī*, vol. 1, 328–29.

145 Ibid., vol. 1, 330–31.

146 See: Al-Iṣfahānī, *al-Mufradāt fī Gharīb al-Qurʾān*, 208.

147 Aḥmad (no. 23965), Shaykh Shuʿayb al-Arnaʾūṭ ranked it as *ṣaḥīḥ* (authentic).

148 Ibn ʿĀshūr, *al-Taḥrīr wa-l-Tanwīr*, vol. 2, 502–3.

149 See: Chauki Lazhar and Khadija Tamaazousti, *al-Umūma wa-l-Unūtha fī al-Islām*, 20.

150 Aḥmad (no. 8952), and al-Bukhārī in *al-Adab al-Mufrad* (no. 273).

151 Al-Iṣfahānī, *al-Mufradāt fī Gharīb al-Qurʾān*, 636.

152 As for the manifestations of environmental degradation that have reached the atmosphere, and even space, this is only a result of the imbalanced human utilisation of the resources of the earth, or the imbalance in the harmony of human society.

153 Al-Iṣfahānī said, "Strive struggle and hard work." Al-Iṣfahānī, *al-Mufradāt fī Gharīb al-Qurʾān*, 704.

154 Muslim (no. 2749).

155 The first quoted verse, for instance, "We created the human being in the finest symmetry, then reduced him to the lowest of the low," denotes that the human being spontaneously turns away from his sound nature, which is due to the fact that from the moment he is in this life, he or his tutor (and not God) is responsible for maintaining his inner and social balances (and helping intellectually immature people with the same), unlike the balance established in the environment.

156 Therefore, the command to maintain the balance that came after the command to restore it does not reduce that maintenance to a part of the cosmic balance, in contrast to the first command ("in the Balance"). This is because the first command is about the cosmic balance in its entirety (spiritual and collective balances included), while, as noted, its full maintenance is not possible. The second command, however, is specifically about the maintenance of the spiritual and collective balances, the full disturbance of which is within the reach of the human being; hence the maintenance thereof was not limited to a part of it. Furthermore, the second command is about the maintenance of the balance after it has been disturbed by ways of transgression and restored by the human being as is understood from the sequence of the verse, while the first command is about the maintenance of what is already standing of that balance, as is clear from the preceding verse stating that it is God who had set up that balance. This, again, supports the idea that the second command is specific to the spiritual and collective balances as those are to be restored in a perpetual fashion as soon as the human being comes to this worldly life, even though they are initially inscribed in his *fitra* as hinted to by their inclusion in the first command. This is in contrast to the environmental balance, which is standing without a systematic disturbance from the day the human being assumes his task, and which the human being is not tasked to perpetually restore. Another reason that explains the reduction of the first command to a part of the cosmic balance, in contrast to the second one, is that the diminishment that occurs in the balance is only a result of a transgression in it. Hence, the diminishment must be restored in the absolute sense without restriction, as all existing dimin-

ishment is already restricted to the preceding transgression. As for the application of both transgression and diminishment to the spiritual and social balances contrary to the environmental balance that is only included in the first commend (i.e., to avoid transgression), this may be attributable to the fact that the logics of transgression that leads to systematic diminishment (which is also applicable to the environment) is already avoided by the preservation of the environment by abstention of transgression without the human being taking responsibility for restoring the weight of the environment as an initial, perpetual and active function, as explained. Hence, the first two responsibilities (spiritual and social balances) are active and perpetual ones, while the third (environmental balance) is initially a passive and accidental one, as there is (initially) no perpetual need for restoring the measurements and compensating for the diminishment.

157 It may be understood from ibn ʿĀshūr's arguments that he holds an opinion opposite to ours. Commenting on the angels' dialogue with God in Q 2:30, ibn ʿĀshūr says, "The angels' words 'Will You place in it one who causes corruption therein' is a proof they knew that God's purpose of creating the earth is its goodness and the orderliness of its affairs, otherwise, they would not give such exclamatory interrogation. They knew God's intent either directly from Him or from understanding the requirements of vicegerency. They may also have understood this from the indications of God's care for the earth and the order He set in it, which denote that God wants the earth to last for a defined period of time. Many verses have shown that the goodness of the world is a purpose for God, as He said, 'Is it possible that if placed in authority you will create disorder in the earth and sever your family bonds? They are those who were condemned by God.' (Q 47:22–23, b.o. Ahmad Ali). God also said, 'When he leaves, he sets out to spread corruption in the earth, destroying crops and live-stock – God does not like corruption.' (Q 2:205, b.o. Wahiddudin Khan)." Ibn ʿĀshūr, *al-Taḥrīr wa-l-Tanwīr*, vol. 1, 403. After a long discussion, ibn ʿĀshūr adds, "Vicegerency in the earth is on behalf of God to establish *ʿumrān* (investing, constructing, thriving… the earth) in all of its forms. That means God entrusts humans to fulfil His intent in the world, and in this sense, the human being's actions vis à vis the earth are on behalf of God [...] As for angels, they were not created qualified for this duty to the extent that they could not give names for the objects. They are naturally inclined to one attribute, namely goodness, which does not change or fall short. Therefore, they were not qualified to subtract the unknown information from the known facts in a way that could perpetuate their knowledge. Moreover, they are not sources of evils, which are necessary for the reformation of this world; their goodness, though suiting their pure world, does not suit the order of a mixed world." Ibid., vol. 1, 418–19. It seems that ibn ʿĀshūr means that the reformation (*iṣlāḥ*), i.e., the instauration of the goodness (*ṣalāḥ*) of the earth, in the material sense, is one of the duties entrusted to the human being. This appears from the possibility he presented that the angels understood that this reformation is a requirement of vicegerency. It also seems that he considers that the world and the earth were not initially created in a state of orderliness and goodness, but it is the human being who is entrusted to achieve this. This is understood from his statement, "does not suit a mixed world" meaning that the earth is in a blended state of goodness and corruption. However, the Qur'an explicitly indicates that the basic condition of the earth is goodness and orderliness, as noted above. Moreover, we did not find evidence in his arguments that the reformation of the earth in the material sense is a human duty. As for the angels' saying, "causes corruption therein and sheds blood," it proves that the earth was in a state of goodness before the advent of the human being, and not that reforming it is one of his duties. It may even indicate the opposite (that is, reforming it is not one of its duties); indeed, how could he be entrusted to do something which is already done? Moreover, we find no justification to investigate how the angels "knew that God's purpose of creating the earth is its goodness and the orderliness of its affairs,"

as this does not need a supporting proof at all. This is just a consequence of the Divine perfection, which entails that everything He does in His creation is (ultimately) good, i.e., it is a requirement of His Lordship. The angels were not surprised by the goodness of the earth. Rather, they were surprised by the opposite, i.e., corruption that will inevitably occur due to the duty entrusted to the human being and, hence, contradict that norm. The reason that angels were not qualified to perform the duty entrusted to the human being, or rather, the reason that their function in the universe does not compensate for the human function, is not their inability to do evil. The angels are able to do whatever God commands them, either reformation or destruction and bloodshed. This is supported by many texts that record stories where the angels were sent by God to destroy whatever and whomever He commanded them. Rather, the reason why their actions in the universe would not compensate for human actions (which is the reason explicitly stated by the Qur'an) is that their knowledge is limited to that which God taught them. Therefore, they have no way to act on behalf of God in maintaining the balance, because acting on behalf of God requires freedom of will and the ability to depart from the known to reach the unknown as stated by ibn 'Āshūr himself. Evil is not required to reform (establish goodness in) the world as claimed by ibn 'Āshūr, as the world was originally balanced before the advent of the human being's evil deeds, as we have explained. Evil, however, is an inevitable consequence of granting free will to a being that lacks Divine perfection, and not a requirement of reformation. Perhaps ibn 'Āshūr intended that reformation takes place after the occurrence of evil and corruption, and indeed, in this case, there must be evil in order to proceed to reformation. However, this is a weak possibility, as he stated that angels were not created for a world where evil is mixed with goodness, and therefore they were not qualified for vicegerency. The angels' incompetence for this duty became obvious before the human being's descent to Earth and his corruption. Thus, the mixed state of good and evil was present on Earth, in his view, even before the human being and thus, evil must occur from the vicegerent in order to reform that. As for the other verses he cites, they, at best, forbid corruption on the earth, i.e., they order to preserve it, and there is nothing in these verses denoting a command to reform it, unless ibn 'Āshūr meant by the establishment of its goodness (*salāḥ*) the preservation of the existing order (though his arguments denote the initialisation of goodness). While the objectives of Revelation unquestionably support the objectives of creation, the goodness of the earth, in the sense of establishing its balance and harmony, is only a direct objective of the Divine cosmic will. We find nothing in the Divine revealed will (the *Sharī'a* objectives) more than the objective to preserve that existing goodness.

158 See for instance: Ṭāhā Jābir al-'Ulwānī, *Issues in Contemporary Islamic Thought* (Herndon, VA: International Institute of Islamic Thought, 2005), 134.

159 Fatḥī Ḥasan Malkāwī, *Epistemological Integration, Essentials of an Islamic Methodology* (Herndon, VA: International Institute of Islamic Thought, 2014), 216.

160 Al-'Ulwānī, *al-Tawḥīd wa-l-Tazkiya wa-l-'Umrān*, 23.

161 Ibid., 119.

162 We have mentioned in the third chapter of this study that al-Iṣfahānī has argued that *'imārat al-arḍ* is one of the functions for which the human being was created. However, what comes out from al-Iṣfahānī's arguments is that he sees it as an existential function towards which the human being is instinctively guided the same way animals are. Nevertheless, he believes it will be rewarded and can even be counted as worship if it is performed in the right way and with the right intention, for the sake of God and for serving his fellow human beings. Furthermore, he describes *'imārat al-arḍ* as something indispensable to live on the earth, and not as a purpose. In his entire book, al-Iṣfahānī says about *'imārat al-arḍ* not much more than the following words: "As for *'imārat al-arḍ*, it is to attend to that which drives the lives of people and provides their livelihood. An individual is not tasked to take care of his livelihood on his own in terms of food, clothing and shelter. He has no other choice in order

to live decently in this world but to satisfy his hunger, cover his nudity and protect himself from heat and cold. He has no choice but to achieve that in a permissible way. Therefore, God said: 'Verily you will have no hunger or nakedness there, nor thirst nor exposure to the sun.' (Q 20:118, Ahmad Ali). If the human being strives to achieve that as per what is required, his endeavour will be considered an act of worship and a *jihād* for the sake of Allah, as the Prophet (ﷺ) said: 'Whoever seeks his livelihood in an appropriate manner is in a state of *jihād* and who does not do that properly, his endeavours are in vain.' God said: 'Say: "Shall I tell you whose labour will be wasted? Theirs whose effort is misspent in pursuit of the pleasures of the world, even though they think they are doing good things."' (Q 18:103–104, Ahmad Ali). The human being is in the service of people in these endeavours, and he is subjugated for their benefit without his will, it is as if he is among the animals that God has subjugated for the human being, reminding them of one of His favours as in His saying: 'He created horses, mules and donkeys for riding and for splendour.'" (Q 16:8, Ahmad Ali). Al-Iṣfahānī, *al-Dharīʿa ilā Makārim al-Sharīʿa*, 85–86. Hence, it is clear that al-Iṣfahānī considers *ʿimārat al-arḍ* as an existential function that is inevitably performed by the human being by virtue of the cosmic will and not the revealed one. Furthermore, he does not give this concept any inherent Qurʾanic value nor does he even say that *ʿimārat al-arḍ* is a religious obligation. Moreover, he even explicitly states that the Qurʾan may praise *ʿimārat al-arḍ* if it is done in a beneficial way, or it may blame it if that is taken as an objective, quoting a saying that he attributes to the Prophet: "Life is a bridge, cross it but don't construct it (*lā tuʿammirūhā*)." Ibid., 280–81. Clearly, this view is light years away from the thesis of al-ʿUlwānī and other contemporary scholars around this concept.

163 Al-Najjār, *Fiqh al-Taḥaḍḍur al-Islāmī*, 22–23. In his latest research, however, al-Najjār maintains that the mission for which man was created is *ʿimārat al-arḍ*. See: al-Najjār, "Maqāṣid al-Qurʾān fī Tazkiyat al-Insān," 107.

164 Fatḥī Malkāwī, *Manẓūmat al-Qiyam al-ʿUlyā: al-Tawḥīd wa-l-Tazkiya wa-l-ʿUmrān*, 133–34.

165 Ibid., 139.

166 Ibid., 136.

167 Ibid., 131.

## Bibliography

Ibn ʿĀshūr, Muḥammad al-Ṭāhir. *Al-Taḥrīr wa-l-Tanwīr [The Verification and Enlightenment]*. Tunis: al-Dār al-Tūnisiyya, 1984.

Ibn ʿĀshūr, Muḥammad al-Ṭāhir. *Maqāṣid al-Sharīʿa al-Islāmiyya [The Objectives of Sharīʿa]*. Edited by Muḥammad al-Ṭāhir al-Misāwī. Jordan: Dār al-Nafāʾis, 2nd ed. 2001.

Al-Ghazzālī, Muḥammad Abū Ḥāmid. *Shifāʾ al-Ghalīl fī Bayān al-Shabah wa-l-Mukhayyal wa-Masālik al-Taʿlīl [The Satisfaction of the Thirst in Explaining Resemblance, Ambiguity and the Methods of Rationalization]*. Baghdad: Maktabat al-Irshād, 1971.

Ibn Ḥanbal, Aḥmad. *Musnad al-Imām Aḥmad ibn Ḥanbal*. Edited by Shuʿayb al-Arnaʾūṭ and ʿĀdil Murshid, et al. Beirut: Muʾassasat al-Risāla, 2001.

Idris, Jaafar Sheikh. "Al-Taṣawwur al-Islāmī li-l-Insān Asāsun li-Falsafat al-Islām al-Tarbawiyya [The Islamic Perception of the Human being as Basis for an Islamic Educational Philosophy]." *Al-Muslim al-Muʿāṣir*, 12 (September 1977): 61–80.

Al-Iṣfahānī, al-Rāghib. *Al-Mufradāt fī Gharīb al-Qurʾān [The Dictionary of Complex Qurʾanic Terminology]*. Edited by Ṣafwān ʿAdnān al-Dawūdī. Damascus-Beirut: Dār al-Qalam, al-Dār al-Shāmiyya, 1412 AH.

Al-Iṣfahānī, al-Rāghib. *Tafsīr al-Rāghib al-Iṣfahānī, [The Exegesis of al-Rāghib al-Iṣfahānī]*. Edited by 'Ādil ibn 'Alī al-Shādī. Riyadh: Dār al-Waṭan, 2003.

Al-Iṣfahānī, al-Rāghib. *Al-Dharī'a ilā Makārim al-Sharī'a [The Book of Means to the Noble Qualities of Sharī'a]. Edited by Abū Zayd al-'Ajamī*. Cairo: Dār al-Salām, 2007.

Kāẓim, Aṣīl Muḥammad and Maḥmūd 'Abd Ḥamad. "Asālīb al-Ta'līl wa-Dalālatuhā fī l-Qur'ān al-Karīm [The Methods of Rationalization and their Meanings in the Noble Qur'an]." *Journal of al-Qādisiyya fī l-'Ādāb wa-l-'Ulūm al-Tarbawiyya* 4 no. 2 (Sept. 2005): 161–170.

Ibn Khaldūn, 'Abd al-Raḥmān. *Dīwān al-Mubtada' wa-l-Khabar fī Tārīkh al-'Arab wa-l-Barbar wa-Man 'Āṣarahum min Dhawī al-Sha'n al-Akbar [Book of Lessons, Recordings of the Beginnings and Events in the History of the Arabs, the Berbers and their Powerful Contemporaries]*. Beirut: Dār al-Fikr, 1988.

Lazhar, Chauki and Tamaazousti, Khadija. *Al-Umūma wa-l-Unūtha fī al-Islām wa-l-Tamyīz bayna al-Mar'a wa-l-Rajul fī al-Aḥkām al-Shar'iyya [Motherhood, Femininity and Gender Differentiation in Islamic Provisions]*. Doha: Hamad Bin Khalifa University Press, 2019.

Lazhar, Chauki and Tamaazousti, Khadija. *Maternité et Islam*. Doha: Research Center for Islamic Legislation and Ethics, College of Islamic Studies, 2018.

Malkāwī, Fatḥī Ḥasan. *Manẓūmat al-Qiyam al-'Ulyā: Al-Tawḥīd wa-l-Tazkiya wa-l-'Umrān [The Higher Value System: Monotheism, Purification and Civilization]*. Virginia: International Institute of Islamic Thought, 2013.

Malkāwī, Fatḥī Ḥasan. *Epistemological Integration, Essentials of an Islamic Methodology*. Virginia: The International Institute of Islamic Thought, 2014.

Ibn Manẓūr, Muḥammad ibn Mukram. *Lisān al-'Arab [The Tongue of the Arabs]*. Beirut: Dār Ṣādir, 3rd ed., 1993.

Mujāhid, Abū al-Ḥajjāj al-Makhzūmī. *Tafsīr Mujāhid*. Edited by Muḥammad 'Abd al-Salām. Egypt: Dār al-Fikr al-Islāmī al-Ḥadīth, 1989.

Al-Najjār, 'Abd al-Majīd. "Maqāṣid al-Qur'ān fī Tazkiyat al-Insān [The Objectives of the Qur'an in the Purification of Man]." In *Sūrat al-Insān bayna al-Marji'iyyatayn al-Islāmiyya wa-l-Gharbiyya*, edited by Rā'id 'Ukkāsha and 'Ā'isha al-Ḥaḍīrī. Virginia: The International Institute of Islamic Thought, 2020.

Al-Naysabūrī, Muslim ibn al-Ḥajjāj. *Ṣaḥīḥ Muslim*. Edited by Muḥammad Fu'ād 'Abd al-Bāqī. Beirut: Dār Iḥyā' al-Turāth al-'Arabī, n.d.

Al-Qaraḍāwī, Yūsuf. "Qīmat al-Insān wa-Ghāyat Wujūdih fī Ḍaw' al-Qur'ān wa-l-Sunna [The Value of the Human Being and the Purpose of his Existence in the Light of the Qur'an and the Sunna].: *Journal of Buhūth al-Sunna wa-l-Sīra, Qatar University*, no. 5 (1991): 13–29.

Ibn Qayyim al-Jawziyya, Shams al-Dīn. *Shifā' al-'Alīl fī Masā'il al-Qaḍā' wa-l-Qadar wa-l-Ḥikma wa-l-Ta'līl [Healing the Sick about the Issues of Predestination, Wisdom and Rationales]*. Beirut: Dār al-Ma'rifa, 1978.

Ibn Qayyim al-Jawziyya, Shams al-Dīn. *Madārij al-Sālikīn bayna Manāzil Iyyāka Na'bud wa-Iyyāka Nasta'īn [The Wayfarers' Stages]. Edited by Muḥammad al-Mu'taṣim Billāh*. Beirut: Dār al-Kitāb al-'Arabī, 1996.

Ibn Qutayba, 'Abd Allāh ibn Muslim. *Gharīb al-Qur'ān [Lexical Complexities in the Qur'an]*. Edited by Aḥmad Ṣaqr. Beirut: Dār al-Kutub al-'Ilmiyya, 1978.

Riḍā, Muḥammad Rashīd. *Tafsīr al-Manār [Interpretation of the Illuminator]*. Cairo: al-Hay'a al-Miṣriyya, 1990.

Al-Shāṭibī, Abū Isḥāq. *Al-Muwāfaqāt* [The Reconciliation]. Annotated by Mashūr ibn Ḥasan. Cairo: Dār ibn 'Affān, 1997.

Al-Subkī, Tājj al-Dīn. *Al-Ashbāh wa-l-Naẓā'ir [Similar Legal Maxims and Norms]*. Beirut: Dār al-Kutub al-'Ilmiyya, 1991.

Al-Ṭabarī, Muḥammad ibn Jarīr. *Jāmi' al-Bayān 'an Ta'wīl Āyī al-Qur'ān [The Comprehensive Exposition of the Interpretation of the Verses of the Qur'an]*. Edited by Aḥmad Muḥammad Shākir. Beirut: Mu'assasat al-Risāla, 2000.

Ibn Abī Ṭālib, Makkī. *Al-Hidāya ilā Bulūgh al-Nihāya fī 'Ilm Ma'ānī al-Qur'ān wa-Tafsīrih wa-Aḥkāmih, wa-Jumal min Funūn 'Ulūmih [Qur'anic Lexicography, Exegesis, Jurisprudence and Disciplines]*. Sharjah: Faculty of Sharī'a and Islamic Studies, University of Sharjah, 2008.

Ibn Taymiyya, Taqī al-Dīn. *Bayān Talbīs al-Jahmiyya fī Ta'sīs Bida'ihim al-Kalāmiyya. [Exposition of the Falsehoods of al-Jahmiyya in the Establishment of their Theological Innovations]*. Medina: King Fahd Complex for the Printing of the Holy Qur'an, 2005.

Ibn Taymiyya, Taqī al-Dīn. *Majmū' al-Fatāwā [The Compilation of Fatwas]*. Medina: King Fahd Complex for the Printing of the Holy Quran, 1995.

Al-'Ulwānī, Ṭāhā Jābir. *Al-Tawḥīd wa-l-Tazkiya wa-l-'Umrān: Muḥāwala fī l-Kashf 'an al-Qiyam wa-l-Maqāṣid al-Qur'āniyya al-Ḥākima [Monotheism, Purification, and Civilization: Attempts to Reveal the Ruling Qur'anic Values and Objectives]*. Beirut: Dār al-Hidāya, 2003.

Al-'Ulwānī, Ṭāhā Jābir. *Issues in Contemporary Islamic Thought*. Virginia: The International Institute of Islamic Thought, 2005.

# Conclusion

This study departed from the assumption that contemporary Islamic scholarship suffers from the absence of theorisation about vicegerency as one of the most prominent dimensions in the field of Islamic worldview. After the treatment, categorisation and analysis of the collected data on the subject matter, in both classical and contemporary literature, this hypothesis was confirmed by the current study.

Besides the strong expectation that this hypothesis would be confirmed, it was also expected that the sum of contemporary studies in the field would provide a fertile ground to develop the said theory. However, the study ended up proving the opposite, i.e., the impossibility of building on previous studies in the field, as they are not based on solid Qur'anic grounds, some of them even being in flagrant contradiction with the Qur'anic worldview and even its letter. Nevertheless, critical engagement with these studies proved to be fruitful in identifying and developing the methodological and epistemological entries that this study relied upon in order to overcome the shortcomings that prevented the development of the said theory.

The main objective of this study was to fill the above-described gap by establishing the contours of a Qur'anic theory of vicegerency as a human existential function. Based on the analysis and critique of both classical and contemporary views on the subject matter and on the systematisation of the related Qur'anic concepts, this study has established the outlines of an organised structure in which vicegerency operates and defined its precise meaning accordingly.

One of the starting points of this enterprise consisted in investigating the Qur'anic conception of worship as a function common to all the existents of the universe, including human beings. This allowed us to consider the human existential function within the cosmic scheme in which it operates. According to the Qur'anic outlook, worship, religion, revelation, Islam and Divine guidance are not human prerogatives but common to all elements constituting the universe. Hence, Islam, in the Qur'anic worldview, is not limited to scriptural revelation but is rather an overall cosmic order, which Revelation enables the human being to enrol in. Accordingly, the human being shares the same overall existential function, means and objective with the universe. That existential function is worship, the means is guidance and the existential objective is cosmic Islam, in terms of surrender to God (*istislām*) leading to the soundness (*salāma*) of the natural constitution, resulting in peace (*salām*) with the self and the surroundings.

After having drawn up this cosmic sketch, our focus turned to the examination of the specific function that distinguishes the human being from other creatures as to the realisation of that cosmic Islam. The key entry of this investigation was to understand the meaning of *khilāfa* as presented in the vicegerency verses in *sūrat al-Baqara* (Q 2:29–38) in the light of the verses of *sūrat al-Raḥmān* (Q 55:1–13). This further defined the object of the vicegerency of the human being, that is his existential function, as the maintenance of the harmony that God has placed in the universe, or, in other words, the cosmic balance. However, this overall function needed further refinement as that maintenance does not include all aspects of the cosmic balance maintained by God, as indicated by Q 55:8. Hence, the outstanding issue was to explore the specific aspects of the cosmic balance that the human being has been entrusted to preserve on behalf of God. This issue was addressed by enumerating and categorising all the concepts and principles explicitly used by the Qurʾan as the rationale behind the revelation of Scripture and the creation of man and universe. Those concepts were referred to by this study as the Qurʾanic teleological concepts. After reading through the Qurʾan verse by verse we found about two hundred verses that explicitly establish the teleological reasons behind those three existential phenomena, through approximately 60 principles or concepts. Those concepts were considered to be the higher Islamic principles making up the Qurʾanic worldview. After sorting out these principles according to their relation to the deputisation on behalf of God in the maintenance of the cosmic balance, we could classify them into eight categories or topologies. Only the eighth category includes the principles that fit as a direct expression of one of the aspects of the cosmic balance that the human being is assigned to maintain on behalf of God. Out of the 60 identified teleological concepts or principles, two proved to be suitable for this category, namely the purification of the heart and judging among people, representing, respectively, the maintenance of the spiritual balance and the maintenance of the social balance. A third principle was added to those two as it was shown to be a suitable object of vicegerency, namely the maintenance of the environmental balance.

The rest of the study was then devoted to the examination of the specific aspects of the cosmic balance that the human being has been entrusted to maintain, as the existential function for which he was created, through the methodological and epistemological entries elaborated before. Furthermore, these aspects were related to the other Qurʾanic teleological concepts. All these concepts were organised and linked with the cement of deputisation on behalf of God in maintaining the cosmic balance, thus revealing a consistent whole capable of framing all teachings of Revelation. The overall outcome of this investigation suggests that it is God, initially, who maintains the natural balance and measures, in the sense of the naturel soundness, that He has installed within the human self, in terms of the equilibrium between all human aspirations and faculties. This also applies to human society, in terms of the equilibrium in the human community between its members and their different types of interactions. However, God has mandated the human being to act on His behalf in the preservation of this natural equilibrium. Furthermore, the human being is mandated to act on behalf of God in the preservation of the inherent equilibrium of his natural environment when engaging in its utilisation. By performing this task (i.e., the maintenance of the three equilibriums), the human being is enabled to join cosmic Islam, which is the broader purpose behind his specific function. This, in turn, will offer him an interim alternative for the satisfaction of his ontological infinite aspirations, which is only possible in the Hereafter. All other Qur'anic teleological concepts identified by this study were found to be referring to the means, attributes, objectives, consequences, outcomes or ontological reasons of this main function. It is the identification of and elaboration on this dialectical convergence that has drawn the contours of an integral Qur'anic vicegerency theory. Before arriving at the findings described above, which answer the principal question of this study, several other key questions were explored, shaping this study in the following structure:

In the **first chapter** of this study, the introductory notes gave an overall idea about the importance of the concept of vicegerency and its relevance to contemporary Islamic scholarship. The main hypothesis, research questions, methodological approach and focus adopted in this study were highlighted, followed by a brief overview on the early modern reform endeavours concerned with knowledge integration in general and Islamic worldview as a main solution in particular.

The **second chapter** gave an idea of the contemporary context in which the idea of the Islamic worldview developed. It became clear that the radical epistemic and social changes induced by modernity have revealed the structural deficiency of traditional Islamic sciences. The classical methodological apparatus, which was designed to cope with atomistic changes, could not introduce Islam in the era of modernity. This also applies to the traditional epistemological patterns, which were thought to be deviating from the Qur'anic epistemology. Consequently, the idea of Islamic worldview came, under different denominators, to the forefront as a promising horizon. The revival of many traditional concepts arose in attempts to overcome the epistemological and methodological disintegration of Islamic thought and to catch up with Western progress. It is in this context that the idea of vicegerency as the human existential function gained popularity. It also became clear that the idea of Islamic worldview itself, its applications and its development remained vague among its early advocates.

It appeared from the **third chapter** that the idea of vicegerency as human existential function, in the way advocated by the majority of contemporary reformists, is not alien to Islamic heritage. One of the main differences, however, is that classical scholars who espoused it did not elaborate much on the idea but only referred to it in passing, usually when interpreting the Qur'an. It turned out that the question of human existential function was not an important issue in Islamic intellectual heritage, mainly because of the ideological disputes between the different schools of theology based on their epistemological patterns and the subsequent defensive reactions to them. Another important finding of this chapter is that classical scholars never problematised the idea that the human being could be the vicegerent of God on the creedal level outside the context of the critique of pantheist doctrines. This challenges an established consensus among both contemporary advocates and detractors of the idea of vicegerency on behalf of God. Indeed, both of them assume that the classical controversy was of creedal nature and that ibn Taymiyya rejected the idea of the human being's vicegerency of God in an absolute and categorical manner, an idea that this study has debunked. Another opinion that this chapter has challenged is the prevailing view, among contemporary critiques of vicegerency, that the idea of the human being's vicegerency on behalf of God as it is articulated within contemporary reformism is unprecedented in classical scholarship.

The **fourth chapter** showed that when most contemporary reformists adopted classical definitions of vicegerency, they did not attempt to assess those traditional views, nor did they re-establish the concept within Islamic creed and Scripture. The contemporary advocates of vicegerency did not root the concept in the Qur'anic worldview, did not approach it from a clear methodological and epistemological framework, nor did they adopt a classical hermeneutical approach. Most of the contemporary apologists of the concept used it in reaction to what they considered to be the Western worldview of civilisation. They tried to present an Islamic alternative by projecting (both classical and modern) pre-established concepts on the Qur'anic texts. The distortion of the concept of vicegerency and its deviation from the Qur'an, or its loose, pointless use, appeared in many aspects. Among these problematic aspects figures the relationship between the functions of vicegerency and worship, the question of how the human existential function relates to deputisation on behalf of God, the issue of the position of vicegerency within the Islamic worldview, and its relationship with the other major Islamic concepts and principles, among many other unresolved issues. As a result of all these diagnosed flaws, none of the contemporary studies succeeded in clearly and accurately defining the very nature of the human existential function. Furthermore, none of them have developed a vicegerency theory. We were able to affirm the latter statement with confidence based on several criteria that define whether the presented theses can pretend to the status of a theory or not. The same criteria were relied upon in the following chapters in the attempt to develop the outlines of a theory. Among the hypotheses that we have formulated in the introduction of this study that were verified and confirmed by this chapter is that vicegerency did not play a significant role in literature on Islamic worldview, despite the fact that it was considered one of its major features, or even its overarching principle.

The **fifth chapter** dealt with the gaps we had identified in the literature on vicegerency by laying some epistemological and methodological entries the implementation of which could overcome those shortcomings. While examining the way in which contemporary advocates of vicegerency try to relate the concept to the Qur'an, it was confirmed that none of the approaches used by them could be relied upon, considering the fact that, besides the superficial quotation of, often unrelated, Qur'anic verses, no holistic methodological and epistemological approach nor clear hermeneutics was adopted in the process. This observation required the clearing of new ground for rooting the concept in the Qur'an. Before engaging in this exercise, this chapter provided an in-depth analysis of the issue of who or what the human being is vicegerent of. Through a thorough examination of the views around the question in the light of the relevant Qur'anic verses, this chapter demonstrated that vicegerency is a function that the human being performs on behalf of God. Among the key entries to overcome the identified shortcomings in view of developing a holistic outlook on vicegerency is the reading grid of the Qur'anic conception of the function of the universe, the nature of the human being and his existential relationship with the universe. This reading grid was introduced by this chapter to approach the human existential function from an overall Qur'anic perception or a "worldview exegesis." This further helped to fill some of the main gaps identified in the previous chapter, among which was the unresolved question of the relationship of worship as a function and vicegerency as a function. It appeared that, in contrast to the theologically problematic responses that have been criticised in the previous chapter, and as per the above Qur'anic reading grid, vicegerency is neither a part of the worship for which the human being was created, nor is worship a part of vicegerency, nor is vicegerency a synonym for worship, nor are they two distinct functions. As per our Qur'anic framework, vicegerency is a worship specific to human beings. Furthermore, this approach also provided an answer to the issue of the teleological relationship between the human being and creation. Another epistemological entry developed in this chapter through a Qur'anic approach is the establishment of the ontological relationship between God, human nature, universe, Revelation and the human existential function by integrating these concepts in their overall cosmic context.

The **sixth chapter** was the final phase in addressing the main question of this study. This enterprise was undertaken by tracing and listing all the Qur'anic verses that explicitly stipulate the reason behind the creation of the human being and the universe and the revelation of Scripture (the three major existential phenomena). This chapter considered the concepts and principles explicitly recognised by the Qur'an as rationales behind the existence of the human being, universe and Revelation as "the major concepts of Islam" constituting its worldview. These principles were classified in different topologies in the light of the previously defined methodological and epistemological entries. This classification drew up the coordinated relationship between those principles under the umbrella of vicegerency and organised them in a coherent and systematic theory. After the identification and categorisation of those principles, this chapter proceeded to the elaboration of the principles that express the very nature of the human existential function (the object of vicegerency) and scrutinised their correlation with the other major concepts that constitute the Qur'anic worldview. This enabled us to capture a precise and coherent conception of the human existential function and its features within the Qur'anic worldview.

By and large, this study revealed that the problem of the fragmented and atomistic approaches in Islamic thought and, particularly, in reading the Islamic Scripture, is far from being resolved, despite the strong emphasis on the issue of knowledge integration and the holistic view of Revelation. This was blatantly apparent from the fact that contemporary scholars of different reformist backgrounds failed to identify the Qur'anic perception of the human existential function beyond the reliance upon one or two isolated verses. Therefore, the main contribution of this study is that it has proposed a new approach for understanding the human existential function from within the Qur'anic worldview. This study offered, for the first time, an integral induction and categorisation of the Qur'anic teleological concepts and related them within a coherent framework that reveals the outlines of a vicegerency theory and a Qur'anic worldview. Besides this main contribution, various gaps in Islamic scholarship on the subject matter have also been addressed. For instance, this study is the first in its genera to not only map contemporary theses on vicegerency as an existential function, but also to perform categorisation and comparative and critical analysis of them. The gaps that were observed during these discussions were filled in the following attempts to fulfil the main objective of the study. Furthermore, this study has challenged the mainstream perception of contemporary Muslim reformists regarding the human existential function, i.e., *ʿimārat al-arḍ*, by deconstructing its theological basis and demonstrating that this idea is not supported by the Qur'an, neither as a human existential function nor even as a mere religious requirement. Additionally, while contemporary studies on the Islamic worldview and vicegerency present what they consider to be the overarching or governing Islamic concepts or principles by making a list of principles without clarifying the criterion on which these were chosen to the exclusion of others (and without relating them to each other ontologically), this study proposed a set of clear criteria for that purpose.

While the importance of this study resides in the new horizons it opens for Islamic worldview studies, we believe that the outlined theory proposed in this study has the potential to overarch all Islamic disciplines and serve as their frame of reference. This is because the human being's existential function and related purposes are ultimately the supreme purpose that governs the teachings of Revelation and subsequent Islamic thought, sciences and *ijtihād*; it is, in other words, the core of its philosophy or worldview.

Since the scope of this study was not wide enough to address the concrete articulations of the proposed theory in the reform of contemporary *ijtihād* and Islamic sciences and thought, we encourage further research to focus on the role of the human existential function in the epistemological and methodological reform of Islamic sciences and contemporary Islamic knowledge production. This is all the more important given that the absence of any study interested in the appraisal and reform of Islamic sciences on the basis of the Islamic worldview is a major gap that this study has identified in Islamic literature. There is a pressing need for further studies to relate contemporary religio-ethical reasoning and Islamic sciences to an overall Qur'anic worldview in which they can operate to overcome fragmentation and atomistic approaches to Scripture. We consider the outlines developed in this study to be a first step in this process. We hope this study will pave the way for further academic interest in vicegerency and human existential function in general as a key element in contemporary Islamic epistemological reform endeavours.

# Index


ʿAbd al-ʿAzīz, ʿUmar ibn 54
ʿAbd al-Raḥmān, Ṭāhā 12
ʿAbduh, Muḥammad 6, 28, 51, 88, 90, 96, 128
Abū Ḥayyān 50, 59
Abū Sulaymān, ʿAbd al-Ḥamīd 12, 32, 88, 126; on Bedouin influence on Islamic political life 33; on building of Islamic social sciences 34; on positive worldview 33
act(s) of: grace 72; naming 97; supererogation 72
"action-attributes" (*ṣifāt fiʿliyya*) 110
ʿĀd 230, 243
Adam as vicegerent 64
Ahl al-Sunna on worship 83n136
Akbarian: idea 121; scholar 97; thought 115; tradition 97; view 154; writings 97
al-Afghānī, Jamāl al-Dīn 6
al-Aḥmar 111; and division of vicegerency 111; on jinn and freedom of choice 111; on vicegerency and Islam 112
al-Ālūsī 50, 60
al-Ashʿarī on purpose of creation 68
al-Baghawī 47, 49; on *khalīfa* 59
al-Baṣrī on vicegerency of God on earth 61
Al-Bayḍāwī 59, 62, 120; on *khalīfa* 59
al-Brūsawī 120
al-Busrī, Abū ʿUbayd 61
al-Dasūqī 96; on the objective of human existence 93; on religion and world 93; on servitude (*ʿubūdiyya*) and lordship (*rubūbiyya*) 92, 153; on vicegerency 92; on Western vicegerency 92–93
al-Faḍl, Munā Abū 88, 125; and four Islamic pillars 125
al-Fārūqī, Ismāʿīl 9, 26, 88, 114; on *khilāfa* and political responsibility 119; on vicegerency 114
"al-Furqān" (the standard of right and wrong) 217
*al-Futūḥāt al-Makiyya* (the Meccan Revelations) 48
al-Ghazzālī 58
al-Ḥarālī 57
al-Iṣfahānī 49, 54, 58, 66, 101, 233; on human existential mission 66; on *istikhlāf* 67; on object of vicegerency 62; Qur'anic refutation of 72; and separation of ethics and worship 71; on vicegerency 63; on vicegerency and emulation of God 121; on wazn (weight) 206; on worhship and the Hereafter 71; on worship and vicegerency 69; on worship and virtue 70; on worship as purification of the soul 71
al-Isnawī 162
al-Jabriyya (determinists) 80n136
al-Jawziyya, ibn Qayyim 50
al-Karrāmiyya 80n136
al-Khūlī, al-Bahī: nature of vicegerency 114; on vicegerency and worship 118
al-Maʿāfirī, ʿAbd Allāh ibn Naʿīm 52; on vicegerency 61
al-Makkī, Abū Ṭālib 68; on creation and worship 67–68
al-Masīrī, ʿAbd al-Wahhāb 88, 90
al-Māwardī 47
"*al-milla*" system 25
*al-Mustakhlif* (God Almighty) 122
al-Muʿtazila al-Qadariyya (adeterminists) 80n136
al-Najjār, ʿAbd al-Majīd 5, 103, 241; and jurisprudence of *khilāfa* 103; and vicegerency and worship 105
*al-naẓariyyāt al-fiqhiyya* (legal theories of jurisprudence) 7
al-Nūrsī, Badīʿ al-Zamān Saʿīd 88, 102

al-Qaṣṣāb, Aḥmad 58
al-Qaṣṣāb, Ahmad on Q 24:55 and *istikhlāf* 58
al-Qūnawī, Ṣadr al-Dīn on servanthood and lordship 97
al-Rāzī on Q 24:55 58
al-Ṣadr, Muḥammad Bāqir 88, 122–24, 155; on object of vicegerency 155
al-Samʿānī 47, 49; on *khalīfa* 59
Al-Samarqandī on vicegerents of God 61–62
al-Sayyid, Raḍwān 128
al-Shāṭiʾ, ʿĀʾisha Bint 88, 108
al-Shāṭibī 39, 57
al-Sulaymī, Abū Ḥabīb 52; on vicegerent of God on earth 61
al-sunan al-kawniyya (cosmic norms) 7
al-Ṭabarī 46–47, 49–50, 208, 215; on object of vicegerency 61
*al-taḥsīn wa-l-taqbīḥ* (the intellectual inability to identify good and evil) 80n136
al-Thaʿālibī, ʿAbd al-ʿAzīz 30
al-Ṭībī, Sharaf al-Dīn 57
al-Ṭūfī, Najm al-Dīn 162
*al-ʿubūdiyya* (total devotion to and worship of God) 66
al-ʿUlwānī, Ṭāhā Jābir 11, 88, 241
al-Zamakhsharī on Q 2:30 98; on vicegerents of God 61
al-Zaylaʿī, Fakhr al-Dīn 57
*amāna* (trust) 1
anthropomorphism 48
Ashʿarī: epistemology 32, 70, 71, 91, 118; school (of thought) 68, 71; on worship 70
attributes of God: Bringer of Judgement (al-Ḥasīb) 225; Grateful (al-Shakūr) 225; Living One (al-Hayy) 224; Pardoner (al-ʿAfuww) 225; Responder (al-Mujīb) 225; Watchful One (al-Raqīb) 225
ʿAwda, ʿAbd al-Qādir 90, 128–29; and definition of vicegerency 96
*awlawiyyāt* (priorities) 7

Bāshā, Muḥammad ʿAlī 38
bearing glad tidings 220, 222
bearing of responsibility (*amāna*) 10
Bible chapters/verses: Genesis 1:26 97; Genesis 1:26-30 98; Genesis 1:28 97
The Book of Means to the Noble Qualities of Sharīʿa (Al-Iṣfahānī) 58, 65
building and populating (population of) the earth (*ʿimārat al-arḍ*) 90, 100, 102, 148

Center Leo Apostel (CLEA) 8
civil *dominium* and Christian *dominium* 98
civilisation: human existence and 65; Islamic sciences and 32; Islamic thought and 88; Islamic worldview of 127; jurisprudence of Islamic 127; principles of 104; and umran 157
"comprehensive interpretation" (*al-tafsīr al-shāmil*) 8
conceptional intertextuality 163
concoction (*talfīq*) 28
contemporary Islamic thought 1, 34, 124
contemporary reformists 1, 88, 90, 266
contextual intertextuality 163
corruption (fasād) 243
cosmic balance 116, 158, 163, 176, 178–79, 194, 196–97, 204, 207, 210, 224–27, 234, 240, 244, 264; aspect(s) of 204–6, 226, 239–40; on Earth 239; maintenance of 200, 205, 210, 247, 264; preservation of 238, 239
cosmic duties (*taklīf kawnī*) 157
cosmic fate 150, 156
cosmic Islam 116, 158, 163, 171–73, 176, 179, 196, 210, 222, 245–47, 264–65; components of *247*; discussion on 196; enrollment in 196; as existential objective 263; joining 172–73, 222, 247, 265
cosmic will 81, 93, 102, 118, 150, 157–59, 216, 225, 230
creation of the human beings (reasons of) 199–200
Critique of Judgment (Kant) 8
"cultural mandate" (*dominium terrae*) 97
customary convention (*al-ḥaqīqa al-ʿurfiyya*) 162

Day of Resurrection 72, 206, 221, 232, 242
deduction (*istimbāt*) 6
delegated sovereignty (idea of Webber, Robert) 97
delusion (ghurūr) 220
demise of the "Companions" 33
deputisation: on behalf of God 101, 104, 121–22, 148, 155, 157, 159–60, 165, 196, 197, 214, 224, 227, 232, 264, 266; of God 104–5, 114, 125, 156; human being's 100, 158
Divine: acknowledgement 156; act 109–10, 165, 176; action 101, 158, 165, 177, 179, 204, 208, 239, 244; attributes 63–64, 114, 117, 118, 158–59, 222–25;

blessing 244; breath 117; command 14, 106, 156; cosmic will (*irāda kawniyya*) 102, 216; deputization 121; determination 209; ethics 117, 118, 122, 154; functions 121, 200; generosity 213; guidance 116, 167, 172, 176, 178, 216, 263; harmonisation 209; image 224; insufflation 159, 216, 224; mission 110; norms 236; objectives 113; order 175, 243; perfection 202–4; purpose 63; purposiveness 115; realisation of ethics 117; sovereignty (*ḥākimiyya*) 58, 110; task 216; testing 241; vicegerency 122, 128
Divine will 102, 115, 117–19, 156–57, 165; execution of 108; fulfilment of 114, 118; imperatives of 115, 118; as object of vicegerency 102; violation of 109
Drāz, Muḥammad ʿAbd Allāh 6, 128–29

endeavours in religio-ethical reasoning 1
environmental balance 243, 246–47; disturbance of 246; maintenance of 245, 264; preservation of 240
epistemic deficiency 24
epistemological integration 12, 129
epistemological paradigms 3
ethical purpose 115
ethical responsibility 13
ethicisation' (*takhalluq*) 13; external 13; internal 13
euromodernity 14
European modernity 3, 23–24, 26, 28
evangelical lordship and servitude 98
evidence-based reasoning (*burhān*) 68
existence and cosmos in Qurʾanic conception 3
existential function: human being's 113, 165, 196–97, 204, 268; nature of 4; theorisation of 2, 68; vicegerency as 89–90; worship as 66; *see also* vicegerency
"explanatory model" (*al-namūdhaj al-tafsīrī*) 8

faith (*ʾīmān*) 100
"faith-based" (*istikhlāf ʾīmānī*) 110
false gods (ṭāghūt) 214
Faraḥāt 106–8; and division of vicegerency 110; on vicegerency 106
fasād (corruption) 237
fāsiq (transgressor/pervert) 208
fāsiqūn (perverts/trespassers) 245
*fatwā* (non-binding legal verdict) 10
Fazlur Rahman 25, 27, 29, 32, 36; on Islamic and modern sciences 35
*fiqh: al-nawāzil wa-muwākabat al-mustajaddāt* (methodology for resolving new legal incidences and reality-treatment) 7; *al-tanzīl* (methods of applied *fiqh*) 7; *al-wāqiʿ* (methodology of considering reality in *ijtihād*) 7; councils (cross-doctrinal) 28
fisq (perversion) 207
*fiṭra* (human nature/natural constitution/natural human disposition/natural inclination/unspoiled nature) 1, 13, 102, 119–20, 159, 172, 176, 178, 208, 210–11, 219; restoration of 229
foundational Islamic texts 15n2
fragmentation problem 30–32, 35–36, 129
free will 68, 117, 153, 160, 165, 172

generations: ancient 57; human 47; Muslim 50; previous 160–61; *salaf* 52; succession of 108, 156–57, 159–60
giving charity 233
god-consciousness (taqwā) 212
God's Most Beautiful Names 174, 202, 204, 222
good and evil 39, 71, 80, 95, 109, 165; choice between 111, 113
goodness (khayr) 228
Governing Value System (al-ʿUlwānī) 11
Greek philosophy and Islamic principles (reconciliation of) 30

*ḥadd* (legally prescribed penalty) 35
Ḥājj Ḥamad, Muḥammad Abū al-Qāsim 96; on political authority 96
Ḥanafī: jurisprudence 27; school 28
"Hands of the Truth" 64
His: image (*be-tsememū*) 98; way (*ki-demūtenū*) 98
human being: existential function of 2, 4, 108–9, 161, 174, 231
human civilisation: building 12; establishment of 230; Western view of 127
human existential: function 66, 120, 177, 213, 238, 263; mission 63, 66, 215; nature of the 110, 266; in Qurʾanic worldview 268; and sinning 239

ibn Abbās 47, 209
ibn Abū Ṭālib 211
ibn al-Aʿrābī 208

ibn al-Jawzī 50, 58
ibn al-Qayyim 50, 52–53, 57; on man as *khalīfa* on earth 57
ibn ʿArabī 64, 72, 97, 120; on *istikhlāf* 63
ibn ʿĀshūr, Muḥammad al-Ṭāhir 24, 26–28, 31, 50, 88, 101–2, 168
ibn ʿAṭiyya 168
ibn Bādīs, ʿAbd al-Ḥamīd 90
ibn Juzayy 168
ibn Kathīr 209
ibn Khaldūn 47, 53, 56, 57, 60, 64, 101, 121, 231; and concept of *istikhlāf* 64; on *istikhlāf* 57, 60; and *istikhlāf* as a fact 65
ibn Masʿūd 47
ibn Miskawayh on vicegerents of God 61
ibn Taymiyya 27, 32, 47–50, 53–56, 68, 80–83, 162, 196, 223, 228, 266; on existential purpose 68; and Qurʾanic epistemology 68; on vicegerency 61
ibn ʿUmar 51
IIIT *see* International Institute of Islamic Thought
*ijtihād* (religio-ethical reasoning) 2, 9, 28; atomistic 28; classical atomistic approach to 36; conception of 9; contemporary 9, 31, 268; contemporary applied 30; emergence of absolute 24; fragmentation in 2; holistic meaning of 31; methods of 6; as an a posteriori process 30; traditional methods of 31
Imago Dei 98
ʿimārat al-arḍ (constructing and populating the earth) 1, 58, 69, 90, 100, 102, 148–49, 205, 241–43, 245
Imitatio Dei 98
imitation (*taqlīd*) 26
industrial and technological progress (as a function of vicegerency) 152
infinitives denoting justification (al-taʿlīl bi-l-maṣḍar) 198
"injunctive jurisprudence" (*fiqh iʿtimārī*) 13–14
innate faculty (*fiṭra*) 178
innate nature (fiṭra) 207, 209, 226
interest(s) (*maṣlaḥa*) 39n6, 69
International Institute of Islamic Thought (IIIT) 7, 10, 88, 113
inter-people acquaintance 200
Iqbāl Muḥammad 6, 88, 121, 128
*irāda* 102, 157, 158, 216
Islamic: concepts and principles 247; convention (*al-ḥaqīqa al-sharʿiyya*) 162; doctrinal schools (*madhāhib*) 24, 28; epistemology 3, 7, 10, 14, 38; founding texts 4, 6; intellectual heritage 88, 124, 265; intellectual legacy 11; intellectual production 5, 7; jurisprudence (*fiqh*) 11, 13, 27; meaning (*al-maʿnā al-sharʿī*) 162; methodology and epistemology 2, 31; reformism contemporary 2, 32; reformist movement 38, 88; teachings 2, 5, 7, 24, 65, 124, 126, 148; theology 4, 66, 89, 115, 165; value system 1, 26; vicegerency 4, 106, 107
Islamic civilisation 103, 104; and sciences decline 23
Islamic knowledge: construction of 7; framework for 10; new 10; sources of 10
Islamic sciences: and civilisation decline 32; fragmentation in 31, 38; internal integration of 36–38; stagnation of 27, 31; traditional 29, 265
Islamic thought: and civilisation 5, 88; contemporary 147; governing 5, 6, 88; methodological reform of 3; problem of fragmentation in 37; realistic 37; reform of 36
Islamic thought and sciences: crisis of 37; fragmentation of 32; restructuring 14
Islamic worldview 197; distortion of the 33; integral 38; primacy of the 32; theory of the 2
Islamisation of knowledge (project) 7, 9–10, 31, 37, 88
Islamisation of Knowledge: General Principles and Work Plan (al-Fārūqī) 9
*isrāʾīlīyyāt* (narratives imported from Judeo-Christian sources) 33, 47
*istikhlāf* 1, 14, 38, 56; concept of 1–4, 46, 63, 65–66, 69, 88–89, 96, 101, 128; contemporary perceptions of 90; as an existential (human) function 4, 46, 66, 72, 89; as a human existential function 89; interpretation of 54; meaning of 2, 58, 65, 108; ontological foundations of 1–3, 15n4; polemics of 56; as a purpose of human creation 64; as succession of generations 160
Izutsu, Toshihiko 118

jihad 103, 233–35: intellectual 234; meaning of 234; rationale behind 235; spiritual 235
jurisprudence 10, 39
Jurisprudence of Islamic Civilization (al-Najjār) 104
jurisprudential: issues 9, 28; provisions 36; scholarship 25; sciences 9

jurisprudential analogy (*qiyās fiqhī*) 9
justly balanced 232–34

*kalām* (speculative theology) 32
Kant, Immanuel 8, 115
Kant's moral philosophy 115
*kashf* (Divine knowledge unveiled to the heart) 64
*khalīfa* (successor/substitute/deputy/stewar d/vicegerent) 4; meaning of (in Qur'an and Bible) 98
*khalīfa* and *imām* difference 53
*khalīfa* as a creation of God (*khalīfa minnī*) 50
*"khalīfat Allāh"* (vicegerent of God) 54
*khilāfa*: linguistic definition of 155; linguistic meaning of 160; as succession of generations 156
knowledge fragmentation 7, 88
knowledge integration: external 37; lack of 31; problem of 36
Knowledge Integration Project 32, 37

Last Day 154, 227
lineal identity (nasab) 229

*ma'ālāt* (ultimate consequences of actions) 7
Majallat al-Aḥkām al-ʿAdliyya (Mecelle) 27–28
Makkī, Abū Ṭālib 68, 168
Mālik bin-Nabī 6, 23, 26
Malkāwī, Fatḥī on ʿumrān 242
man's existential function 66, 94–95, 108–9; epistemic theorisation of 68; in Islam 15; view of 120; vision of 112
*maqāṣid al-Sharīʿa* (Islamic objectives) 6–7, 31
maʿrūf (known to be good) 227
material progress of the West 129, 241, 244
Māturīdī on worship 70
Mawdūdī 58, 88, 102, 128
microcosm (al-'ālam al-saghīr) 55
modernity: critique of 13; and epistemic and social changes 265
modern reformist movement 5, 6
modern reform movement: emergence of the 24
modern sciences and Islamic sciences 27
monotheism (*tawḥīd*) 71, 93, 104, 119, 210; principles of 10
"monotheism of lordship" (*tawḥīd al-rubūbiyya*) 99
mujāhid (the one who performs jihād) 82, 195, 234
munkar (known to be rejected) 227
Muslim reformist: contemporary 96, 128, 244, 268; modern 6, 27
Muslim scholars: classical 98, 113; contemporary 89, 241
Muslim *umma* (community) 12
*mustakhlaf* (succeeded/deputised) 54
Muṭahharī, Murtaḍā 88
mutual deterrence (tadāfuʿ) 235
*muwāzanāt* (the legal balance between benefits and harms) 7

Nasr, Seyyed Hossein 96
natural determinism 80n136

object of vicegerency (*al-mustakhlaf fīhi*) 4, 46, 59, 89, 147; attributes of 201; on behalf of God 239; as fulfilment of God's will 153; identification of 120; methodological entries of 165
Ottoman: Caliphate 24; Empire 24–25; parliament 25; reforms 25

pantheism 48–49, 54–55
People of the Book 227
performance of prayer 213, 231, 233
permissibility (ibāḥa) 229
personal status laws 24, 28
Pharaoh 49, 58
piety (taqwā) 210, 216
political Islam 13
polytheism 47–50, 53–54, 56, 92
"positive vicegerency" (*istikhlāf waḍʿī*) 110
praise (ḥamd) 215–16
preaching literature 88, 90
pre-Islamic (*jāhiliyya*) worldview 33
prepositions denoting justification (al-taʿlīl bi-l-ḥurūf) 198
prophet Hūd 243
purification of: the heart 264; the soul (tazkiya) 71, 105, 205, 210, 218–19, 227
purposes of creation of the earth (in Qur'an) 149

Qadarites (determinists) 49
Qur'an chapters and verses: Q 2:10 211; Q 2:10–12 246; Q 2:143 232; Q 2:151 218; Q 2:203 218; Q 2:208 116, 246; Q 2:213 226; Q 2:223 218; Q 2:231 218; Q 2:233 218; Q 2:235 219; Q 2:251 235; Q 2:26 219; Q 2:262–64 223; Q

2:282 218; Q 2:29 152, 244; Q 2:29–38 264; Q 2:30 46, 56; Q 2:30 48, 53, 59–61, 65, 152, 156–57, 194, 224, 241; Q 2:30–34 219; Q 2:31 48, 152, 175, 213; Q 2:31–32 158; Q 2:33 159; Q 2:60 238; Q 3:104–5 228; Q 3:108 116; Q 3:110 227, 233; Q 3:113–14 228; Q 3:185 221; Q 3:7 219; Q 3:79 219; Q 3:79–85 246; Q 3:82 171; Q 3:83 115, 116, 167; Q 4:105 226; Q 4:135 232; Q 4:170 116; Q 4:28 239; Q 4:5 179; Q 4:53 99; Q 5:15–16 214; Q 5:8 232; Q 6:122 211; Q 6:130 220; Q 6:133 106; Q 6:141–42 238; Q 6:165 53, 57, 62, 236; Q 6:165 56; Q 7:10 151; Q 7:11 220, 223; Q 7:129 58, 106, 154; Q 7:157 229; Q 7:169 161; Q 7:172 82n136; Q 7:172 215, 226; Q 7:199 229; Q 7:31 238; Q 7:32 221; Q 7:56 116, 237; Q 7:69 106; Q 7:74 150, 243; Q 7:8 206; Q 8:24 211, 214; Q 8:29 217; Q 9:125 212; Q 9:38 221; Q 9:97 231; Q 10:108 116; Q 10:16 246; Q 10:19 239; Q 10:25 214, 246; Q 10:57 240; Q 10:57–58 211; Q 11:105 221; Q 11:107 109; Q 11:118–19 239; Q 11:118–119 228; Q 11:61 149–50, 243; Q 11:7 195; Q 12:111 218; Q 13:15 167; Q 13:8 208; Q 14:32–34 151; Q 143:2 233; Q 15:19 206, 208; Q 15:28–29 220; Q 15:82 150; Q 16:90 70; Q 16:36 214; Q 16:44 213; Q 16:48–49 169; Q 16:52 167, 171, 227; Q 16:78, 217; Q 16:81 169; Q 16:89, 218; Q 16:90 72; Q 17:105, 116, 171; Q 17:42–44 169; Q 17:44 170, 215; Q 17:85 220; Q 17:9–10 219; Q 18:105 206; Q 19:76 212; Q 19:93 166, 171; Q 20:124 242; Q 20:14 214; Q 20:50 115, 167, 171, 172, 175; Q 20:76 210; Q 20:81 238; Q 21:10 212; Q 21:27 156; Q 21:47 206; Q 22:77 72; Q 22:18 167–68; Q 22:40 235; Q 22:6 202; Q 22:61 202; Q 22:77 70; Q 22:78 232–34; Q 23:1 214; Q 23:11 214; Q 23:52–53 239; Q 23:70–71 171; Q 23:71 116, 212; Q 23:91 169; Q 24:22 223; Q 24:35 117; Q 24:41 168, 172; Q 24:41–45 171; Q 24:55 52; Q 25:2 208; Q 25:52 234; Q 26:128–31 243; Q 26:88–89 210; Q 28:68 109; Q 28:77 104; Q 29:6 234; Q 29:61 82n136; Q 29:64 221; Q 29:69 234; Q 30:30 120; Q 30:30–32 227; Q 30:41 240; Q 30:7–8 221; Q 30:9 150, 242; Q 31:20 151, 244; Q 31:30 202; Q 31:33 221; Q 32:18 208; Q 32:5 118, 224; Q 32:9 217; Q 33:45 232; Q 33:72 173, 239; Q 35:1 120; Q 35:41 155; Q 38:26 98; Q 38:71–72 220; Q 39:5 116; Q 40:11 48; Q 40:67 213; Q 41:33 52; Q 41:44 211; Q 42:13 232; Q 42:17 116, 179; Q 42:27 236; Q 42:52 211; Q 43:71 221; Q 44:58 212; Q 45:12 151; Q 47:17 212; Q 47:19 219; Q 47:29 211; Q 49:13 236; Q 50:31–34 224; Q 51:56 105; Q 51:56 66, 68, 91, 94, 166, 172, 195–96; Q 54:49 206; Q 55:1–8 197; Q 55:1–13 174, 264; Q 55:4 218; Q 55:7 116, 205, 208; Q 55:8 116, 264; Q 55:8–9 240; Q 55:9 205; Q 57:1 167; Q 57:25 179; Q 57:7 61; Q 59:19 214; Q 59:24 203; Q 64:14 223; Q 64:3 171; Q 65:12 195; Q 66:6 157; Q 67:2 236; Q 67:3 170; Q 76:3 154, 217; Q 79:27–28 208; Q 84:6 239; Q 87:1–3 208; Q 87:14 210; Q 87:2–3 173, 175; Q 89:27–28 210; Q 90:8–10 154; Q 91:7 209; Q 91:7–10 154; Q 91:8–10 209; Q 95:4 209; Q 95:4–5 239; Q 96:1–6 203; Q 96:5 218; Q 96:6 239; Q 98:5 213; Q 102:1–2 222; Q 103:2 239; sūrat al-Aʿrāf 223; sūrat al-Baqara 4, 48, 177–78, 264; sūrat al-Dhāriyāt 105, 195; *sūrat al-Ḥajj* 72; *sūrat al-Raḥmān* 174–79, 194, 264
Qurʾanic: norms (*sunan*) 6; philosophy 6, 37
Qurʾanic concepts: ijtibāʾ (being chosen) 232; Islam (surrender) 232; jihād (struggle) 232, 234; qisṭ (equity justice fairness) 232, 234; wasaṭiyya (to be balanced) 232, 233
Qurʾanic epistemology 27, 32, 68, 265; theorisation of 27
Qurʾanic worldview 12, 33, 210; distortion of 33; and higher Islamic principles 264
Quṭb, Sayyid 7, 88, 90, 96, 128, 152

rationales of creation: inter-people acquaintance 235; mutual aid between humans 236; trial 236
"reasonableness and permissibility" (*taʿlīl* and *tajwīz*) 80n136
reductionist: approach 1, 100; model 31; perspective 5
reformers (*al-muṣliḥūn*) 61
reformist movements 6; modern Muslim 90
religion and science relationship 28
religion and the state relationship 28

religious and secular education dichotomy 37
religious responsibilities (*taklīf shar'ī*) 157
religious thought in Islam 6
revealed will (*irāda shar'iyya*) 102
revelation: advent of 163, 196–97, 200, 205, 212–13, 217, 234; epistemology of 72; ontological reasons of 201–2; purpose of 233; reason for 198–99, 237; teleological purpose of 240
rhetorical question (*istifhām 'inkārī*) 168
Riḍā, Rashīd 6, 50, 88, 128, 150, 160, 208

*salāt* (prayer) meanings 162–63
scene of vicegerency (*mustakhlaf 'alayhi* i.e., the world) 59
Schenzle on Biblical and Qur'anic vicegerency 98
"schizophrenia" at the social level (Fazlur Rahman's usage) 25
sciences of Revelation 67; *see also* Islamic sciences
secondary acts of grace 71
self-accomplishment through annihilation (*fanā'*) 67
"self-attributes" (*ṣifāt dhātiyya*) 109–10
Sharī'atī, 'Alī 88, 108
*shirk* (polytheism) 47
social balance 230–32, 237, 247; maintenance of 264
specific rulings (*aḥkām juz'iyya*) 10
spiritual balance 163, 207, 210–13, 217–19, 222, 224–25, 231, 235, 246–47; maintenance of 210, 213–14, 217–18, 231, 234, 244, 264
spiritual elevation 99, 100, 104
spiritual purification 163, 202, 205–6, 216
subjugation of the universe 215–16
"subsequent interests" (*maṣāliḥ 'ājila*) 40n11
succession: generational 107, 108; human being's 160; intergenerational 107, 158
Sufis and worship 81n136
Sufism 15, 65, 66, 69; radical views of 48
*sunna* (path) 119
Sunni reformists 88
supererogatory act 69
*sūra* (image/shape/form) 159, 223

taḥliya (replenishment) 10, 207
*taḥliya* (securing the best development) 10
takhliya (purging the soul) 207
*takhliya* (the purgative habilitation) 10
tanzīh (transcendence) 223
*Tanzīmāt* (organisations/regulations) 24–25
taswiyya (harmonisation) 209
*tawḥīd* (monotheism) 1, 9, 11, 242
Tawḥīd: Its Implication for Thought and Life (Fārūqī) 10
tazkiya (purification of the soul) 1, 11, 206, 242
teleological reasons for sending messengers 218–19
Thamūd 150, 230, 243
three equilibriums 265
traits/duties of vicegerency 62–63
transgression (ṭughyān) 215
trusteeship: *Al-āyatiyya* (signing) 13; *Al-fiṭriyya* (innateness) 13; *Al-idā'iyya* (depositing) 13; *Al-jam'iyya* (wholeness) 13; *Al-shāhidiyya* (witnessing) 13; five principle of 13
"trusteeship jurisprudence" (*fiqh i'timānī*) 13–14
trusteeship paradigm ('Abd al-Raḥmān's concept) 12–14; main components of 14
Twelver Shias and vicegerency 123

Umayyad dynasty 33
*umma* (nation, community) 11–12, 32, 53, 58, 124–25, 228
'umrān ((establishing) civilisation, urbanisation) 11, 231, 242
'umrān and capitalist economy 242
"unwitnessed" (*ghayb*) 9
usury (*ribā*) 35

'vicegerencial' (*khilāfī*) 104; elevation 104
vicegerency: as adherence to God's commands 90; and balance 177; on behalf of God (of man) 54–55, 101, 103, 237, 266; civilizational 96; concept of 88; contemporary advocates of 90, 149, 155, 266; contemporary critiques of 266; cosmic 96, 106–8, 164; doctrine of 104; and evil 225; and freedom of action 111, 154; fulfilment of 125; function of 11, 91, 102, 103, 106, 107, 111, 114, 148, 165, 179; as a function of human being 267; in Greek mythology 160; as human existential function 101; as a human function 101, 147; as inevitable fate 94; Islamic theory of 3; jurisprudence of 103, 104; and maintaining environmental balance 237; as manifesting Divine attributes 90; mission of 106–8, 113, 152, 157;

and natural resources 237; and natural surroundings 238; notion of 3; object of 89, 101, 102, 114, 148, 155; in Persian mythology 160; and purification of the Soul 65; Qur'anic theory of 46, 263; as responsibilities of free choice 90; and subjugation 152; theoretical foundations of 6; theorisation of 263; theory of 2, 14, 89, 104, 120, 124; and trust 173, 174; and ʿumrān 243; as voluntary worship of God 106; and worship 105–7, 118, 266
Vicegerency of Man Between Revelation and Reason (al-Najjār) 104
vicegerency theory 247, 266, 268; contours of 232; development of a 148; Qurʾanic 4, 155, 179, 196, 205, 265
vicegerent (*mustakhlaf ʿanhu*) 46
vicegerent himself (*khalīfa*) 46
vicegerent of Allah (as political title) 99
vicegerent on behalf of God (*khalīfa ʿannī*) 50

Wahb ibn Munabbih 81n136
*waḥdat al-wujūd* (oneness of existence) 48, 64
*wālī* (governor) of God 95
Weltanschauung (worldview) 8
Western: colonialism 23; colonisation 23; development 29, 30; knowledge 7, 29; modernity 27, 29, 31, 38; progress 30, 129, 153, 265
*wilāyat al-faqīh* (guardianship of the Islamic jurist) 123
"witnessed" (*shahāda*) 9
worldly causes and interests 71
worship (*ʿibāda*) and interest (*maṣlaḥa*) dualism 91
worship as existential function 66
Wycliffe, John 98

Zarmān, Muhammad 99; and major worship 99–100; and minor worship 99, 100; on vicegerency 99–100